Souls in the Kalyug

HEDGEHOG AND FOX

HISTORY AND POLITICS SERIES

"The fox knows many things,
but the hedgehog knows one big thing"

General Editor

RUDRANGSHU MUKHERJEE

Related Series Titles

Sudipta Kaviraj TRAJECTORIES OF THE INDIAN STATE
Sumit Guha BEYOND CASTE
Akeel Bilgrami CAPITAL, CULTURE, AND THE COMMONS
Pulapre Balakrishnan INDIA'S ECONOMY FROM NEHRU TO MODI
Syed Sayeed REFLECTIONS ON AMBEDKAR'S "ANNIHILATION OF CASTE"
Nivedita Menon SECULARISM AS MISDIRECTION
Chandi Prasad Bhatt GENTLE RESISTANCE: AN AUTOBIOGRAPHY
Charu Gupta HINDI HINDU HISTORIES
Tanika Sarkar RELIGION AND WOMEN IN INDIA
Partha Chatterjee FOR A JUST REPUBLIC
Ranajit Guha THE SMALL VOICE OF HISTORY

SHANKAR RAMASWAMI

Souls in the Kalyug

THE POLITICS AND COSMOLOGIES OF MIGRANT WORKERS IN CONTEMPORARY INDIA

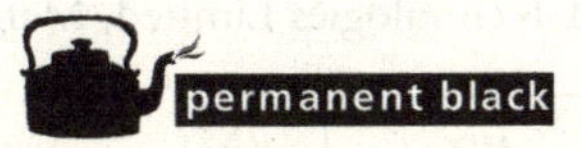

and

Published by
PERMANENT BLACK
'Himalayana', Mall Road, Ranikhet Cantt,
Ranikhet 263645
Email: perblack@gmail.com

and

Distributed by
ORIENT BLACKSWAN PRIVATE LIMITED
Bangalore Bhopal Bhubaneshwar Chandigarh Chennai
Ernakulam Guwahati Hyderabad Jaipur Kolkata
Lucknow Mumbai New Delhi Patna
www.orientblackswan.com

ISBN 978-81-7824-719-9

FOR SALE ONLY IN INDIA

First published by University of Pennsylvania Press

Printed and bound by Manipal Technologies Limited, Manipal

CONTENTS

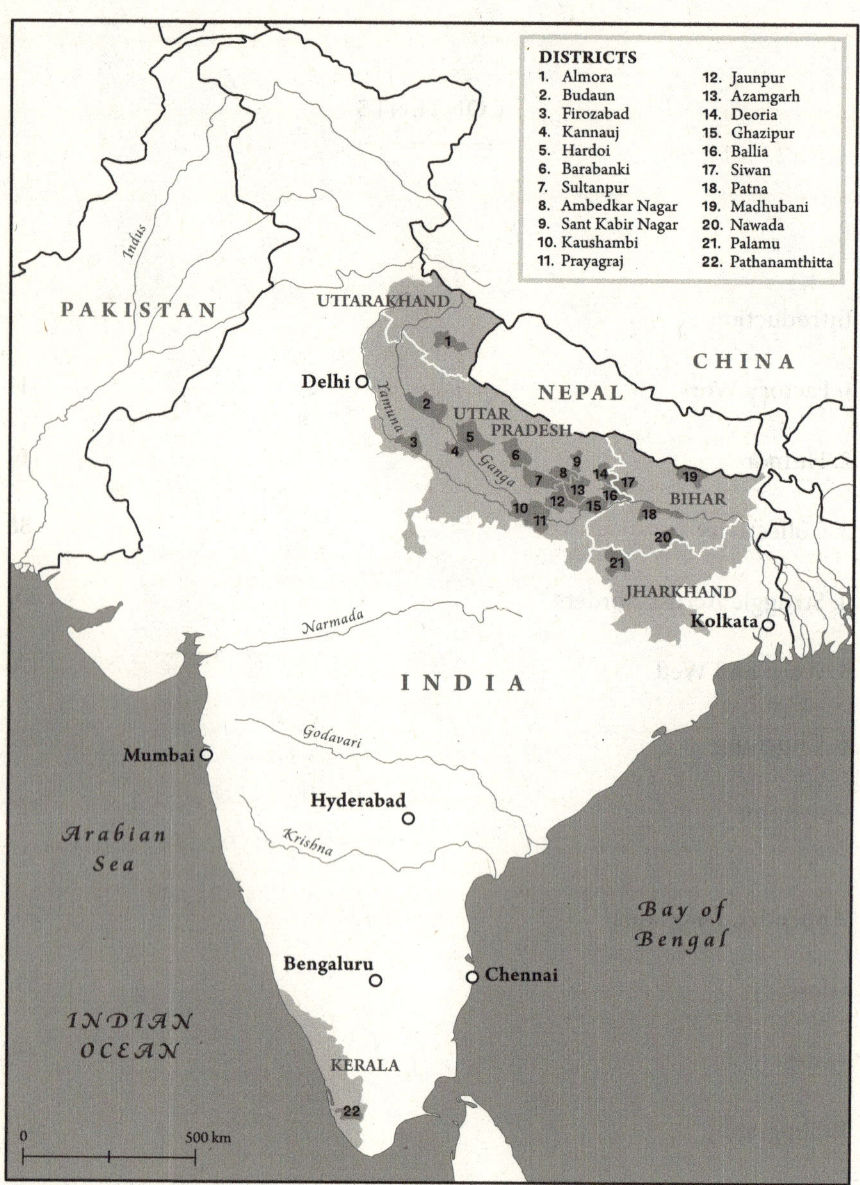

Map 1. India, with migrant workers' home districts, as mentioned in the book. The map shows India's borders according to the Government of India.

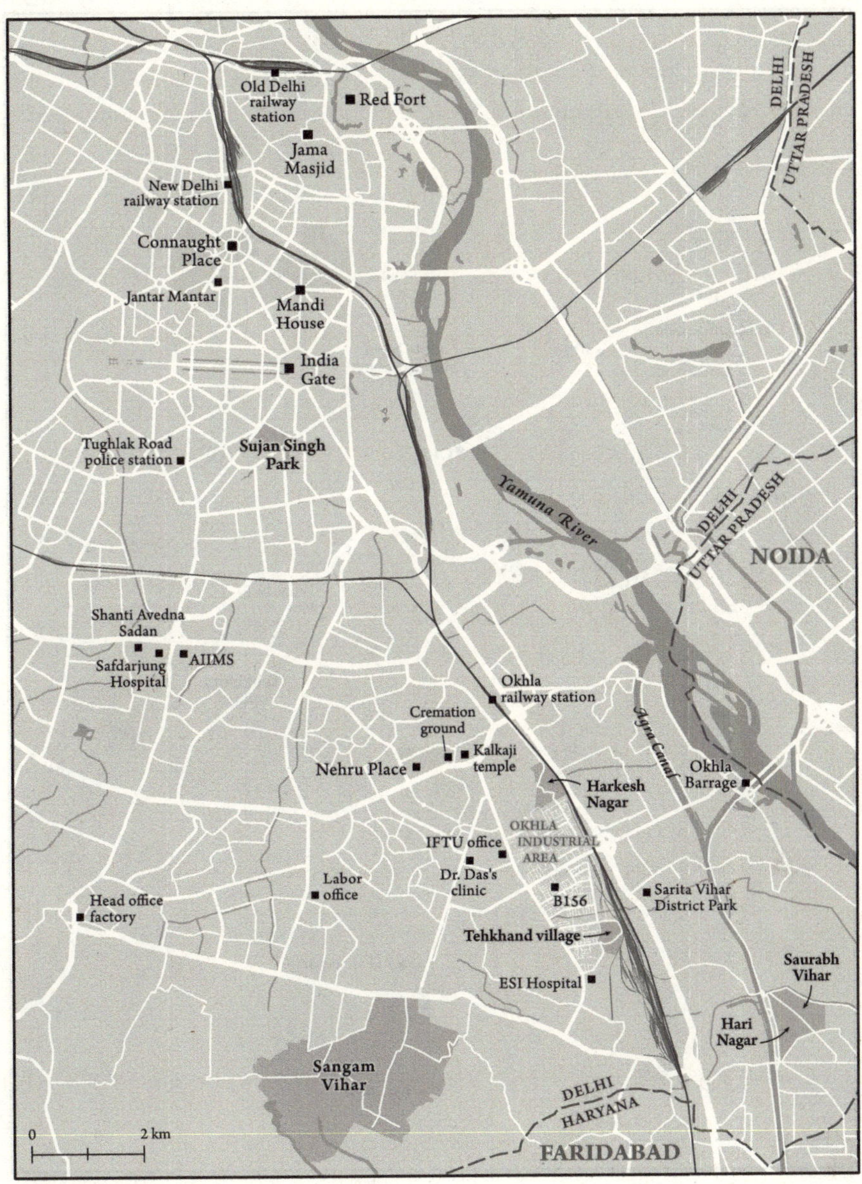

Old Delhi railway station
Red Fort
Jama Masjid
New Delhi railway station
Connaught Place
Jantar Mantar
Mandi House
India Gate
Tughlak Road police station
Sujan Singh Park
DELHI
UTTAR PRADESH
Yamuna River
NOIDA
Shanti Avedna Sadan
Safdarjung Hospital
AIIMS
Okhla railway station
Cremation ground
Kalkaji temple
Nehru Place
Agra Canal
Harkesh Nagar
Okhla Barrage
OKHLA INDUSTRIAL AREA
IFTU office
Dr. Das's clinic
Labor office
Head office factory
B156
Sarita Vihar District Park
Tehkhand village
ESI Hospital
Saurabh Vihar
Hari Nagar
Sangam Vihar
DELHI
HARYANA
FARIDABAD
0
2 km

Map 2. Delhi.

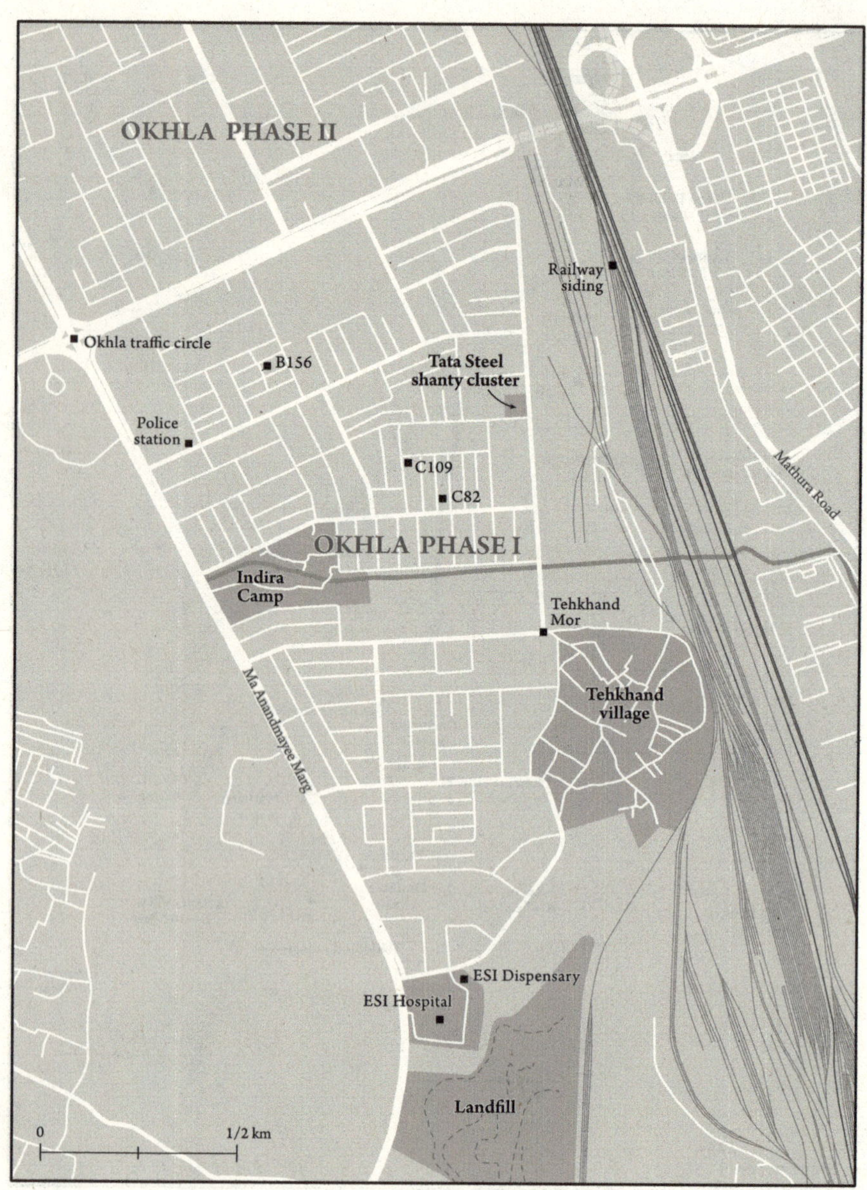

Map 3. Okhla Industrial Area.

Introduction

The development process in India, along with its alleged achievements, has induced multiple difficulties and hardships for poor and working people. In villages, farming families confront an agrarian crisis, with rising costs of seeds, fertilizers, and pesticides, inadequate irrigation facilities, low prices for their crops, grave indebtedness, and ecological damage to the soil, water, and forests. Due to a paucity of jobs in the countryside, many are compelled to migrate to cities for work.[1]

Once in the city, migrants confront many difficulties. In workplaces, they contend with low-paid, insecure, exhausting, and hazardous work.[2] In neighborhoods, they deal with congested living conditions, poor qualities of air, water, and sanitation, vulnerabilities to illnesses, and separation from their families in the village.

This book pursues the following inquiry. How are migrant workers confronting these myriad difficulties and hardships, in ways that are less injurious and more life-promoting? The book proposes an answer in three parts. In a metal factory in Delhi, the anchoring ethnographic site of this book, migrant workers engage in resistances and collective struggles against perceived oppression and injustice. In the city and village, they weave integrative filaments to one another, in empathetic closeness and fellowship. In the cosmological domain, they attempt to resist soul-distorting processes in present, decivilizing times. Through these activities, migrant workers strive toward, and at times realize, elements of a good life.

A Factory in Okhla

Metal Artware Exports began functioning in the early 1990s, manufacturing metal artware through vendors in north India, and later, through its own production units in Delhi. While some of its goods were sold in India, the bulk of its orders were exported to its parent company in America, for sale to department stores, art galleries, and boutiques in America, Europe, and elsewhere. The company's purported vision was to create goods that brought together unique artistic designs with metalworking craft traditions in India. By setting up its own factories and hiring up to 450 direct employees, the company sought to lower costs, protect its designs, and enhance quality. Between 1997 and 2001, the company's annual turnover grew from $800,000 to $1.73 million.[3] Given its success with steel designs, the company set up a metal factory in the Okhla Industrial Area, B156, in March 2001, for the polishing of steel artware goods.[4]

The Okhla Industrial Area is located in southeast Delhi, in the region bounded by the Okhla railway station, the Kalkaji temple, the Employees' State Insurance Hospital, and Tehkhand village. Okhla developed in stages: Phase III in the late fifties, and Phases I and II from the early seventies. The industries in Okhla include garment exports, engineering, paper and printing presses, pharmaceuticals, electronics, and plastics.[5] Plots are also occupied by software and telecommunications companies, call centers, advertising agencies, and automobile dealers. Okhla is a turbulent space, with companies seeking to replace regular workers with casual and contract workers, hiring and terminating workers with vicissitudes in export orders, and closing and relocating factories to Faridabad, Gurgaon, and Noida in the neighboring states of Haryana and Uttar Pradesh.[6] While unions are active in Okhla, they are largely seen to broker termination settlements with managements for commissions.[7] Large numbers of working-class people reside in shanty clusters in Okhla such as Indira Camp and Sanjay Colony, and in rented rooms in the urban villages of Harkesh Nagar and Tehkhand.

The B156 manager recruited workers through his contacts with metal polishers in Okhla. Those who were initially hired were employed as regular workers of Metal Artware Exports and paid Delhi minimum wage grades, with state health insurance and other legal benefits.[8] A couple of months later, more workers were hired as casual workers under a different company name, Artistic Goods, and paid less than minimum wages, without health and other benefits. In September 2001, the manager began a night shift of mostly casual workers, and the factory's workforce grew to about sixty workers. The B156 workers were male migrants, aged in their late teens to mid-forties, mostly from villages in Uttarakhand, Uttar Pradesh,

Bihar, and Jharkhand, and from varied backgrounds of caste and religion (e.g., Other Backward Classes, Scheduled Castes, Scheduled Tribes; Hindus, Muslims, Buddhists).[9] They lived in shanties, rented rooms, and constructed houses in neighborhoods of south and southeast Delhi, Faridabad, and Noida.

Metal polishing is dirty, difficult, and dangerous work. The polishing process generates a gray-black, malodorous, foggy haze of metal dust, debris, and buff fibers that rises from the machines. The shop floor is a difficult space to inhabit, with overhead fans blowing particles, debris, and smoke into one's face and nostrils. Workers' clothes, masked visages, and bodies are blackened throughout the shift by the dust and grime. Amid the high-pitched whirring of the belt grinder and the subterranean rumbling of the exhaust fan, one hears the sounds of coughing, hawking, and abusing, as polishers spit out blackish phlegm into the piles of debris that accumulate in the ducts beneath the machines. Workers' bodies, while muscular, are often thin and angular, bearing the signs of physical exertions, austere diets, and chronic ailments. Colds, coughs, fever, stomach disorders, chest pains, jaundice, and tuberculosis are common among the workers, making doctors' clinics and government hospitals a third coordinate, along with the factory and residence, in the orbits of their lives. Stimulants and tranquilizers for ailing bodies are procured from liquor and tobacco-*biri-pan* shops, which form a fourth coordinate in migrant lives in the city.[10]

I came to B156 on a night in December 2001. I was brought there by a metal polisher whom I had been interviewing in Tehkhand village, who was a casual worker on the night shift. I got to see the dark, dirty, and grim work environment. I wondered how the workers could withstand such a place. I went to the company's head office in Lado Sarai, and met the two American and Indian directors, who generously gave me access to B156. I began coming to the factory, observing activities, and interviewing workers. Beneath the surface of monotonous and repetitive production, I gradually began to see that there was a deep, unrelenting, turbulent politics of machinations and agitations. It was an ongoing battle, a ground-level *Mahabharata* in the making, with ephemeral pauses and breaks, but never a lasting peace. Beneath the grimy masks, I could also see that the B156 workers were diverse, colorful, wise, and articulate characters, with deep understandings and critical visions of the factory, the world, and themselves. As I witnessed unfolding developments in this battle, my questions kept growing.

I began fieldwork at B156 in January 2002, and kept coming back until January 2006.

Contrary Processes

In this book, I address the following specific questions. What is the nature of the work activities, social relations, resistances, and struggles of the B156 workers? What are their experiences of illnesses, hospitals, family life, and neighborhoods in Delhi? What are their understandings and visions regarding the sources of difficulty in their lives, the nature of God, and the possibilities for justice in the world?

In responding to these questions, the book presents a picture of contrary processes of entanglement and noncooperation in multiple domains of workers' lives. In the world of the factory, workers become entangled in managerial machinations, active collaboration, and competition, which give rise to work intensification, bodily hazards, surface-level respect, and hostile envy. In the social worlds of the city and village, migrants become caught up in disintegrative processes to do with efforts to accumulate savings, discord in the family, and insularities of caste and religion. More deeply, in the cosmological world, according to migrants' implicit visions, they become entangled in an interplay of souls and the present, decivilizing epoch (the *Kalyug*), in which thoughts, feelings, actions, and dealings become distorted by egoistic and demonic proclivities. In the factory, noncooperation manifests in resistances at the machines, auto-critique, and collective struggles. In the city and village, noncooperation emerges in empathetic closeness and fellowship, within and across boundaries of caste and religion. In the cosmological world, migrants noncooperate with the distorting interplay of souls and time in the weaving of integrative filaments to one another and the divine, in resistances, struggles, lateral bonds, and devotional practices.

Within the contrary processes, one sees multiple, simultaneous, and at times internally conflicting strivings of migrant workers, which together suggest the contours of an implicit vision of a good life, however distant and elusive it might be under the given circumstances.[11] These strivings include material well-being, bodily health, mental peace, respect, justice, and togetherness.[12] Guided by an understanding of these strivings, it becomes possible to speak of workers' activities that are injurious and life-promoting. In entangling processes, migrant workers injure themselves and others. In noncooperation, they move closer to the realization of diverse elements of a good life.

The picture of contrary processes, I believe, enables the inclusion, juxtaposition, and understanding of important phenomena in migrant workers' worlds. First, the attention to processes emphasizes movement, turbulence, and flux in workers' worlds. Nothing seems to ever be calm, quiet, or still in these lives. One also sees that migrants are diverse persons, with their own ways of thinking, feeling, speaking, and acting, even in small groups, who can alter their behaviors and activities over time. For example, those who initially exhibit vertical loyalty and pursue speed in the factory, might become disillusioned, and morph into active members in struggles. Along with these movements, one gets to see migrant workers as critically sensitive beings, who are continually drawing on multiple inheritances, including epics, medieval devotional (*bhakti*) poet-saints, spiritual discourses, cinema, the news media, and their ongoing experiences, in describing, interpreting, and critiquing their worlds and themselves. Second, the picture enables the juxtaposition of seemingly contradictory phenomena. For example, while workers express respect for the machine and the associated divinity, Vishvakarma, they might also engage in machine sabotage. While they might joke and feel hostility toward workers from other regions and religions, they also develop close neighbor relations and friendships across these boundaries. Third, while I use the terms "collaboration" and "resistance" to describe certain activities (e.g., informing and reporting to the management, regulating quantities at the machines), the categories of entanglement and noncooperation permit the inclusion of activities that are not clearly describable in these terms, but that might align with managerial objectives and disintegrative forces (e.g., speed contests, hostile joking, untouchability) or militate against them (e.g., the deepening of lateral bonds).

In adopting the categories of entanglement and noncooperation, I am drawing from workers' discourses and proximate sources. To describe feelings of getting caught up and lost in activities (e.g., body-depleting work, looking after families), workers used words conveying senses of entanglement (e.g., *phamsna* [to be caught, stuck, entangled], *uljhan* [confusion, entanglement], and *cakravyuh* [circular maze] in Hindi).[13] They used certain words that resonate with the idea of noncooperation, in describing auto-regulated working (*hisab se kam karna*), the seeking of justice (*haq*), the method of nonviolence (*ahimsa*), and the duty to oppose and not endure oppression and wrongdoing (*atyacar, zulm*). I also draw instruction from the Noncooperation

Movement during the freedom struggle in India, in which Gandhi and the Congress advocated the boycotting of government (e.g., elections, courts, schools) and promoted a constructive program of spinning cloth, forging Hindu-Muslim unity, and abolishing untouchability. During this movement, peasants, *adivasis* (original inhabitants), and workers engaged in nonviolent agitations (e.g., for fair rents, access to forests, and better wages), utilizing their own idioms and vocabularies, including religious imageries, and not always with the support of the Congress.[14] For Gandhi, noncooperation also meant the duty to refuse to participate in ethical wrongdoing in one's milieus, and to not acquiesce to one's own egoistic motivations.

Plan of Work

The first two chapters of the book explore everyday processes and social relations at the metal factory. In Chapter 1, "Factory Work," I begin with a description of the rhythms of the workday, the night shift, and payday. A work-intensifying process arises, I argue, through the interplay of managerial machinations and workers' active collaboration, competitive pursuit of speed, modifications of work methods, beliefs in the virtues of hard work, and desires for advancement and the rapid accumulation of savings ("looting" mentalities). This process confronts resistances from resting, shirking, and the practice of auto-regulated working, in which workers coordinate among themselves to adjust quantity, speed, and quality, so as to conserve bodies, protect jobs, maintain respect, and avoid causing harm to others. The chapter then delves into the relations of work and respect (*izzat*). I describe workers' embarrassment about the dirtiness of polishing work and attempts to camouflage the nature of their work to others; their respect for the machines and divinities, as exhibited in prayer, worship, and avoiding sabotage; and their dealings with the management and with one another, in which instrumentality and envy give rise to surface-level respect. Workers express anxieties of getting caught up in a hazardous, vitality-eroding work process, and seek ways to alter their working styles, develop deeper relations, and prolong life.

Amid black dust, noise, and rising workloads, there is a vibrant life of humor and joking (*mazak*) at the factory. In Chapter 2, "Humor," I investigate the themes, motives, and effects of these practices. Workers engage in horseplay, erotic joking about genitalia and buggery, and joking about women as objects and submitting machines, which might reveal anxieties about losses of male control in domestic gender equations. To observe respect, workers avoid vulgar joking around elders and certain relatives, and in the worlds of the residences. Workers invoke slurs and negative stereotypes about migrants from Bihar and Muslims, which express a mélange of envy, hostility, and friendly feeling. But workers also allege that persons from a given region or religious community are diverse, distinctive, and difficult to generally describe. Humor assists the production process, by allowing workers to get into the work, and distracting them from tensions, boredom, and fatigue. But through humor, workers also create a theater of play, develop closeness, articulate a critique of factory oppression, and engage in an auto-critique of their own qualities of egoism, submissiveness, and insularity. In humor and joking, workers attempt to realize a bit of joy in the present, and not defer it to a future in the village.

Chapters 3 and 4 examine developments over time in managerial activities and workers' struggles. In Chapter 3, "Collectivity," I begin by describing the work-intensifying process that arose from the interplay of managerial machinations and workers' loyalty and envy. This process confronted turbulence due to workers' disillusion amid depressed wages, job threats, injuries, and illnesses. A process of collectivity emerged, guided by unity politics, in which workers held park meetings, looked to proto-leaders for guidance, and engaged in refusals of transfers, reduced bonuses, and overtime without perquisites, partly motivated by the quest for justice (*haq* [right, just due]). These collective refusals could disintegrate due to machinations, the actions of proto-leaders, the influence of workers' social circles, and the willingness to capitulate to existing conditions. I turn to a discussion of workers' critical discourses on oppression, and an implicit view of its deeper sources, rooted in a distorting interplay of souls and the *Kalyug*, which induces multiple activities observed in the factory. In cursing, sabotage, and restrained working (an extreme version of auto-regulated working), workers articulated discontent and opposed oppressive factory practices. The chapter then describes a sequence of events in which workers resumed unity politics, joined a militant ultra-left union, and contested a lockout, eventuating in the restarting of work with a reduced workforce. During these contestations, the politics of synchrony (*talmel*), a more autonomous, horizontal, improvisatory form of collectivity, critically contributed to protecting jobs, by amplifying protest (through a poster campaign) and averting a complete exodus. In the politics of collectivity, workers were attempting to noncooperate with oppression and injustice, and the soul-distorting interplay that bolstered them.

Chapter 4, "Struggle Across Borders," describes a sequence of events in which a legal dispute between the directors led to a work stoppage in the company's factories, unpaid wages, retrenchments, and closures. The workers sought alternatives to the union's protest repertoire of a militant gate struggle followed by long court cases. Drawing on past experiences of workers in Faridabad, the B156 workers composed placards, detailing ongoing events, and stood silently on the roads of Okhla and other parts of Delhi, in an expansion of synchrony politics. I describe the workers' motives of restoring jobs, pursuing justice, and keeping their microsociety (*samaj*) alive, and their methods of nonviolence (*ahimsa*), which allowed them to sustain a visible, disturbing presence on the streets of Delhi. As the struggle continued, the workers confronted material strains, their own uncertainties, and discouragement in their residential milieus. The motives and methods of the protests catalyzed empathetic bridges and practical linkages across multiple borders in Okhla, in Delhi, and beyond India, leading to a global grassroots boycott of the American company's goods and the absorption of the workers into a new Okhla factory. This struggle of workers, acting together with others, gave rise to a glimpse of forces of truth, which at times can constrain the workings of global capital.

The final two chapters shift focus to workers' neighborhoods and cosmological visions. In Chapter 5, "Warp and Weft," I explore the worlds of two B156 workers, Naresh and Varmaji. I begin by describing Naresh's childhood in Jharkhand, his experiences of working and living in Okhla, the joys of being together with his relatives and family members, and the difficulties in pursuing medical treatment for an aunt in government hospitals. I then discuss Varmaji's journey from Uttar Pradesh, his past practices of excessive drinking, his tensions, duties, and attachments in the family sphere, and the discord and closeness with his wife, Durgawati. I then examine practices of fellowship (*bhaicara*) within and across boundaries of caste and religion. In neighbor relations, the hosting of other migrants, and mixing with other B156 workers, Naresh loosened his adherence to village norms to do with caste dealings. Despite past involvements with communal politics in the village, Varmaji developed close relations with his Muslim neighbors. At the festivals of Holi, Muharram, and Eid, one witnessed the intensities of conviviality, friendship, and the hosting of one another. Amid the disintegrative forces of the development process, insularities, and hostilities, migrants weave integrative filaments in the social fabric (*tana bana*) of the city and village, through empathetic closeness and fellowship. In this weaving work, migrants construct fragile dwellings, in which they experience a bit of the good life, while in prolonged exile from the village.

Chapter 6, "Churning," delves further into workers' understandings and visions of their lives, the world, and the future. I begin by discussing workers' views on the deeper sources of difficulty and hardship in their lives, involving ideas of fate, action (*karm*), God, and the world as a festive gathering (*mela*). In making sense of the magnitude of difficulties, narratives direct attention to the interplay of souls and the *Kalyug* (or the *Qayamat* [doomsday] among Muslim workers), which gives rise to distorted activities in multiple spaces, including factories, the state labor department office, city streets, government hospitals, neighborhoods, residences, and the village, with the possible assent of God. In confronting such a world, workers advocate engaging in good actions that can decelerate the progress of the *Kalyug* toward dissolution and doomsday. One witnesses implicit anti-decivilizing activities, I suggest, in noncooperation with destructive processes, the weaving of integrative filaments, and devotion to the divine. One might see the relation of decivilizing processes and anti-decivilizing activities as a churning (*manthan*) of souls, the world, and time. Within these agitations, workers struggle to make the world less oppressive and more life-promoting, and more aligned to the hope of a deeper, *karmic* justice.

Sources and Methods

The fieldwork and writing of the book have been guided by a range of sources.[15] First, I have been influenced by writings on autonomous politics. This politics focuses on the activities through which ordinary people exchange, discuss, deliberate, and take their own, improvised steps, often at a remove from leaders, political parties, and hierarchical unions, to oppose perceived oppression and injustice. I have been instructed by studies of the resistances, protests, and struggles of peasants, workers, and other groups,[16] and the emergence of horizontal movements, occupations, and decentralized networks of protest and constructive activity.[17] I have also been inspired by urban ethnographies that have disclosed the capacities of ordinary people to exhibit respect, ethical awareness, empathy, and compassion, within contexts of difficulty and deprivation.[18] In India, my understandings of workers have been informed by writings on work processes, neighborhood worlds, and struggles,[19] and by depictions of the experiences, languages, and politics of villagers, migrants, and workers in Hindi cinema and documentary films.[20] I have also been critically educated by the reportage and analyses in the *Faridabad Workers Newspaper* (*Faridabad Majdoor Samachar*, or *FMS*), a Hindi newspaper, which is brought out and distributed by a vibrant group of workers, activists, students, and others. *FMS* reports on workers' thoughts, experiences, resistances, and struggles in the greater Delhi region and the world, and has closely documented workers' practices of autonomous, horizontal collectivity (*talmel*) since the mid-nineties.[21] *FMS* played a vital, catalytic role in the development of the B156 workers' understandings, resistances, and struggles.

Second, the book has been informed by works that have explored the connections between religion and transformative politics. I have been instructed by writings that examine the ways in which religion might ground, motivate, and critically assist a politics of justice, democracy, nonviolence, and social transformation.[22] In India, historical writings have given glimpses of the role of religion in animating struggles against perceived oppression and injustice: *adivasis* referenced divine commands and impending epochal transition beyond the *Kalyug* (*Kaljug*) in movements and rebellions; peasants invoked Ram and Sita of the *Ramayana* and gestured to a more fair, just society of Ram's rule (*Ramraj*) in agitations against landlords; lower caste groups drew upon alternative histories, devotional poet-saint traditions (e.g., Kabir and Ravidas), and spiritual practices in refusing customary work and social dealings; and Muslim artisans and workers articulated understandings of themselves as good, respectable, devout people and followers of an egalitarian Islam in combating deprivation and exploitation.[23] The book also builds upon works that excavate and describe ideas and practices of nonviolence, tolerance, and togetherness among Hindus, Muslims, and others, amid the ideologies and workings of religious nationalism and communal violence.[24]

Third, the motives for the fieldwork, and the nature of the descriptions in the book, owe a good deal to the ideas and visions of an eclectic set of thinkers. From Marx, I have developed understandings of alienation and exploitation; the visible and hidden worlds of circulation and production; and plural, emancipatory trajectories of societies beyond capitalism.[25] From Dostoevsky, I have gained insights from the depictions of the complex contradictions, motives, and proclivities within persons and souls; the diversity of personalities and viewpoints within small groups; the constriction, hardship, and conviviality in the world of a Siberian prison; the elitist, secretive, and violent dimensions of revolutionary ideologies and activities; and the mystical vision of salvation through suffering, self-emptying (*kenosis*), and love.[26] From Weil, I have been influenced by the descriptions of factory work and its consequences for bodies, minds, and souls; the vital importance of rootedness for human beings; the category of force (which induces precarity in the world) and the counterforce of *metaxu* (bridges of the spirit that sustain and promote life); and a tragic vision, involving the recognition of radical suffering, attention to afflicted beings, decreation (self-surrender), and the possibility of grace through a distant, elusive God.[27] From Gandhi, I have been instructed by the critique of modern civilization; the vision of *svaraj* (autonomy), which would include material prosperity, social bonds, and ecological sustainability, without mass migrations to cities; the adoption of nonviolence (*ahimsa*) and noncooperation (*asahyog*) as methods in opposing oppressive, unjust regimes; the understanding of a play of contesting forces in the world (e.g., brute force, soul force) and vying tendencies in souls (e.g., divine and demonic potentialities); the commitment to fellowship (*bhaicara*) among religious communities, from a rootedness within religions, against the divisive workings of communal politics; and the devotion to an indwelling, benevolent, but potentially fearsome God.[28]

During my fieldwork, I spent time observing, listening, and speaking with workers in various spaces of the factory (e.g., at the machines, outside the gate, in the welding room and storeroom, in the upstairs office). I also interacted with the managers, supervisors, quality checkers, and security guards. Beyond the factory, I observed and interacted with workers and others in neighborhoods, residences, streetside eateries, music programs, park meetings, union offices, demonstrations, processions, street protests, state labor department offices, doctors' clinics, hospitals, the Kalkaji cremation ground, temples, mosques, shrines, religious gatherings (*jalsas*), train stations, and towns and villages in Uttar Pradesh (Ambedkar Nagar, Budaun, Sant Kabir Nagar, and Sultanpur districts), Bihar (Nawada district), and Jharkhand (Latehar and Palamu districts). In these spaces, I recorded exchanges, conversations, and discussions on audio cassettes, using a Sony WM-D6C Pro Walkman and a condenser microphone.

I also conducted interviews with sixty-five persons who worked at B156. I interviewed each of these persons once or twice, on their migration trajectories, work experiences, and thoughts and feelings about B156. With twenty workers, I conducted multiple interviews on a range of subjects, including factories, neighborhoods, residences, family relations, the city and village, and religious ideas and visions.[29] Many of these interviews were conducted in a rented room in Tehkhand village, close to the residences of a cluster of B156 workers, along with a research assistant.[30] I also interviewed the B156 managers, supervisors, and checkers, state labor department officials, police officers, political leaders, union leaders, doctors, traditional healers, landlords, shopkeepers, wives, other close relatives, and polishing workers in other Okhla factories. These interviews were also recorded on audio cassettes.

Throughout the fieldwork, I took photographs of workers and others in multiple spaces, using an SLR camera and black-and-white film. These photographs were of great assistance in developing understandings during the fieldwork and while writing the book. I hope that the photographs can diminish distances to the persons, spaces, activities, and events described in the book, and enable their own insights into these worlds.

In writing the book, I have tried to work closely with migrant workers' language (e.g., categories, idioms, and imageries) when describing and giving readings of their lives, activities, thoughts, and feelings.[31] The workers' quotations have been translated into English, with the Hindi (a lingua franca among migrants in Delhi, inflected by words and idioms of their regions and villages) in the endnotes, for bilingual readers. These quotations have been selected from my direct witnessing, interviews, and reported speech (by the speakers or others), and have sometimes been edited for clarity. Some categories of vital importance in workers' discourses, which are difficult to concisely translate without significant losses in meaning and political possibility (e.g., *izzat*, *haq*, *Kalyug*), often appear without translation.[32] I have transliterated Hindi words according to the style of *The Oxford Hindi-English Dictionary*, omitting diacritics.[33]

Regarding naming practices in the book, I have largely avoided anonymity. I have given the names of most persons and of places in Okhla, Delhi, India, and America, along with photographs. I adopted this method after seeing Mitchell Duneier's ethnography of sidewalk vendors in New York (with Ovie Carter's photographs), which follows a practice of identifying persons and places to enhance accuracy, accountability, and credibility.[34] From early on, I also observed that the workers were not asking for anonymity; indeed, they were often seeking ways to overcome it, by communicating information about their conditions to others beyond the factory gate, in writing letters to the company directors, pursuing legal complaints at the state labor department office, holding placards on streets, giving interviews to journalists, and participating in documentary film shootings. But given certain activities that impinge adversely on the workers (e.g., legal violations, medical negligence), I have given generic names for the metal companies (e.g., Metal Artware Exports, Artistic Goods) and have withheld the names of the company directors, state labor department officials, police officers, and government hospital doctors.

Decelerating Time

One of my favorite places in Delhi is the monument India Gate, a grand, majestic arch of sandstone surrounded by lawns, trees, and water bodies, in the center of the city. It was built under the Raj to commemorate the soldiers of the British Indian army who fought and died in the First World War and the Third Anglo-Afghan War. Some decades later, in Independent India, a memorial was installed under the arch, comprising a black marble cenotaph, a soldier's helmet and rifle, and a burning flame, to honor the soldiers of the armed forces who died in India's third war with Pakistan.[35] I have always been drawn to this place. I wonder about all that this monument has witnessed in its lifetime, such as Gandhi's funeral procession winding its way to Rajghat, massive rallies of farmers and workers at the Boat Club in the seventies and eighties, gatherings of the Vishva Hindu Parishad before the demolition of the Babri mosque in Ayodhya, and the thick, gray, choking pollution that now envelops Delhi in winters. When I see the word INDIA engraved above the arch, I cannot but think that the monument stands not only for fallen soldiers, but also for the struggles, past and ongoing, of poor and working people of the country.

This book is about a group of such people, the B156 workers, the injurious forces they confront in the factory, city, and village, the ways in which they get caught up in work-intensifying and divisive processes, contributing to their own difficulty and hardship, and their attempts, however fragile, ephemeral, and uncertain in their effects, to sustain and promote life. In these efforts, they seek to slow down the pace and intensity of oppressive and unjust practices in the factory, the disintegrative workings of insularity and hostility in the social fabric, and the progress of cosmological time toward the cataclysmic destruction of the human and ecological world. They do so, to defer death and live a bit better in the present. They also do so, to bring the world closer to justice, and to allow it to survive a bit longer than might be its current fate. This monument, I would like to think, honors these migrant workers, and many others like them in the world, who are trying, against grim, formidable forces, to promote and not destroy life.

CHAPTER 1

Factory Work

Forces of life and death jostle in the world of the metal factory. The management makes ongoing attempts to increase production and improve quality. Some workers actively assist and facilitate these goals, for multiple motives. Others attempt to conserve bodies and avoid harming others.

In this chapter, I discuss everyday work processes and activities in the initial phases of the factory's functioning (2001–2003). I begin by describing the workday, the night shift, and payday. I then examine managerial techniques for raising production, and workers' active collaboration, pursuit of speed, and modifications in methods, which together contribute to what one might term a thanatic, work-intensifying process. Some workers try to restrain this process by adjusting quantity, speed, and rest, in the practice of auto-regulated working, which exhibits the politics of synchrony (*talmel*). I then explore workers' feelings and practices of respect with regard to polishing work, the machines, the management, and coworkers. The workers are tragically aware, I conclude, of being caught up in a perilous, vitality-depleting process, within their migrant odysseys.

Work Rhythms

The workday involves an ebb and flow of intense work and rest breaks within a dark and polluted atmosphere. Night workers contend with sleep deprivation and bodily losses. Payday is an occasion for modest joys.

The Workday

The metal polishing factory of Metal Artware Exports is located in a narrow, dusty lane of the DDA Sheds in the Okhla Industrial Area Phase I. Neighboring sheds are engaged in the production of metal casings, bottle caps, and plastic bags, the distribution of computer hardware, industrial irons, and printing paper, the storage of industrial gas canisters, and the repair of automobiles. Along the lane, one sees rows of cycles, parked vehicles, cycle rickshaws, generators, a tea shop, a *pan* shop, stray dogs, and clusters of workers engaged in welding, hammering, and the loading and unloading of trucks. The factory, which began functioning in March 2001, employs about sixty workers.

Workers begin to arrive at the factory at about 8:30 a.m., on cycle and on foot, from urban villages, shanty clusters, and other working-class colonies in Okhla, Govindpuri, Sangam Vihar, Madanpur Khadar, Badarpur, Faridabad, and Noida. They stack their cycles along the wall of the vacant neighboring shed, and stand or squat in small clusters, chatting, rubbing tobacco in the palm, smoking *biris*, glancing at one another's watches, and peering through the gate at the clock on the back wall of the factory.

At 9 a.m., the shift begins, and workers shuffle through a gray-blue metal door, the factory gate, bearing the address, B156, painted in dark-blue strokes. They remove their shirts and trousers, and push and shove to get to their work clothes, which are kept in plastic bags and sacks inside a wooden crate in the cramped six-by-eight-foot welding room. They move out to the shop floor, a twenty-by-forty-foot room with slanting roofs reaching twenty feet in height, and gray walls with streaks, blotches, and chipping paint. There are eight olive-green polishing machines arrayed in two rows and a belt grinder machine in the back-right corner.[1] Each machine has a left and right workspace. Metal ducts connect the polishing machines to the exhaust fan-filter system at the center of the floor. Some polishers change their clothes right away, while others sit at their stools, yawning, stretching, trying to wake up more fully, watching the bustle of activity. Vijay, a supervisor from Almora, Uttarakhand, who was promoted from the position of polisher, directs helpers to bring specific quantities of metal artware pieces, such as platters, bowls, trays, vases, and wine coolers, to each machine. As workers joke and shout across the floor at one another, they closely watch, with anxiety and tension, as these quantities are set out.

Figure 1.1. The DDA Sheds, Okhla Industrial Area Phase I.

Work clothes exhibit many variations. One sees full shirts, short-sleeve shirts, polo shirts, and T-shirts, with logos of rock bands or words like "I Love NY," purchased from street vendors of export surplus in Okhla. They wear pleated tericot trousers, track pants, or pajamas, with slippers, sneakers, or shoes. There are rips, tatters, and holes in these clothes, especially on the forearms, elbows, knees, and thighs, caused by the abrasions of the polishing process. Workers try to squeeze a bit more life from these clothes by affixing layers of packing tape over the tears and holes. Trousers sometimes sport a permanently open fly, due to wrong sizes, broken zippers, and dislodged waist clips, requiring the tying of a string as a belt. Whatever are the original colors of these clothes, after a few days on the shop floor, they acquire a similar mélange of gray, sepia, and black tones, with dark accumulations of dust, debris, and polishing compound residues. The supervisor wears a blue short-sleeve shirt and trousers supplied by the company.

Ten minutes into the shift, Vijay directs a helper to switch on the exhaust fan, whose sudden rumbling interrupts the flows of conversation and joking.

Figure 1.2. The shop floor.

It becomes difficult to hear anyone beyond a few feet. There is an immediate awareness of the imperative of production. "Hurry up, guys! What are you doing?! Start your machine!"[2] Vijay shouts, as polishers pack their bags under the machines and settle onto their wooden stools. Workers don cotton *sari* fragments (*dhotis*), distributed each week as crude face masks. Some tightly cover the nose, mouth, and head, while others tie them in a village-style turban, leaving the face open, as they do not like the constricted breathing and the smells of the grime in the *dhotis*. They put on two sets of thick cotton gloves. Since only one pair is distributed each week, they must protect them from pilfering.

Polishers gesture to the machine with the right hand, then to the forehead and chest, in obeisance to the machine and to deities such as Vishvakarma and Allah. At 9:15 a.m., the machines start coming on. One hears the sounds of emery granules grating into steel, and sees sparks flying into the air. The belt grinder crescendos to a high-pitched whirring as metal pieces are

Figure 1.3. Front side of the shop floor.

pressed into the emery-coated belts, spewing more sparks. The machines are all running by 9:30 a.m. Buzzing sounds can be heard from the welding room, where two welders use argon gas and steel rods to shape beads along the edges of platters and trays.

The polishers push and press into the buffing wheels, undulating back and forth, pausing to gaze down at fine imperfections. A thick, gray-black haze of dust and debris rises and hovers above the shop floor. The grimy overhead

Figure 1.4. Back side of the shop floor.

fans blow the dust and haze in all directions. Dim, gloomy fluorescent lights gently sway above the machines. Torn and tattered posters of the labor laws on the left wall flap about in the dusty breeze. Dense particles dance in a frenzy inside the rays of sunlight that shoot across the ducts to the belt grinder. The noises of the exhaust system, belt grinder, and polishing machines blend together into a strange congruity. As Weil writes, on factory noise, "All noises have their meaning, they are all rhythmic, they fuse into a kind of giant respiration of the working collectivity . . . metallic noises, the turning wheels, the bite of metal upon metal; noises that speak neither of nature nor of life, but of the serious, steady, uninterrupted acting of men upon things."[3]

Outside the gate, strong, foul odors emerge from a round pot on a kerosene stove, in which solid chips of adhesive, made of tallow, are dissolved in water and cooked into a thick, bubbling, dark-brown goop. Helpers dip the edges of cutting buffs into the pot, spread the glue with their fingers, then apply coats of emery granules, pressing with the fingers and pounding the edges

Figure 1.5. Vijay, the supervisor, standing behind the machines.

with their palms. Their hands grow thick, hard, and calloused from this work. On the porch, helpers place metal pieces into a tub of diluted sulfuric acid to remove dark carbon residues on the welded edges. They handle these pieces with ordinary rubber gloves. The noxious acid fumes add to the bouquet of odors emanating from the factory gate.

Beneath the appearance of calm at the machines, the polishers are nervously deciding how many pieces to make. They use hand gestures and fragmentary verbal exchanges to communicate and coordinate with one another. It is the most tense part of the day, as some polishers might unexpectedly raise production, while others might invite quarrels with the supervisor for removing extra pieces.

Metal polishing comprises a sequence of operations. A wire buff is used briefly, when necessary, on the steel beads of pieces. Polishers wear goggles for this, as arrow-like bristles can jettison into the eyes. Otherwise, polishers begin with cutting (*katai*), using a leather and cloth buff coated with black, coarse emery granules. After this is fine cutting (*ghotai*) with a leather buff

Figure 1.6. Tea break. Front, left to right: Hanif, Achaibar, Sivam. Back, left to right: Sundar, Bhagvati, Uday, Govind, Vijay II, Krishna, Rajender, Mithilesh.

coated with tan fine-grade emery. Polishers hold the piece horizontally and cut in an up–down motion, then orient the piece vertically and cut in a right–left motion. Fine cutting is followed by polishing (*fiber*), using a buff with bristles of bamboo or coco fibers, and then, jean buffing (*saplai*), with a soft buff made of army denim cloth scrap. In these operations, polishers hold the pieces horizontally and then vertically, using a right–left motion each time. Helpers clean the pieces (*dhulai*) in kerosene and return them to the machines. Polishers do final polishing (*camak kholna*) with the denim buff or a soft cotton buff, orienting the piece vertically and using a right–left motion. During each operation, polishers remove a range of surface imperfections, such as bumps, holes, iron and carbon residues, waves, and buff marks. Polishing compound bars (*masalas*), made of quartz powder, tallow, wax, and other ingredients, are used as lubricants. Polishers at a machine work together on the pieces, with each partner specializing on the inside or outside portions of pieces.

As the clock reaches 11 a.m., polishers begin peering out of the gate and lingering a bit longer at the water jug near the entry. Tea is brought in a large kettle from a streetside eatery (*dhaba*) in the next lane. Metal pieces are set down, the machines are switched off, and *dhotis* are unraveled. "Hey, you shirkers, drink some tea!" Babloo Khan, a polisher from Budaun, Uttar Pradesh, might cry out.[4] The polishers quickly dust off their shirts and trousers, wipe sweat and grime from their faces, and move outside for the fifteen-minute tea break.

They huddle around a plastic bucket of brown-and-white cups, get tea, and gather in clusters, sitting or squatting along the walls, on the backs of cycles, on the footboards of scooters, and under a large rosewood tree to the right of the gate. The tea is watery and sweet. Motorcycles, cars, and trucks kick up dust in the lane. The pulsating pounding of power presses, the buzzing sounds of welders crouched on the sidewalk, and the harsh clanging of hollow gas cylinders unloaded from trucks down the lane provide the sonic backdrop for the rest break, augmented by the puffing of generator sets during power cuts. It is a good time for joking and discussing. Once tea is over, it is time for tobacco and *biris*. Inside, the helpers, with *dhotis* over their faces, sweep under the machines and collect piles of dust, debris, and waste into sacks. This is the most detested part of their jobs. "Come on, guys, time's up," says the guard, a few minutes before the break is over.[5] The polishers slowly get up, mumbling abuses. As they move inside, the helpers come out for their tea break.

At their workspaces, polishers stretch the break a bit, sharing tobacco, and taking one's time to put on *dhotis* and gloves. The exhaust fan rumbles again. The undulations resume in this rhythmic, pulsating danse macabre of brute force and subtle grace. Polishers bend forward and back, and sway side to side, cradling pieces with the chest and stomach, pushing with the knees, thighs, and calves. Tattered and frayed cardboard pieces affixed to the ducts, above the buffing wheels, act as crude dust shields. Gloved hands go close to the buffs when polishing the insides of items. Grimy visages are illuminated, ever so briefly, by the shimmering reflections of the overhead lights, when polishers pause to study imperfections, dab the buffs with compounds, and adjust their grip on the pieces.

Uday Singh, a young polisher from Palamu, Jharkhand, works with force and speed, lifting the insides of pieces into the buffs, rocking the machine on its foundation.[6] He wears an army-green cap, with his initials written in red across the front, to cover his hair and block the glare from the lights onto the pieces. Naresh Singh, his machine partner and relative, in his early twen-

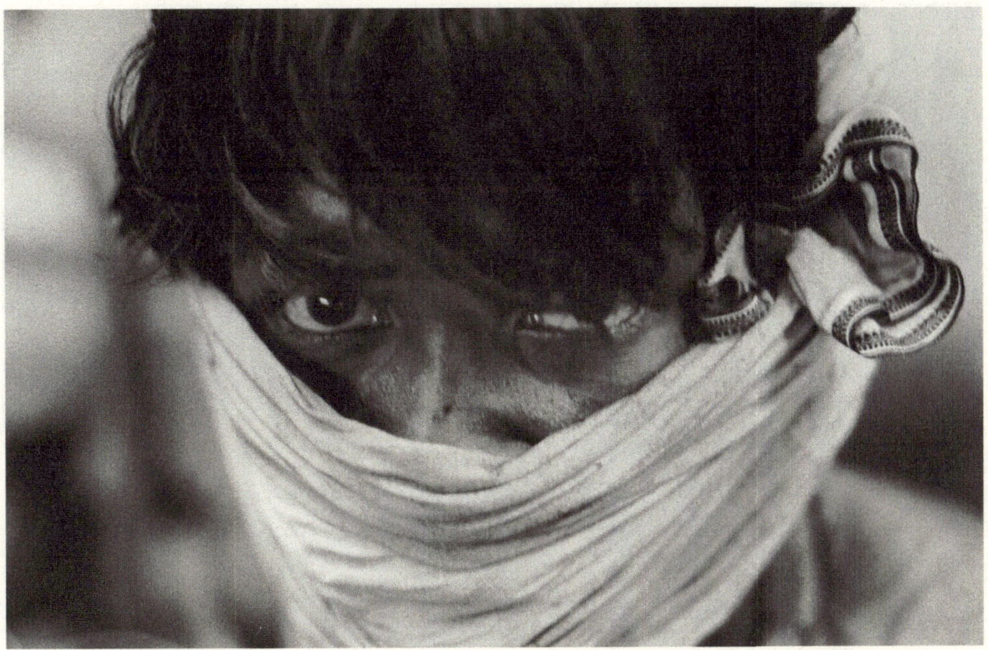

Figure 1.7. Uday.

ties, deploys more calm, smooth, and elegant motions. He wears an army-green cap without any initials. Across from their machine is Amlakant, an elder polisher from Ballia, Uttar Pradesh, whose movements are slow, steady, and meticulous. Babloo Khan, who does repairs of night-shift pieces at the machine to the right of Amlakant, bends in close, pressing pieces to the buffs with a stoic calmness.

After the tea break, as polishers progress to fine cutting, a new source of tension arises, with the prospect of the appearance of Khan sahab, the B156 manager. When he arrives at the gate, on a Hero Honda motorcycle, any workers resting near the entry quickly disperse. The guard carries his helmet inside and takes it to the upstairs office. The manager walks in, stops at Amlakant's machine, which is closest to the gate, and surveys the shop floor with a cold, blank expression. He is slim, in his early forties, and wears crisply ironed shirts, trousers, and shiny black shoes. He carries his motorcycle keys and mobile phone in his hands. He moves across the floor, lingers at the belt grinder, then climbs the stepladder to the office, a six-by-fourteen-foot room

Figure 1.8. Lunch in the welding room. Left to right: Amlakant, Sundar, Achaibar, Mithilesh, Premchand.

with a desk, metal closet, checker's table, and water cooler. He sits at his desk in a red high-back chair, under a low, slanting ceiling, and attends to paperwork and phone calls. While Khan sahab is in the factory, workers remain watchful and alert. Polishers restrain their movements away from the machines.

A few minutes before 1 p.m., the polishers put down their pieces and get up from the machines. They scrub their hands with soap at the water tap near the latrine, retrieve their lunch boxes, and move outside. They spread out sacks and newspapers on the ground and sit in small clusters, on the porch, near the glue pot, next to the cycles, and across the lane. A few find space inside the welding room and storeroom amid metal pieces, buffs, and compounds. Workers bring *rotis* (round flatbread) and *sabzi* (vegetable curries) or *dal* (lentils) for lunch. The curries usually contain potatoes, tomatoes, and other vegetables, and are prepared with generous amounts of oil and spices. Some buy a small plate of dry, spicy chickpeas and onions from a street vendor and *rotis* from the *dhaba*. Those who share their vegetables take out a portion

Figure 1.9. Ramparvesh.

and place it on the inverted lids of one another's containers before eating, to avoid transfers of saliva, though some do not observe such rules, and go directly into others' containers. As they eat, they wave off buzzing flies around the *rotis* and vegetables.

They finish quickly, go inside to wash their hands and lunch boxes, and come back out. Some sprawl on the ground, sit on cycles, or lean over scooters, and try to sleep, amid the dust and noise. Others chat about sports, politics, films, and goings-on in the company, and share stories from the neighborhood and village. Before long, one sees puffs of smoke from *biris* and the rubbing and clapping of tobacco in the palm. Khan sahab might come outside at this time, and sit in a chair near the polishers. Humorous exchanges might ensue, or at times, tense discussions about production increases, wage hikes, and overtime perquisites.

Inside, the helpers are at work, sweeping the floor and ceiling fans, cleaning the ducts, shaking dust from the filter, removing debris from the base of the fan-filter system, and collecting it all into large sacks. Before 1:30 p.m., the guard begins to prod the polishers to get up. They wipe their faces and necks with their *dhotis*, and move back inside with dragging, sluggish steps.

The afternoon is long, difficult, and tedious. Polishers shift to fiber buffing, which for many, is the most grueling work of the day. The haze blackens. The atmosphere becomes dark, gloomy, and grim. Amid the noise, one hears the sounds of polishers coughing, hawking, and discharging dark phlegm into the ducts. Cascading sweat on the brow and nose is wiped away with the backs of dirty gloves. Polishers call helpers to bring drinking water to the machines. This water, supplied by private tankers and stored in a roof tank that is not regularly cleaned, is of dubious quality. One occasionally sees small worms swimming in the clear plastic bags through which they drink. When these were shown to the manager, he responded, "You guys eat meat at home, which is much larger than this. Eat this too."[7]

During denim buffing, one hears reverberating sounds of gnawing and buzzing. The buffs eject olive-green cloth tendrils onto faces, bodies, and clothes. As polishers dab compounds and apply pressure, the buffs secrete black smoke. One takes special care in this operation, as the jean buff can pull in one's glove and injure the wrist or arm. When a polisher breaks in a new denim buff, by leveling the edges and opening its layers with a brick and blade, fibers spew in all directions, covering the polisher and blowing through the ducts, forcing others to get up and back away, waving their hands and muttering abuses.

By the 4 p.m. tea break, there is a sense of relief. Much of the difficult work is done. In the winter, polishers sit along the opposite wall and take in a bit of scarce, receding amber sunlight.

After the break, as denim buffing is completed, helpers wash the pieces in a tub of kerosene to remove compound residues, and dry them in a tray of wood shavings. This is a chance for polishers to rest for a few minutes, without being told anything by the supervisor, who is busy trying to rush the helpers through this work. Polishers don clean, white cotton gloves, dust them with dolomite powder, and do final polishing, using smooth, gentle, and precise movements. Finished pieces are set on the ducts or handed to helpers, who hold them carefully by the edges and bring them to the office, where they are cleaned with thinner and a soft cotton cloth. The checker stands at a small table, closely examines pieces under a tube light, marks unacceptable imperfections with a red pencil, and sends "failed" pieces back to the machines. Pieces that "pass" are placed in clear plastic bags and packed in old newspapers, by a helper seated on the floor in front of the manager's desk. Polishers get their failed pieces back, look at the red marks, do repairs, and send them back upstairs, sometimes more than once. The atmosphere becomes hectic and tense, with Vijay shouting orders, the helpers shuttling pieces to and from the checker, and polishers racing to do final polishing. Once one's pieces pass, Vijay gives them fresh pieces to work on for the remainder of the shift.

The day shift runs until 6 p.m., and with overtime, to 8 or 9 p.m. Toward the end of the shift, the polishers watch the clock closely. Fifteen minutes before the shift end, they turn off the machines. The belt grinder winds down. The exhaust fan shudders to a stop. The room is suddenly quiet. One can hear one another again.

Polishers quickly undress, shake out their shirts and trousers, and stuff them back into their bags and sacks. Some stretch their arms. Others dust and wipe their machines with *dhoti* fragments. One sees thin, angular, and gaunt bodies, visible rib cages and vertebrae, and indented stomachs, along with muscles in the arms, shoulders, and thighs—a strange juxtaposition of emaciation and strength, characteristic of proletarian bodies. They climb across the ducts and move toward the bath.

They take out soap bars and plastic sack fragments from their bags and plunge into the bathing area, which comprises a three-by-three-by-seven-foot single-person latrine that gives off a horrible stench during the daytime, and a three-by-six-by-eight-foot adjoining chamber with water taps and plastic buckets.[8] About twelve workers bathe at once, shoving and jostling for space. Some spill out into the entry area. In the hot months, they sweat profusely from the proximity of so many bodies. In the winter, they shiver in their underwear and cry out, "Ram, Ram! Oh, Mother Ganga!"[9] They plunge mugs into the buckets, throw water onto themselves, and soap aggressively, scrubbing with both hands, pulling sack fragments across the chest and back, dislodging layers of grime. Elbows swirl as they scratch and scrub the scalp with vigorous movements. Bits of pungent, gray-black foam fly in different directions. Grimy water splashes onto each other's heads, backs, and bodies. Lacking room or sack fragments, some subtly scrub their soapy backs against the chamber wall, as others angrily scold them, "Hey, look how much you're dirtying the wall! Did you come here to mess the place up or take a bath?!"[10] Some reach down to wash one foot, while precariously balancing on the other, as others squat and sit in the dark water, cleaning the legs and feet. They shout for soap and sack fragments, for one's back to be scrubbed, for mugs of water to be poured onto them, and to give more space, pushing, pushing back, sometimes tottering onto one another like dominoes. When someone tries to move toward the buckets, there is a cacophony of resistant responses, such as, "Where do you think you're going?! Wait a minute, brother! There's no room, man!"[11] When a worker bends or stoops, others might pinch, tweak, or goose him, or suddenly pull down his underwear, exposing his backside, inducing riotous laughter and cries of glee that resound in the chamber, as he struggles to pull it back up. One otherwise tries not to reveal one's genitalia, washing on the outside of one's underwear, discreetly soaping and emptying water inside the loose elastic bands. Amid sounds of hawking, spitting, and nose blowing, some sing verses of film songs. There are eerie, unexpected moments of calm and peace, abruptly interrupted by angry exclamations of those outside, who shout, "Come on, brother, get out! What the heck are you doing? You've taken a long time! Only you guys are going to take a bath and we won't? Let others bathe!"[12] Bathers push their way to the buckets, throw mugs of water over the body, and gingerly exit the chamber, trying to avoid touching the grimy bodies of others.

Inside the welding room and storeroom, with the doors closed, polishers don long-sleeve shirts over dripping bodies and use a spare underwear, or the existing one, to vigorously dry the hair, face, and body, amid knocking, pounding, and shouting by others to get out quickly. One witnesses a dramatic renewal of appearance, as bright, clean faces emerge from these underwear-towels with guttural exhalations of satisfaction. Colors suddenly appear in clothing—red, burgundy, indigo, olive, dark green—for the first time since morning. They look over one another's shoulders into the small wall mirror near the stepladder, sharing combs, and arranging strands of hair with the fingers. They pick up hard chunks of jaggery (*gur*) set out at Amlakant's machine, provided by the company, which is believed to cleanse the throat of dust and fibers. When eyes become watery and red, they bring a medicine bottle from the office, hold each other's eyelids open, and squeeze drops into the eyes.

They retrieve their lunch boxes and move toward the gate, grabbing and pulling up their trousers as they delicately step across the puddles near the entry. The guard runs his hands over the body, checks the pockets, lifts the lunch boxes, and says, "Go on, brother."[13] They wipe down their cycles, and sit for a bit, resting, smoking *biris*, and waiting for others to come out. They disperse in pairs and clusters, on cycle and on foot. They go to the vegetable market, one another's rooms, or directly home. Some head to liquor shops to "open their accounts (*khata kholna*)" for the evening, invoking a cricket expression for when a batter begins to score runs in a match. Meanwhile, workers on the night shift are getting out of bed, readying themselves, and making their way to the factory.

Night Work

The night shift begins at 9 p.m.[14] The night workers arrive, get into their work clothes, and dust off the machines. The machines are all running by 9:30 or 9:45 p.m. The night shift, which began in September 2001, includes relatives, neighbors, and other contacts of the day-shift workers. The night workers were mostly hired as casual workers, under a different company name, Artistic Goods.

Night workers must struggle not only with production norms and quality standards. Throughout the night, they wrestle with drowsiness and grogginess. The first bouts occur before midnight. Polishers get up and move about, wash their faces, smoke *biris*, and in the winter, warm their bodies by a fire of old, burning buffs outside the gate. After a few minutes, Ramkumar, a regular helper who supervises the gate, prods them to get back inside. Around this time, Govind, the night-shift supervisor (and Vijay's relative from Almora), who was a polisher in the early days of B156, sprawls out on two chairs in the office, with his feet up, covers his face with a *dhoti*, and goes off to sleep. There is no other management presence on the shift. Ramdev, a thin, quiet, regular helper from Madhubani, Bihar, stays awake and watches over the shop floor through a window above the checker's table.

A kettle of tea is left at the gate when the *dhaba* closes at night, and is reheated on the stove for the 1 a.m. break. Polishers come outside, pour cups of tea, and sit in the dim glow of the tube light above the gate, around the fire, and in patches of darkness along the opposite wall. No other sheds in the lane operate in the night. There are no other noises, except of soft voices,

Figure 1.10. The night shift. Madan and Rambachan II.

Figure 1.11. The welding room. Tulsi and Rambachan.

Figure 1.12. Varmaji.

occasional hawking, and mosquitoes buzzing close to the face. Before long, one sees bodies lying close against one another, along the far wall, down the lane, with teacups strewn on the ground. Some sleep. Others rest, eyes closed. There is an eerie stillness and silence. By quarter past one, Narayan, a stocky, elder polisher from Nawada, Bihar, who likes to boss others around, begins to shout at the lying bodies in a bellowing voice, "Come on, get up! What are you guys doing?! Let's go!"[15] The polishers slowly rouse themselves and stagger inside. Before long, the machines are running again.

After the break, as polishers shift to fiber buffing, others are hit hard by sleep. Due to the disturbing noises of the welding process, the welders stop their work and sleep at the same time, in their chairs, sometimes putting up their legs on the worktables. Inside the storeroom and outside the gate, helpers lie down on wooden crates, stacks of cutting buffs, and sacks of compounds. There is sometimes no one to attend to the shouting requests of polishers for materials and drinking water.

As it gets to 4 a.m., the specter of sleep begins to visit the machines. Eyelids close and heads drop, pieces still in hand, with fingers only inches away from the spinning buffs. When a polisher's head lowers, Narayan, who might be moving about the floor, shouts and slaps him hard on the shoulder, jolting him awake. Ramesh, a young, thin polisher from Deoria, Uttar Pradesh, who has been working in factories since his late teens, fights off sleep by singing film songs, such as "*Sajan re jhuth mat bolo, khuda ke pas jana hai* (Dear one, don't tell lies, you'll have to face God someday)," from *Teesri Kasam* (1966).[16] He never quite makes it to the somewhat unfitting verse, "You lost your childhood in play, slept through your youth, and cried when you saw old age."[17]

More pathetic scenes are witnessed at the machine of Varmaji, an elder polisher from Sant Kabir Nagar, Uttar Pradesh, who often drinks liquor before the night shift. When he gets drowsy, his chin drops, and subsequently, his pieces drop, one by one, into the duct. He reaches for more pieces, eyes closed, presses and drops them, until there are no pieces left. His partner, Mohan, an elder, husky polisher from Ballia, Uttar Pradesh, might poke him with a metal rod, bang it on the duct, and throw white powder on his face to rouse him. Varmaji awakens, walks outside, collapses onto his back, and descends into a deep, snoring sleep. The young Jharkhandi brothers and cousin-brothers of Naresh sit at the machines at the back corner of the floor, and work quietly and diligently through the night with solemn, stoic faces. As they get to jean buffing, they sometimes doze off, one after another, reclining on their stools, backs on the wall, legs stretched out, and grubby feet on the ducts. One sees strange sights, such as Tapesvar, with a *dhoti* over his head and face, pouring tobacco into his palm, with fingers on the cap of the slaked lime bottle, drifting back into sleep. There are dangerous glimpses of polishers with eyelids lowered and mouths open, working the denim buff, not fully awake or asleep, risking injuries.

As the clock crosses 5 a.m., things begin to change. Govind awakens and groggily comes down to the floor. His hair is disheveled and his face is puffy.

Figure 1.13. Govind, the supervisor, addressing Madan.

He makes a round of the machines, pausing behind polishers (some of whom are still struggling with sleep), watching hand movements, requesting status reports, scolding those who are dragging behind, and acting, polishers say, like a mad elephant (*pagal hathi*). He goes to the storeroom, pushes open the door, and shouts at sleeping helpers to get up. They hastily comply. He checks on the welders' progress and on the helpers outside, who quickly rouse themselves and get to work.

Before long, the polishers are working intensely again, bobbing up and down, pushing, pressing, looking up at the clock, dabbing compounds, and pressing some more, in a whirlwind of undulating figures. Glimmers of dawn light come through the open gate. Though drowsiness has not fled, and pieces still have to be completed, the worst of the night is over.

The pace of activity now becomes more frenzied and frantic. The dawn light illuminates imperfections that were missed during the night, which polishers try to remove with anxious and vigorous denim buffing. Helpers wash pieces, polishers put on clean gloves and complete final polishing,

Figure 1.14. Avdesh passing a platter upstairs for checking.

and finished pieces are relayed upstairs. "Finish the final polishing fast!" Narayan shouts.[18] The pieces are checked by Ramdev, who is seen to be excessively exacting, so as to impress Khan sahab and get promoted from the post of helper. Many pieces are sent back to the machines, and sometimes many times, provoking anger among the polishers. One hears volleys of abuses and threats directed at Ramdev, referred to as *mariyal* (feeble, sickly, quasi-dead), due to his wiry, gaunt frame. "You jerk, *mariyal*, you failed my pieces?! I'll grab him from upstairs and throw him down here! Bring him to me!" they shout, with gesticulating fingers.[19] Once their pieces pass, the polishers help in repairing others' pieces and relaying them for checking. In these activities, they exhibit a camaraderie that is not seen on the day shift. When there is time left, Govind gives them more pieces.

As final repairs get done, and workers get ready to bathe, tea comes from the *dhaba*, along with *samosas* or bread *pakoras*.[20] They come outside in various states of undress, and gather around the gate. Sweepers in the lane throw up dust and burn piles of garbage. Some polishers go back to the machines to finish repairs. Others go straight to the bath. As they bathe, dress, and leave, after shifts with overtime, day-shift workers begin arriving at the factory. There is congestion and collision in the entry and the changing rooms as workers try to get in and out at the same time. A few night workers linger outside, waiting for Govind, who can provide cash advances, to join them as they make their way to the liquor shop to open their accounts for the day.

Once night workers get home, they have serious difficulties. A consequence of night work, for many, is a loss of appetite, and they often do not eat much before going to sleep. In Tehkhand village, where the Jharkhandi workers cluster together in tenements, by late morning, one sees dark rooms of corpse-like figures shrouded under sheets or quilts, or arrayed in close lines on the terraces. Due to the heat, the noise of household activity, and the presence of small children, night workers often can only sleep until 4 or 5 p.m. They sit up, half-awake, with droopy eyes and listless expressions, drifting in and out of sleep. They try to eat, but might not feel hungry. They lie down again and struggle to get up for duty. This is a fertile time for quarrels with wives, who might not like staying alone during the long nights. On occasions when there is sexual activity, "You can figure that night will be an absence from work," says Rambachan II, a night polisher who cycles a long distance from Faridabad.[21] When a night worker does not turn up for work, and others know that his wife is in Delhi, they joke that he must be doing "double duty."

Due to these difficulties, night workers incur four to five absences a month, and sometimes more. An exception is Ramesh, who rarely misses duty, because of the diligent efforts of his sister-in-law to get him up and push him out of the room each evening. On his zombie-like walk to the factory every night, along the busy Okhla roads from Harkesh Nagar, his eyes droop, and he occasionally knocks into cycles and pedestrians, provoking heated exchanges and abuses. As night workers, it also becomes difficult to meet others, because of conflicting schedules. Distance enters into one's relations with friends, neighbors, and relatives. One becomes a ghost-like presence in the neighborhood, apparently residing there, but invisible to others.

Bodily losses, wage losses (due to absences), domestic tensions, and a resistance, more deeply, to living as quasi-corpses, zombies, and ghosts create discontent on the night shift. They make repeated requests to Khan sahab for shift rotation, as was the initial practice. The manager defers promises to do so. The night workers grumble but adjust. Some take the loss of appetite as a boon, as it means savings on food expenses. A few give up daytime sleep to work extra hours in workshops. There is also a sense of freedom (*azadi*) on the night shift, in the absence of the manager. They can come late, move about, shout abuses, rest, and even sleep at times, in ways that are not permissible in the day. This freedom allows them to tolerate and even partly enjoy working on the night shift.

But the acquiescence and adjustment are never complete, and do not come without anxieties. "The night is made for sleeping, not for working," night workers say.[22] Only demons (*rakshasas*) and devils (*shaitans*) stay awake at night, not human beings (*insan*). The bodily effects of working a continuous night shift were visible in weight losses and illnesses such as fever, jaundice, and tuberculosis. The subtle awareness of what was happening to them, and of their collaboration in this process, might partly explain why intoxicants and tranquilizers like liquor, tobacco, *pan*, and *bhang*[23] were so important in night workers' lives.

Payday

Wages are disbursed as early as the seventh and as late as the twelfth of the month. No explanations are given for delays.[24] On paydays, the cashier from the head office arrives toward the end of the day shift, and goes up to the office. Workers go upstairs, a few at a time, and collect their cash envelopes. During the first year, regular (or "permanent") workers receive monthly wages of $54 (Rs. 2,592) for helpers and $57 (Rs. 2,758) for polishers, which were the unskilled and semiskilled Delhi minimum wage grades as of August 2001; $68–79 (Rs. 3,300–3,800) for supervisors; and $83 (Rs. 4,000) for welders. There are deductions from these wages for state health insurance (Employees' State Insurance [ESI], 1.75 percent) and provident fund (Employees'

Provident Fund [PF], 12 percent) benefits. Casual workers receive less than minimum wages ($31–46 [Rs. 1,500–2,200] for helpers, $50 [Rs. 2,400] for polishers), without health insurance and provident fund.[25] Regular workers sign on the company muster roll of Metal Artware Exports, while casual workers sign on loose paper spreadsheets of Artistic Goods.[26] When collecting their payments, workers might get into quarrels with the cashier about amounts cut for absences and advances.

Outside the gate, they ask about each other's payments. They show their envelopes, express doubts and suspicions, and make calculations. There are rapid exchanges of notes as they settle debts with one another. Those who incurred many absences gaze down at their envelopes with fallen faces. One also sees the rare meeting and mingling of workers of both shifts, despite undercurrents of competition and hostility. When night workers go in to collect their wages, they might pause at the machines to greet, chat, and joke with day-shift polishers. Paydays offer glimpses of less divisive sentiments among workers, assisted by the shared joys of getting paid.

The workers disperse, with many going to nearby liquor shops and street vendors for meat and drinks. Over the next days, they settle payments with landlords, shopkeepers, life insurance agents, moneylenders, and other creditors in their neighborhoods. Many night workers who live far from Okhla do not return for duty that night. Only half of the machines run, operated mostly by the young Jharkhandis. Some night workers, who have drunk heavily and do not feel up to going home, turn up at the gate in the late night. They are not there for duty, but for refuge. They find a safe, quiet place, on top of the generator casing or under a tree, and crash for the night. At dawn, they get up, wash their faces, get on their cycles, and take their lightened pay packets home.

Danse Thanatique

The supervisors continually attempt to raise production and enhance quality. The polishers respond by active collaboration and pursuing speed and modifications of methods, guided in part by beliefs in the virtues of hard work and desires for the rapid accumulation of savings. Workers also seek ways to rest. Some engage in auto-regulated working, in which they coordinate to adjust quantity and speed.

Machinations

At the start of the shift, the supervisor often tries to get polishers to accept more pieces than prevailing norms. This is not easy to do. He uses a gentle tone, addresses them respectfully as master craftsmen (*ustadji*), and asks them to try. He appeals to their egos, invokes examples of others who have already made the higher quantity, and warns them that if they don't raise production, the company might close down. He might apply pressure, display anger, and threaten to make reports to Khan sahab, using an oft-heard phrase, "A job means saying yes, otherwise you can go home!"[27]

Once quantities are settled, the supervisor focuses on discipline. Vijay stands behind the machines, surveying the floor. Though he does not approach polishers while they are working, if they go to the latrine and linger at the water jug, he pressures them to return to their machines. After doing repairs on batches of pieces, Babloo Khan likes to smoke a *biri* in the welding room. The supervisor goes after him, sometimes jestingly pulling him by the shirt to get him back to the machine. Due to the excessive pollution and the limits on movements, polishers speak of feelings of suffocation (*ghutan*) and confinement (*bandish*) inside the factory.

As the polishers complete denim buffing, the supervisor tries to hasten the pace so the pieces will be finished and repaired by the shift end. He rushes them along by pointing to faster polishers. "See, their pieces have been completed quickly! Yours still aren't done! Come on, do the final polishing!" he says.[28] After one's pieces pass, he returns to gentle, coaxing speech to get them to work on fresh pieces, which he might say, is just to pass the time (*timepass karna*). The objective is to keep them busy at the machines.

When a large number of a polisher's pieces fail, Vijay might call him to the office, show him the defects, and say, in the presence of Khan sahab, "Your pieces didn't pass. What is it you do, man? What sort of a craftsman are you? Tell me, what should I write for your production? No work got done today!"[29] News of such exchanges spreads rapidly across the shop floor, enhancing one's sense of embarrassment and disgrace (*beizzati*). To avoid such encounters, polishers work hard to get their pieces passed.

To raise production, the supervisors do not rely only on negotiations at the machines. They make efforts with polishers outside of shift hours. They cultivate active collaborators (*camcas*), who will obey managerial directives and give information and reports on what workers are saying and doing, such as piece removals and oppositional language. In exchange, collaborators might be given slight wage increases, cash advances, less restrictions in moving about the factory, ease in getting leave, and leniency in returning late from the village. At critical junctures, they do not refuse to take on extra pieces.[30] Active collaborators are set up and operate secretively, so it is not always known with certainty who they are. Supervisors also cultivate loyal (*vafadar*) workers who do not give reports, but work quickly and raise production, for similar benefits. Supervisors might invite loyal workers to a nearby *dhaba*, and with meat, *rotis*, and liquor, try to persuade them to take on more pieces. They butter them up (*makkhan lagana*) by praising their skills and capabilities. They tell them of the pressures they are facing to increase norms. If they agree to take on extra pieces first, others will follow. For those requiring cash advances for liquor, such entreaties are difficult to refuse.

Once a polisher agrees to accept more pieces, the checker's assistance might be enlisted to relax quality standards and give the appearance of passing the higher quantity for a few days. Meanwhile, Babloo Khan, a suspected collaborator, discreetly repairs the pieces at his machine. The supervisor pressures others to follow the polisher's example. Once they do, and the higher norm is established, the checker gradually raises the finishing standards back to the proper level.

Machinations generate pervasive tensions, not just workload increases. From the start of the day, polishers feel apprehensive about the verbal tussles (*jhik jhik bazi*) that may occur with the supervisor, should they choose to remove extra pieces. When such quarrels arise, "First thing in the morning, your whole mood gets spoiled," they say.[31] Polishers do not like the supervisor standing behind their rear ends, pushing and prodding them as if they are oxen. When they get rushed at the finishing stage, they might direct tension at their machine partners, shouting at one another to speed up their work. This tension does not necessarily result in better production. In their haste, polishers leave imperfections on pieces.[32] "There is a lot of headache here," says Sivam, a polisher from Kannauj, Uttar Pradesh, with a volatile temper. "You have to complete your production. Get your pieces passed. Watch the clock. Complete everything by the shift end. And listen to the critical things they all say. Compelling difficulty (*majburi*) makes one do all this!"[33] After a tough day's work, if the supervisor makes disparaging remarks, "Your mind gets ruined. This is the situation: do the work, and afterward, get kicked in the ass too."[34]

The supervisors also incur tension in trying to get workers to work. They feel fatigued by the shift end from the tussles, quarrels, and mental work (*mansik mehnat*), as Govind puts it, of trying to get work done from workers.[35] They had worked alongside many of the polishers in other factories. A few years earlier, seven of them had fought a union struggle together at D45, that ended in exodus and dispersal. Their relations were suddenly different at B156. Partly due to the tension of managing workers, Govind and Vijay drank regularly.

Tensions produced from above, and felt by everyone, make the factory a space that assaults not just the body but also the mind. "Body may often be exhausted evenings upon leaving the factory, but mind is more so and invariably so," Weil observes.[36] After duty hours, substratum tensions besiege exhausted psyches about what transpired that day, what machinations might be going on offstage, and what might occur in days to come.

Speed, Modifications, and Looting

Polishers pursue dangerous working styles that contribute, wittingly or otherwise, to greater workloads and tensions. When Uday and Naresh began at B156, in mid-2001, the supervisor and a few other polishers had doubts about whether they would be able to handle the work. At T7, where they had been working, they had mostly polished brass with softer buffs. Steel polishing at B156 required more operations, stronger exertions, and higher quality. They were kept off the muster roll, and there were hints that Uday, due to his young appearance and thin body, might be let go. They struggled to learn the work. By applying heavy force, doing thorough cutting, and postponing rests, they began finishing their pieces quickly, ahead of others, and to the checker's quality standards.

They pursued this working style for certain reasons. They wanted to prove themselves, create a good image with the management,[37] get their wages increased, and become regular workers. In offstage dealings, Vijay encouraged Naresh and Uday with vague promises of wage hikes and regularization. Due to the rare possibilities of becoming regular workers in Okhla metal factories, they also wanted to get jobs at B156 for multiple relatives (a kin reserve army of sorts) who were working elsewhere as casual or contract workers. Seven relatives were hired in their first eighteen months. More were waiting.

Speed is contagious at the machines. Guptaji, Amlakant's partner, does not like being upstaged by the younger Uday. He closely watches Uday's polishing wheel, across the duct, and tries to keep pace, sometimes rushing operations and using extra force. Hanif, to Uday's left, also gets into the chase. Ego, competitiveness, aggression, and humor animate these contests. As they complete jean buffing, they cast their pieces onto the ducts, creating loud noises, signaling to others that they are almost done. After final polishing, Uday's pieces pass quickly. He sits back, crosses his legs on the duct, rubs tobacco, and watches, as others get their pieces returned with red marks, for imperfections neglected in haste.[38]

The contagion could induce injuries. Rajender, a tall, thin, elder polisher from Ghazipur, Uttar Pradesh, who ordinarily works slowly, decided one day to pursue Uday. He chased him as best he could, all day, muttering, "Damn it, today I'll see if that Jharkhandi gets ahead of me!"[39] "I'm going to get this guy injured today," Uday told Naresh, as he shifted to denim buffing, exerting force and kicking up smoke.[40] Rajender followed. His piece slipped, and the buff pulled in his glove, badly flaying his wrist. He gazed down at the wound, in silence and dismay, slowly got up, and made his way to the office for the first aid kit. Uday was smiling. But speed also punishes those who are accustomed to it. One day, in Uday's absence, Naresh was polishing the inside of pieces, which was not his specialty. As he tried to catch up to his partner during denim buffing, the piece slipped (as in Rajender's case), the buff caught his glove, and cut his wrist.

Speed contests raise production, by displaying slack capacity, enabling the supervisor to increase norms at the start of the shift. The polishers were aware of this. On why they engage in such contests, which increase workloads for everyone, Umesh, a night polisher from Madhubani, Bihar, says, "Competing in this way, people want to kill themselves."[41] Speed is destructive and self-destructive.

Polishers also engage in modifications of methods and implements (*jugad*), which assist managerial objectives of increasing production and quality. They modify the sizes of buffs, create tiny buff-like devices by affixing emery belts or cotton to the machine shaft, and experiment with different, nonobvious choices of buff types and sizes. They introduce new processes such as the acid bath, revise the order of procedures, and do away with operations. They evolve methods of holding, manipulating, and pressing pieces, using certain motions, angles, and sequences. They develop these modifications to avoid injuries, ease work, get one's pieces passed, increase speed, and improve quality.[42] Modifications also create hazards. The acid bath gives off noxious fumes. Emery belts can unravel and customized buffs can fly apart, injuring the face and eyes. But the company is able to save production costs of purchasing safer, durable, and proper-sized buffs and conserve materials such as polishing compounds.

More significantly, through modifications, the management acquires knowledge of how production and quality may be improved. The supervisors and checkers do not always have deep knowledge of how to remove fine imperfections from the pieces. By closely observing and discussing with polishers, and expecting them to engage in modifications, without guidance, the supervisors and checkers learn many things.[43] "They hire you to extract something from this," Varmaji says, showing grasping fingers over his scalp.[44] They recognize that polishing involves not only brute force and physical strength, but also intelligence, creativity, and artistry. A *karigar* (craftsman, artisan, skilled worker) in the metal polishing line is a respected title, connoting one who knows what methods, implements, and modifications to utilize to polish metal pieces easily and quickly, with proper quality, while conserving materials. Out of desires for safety and ease, and also to prove one's abilities, display one's artistry, and enhance one's image as a craftsman, polishers develop modifications that wittingly or otherwise, bring about new hazards, the gifting of knowledge to management, and greater workloads. The supervisor is able to put down more pieces. The checker is able to circle more imperfections. To mitigate the new strains, polishers must struggle to develop more modifications.[45] While the practice of *jugad* is often praised in the business media and elsewhere, as ingenuity amid constraints, it is difficult to only celebrate it at B156, given its diverse motives and consequences.[46]

One reason that some migrants work so intensely is ideas and beliefs about hard work (*mehnat*). In discussions, the B156 workers affirm that hard work is a good thing, that one should work hard to earn one's living, rather than engage in theft, dacoity, dishonesty, or muscle force, and that if one does hard work, one will get good fruits (*acche phal*).[47] Among these good fruits are a strong, healthy body, legitimate earnings, mental peace, and respect. "Hard work is the principal basis of human life. One can get everything from it. One cannot get anything without it," Varmaji says.[48]

Migrants often come to Delhi with the goal of working hard, accumulating savings, contributing to expenses in the village home for farming, house building, and marriages, and setting up a small business in or near the village, such as a general store or a vehicle for hire. In Okhla, they confront insecure and turbulent work situations. Even if one manages to get regularized, there is anxiety about the longevity of one's job, given the frequency and ease with which companies terminate "permanent" workers and shift or close factories. "There is no certainty with a private sector job. It's here today, gone tomorrow," migrants say.[49] A factory is seen as a temporary, fragile, and precarious dwelling. "The factory is like a bird's nest for us. When a windstorm comes, that nest gets destroyed. Then we'll go somewhere else and build another nest. If not here, then there, or someplace else," says Arun, a regular polisher from Nawada, Bihar.[50] At B156, workers continually engage in speculations and discussions about how long they might survive in this nest, express hopes of making it to the next Holi, Divali, or Eid, and exchange information about other such nests in Okhla, Delhi, and elsewhere, where they might go in the event of destructive turbulence.

Work ethics, accumulation desires, and precarity can come together in dangerous ways. One might accept difficult working conditions, work diligently and quickly, avoid conflict, and try to create a good image so as to extract whatever one can while a given job lasts, through the alchemy of hard work into wages. This working style is described by Naresh, ironically, as looting (*lutna*). "One thinks, okay, I've come to earn. I have to withstand hardship (*kasht*) for one or two years. I'll endure it. Try to earn quickly, put together some capital," he says. "It's like one is looting, somehow loot money! So long as the opportunity is there, one loots. Who knows what will happen tomorrow, given the situation we're seeing here."[51] One tries to work as many hours, at given wages, as one can get. Some night polishers, after working a twelve-hour shift, seek more work during the day. Not everyone does this "looting" for accumulation. Madan, a younger brother of Naresh, works extra hours in Tehkhand workshops, less to save, but so as to be able to spend freely and "blow up (*urhana*)" money on liquor and meat, and at times, on new, colorful clothes, which might get quickly looted by younger relatives. In such routines, one sees a reckless, frenetic cycle of hard work–wages–intoxicants–hard work. . . . [52] Madan rarely slept.

But all act recklessly in the ethos of looting, by working intensely under hazardous conditions and avoiding giving thought to the strains and dangers to one's body. It is only for a short time, says Naresh, until one accumulates enough, or one's body gives out, and one returns to the village. After that, there will be actual "life" (*zindagi*), without such hard work, hardship, and separation. "One is not living 'life' here. As soon as one has earned, one will go back to the village, live with all of one's people. It's there only that one is to live life. There's a lot of life ahead there," he says.[53]

By not seeing one's present existence, while working in factories, also as life, albeit difficult and distorted life, migrants think less of conserving bodies, resisting working conditions, and trying to live a bit better now. They adopt working styles that accede to and perpetuate these conditions for themselves and others. Migrants' hard work gives rise to ambiguous fruits: wages, but also sleep loss, injuries, knowledge transfers, and pressures to do more work. In seeking to loot, migrant bodies, minds, and life energies get looted.

Resting and Shirking

Not everyone is so reckless. Workers also seek ways to get some rest and ease (*aram*). One way of doing this is to incur absences, when bodies get exhausted. This often occurs when large items are being made and shifts are running for twelve hours. Despite stern pressures from the manager to work overtime on Sunday, some polishers refuse. Achaibar, a polisher from Ambedkar Nagar, Uttar Pradesh, who stays in a shanty in Faridabad, prefers to rest and meet others on this day. "All the weekdays, the management gets work done as it pleases. One day is our Sunday holiday, brother, it's up to us what we do on that day," he says.[54] "Joys parallel to fatigue: tangible joys, eating, resting, the pleasures of Sunday . . . But not money," writes Weil.[55]

Polishers also rest on the shop floor. They take breaks between operations, and during the washing and checking of pieces. They stand up sometimes to, as they put it, rest their backsides. They move about (*ghumna*) to the storeroom, water jug, and latrine. They go to other workspaces to borrow buffs and share tobacco. These rests are restricted by the supervisor's presence and their own felt pressures to complete their production. They rest after their pieces pass, and they wait to begin on fresh pieces. Polishers see these rests as necessary, to get their work done, and legitimate, if one's pieces pass.

If one seeks more rest than what is necessary or legitimate, it might be viewed by supervisors and workers as shirking (*kamcori*). Suspected collaborators are seen to evade work without punishment. Raju unexpectedly raises production, but might leave the shift early, citing aches and pains, and not return for days. Vijay II works quickly, but not always carefully, and moves about many times in the day. Such polishers might accompany substandard pieces to the office and make requests to the checker to pass them. They use the arts of persuasion, putting blame on the quality of the steel, alleging that extensive efforts have been made, and advising that repairs will be futile and damaging, while plying the checker with tobacco. Their pieces pass.

Narayan and Kalim, suspected collaborators, avoid sitting at the polishing machines on the night shift, preferring to direct the work of helpers and sleep in the office. When they are pressured to do polishing, they are often unable to make the pieces properly. At checking time, they adopt surreptitious methods. As others send their pieces upstairs, they intercept them on the storage ledge, write their own machine number on them, and watch as "their" pieces pass quickly. They abandon their own pieces on the ledge, without numbering them, or write other machine numbers on them so they will be sent to others for much-needed repairs.[56] As an alternative to subterfuge, Narayan might request younger polishers to repair his pieces in exchange for his two bread *pakoras* during the morning tea break. Given Narayan's age and vision difficulties, and their own hunger, they do it.

Shirking by collaborators is more of a perquisite than an act of resistance. But not all shirking is done by them. Balram gets up often and takes rounds to the latrine, and sometimes leaves glaring imperfections on his pieces, much to the rage and shock of his partner, Sivam. Govind teases him, "Shirker! At least do two cents' worth of work!"[57] When Balram's pieces fail, Khan sahab might shout at him, "This won't do! If you don't want to work properly, become a helper!"[58] Balram quietly takes the scolding. Given the high production and quality demands at B156, the wages were too low, he felt. Shirking was also a form of protest.

A master at creating rest and ease is Mithilesh, a young polisher from Kaushambi, Uttar Pradesh, who works the belt grinder, grinding edges and other portions of the pieces before they go to the polishing machines. He carefully adjusts the belt choice, pressure, and pace so as to spread the day's work, which requires one to four hours, across the shift. To rest, pass time, and escape the thick haze in his corner of the shop floor, he gets up many times and takes long rounds to the latrine, water jug, and storeroom, chatting and joking with those he meets along the way. He sits in the welding room with Premchand, a welder from Siwan, Bihar, who quietly listens to his animated gossip, stories, and reflections. He knows how to speak charmingly with the supervisor, who rarely tells him to get back to the machine.

When Mithilesh sees the manager's helmet being brought inside, he quickly dons his goggles and gets to work. Khan sahab comes over to the belt grinder and pauses, closely observing his work, doing what Mithilesh suspects to be a quick time study, to judge whether he has enough work to do. Mithilesh will work slowly on one piece. "If the piece takes one minute, I'll grind it for four minutes. I'll go on rubbing that thing whatever which way.

Go on looking at my 'artistry.' Khan sahab will think, okay, it takes a lot of time to grind this piece. Once he goes, I'll throw that piece down right away," he says.[59] So long as Khan sahab is in the office, Mithilesh runs the grinder so that its sound will be heard whether or not he is doing any work. At the shift end, he works vigorously, so if the manager comes down, he will appear to be working diligently. "Look at the clever one!" the polishers will shout, with smiles. "He was roaming around all day! Now he's doing some grinding!"[60]

If Vijay tries to get him to do more work, Mithilesh finds ways of dealing with him. If asked to remove more imperfections, he might use less pressure to give the impression that they cannot come out without damaging the piece. When asked to grind along the fragile edges of vases, he might apply excess pressure and open the joints, forcing the pieces to be sent for rewelding, prompting Vijay to retract his request. One has to exercise cleverness (*hoshiyari*), he says, and make a fool (*cutiya banana*) of the supervisors. But when polishers bring him pieces and ask him to grind certain portions properly, he does so without objections.

Mithilesh does not deny that hard work is a good thing. "Everyone says the fruits of hard work are sweet. Okay, I get that," he says. But he adds, "By the time a guy gets those fruits, who knows, he might get to his last rites."[61] In factories, one might do hard work, at risk to one's body, but managements will always want more. "Production will always be less for them, it can never be too much," he says.[62] One must find ways to conserve the body (*sharir ko bacana*), guard against efforts to extract more work, and enjoy a bit of rest and ease. For the good fruits of hard work may not be realized so quickly.

Auto-Regulated Working

A group of polishers practices a working style that seeks a path between speed and shirking, called *hisab se kam karna* (auto-regulated working). Its repertoire is to regulate quantity, pace, and resting, while giving proper quality.[63] About half the polishers engage in this practice on each shift, while the other half pursue an unpredictable mix of piece removals, speed, and quantity increases.[64] This distribution is unstable, and shifts along with unfolding turbulence at the factory.

Polishers following this practice regulate quantities by removing extra pieces at the start of the shift.[65] They consult each other at the machines, using covert hand gestures, to coordinate quantities.[66] They speak in fragments, while passing one another on the way to the water jug, or while discussing imperfections in their pieces near the belt grinder. These are concise, rapid exchanges using finger signs, bodies, pieces, and machine noise to avoid discovery by supervisors and suspected collaborators. There are diverse styles of removing pieces, depending on personalities, moods, and the atmosphere in the factory. They might give extra pieces to helpers to take away, set them on the ducts, subtly leave them behind while exchanging pieces at the stock shelf, or keep them in their workspaces to retain ambiguity and delay detection.

Once the supervisor sees polishers removing pieces, he tries to persuade them to accept them. Tense exchanges can ensue. If the supervisor refers to other polishers who have already made the higher quantity, Sivam might show his open right hand, and shout the saying, "The five fingers are not all the same!"[67] The polishers have different capacities, he implies, but also, possible, hidden dealings with the management. Some might angrily reply, "That other guy got himself buggered so I should also do the same?! Go and get the pieces made from him!"[68] Others challenge the supervisors to sit at the machine and show that they can make the higher quantity. They do not have good responses to these challenges. When the supervisors were polishers at the head office factory and at B156, the production levels were significantly lower, and ironically, they too encouraged piece removals. But when some polishers accept extra pieces for consecutive days, due to the supervisors' efforts, others begrudgingly follow, so as to not be targeted for producing less than others.

These polishers also regulate pace. They work with calm and ease (*aram aram se ragarna*), avoid haste and agitation (*jaldibazi, harbarana*), refuse speed contests, and adopt the pace, as Uday puts it, of the tortoise.[69] By working more slowly and exerting less force, one tries to guard against injuries, illnesses, and absences, and conserve one's body and longevity. As Firoz, a young polisher from Jaunpur, Uttar Pradesh, says, "To any craftsman, his life is what is dear to him, not the work."[70] With a slower pace, a polisher also wishes to remove imperfections properly, so that one's pieces pass, and one can avoid rounds of repairs. To achieve such quality, Amlakant works slowly, which forces Guptaji, his partner, to slow down and give attention to imperfections he would otherwise neglect. Their pieces then pass quickly.[71]

They find judicious ways to rest. They get up to stretch the limbs, go to the latrine, and space out production. But they limit their time away from their workspace, to avoid unpleasant encounters with the manager or supervisors.[72]

They rest at the machines, between operations, but do not sit idle for long. Amlakant, whose workspace is the first to be seen when the manager enters the gate, gets up only to spit tobacco into the latrine. His hands are always moving, but at a moderate pace. "I rest while working," he says.[73] At certain times in the shift, polishers slow down, grazing pieces with light pressure, not doing much actual work, so as to not get ahead of others or not complete their pieces too early (the opposite of racing). These are also chances to rest while working.

The polishers avoid sending their pieces too early, to not invite production increases, and avoid sending them too late, to leave time for repairs.[74] When pieces come back and the checker's red marks are seen to be too idiosyncratic or exacting, auto-regulated working sanctions a bit of shirking, as when polishers graze pieces against the buffs to remove the red marks, or rub them off with a soft cotton cloth. Sometimes, such pieces pass.[75]

Others in the factory also practice auto-regulated working. Premchand adjusts quantities according to the norms and wages at the company's welding unit in Lado Sarai, where he was trained. To space out his production and protect against fume-induced illnesses, he takes rests after welding sections of pieces. He stays at his table, chats with those who stop in to rest, and occasionally steps out of the gate. After a year, he brought his friend, Mathew, a welder from Pathanamthitta, Kerala, to work on a second machine. Mathew adopts the same pace. The manager tries to get them to raise production with the promise of better wages, but they are more focused on migrating to the Gulf, where Premchand has done two stints. Rambachan, a helper, learned welding from Premchand and works on the night shift, at helpers' wages. He welds less pieces, never more, than his mentor (*guru*). Helpers also regulate pace by adjusting water quantities and flame intensity while heating the glue pot, and controlling the speed of one's hands while engaged in buff coating and packing of pieces.

In auto-regulated working, workers regulate quantity, speed, and rest, and give proper quality, so as to conserve bodies, maintain one's job, uphold one's respect, and avoid causing difficulties to other workers. They decide how to work, "according to the context and circumstances, taking all things into consideration," Amlakant says.[76] This working style draws on autonomous coordination, through hidden gestures, muted exchanges, and hand adjustments at the machines, which is leaderless, improvisatory, and sensitive to the context of surveillance, collaboration, and competition in the factory. In so doing, auto-regulated working becomes an intimation of the collective politics of synchrony (*talmel*).[77] Auto-regulated working was beneficial to the management in that it yielded high quality, saved on material costs of repairs, and discouraged shirking. But in its restraints on production, and its underlying collective energies, this practice militated against managerial ambitions to intensify work, discipline, and control.

Respect

A category of deep significance in the lives of the B156 workers is *izzat*. This category has multiple valences, including honor, good name, and prestige, and of most relevance in this book, respect.[78] The dirty nature of metal polishing lowers its *izzat*. The workers feel and exhibit *izzat* for the machine. The *izzat* between the management and workers, and among workers themselves, arises in a context of instrumentality, envy, and affective feeling.

Dirty Work

There is respect in hard work and its legitimate earnings. But there is little *izzat* in the dirty nature of metal polishing. The workers must cover their faces with *dhotis*. They wear tattered clothes. Their bodies are blackened. They stop looking like human beings (*insan*) and begin to resemble animals (*janvar*), they say, and specifically, monkeys (*bandar*). They do not like this transformation. When Sivam enters the factory and changes into his work clothes, it feels terrible.[79] He might mutter, "Oh, damn fate! Better to die than live like this."[80] Helpers dislike sweeping the dust and debris on the shop floor and in the ducts, amid the polishers' discharges of tobacco, saliva, and phlegm. At these times, helpers feel very little *izzat* in their work.

To add insult to the low *izzat* of dirty work, they must deal with public exposure during the tea and lunch breaks. They feel embarrassed (*beizzati*) when they are seen in their work clothes by pedestrians and others in passing vehicles. This embarrassment is mitigated by the presence of coworkers, with whom they create a shield of sorts against the gaze of others, and engross themselves in chatting and joking. At dinner breaks, during overtime (when the night shift is not operating), they go to *dhabas* in groups, not alone. They try to avoid touching (and dirtying) the clothes of others while packed together on the closely arrayed wooden benches.

Figure 1.15. Getting up to bathe. Left to right: Amar Singh, Sivam, Balram.

Helpers must also contend with public exposure. A few helpers sit outside most of the day, coating buffs, and are seen by others, including female staff employees of the neighboring offices, who cover their noses with handkerchiefs due to the dust and odors of the B156 gate. They hope that relatives or acquaintances do not show up at the gate and see them in this guise, which can create *izzat* losses in their wider circles. Helpers who cycle to Govindpuri to purchase supplies feel uneasy moving about in dirty clothes. Bhuvan, a young helper (and a relative of Vijay), used to work as a conductor on private buses, and does not wish to be seen in his work clothes by his former colleagues. He takes inside lanes through Okhla, avoiding roads on which the buses operate, and lowers his head when he crosses the main road into Govindpuri. Shopkeepers treat helpers with *izzat*, says Lallan, a helper from Nawada, Bihar, for they are there to buy things, but he feels awkward standing close to cleanly dressed purchasing agents inside small, congested shops. Shop owners' views seem to resonate with workers' own images of themselves. "They look like gray, black-faced monkeys (*lan-*

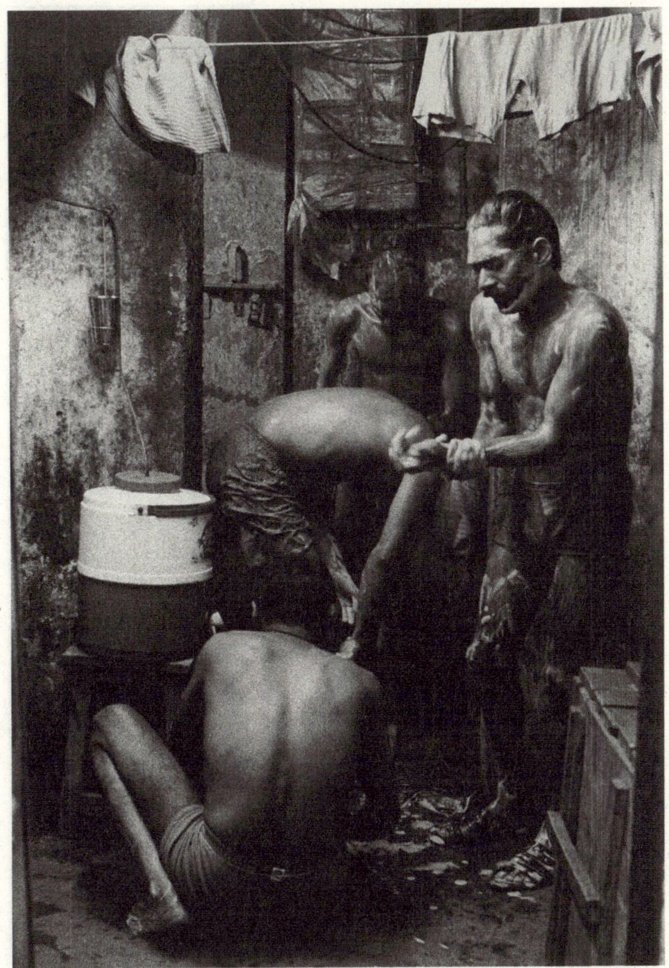

Figure 1.16. The bath.

gurs)," says one shopkeeper in Govindpuri.[81] "But they are poor persons, what to do. There is dust and grime in the factory," another adds.[82] Helpers prefer to get back to the factory, and its dirty work, as quickly as possible.

Bathing at B156 is how workers undo their simian guises. They recover clean, respectable appearances, without any visible or olfactory traces of the dirty work. Once they come out, they blend into a sea of Okhla workers on roads, in markets, and in neighborhoods. They even lose identifying

Figure 1.17. Bathing in the latrine.

markers of being wage workers (*mazdurs*), claims Naresh. "When one leaves the gate, no one can tell if one is coming from a garment factory, or one is a supervisor, or a manager, or works on a computer. One transforms at once," he says.[83] Bathing restores *izzat*.[84]

Once they get home, this *izzat* must be carefully managed. When asked by family members why they come back freshly bathed, they might give vague answers. Helpers often conceal that they do sweeping work, a lowly, stigmatized activity associated with certain Scheduled Castes, saying instead that they work in a storeroom or pack pieces. Sivam once explained to his cousin-brother's wife, with whom he stays, that polishing was done with cloth buffs. She got curious, and asked to see the factory. Sivam got nervous and quickly spun a story, saying that polishing was like her husband's "clean" tailoring work done in garment factories. Drawing on the origins of the denim buffs, he suggested that the factory produced army uniforms, as she had seen on soldiers in *Border* (1997), so there was nothing new to see at B156. His cousin-brother, once briefed by Sivam, collaborates with the story. Despite these efforts, discovery occurs, when unexpected visitors turn up at the factory gate.

Dirty work clothes are visible evidence of the nature of the work, and must be dealt with discreetly. Instead of taking them home for washing, some workers squat and scrub them while bathing, despite management rules against this practice. Others bring them home and wash them secretly at night, so no one will see the black rivulets of water that ooze out of them. Polishers' wives who know of the work might also wash these clothes. They do not necessarily like doing it, as it requires multiple rounds of soaping and scrubbing, and a tolerance for a bouquet of strange, diverse, and foul odors. They might be provoked, at such times, to voice objections to their husband's line of work. When Rajender's wife washes his work clothes inside their shanty, he might tease her, "Look carefully, wash them well!"[85] She might respond, while scrubbing, "Go wash your own clothes! I've told you so many times not to do this kind of work! You can't get any other work in all of Delhi?! Why do you do this rubbish-sorting work?!"[86] To avoid these hassles, some never wash their work clothes. Ramesh goes for weeks, and even longer in winters, without doing so, and does not seem to mind the accumulations of grime that, he says, thicken the clothes. "What's the point of washing them," he figures, as they will quickly get dirty again.[87] Once the clothes become compromised by severe tears and holes, he replaces them with fresh ones, which will never be washed again.

Migrants also practice discretion in the village when describing their work. When they say that they do polishing, it might be confused with polishing shoes on the footpath, which is low in *izzat*. By giving some details, and suppressing others, they try to protect and bolster the *izzat* they have gained by migrating, working, and earning wages in the city. Rajender avoids delving into details of working conditions at B156 and instead, proudly emphasizes, "It is a foreigner's factory and the finished products go straight to

America!"[88] When others press them to get jobs for them at the factory, they might be evasive. This is not just to prevent discovery. They might not wish to draw others into such dirty work.

Some migrants choose disclosure over discretion. Naresh and his brothers describe polishing to their parents, and show them metal pieces they have finished in other factories. There is *izzat* in the village, says Naresh, in working in a factory, where one is not exposed to the harsh elements of sun, wind, and rain that one must endure in farming and construction work.[89] There is more *izzat* in becoming a craftsman (*karigar*) and operating a machine. There is also *izzat* in helping others to come to Delhi, learn polishing, and earn wages. On one occasion, Madan brought his mother to the factory, and asked her to sit close by, with a *dhoti* over her nose and mouth, while he worked at the machine. He wanted her to see the work. Madan, who takes the greatest care with regard to his clothes, hair, and appearance, of anyone at B156, ironically had the least difficulty in revealing his blackened polisher guise. Such revelations generate anxiety and distress among family members about the hazards of the work. But they also exhibit a relation of *izzat* of deeper qualities which is not undermined by the dirtiness of one's work.

Man-Machine

If polishers derive *izzat* in the village from working on machines, they also gain *izzat* within the factory by virtue of the machine. While they are at their machines, aside from the initial and final parts of the shift, the supervisor says very little to them. He leaves them alone to do their work, out of respect for the craftsman and the desire for quality.[90] This is not the case for helpers, who can be directed to do tasks in multiple places through the day. "As long as I am at my workspace, it's my rule (*apna raj*). No one can boss over me," Uday says. "My machine, my workspace, my storage crate—I am the lion (*sher*) of all of these."[91]

The machine is also a space of affective feelings. Once polishers are assigned to a workspace, they make adjustments to the stool height, footrests, and sitting angle, create places to store their modified buffs, and work to get their hands "set" so they can polish the pieces with safety and ease. They gradually develop attachments (*lagav*) for the workspace. For these reasons, they don't like to shift to other machines, and resist doing so.[92] "One's machine is very dear (*pyara*)," says Uday.[93]

The polishers exhibit *izzat* for the machine in gestures, prayers, and worship. Before starting work, they make a gesture (*pranam*) of the right hand to the machine, then to the forehead or chest. They might silently say, "Hail God Vishvakarma,"[94] and pray that the shift passes without injuries. Vishvakarma is the divine, cosmic artisan, architect, and engineer, the originator of artisanal crafts and manufacture, who presides over, protects, enables, and is immanently present in these activities, especially in work involving iron and machinery. Vishvakarma is ambiently present in the factory and dwells within the machines. The polishers' artistry, sustenance, and bodily integrity owe themselves to this immanent divinity.[95] Not everyone prays to Vishvakarma when starting the machine. Some take the name of Bajrang Bali (Hanuman). Muslims might say, "In the name of Allah."[96] But as with Firoz and Hanif, they might also affirm belief in Vishvakarma. Bhagvati, an elder polisher from Sultanpur, Uttar Pradesh, invokes Buddh Bhagvan (Buddha), Ravidas (the medieval poet-saint), and Vishvakarma. At the shift end, polishers dust off and wipe down the machine, using their *dhotis* and gloves, and sweep the foundation and storage crate, as gestures of *izzat*. Many polishers attest that their *izzat* for the machine is greater than the respect they feel for any persons in the factory.

On Tuesdays, a worship ritual (*puja*) is done for Hanuman and Vishvakarma. Toward the shift end, a helper lights incense sticks and gently waves them in front of posters of Hanuman, Vishvakarma, and Ganesh, Lakshmi, and Saraswati, on the back wall near the clock. He recites a few verses of Tulsidas's *Hanuman Calisa*,[97] presses offerings of *bundis*[98] to the mouths of the images, sets a few sweets close to the posters, then distributes the offerings.[99] As the helper moves about the shop floor, polishers pause their work, stop the machine, receive a handful of offerings, place one *bundi* on the machine, and gesture to the machine, before eating the sweets. Babloo Khan often accosts the helper for extra portions. A bag of offerings is left in the office for the night workers.

A more elaborate *puja* to Vishvakarma is done on September 17.[100] In the morning, the machines are cleaned, and new posters of divinities are put up, along with garlands of multicolored tinsel. Tools (such as a hammer, screwdriver, and pliers), flowers, fruits, and *laddus*[101] are set before the posters. Red powder is placed on the foreheads of the divine images. Incense sticks are lit, waved about, set nearby, and placed on each machine, along with flowers. The fruits and sweets are distributed. At the *dhaba* in the next lane, the owner sets up a pavilion with an idol of Vishvakarma, where a priest does *puja* and distributes offerings throughout the day. In the evening, there are cultural programs in Okhla and in working-class colonies, with Bhojpuri singers and dancers, drawing large crowds.

Despite prayer and worship, injuries do occur. A piece can slip, a glove can get caught, and one's hand can get pulled into the machine, causing serious damage. But polishers do not seem to blame the machine or the divine for these injuries. Instead, they tend to blame their own distraction, carelessness, or haste. They might also articulate beliefs that injuries, especially serious, life-transforming ones, occur due to the powers of fate or destiny (*honi, vidhi*). "When an injury is fated to occur, it's going to happen, no matter what divinity you invoke," says Ramakant, a night polisher from Ambedkar Nagar, Uttar Pradesh.[102] But fate, to a considerable degree, is also seen to be shaped by one's good and wrong actions (*karm*), and favorably, by *izzat* for the machine, prayer, and worship, particularly in their noninstrumental valences.

Izzat implies protecting and not damaging the machine. Polishers can blow the machine motor easily, by misusing the power switch, dislodging wires, or applying excessive force while polishing. But to do so, they say, is to subvert the means of one's sustenance and to dishonor one's artistry. It is an affront to Vishvakarma. If one's machine breaks down, for any reason, there are also unpleasant consequences. The polishers are displaced from their workspaces for a few days, while the machine is sent for repairs. They might have to sit at other machines, where they are not used to working. They might get to do lighter work at the belt grinder or in buff coating with the helpers, but must endure the teasing remarks of other polishers, casting their activities as shirking, such as, "You've got it good, brother, you're living it up!"[103] A blown machine creates *izzat* losses. Some try to mitigate the unease by working vigorously at the belt grinder. Others take days off, forfeiting wages, but saving one's *izzat*, until one's machine returns to the factory. When tensions with supervisors escalate over production quantities, one occasionally sees angry polishers deliberately damaging machines. But afterward, as they awkwardly sit about, waiting for repairs, contemplating the consequences of their *izzat* lapse, there can be regrets. Sabotage, even as protest, is not easy to endorse.

The B156 workers do not seem to feel a sense of alienation or antagonism vis-à-vis the machine.[104] They derive autonomy and *izzat* from the machine. They develop affective feelings for the machine. They exhibit *izzat* for the machine and the immanent divine. The machine gives them sustenance and livelihoods. They are not working "against" the machine.[105] Their antagonisms and *izzat* difficulties seem to exist not with the machine, but with the management and with one another.

Surfaces

At B156, instrumentality, egoism, and envy give rise to certain forms of *izzat.* The manager and supervisors use polite, gentle speech with the polishers, praising their work and artistry, and coaxing them to raise production. The polishers prefer this speech to sternness and scolding. But managerial respect, while seen as partly genuine, can also be perceived as surface-level respect (*dikhavati izzat*) and hollow respect (*khokhli izzat*), motivated by desires for production. "It's based only on your work," says Naresh. "If your work is good, they treat you okay. But if it becomes slack, they'll have no concern for you. They'll change their behavior right away."[106] Managerial *izzat*, on this reading, is machinations in respectable camouflage.

Managerial respect is consciously kept within limits. Govind admits that if he gives the polishers the *izzat* they deserve, he will not be able to make them work. As he moves about the factory, he likes to sing "*Ek pyar ka nagma hai* (Life is a song of love)," from *Shor* (1972). But he observes, "If I treat them with love, the company will not be able to function. It will go under."[107] He invokes the saying, "If a horse makes friends with the grass, what will he eat?"[108] Govind sits, drinks tea, and jokes with workers, though Khan sahab advises him not to do so. Deeper valences of *izzat* threaten the instrumentalities upon which the factory depends.

Workers also exhibit *izzat* to the management. In Khan sahab's presence, they bring their feet down from the ducts, avoid smoking *biris*, and restrain vulgar joking. This *izzat* is described in similar terms as the respect they receive from the management, as surface-level, not heartfelt (*dil se*), and as instrumentally motivated, in part, by desires for job protection and advancement. It is respect for the post (*post ki izzat*) more than for the persons. Among themselves, workers might express anger against the management for production pressures, nonrotation of shifts, and delays in wage increases and regularization. But this resentment did not seem to extend higher than Khan sahab, the immediate authority in direct, face-to-face dealings. The American and Indian directors, who rarely visited B156, were endowed with respectable and benevolent qualities.

Amid surface-level respect, there are glimpses of other possibilities in dealings with management. Panditji, a quiet, soft-spoken, elder checker, speaks politely with everyone, shares subtle jokes and exchanges tobacco, acts without airs, and keeps a distance, to the extent possible, from machinations. The polishers feel hassled at times by his fastidious checking, but admit to feeling genuine *izzat* for him. They miss his presence when he is rotated back to the head office, and welcome him with warm smiles, handshakes, and pats on the shoulder when he returns to B156. They wish that he could be given sole charge of the factory.[109]

Among workers themselves, there are *izzat* difficulties. The polishers can look down on helpers and use rough speech when calling them from the machines. "Hey, helper, bring me a buff!" they might shout.[110] If the helpers do not respond, the polishers might utter abuses and throw hard fragments of compound at their backs to get their attention. The addressing and abuses can be tinged with resentment, as helpers are seen to do lighter work, rest excessively, and make comparable earnings. Helpers also desire *izzat*, and respond better when they are addressed politely and by name. The polishers adopt warm and gentle tones, to get through their production. There is not only instrumentality in these dealings. Elder polishers use affectionate terms for sons and young people (*babu, beta, munna*), which the helpers appreciate. Some polishers also train helpers at the machines in polishing.

Deeper qualities of *izzat* can be obstructed by differing allegiances, ambitions, and working styles. Active collaborating, the pursuit of speed, and the raising of production engender *jalan* (jealousy, envy, hostility). This complex of feelings is expressed indirectly in backbiting, verbal abusing, and cursing, and in direct remarks, as when some polishers told the fast-working Uday, at a tea break, "You've screwed all of us. If you get sacked, no one will come to save you."[111]

The polishers recognize the difficulties of trying to get respect from the management and fellow polishers at the same time. Arun works quickly and knows that it creates resentment, but feels it is safer to maintain a good image with the management, as long as the job lasts. If he damages his relations with polishers in the process, he figures that he can repair them later, without difficulty. Uday avoids friendships with slower polishers such as Amlakant, whom he likes and respects, because uncomfortable, empathetic feelings might arise, that he is causing strains and difficulties to his friend. Naresh tries to pursue a moderate strategy, in striving for managerial respect and its benefits, while resisting raising production, due to his existing friendships with Sivam and other polishers. The balance is not easy.

The entangling process of work at B156 gives rise to envy, which enervates and obstructs respect, creating a difficult, tense atmosphere. The respect they share remains surface-level (*upar se*), insubstantial (*halka phulka*), and incomplete (*adhura*), they say. It is an ambiguous and uncertain *izzat*. But in auto-regulated working, workers temper the pursuit of managerial respect, coordinate their work, and avoid generating hostilities. In so doing, they create space for more genuine and deep forms of *izzat* to arise.

Vitality

The B156 workers bear witness to the grinding down of bodies and minds. In the winter season of high export orders, during intense phases of twelve-hour shifts, bodies grow more thin, taut, and muscular. Rib cages protrude. Stomachs become more concave. One sees workers leaving the shift early or vanishing for a few days, due to body aches, breathing difficulties, fever, and sheer exhaustion. Amid the satisfactions of high overtime earnings, workers articulate anxieties about what they are doing, and where it might be leading. They speak of the work as lethal, deadly, and life-taking (*janleva*). "The factory is a dark chamber of death," says Sivam. "When we sit down at the machines, we take a grave risk [we tie funeral shrouds about our heads]."[112] One senses that workers were bearing witness, anxiously, to an unfolding, life-abbreviating work process at B156.[113]

The deeper anxiety, perhaps, was in the awareness of their collaboration in this thanatic process, in speed, modifications, the looting ethos, and beliefs in the virtues of hard work. One could do hard and diligent work, but in the context of B156, it could give rise to self-destructive fruits. "A guy will go on working hard, the company will go on exploiting him, and he's not going to get the good fruits of his work. He'll get entangled, deeper and deeper. One day, his body will be destroyed, and he'll accept defeat, resign, and exit the scene," says Varmaji.[114] One might try to loot wages from the factory, but end up losing bodily strength, vitality, and longevity. It was not just Ramdev, the gaunt, night-shift helper, who should have been seen as *mariyal* (quasi-dead). They were all *mariyals* in the making.

Yet they do not wish to die so quickly. In the stacks of *dhotis* distributed to workers as face masks, one occasionally sees cloth fragments of rough texture, without a border, bearing the strong smell of clarified butter (*ghi*), which is used to anoint bodies before cremation. Volleys of angry abuses break out across the floor at this time, for these are suspected to be fragments of funeral shrouds (*kafans*), removed from bodies that are yet to be cremated, and recirculated through secondhand cloth markets.[115] "Damn it, where did they bring this from? They've given a shroud to cover the face! What sort of bloody company is this?!" they might shout.[116] They might be progressing to death, and will require shrouds soon enough, these abuses seem to say, but right now, they are still alive. By modifying their working styles, amid the entanglements of B156, they find ways to create spaces for themselves, live and breathe a bit better, and defer their migration to death.

CHAPTER 2

Humor

At the metal factory, there is a relentless rhythm of activity directed toward production. The machines gyrate. The exhaust fan rumbles. The polishers press into the buffing wheels, spewing black-gray dust and debris. But along with this activity, there is a continuous, irrepressible flow of humor (*mazak*) at B156. *Mazak* begins at the start of the workday, continues at the machines, during tea and lunch breaks, and at bathing time, and lingers on while walking home. It was striking and intriguing to see the energy, creativity, and vivacity of this *mazak*, within an environment otherwise so dark, gloomy, and hostile to life.

What are the practices, vocabularies, and imageries of workers' *mazak*? What are workers' motives for engaging in *mazak*? What are the messages and effects of this *mazak*? In this chapter, I describe workers' practices of horseplay, vulgar humor invoking buggery and machines, and joking about migrants from Bihar and Muslims. *Mazak* has entangling and noncooperative valences with respect to the thanatic work process. *Mazak* helps workers to work, by distracting them from tensions, ennui, and fatigue. But *mazak* is also a theater, in which workers engage in creative play, entertain one another, draw closer together, and articulate an implicit auto-critique of their own undesirable qualities of egoism, submissiveness, and insularity. In *mazak*, workers seek a bit of fun, conviviality, and life, amid a vitality-enervating process.

Tension

The B156 workers contend with myriad tensions in their lives and worlds. There are the tensions of ongoing managerial efforts to raise production, of verbal tussles with the supervisors, and of finishing one's pieces to the checker's exacting quality standards. There are the travails of attending to living costs in Delhi, illnesses and medical treatments, discord within the family, and duties and responsibilities to the village home. All of these tensions plague the mind while inside the factory.

When working at the machines, workers' thoughts at times drift toward the village. At the belt grinder, Mithilesh cogitates about many things. "My mind goes on thinking about this or that thing. My wife, children, mother, father, brother, sister, village home, relatives, my mother's village, something or the other, some good things, some bad things. I am constantly thinking. How will my life go, what I should do, how can my difficulties be pushed away? It's the *man* (mind, heart). It runs here and there."[1] On the night shift, while polishing pieces, Madan engages in calculations about his wages, monthly expenses, and possible savings for a trip to the village in Palamu, Jharkhand. He imagines what he will do once he gets there. He sometimes goes into a daydream (at night), "travels" to the village, meets people, and exchanges news. "My work is going on, I am not feeling sleepy, news is coming from home and going from here. I go on thinking, how and what must folks be doing at home. The pieces are getting done, one after another, and these thoughts are also going on there [in the village]," he says.[2] When he comes out of the reverie, he might look over to Rambachan II, his partner, who might be puzzled by his prolonged silence, and say, "I went off to the village, buddy. I was talking with everyone."[3] If Madan focuses solely on his work, drowsiness comes quickly. As long as his *man* is in Palamu, his pieces get finished quickly.

When the work is tedious and grueling, the thoughts of Naresh, Madan's elder brother, also shift toward the village, but with a more serious tinge. He wonders if his parents will have enough funds for impending farming operations and whether the coming rains will be adequate. He worries if his mother, wife, or child might be ill, due to the sorcery practices of shamans and relatives. He thinks about how long he will need to work in Delhi, before accumulating enough to return to the village, purchase more land, and begin some small business activity. "I've been in Delhi for this long, and I haven't been able to do anything for the village home. How much longer will I have to do this hard work? How much longer will I have to earn so there will be enough savings? I go on thinking and worrying about all these things," he says.[4] At the machine, his attention (*dhyan*) gets split between the metal piece and the village. Unlike Madan, his pace slows down, forcing him to rush to catch up to others, once his *man* returns, more fully, to the factory.

While resting, tensions can also trouble the mind. One might see a polisher sitting at the machine, staring at the ground with a blank, vague expression, or standing in the entry area and gazing out of the gate, or sitting alone during a break, rubbing tobacco, caught up in some entanglement (*uljhan*) of thoughts. On a trip to the water jug, Arun once paused to ask me, "Brother, please tell me some path such that I can make a basic living easily, without any tension. Give me a way that I can live at home, with ease and mental peace, with the whole family. I want it to be like that."[5] One occasionally sees helpers, between tasks, sitting by the storeroom, squatting on the metal ducts, or leaning against the wall, looking down with grim, solemn visages. At such times, tense thoughts enter the mind, says Sabbir. "If one is idle (*free*), tension is there. Thoughts from here and there come into the mind, like if one were back in the village, one would be with one's family. Or this work is not good. When one is unoccupied, one thinks of all things," he says.[6] Ramparvesh, who is often found in such brooding postures, strongly dislikes the polluted atmosphere and dirty work. Passing the time (*timepass karna*) is not easy, he says. The time feels slow, sluggish, and monotonous.

To avoid such ennui, the polishers engross themselves in the pieces and try to keep their hands moving. The helpers stay busy with their work. They also find other ways to create distance from tensions, in *mazak*. But within the activities of *mazak*, they also address, ridicule, and critique the sources of their tensions.

Vulgarity

The B156 workers engage in a variety of humor practices. I describe their activities of horseplay, buff throwing, and erotic joking on buggery and machines. In the imageries of *mazak*, an implicit critique arises of factory oppression, divisive competition, and submissiveness.

Buggery

Mazak at B156 is most readily visible in horseplay. When workers move around the shop floor to pick up buffs and polishing compounds, rest, drink a glass of water, or go to the latrine, they engage in teasing, banter, and insults, sometimes escalating into wrestling, in which one worker may be brought to the ground as others observe, cheer, and goad them on. A worker who feels he has been outwitted in banter might in frustration grab the other around the chest, pick him up, carry him outside the gate, and drop him on the road. During tea breaks, one might be calmly sitting in conversation one moment, and suddenly see two workers spring up and bolt down the lane, throwing up dust as one chases the other, catches hold of him, brings him to the ground, then sits on him until some apology or request for mercy is exacted. In these ways, the factory becomes a kind of playground for workers, a space not only of grueling and exhausting work, but also of spontaneous, reinvigorating physical play.

At the machines, *mazak* goes on throughout the day, punctuating and embellishing the production process. After a polisher finishes with a buff, he removes it from his machine, and if he feels in the mood, hurls the buff with an arc-like trajectory so that it lands with a huge thud on the exhaust duct hood near the face of the polisher opposite him or at his diagonal. The targeted polisher, bent over his machine, engrossed in his work, jolts at the noise and tremor to the duct. Due to the risks of injury, hurlers of buffs make sure the targeted polisher is not working on the treacherous denim buff at the time. Buff throwing becomes more contagious and unruly toward the shift end, while polishers are engaged in final polishing and repairing, or resting while pieces are being checked in the office, with small denim and cotton buffs spinning and flying through the air, directed at each other's bodies, rather than at the ducts. There is an inclusive promiscuity in this buff throwing, in that anyone might become an instigator or target, whether polisher or helper, whether from Uttar Pradesh or Bihar or Jharkhand, whether Hindu or Muslim, whether located close by or far away on the shop floor. While there is little attempt to hide one's agency in the deliberate, emphatic, and taunting buff throwing that goes on during the day, in this later game, one uses various means and methods to try to hit others with buffs while keeping one's identity obscured, and if need be, implicating others as targets of retaliation. One may hide behind the cement pillar, the fan filter, or another worker's body, or stride purposefully across the shop floor while underhandedly tossing the buff at its target. Timing is everything if one is to remain undiscovered. If one manages to first dab a cloth buff in dolomite powder, it creates an amusing and silly puff of white smoke on impact with

Figure 2.1. Bhagvati embracing Mithilesh behind Amlakant's machine.

the target body. One also wants to be discovered, so targets will be provoked to counterattack, which creates a sense of play.

Much of the fun (*maza*) of these buff-throwing exchanges is in the observation, the targeting, the passionate reactions upon impact, and the subsequent retaliations, either with a buff or by getting up from the machine, pursuing and catching hold of the hurler, and inflicting some punishment, such as a headlock with aggressive knuckle-rubbing on the skull. Although buff throwing is an anarchic affair, there is occasional coordination between persons to attack a target in sync, though without any stable or reliable structure. A person who was collaborating with you a moment ago might unexpectedly hurl a powder-laden buff at you as well, from behind the obscuring duct of his own machine, while maintaining a straight face.[7] A challenge of this game is to execute one's throws and retaliations such that the manager and supervisors, who may unexpectedly descend to the shop floor, do not catch you in the act, which would be taken as an affront to the pretense of discipline in the factory.

Mazak may also take on more vulgar, homoerotic forms, in the flows and economies of touching, feeling, grasping, grabbing, and mock penetrating that goes on among workers. I watched with some astonishment how Mithilesh, arriving at the gate early on a foggy morning, went up to Bhagvati from behind and cheerfully greeted him with a large, circular, swooping motion of his left middle finger directed straight into Bhagvati's rear end. Near the machines, workers may tweak the other's nipples, sometimes lowering their mouth to them, or grasp the other's breast area generously with one's open hand, while making a longing, desirous expression on the face. There is enjoyment (*maza*) in this touching, admits Arun. "Sometimes I grab hold of Mithilesh, it feels like I'm grasping my wife," he says.[8] *Mazak* thrives on a kind of substitution, with male bodies evoking for each other the tactile memory of absent, inaccessible, and desired wives. But the satisfactions may be limited. "When one is very hungry, this [touching] works like *samosas*, that's all," says Amlakant.[9] These *samosas*, while giving some relief (*rahat*) for hungry bodies, Arun says, can also make workers miss wives more intensely.

There is also the sheer delight in the play of touching, grabbing, and displaying the male genitalia, as a way of embarrassing and entertaining each other. At the end of the shift, when workers cram into the latrine and chamber to bathe, one must not only struggle to scrub off the caked dust and grime with detergent soap, while taking care to avoid accidental fingers, elbows, or knees in the eyes within the congested space. One must also keep a check on one's underwear, lest it be pulled down to one's knees by someone or some persons working in concert, followed by wild shouts of delight and triumph, as the hapless victim stoops down to recover his underwear and *izzat*. Babloo Khan avoids these embarrassing possibilities by waiting for the crowd to subside before entering the bath. But he is one of the most mischievous in the group, freely pulling down the underwear of others as they emerge from the bath and rub mustard oil on their bodies, leaving themselves vulnerable to blindside attacks. Babloo also enjoys shocking people while they are changing in the storeroom, by proudly flashing his phallus to whomever may be there, inviting them to be introduced to his "Khan sahab." The spectacle is enhanced by the fact that Babloo Khan is circumcised, a marker of being a Muslim, about which there is much *mazak* in the factory. These viewings (*darshans*) were one of Babloo's ways of retaliating and expressing pride in his anatomy.[10]

I too was not safe or immune from such vulgar behavior, and was treated to many unexpected unveilings of Babloo's Khan sahab if I was in the vicinity. Narayan, a night polisher, would routinely grab at my phallus, posterior, and chest if I happened to pass by his machine. He would do this surreptitiously, unpredictably, and with a stoic face, sometimes not even looking up from his machine. When I would be jolted by these acts and turn toward him in objection and disbelief, he would raise his eyebrows and widen his eyes behind his plastic goggles, in mock surprise and feigned sympathy. But if I did not move away from the area quickly, more jolting acts were forthcoming.

The male genitalia are a constant referent in *mazak*. When a worker is taking too long in the latrine, while someone else is waiting, he might emerge and return to the machine to hear loud speculations, "Come on, it takes time, man, he was jerking off!"[11] The worker himself might offer this as a defense to explain his delay. Naresh II, a night polisher from Hardoi, Uttar Pradesh, treated workers to his modified version of the film song "*Pyar kiya to darna kya* (When you've loved, what is there to fear?)," with the alteration, "*Muth mara to darna kya* (When you've masturbated, what is there to fear?)," to sing in the latrine when one was being hassled by impatient interlopers. Babloo Khan introduced the evocative, parting phrase, "Go on, protect your phallus and get out of here,"[12] which caught on and circulated in workers' exchanges in and outside the factory. In my room in Tehkhand, when there were other workers present whom I wanted to gently ask to leave so I could begin an interview with an individual worker, I needed to only say, "You folks please save [your phalluses and go]."[13] The others would smile, chuckle, and get up, saying, "OK, we're protecting [them and going]."[14]

Besides the phallus, the other male anatomical referent is the *gand* (anus, ass). No matter what might be the topic of conversation, Babloo Khan might unexpectedly interject, in his raspy, deadpan voice, "Ah, stick it in your ass."[15] He might also act out these impulses. In wintertime, when a space heater was used inside the storeroom to dry the emery-coated buffs prepared by the helpers, Babloo and others would gather near the heater at rest times. He once asked the others to put the cord into his *gand* for added warmth, and they obliged, creating a bizarre spectacle. In *mazak* at the machines, one might hear polishers saying, "Come on, give me [your ass] just once."[16] Such requests were made, across long distances between machines, by showing an O shape with the fingers and then the number one with the index finger, accompanied by a pouting expression of desire and hope. If I happened to be nearby while two polishers were bantering in this way, one might appeal to me,

"Brother, I am asking for his [ass] but he is not giving it. You please talk to him for me."[17] Rampal, a night polisher with a warm, buoyant nature, from Azamgarh, Uttar Pradesh, became a favored target of such proposals, buff throwing, and disrobing, in part because he did not seem to take offense at *mazak*, and indeed, was quite adept at initiating and retaliating. Ramakant explained the collective affection for Rampal, saying, "Rampal's ass is the most adored in the company."[18] I once saw Manoj, a night polisher from Hardoi, Uttar Pradesh, working intently on large aluminum vases, and strangely shouting, as if holding an auction, "Come bugger Rampal! Rampal's ass is up for sale! Make your bids!"[19] Such *mazak* also occurred with Govind, the supervisor, who despite his promotion to management, still shared much of the joking culture of the shop floor. One night, Govind was coaxing Rambachan, a helper who was learning welding, and who was also one of his suspected collaborators, to begin work on the welding machine. Rambachan was sitting outside by the fire, as the machine was undergoing repairs. Govind teased him, in a mock angry tone, that he would not get wages for doing no work, and should go back home. Rambachan replied that it was not his fault that the machine was broken, and that he should be marked present in the attendance register. "Your attendance will be marked," Govind said, giggling. "Just give me [your ass] once!"[20]

One of the most favored taunts and threats on the shop floor is, "I'll screw you in the ass! (*Maim teri gand marumga!*)" This could be stated calmly, quietly, or in mock rage, escalating into such colorful utterances as, "I'll toss you up so hard from my phallus that you'll land straight back in Bihar!"[21] In spontaneous wrestling bouts that would break out on the shop floor, vulgar gestures and simulations of buggery would be enacted for nearby onlookers. Once on the night shift, when Madan was nodding off at the machine, Manoj and Rampal lined up behind him, grabbed him around the chest, and simulated vigorous buggery in a line of three, to the amusement of the rest of the weary polishers on the shop floor. Madan woke up with a start. Buggery could also be referred to in the very act of greeting. Rajender, an elder polisher and a master of *mazak*, whose words were often laden with double entendre, would greet me, "How are you, Shankarji? Has your ass [*atthanni* (half rupee coin)] been pounded yet or is it still intact?"[22] At tea break, the respectful act of offering a person a place to sit would be folded into *mazak*, when Rajender would say, "Come, Shankarji, sit on this!"[23] As he said this, he would look me in the eye, with a slight, sharp nod of the head, without gesturing to any actual chair nearby. Sivam, suspecting a double meaning, would lean forward and eagerly ask, "Sit on what?!"[24] "On this chair, man," Rajender would answer with a grin, as he pointed to a nearby chair or got up from the one he was occupying.[25] The expression caught on. If Firoz saw me walking in the industrial area, he might ride up alongside on his bicycle (with a carrier) and greet me with the words, "*Namaste* Shankarji, come sit on this!"[26]

But the imageries of the phallus and *gand* took on particular valences when deployed in relation to the work of metal polishing. When I would greet Bhagvati at his machine, in the early part of the shift, and ask him how he was doing, instead of responding verbally, which would require undoing the *dhoti* fragments covering his face, he would put his left palm under his right elbow and pump his right forearm up and down, simulating an erect phallus. Later in the shift, if I would go by and ask him again, he would put his left palm under his right elbow, and hold his right forearm vertically, with the right hand limp and waving from side to side, as he made a weary, droopy face with what was visible of his eyes and cheeks, signifying a limp, spent phallus. Sometimes other polishers would call over to me, smiling, and make this latter sign, pointing to Bhagvati, to tease and taunt him, implying that he was done for the day, out of strength, and incapable of properly finishing his production. To which Bhagvati would fight back with his erection symbol, vigorously pumping, claiming that he still had life energy (*jan*) left in him, as he leaned into his buffing wheel and kicked up black-gray smoke from the force of his exertions.

Masculinity was partly defined here as the capacity and energy to do hard work (*mehnat*), while avoiding other activities that one might engage in for advantage and mobility in the factory, such as active collaborating. Bhagvati was a suspected collaborator, who was teased for staying on for extra time after the shift end, at the bidding of the supervisor, to finish up repairs on pieces. "After this, he'll go upstairs [to the office] and get screwed in the ass [by the supervisor]," polishers would mutter, as they passed him on the way to bathe.[27] To be a collaborator, this *mazak* suggested, was to open oneself up to possibilities of manipulation, dependence, and humiliation, in one's egoistic quest for advancement. Such perceptions and insinuations about Bhagvati as a collaborator perhaps made it all the more important for him to deploy such masculine, defensive symbols as the erect phallus, as a defiant proclamation of the actual hard work he felt he did at the machines.[28]

The idiom of getting buggered was not reserved only for suspected collaborators.[29] When the supervisor utilized polite, gentle speech to persuade polishers to do extra work, it was spoken of as camouflaged buggery. "If

Vijay has to get some work done from you, he'll speak so sweetly that you won't feel like refusing. He buggers you on the deep inside in such a way that no one can tell what he's done," says Uday.[30] Working on the nonrotating night shift was described in terms of buggering. When Ramakant started his machine at night, he would shout across the shop floor, "Come on, get yourself screwed in the ass!"[31] Mohan, a night polisher, described his work as "getting buggered all night."[32]

Mazak on buggery could also slide into references to *hijras* (third genders), who move about in the industrial area at Holi and Divali to collect customary donations from companies, and who engage in sex work in the evenings at the railway siding, between Okhla and Mathura Road. References to the siding would arise if one asked about the whereabouts of an absent worker, to which the response might be, "Oh, he went to the siding, he's earning a double income these days!"[33] Narayan was once planning to go to the village, and was pressuring Hanif, who was sitting across from his machine, to give him a loan for this purpose. Hanif smiled, gestured with upward-facing palms, and answered, "There's still time. Go to the siding, earn some money, make your 'balance' and go home!"[34] Narayan made a menacing face and shouted back, "If you don't give me some money, I'll ream your ass real bad, Hanif!"[35] Anatomies, genders, and sexualities could flow seamlessly together in the crucible of factory *mazak*, as in the advice given to workers heading to the village, "Go to the siding, get screwed in the ass, earn some money [to bring home], only then will your wife give you her vagina [*cavanni* (quarter rupee coin)]!"[36] But for all the *mazak* about the siding, workers harbored respect and fear with regard to the *hijras*, due to their formidable powers of blessing and cursing. The *hijras* were earning a living (*rozi roti*) at the siding, Uday said, and should be allowed to do so without interference, unless one wanted to provoke dangerous curses.

In this *mazak*, the siding was referenced as a space distant from the factory, at the edge of the industrial area. But one also got the sense that the siding was an analogous image for the condition of working at B156. At the factory, the workers were "getting buggered" by the weighty and hazardous designs of the steel pieces, the high production levels, and the exacting finishing requirements imposed from above. "This is getting-one's-ass-screwed sort of work," Sivam would mutter at his machine, drawing together the siding and the factory.[37] Only that the *hijras* were running their own business (*apni dhandha*), managing their own activities, and making far better earnings.

But there also seemed to be an awareness that workers were actively contributing to this buggering process. In the verbal proposals, threats, and physical simulations of buggery on the shop floor, workers were perhaps articulating and enacting, wittingly or otherwise, not only what they felt was being done to them, but also what they were doing to one another, through collaboration, speed contests, and modifications in methods, which enhanced managerial control and raised workloads. "We are screwing our own asses," Amlakant observed.[38] In the theater of *mazak*, workers seemed to be vividly depicting the nature of their punishing entanglements in the thanatic work process.

Machine

Alongside these styles of homoerotic horseplay and joking, workers engage in heteroerotic *mazak*. Workers affixed photos of film heroines and models to their machines, cut out from old newspapers used as packing material in the factory. Sometimes these pictures were of large-busted models or actresses, wearing bikinis or lingerie, as found in the *Delhi Times* supplement to the *Times of India*. They might strategically amend these photos in vulgar ways and invite others to their machines to rate and comment on their selections and alterations. On the wide, square base of the fan-filter system, near the left wall of the shop floor, where there was no managerial traffic, several photos would be arranged close to each other in a collage. Babloo Khan, whose machine was close to the stairs to the office, cleverly layered the scrap cardboard above his buffing wheel, such that the inside layer had several photos, for his own occasional viewing and displaying, which no one could see unless he lifted the outside layer. Conversations otherwise referenced sightings of female sex workers in the forested areas along the railway tracks, accounts of sexual acts observed there, and discussions of scenes, bodies, and activities witnessed in "blue" (pornographic) films viewed in working-class colonies via cable, video compact discs, and illicit, makeshift theaters. Workers closely scrutinized the photos of one another's wives on Employees' State Insurance cards, voiced desires for introductions, and offered to come along to the village to act as sexual instructors and surrogates. One evening, Sundar, an elder polisher, who was heading to the village in Prayagraj, Uttar Pradesh, was emerging from the bath. On seeing his thin, gaunt body, Babloo advised him, while tugging on the drawstring of his underwear, "You won't be able to [please your wife] with this phallus. Take Shankarji along with you."[39] When a worker was leaving for the village, good wishes would be articulated in the form, "Do it once for me!"[40]

One word that emerges in heteroerotic *mazak* is *machine*. "Bhagvati's machine has come [from the village]!" workers would shout across the shop floor, if they learned that his wife had come to Delhi.[41] Bhagvati might himself call me over and whisper in my ear, "A sugar cane juice-extracting machine (*ganne ka ras nikalnevali machine*) has come to my place."[42] On seeing women on the roads of Okhla, workers might comment to each other, "A fine machine is going by," "I need a machine," and "I'll have to bring my machine [from the village]."[43] Women workers who operated Juki sewing machines in garment factories, and women more generally, might be referred to as *jhuk machines* (bending, stooping machines), conjuring a rear-entry sexual position (*asan*). Women are submissive sex machines in this *mazak*.

But I also heard the word *machine* used for the male body, as when a worker from another Okhla factory was standing in the back of a jam-packed truck returning from a union demonstration in central Delhi, and was bizarrely bumping his pelvis alternately into the posteriors of two others in front of him, while saying, "Now tell me, which machine should I stick [my phallus] into, this one or that one?"[44] Babloo Khan's advice to workers, if they were showing boil-type skin eruptions, was, "Get rid of your heat. Go find a woman, change your motor oil."[45] The male body here is compared to a machine, a vehicle, whose smooth running requires periodic servicing and maintenance. When Hanif was getting ready to go to the village in Barabanki, Uttar Pradesh, to assist with harvesting paddy in his family fields, he told me that it would be very difficult work, in which one had to bend, stoop, and cut for hours at a stretch. With a chuckle of discovery, he said, "A man too has to become a *jhuk machine*!"[46]

In this *mazak*, workers seemed to be developing on buggery as a cognate image for working at B156. The polishers, bending, leaning, and inclining their bodies into the buffing wheels, rhythmically, back and forth, with the supervisors on their backs, prodding them to go faster, could be seen as *jhuk machines* of a kind. This self-referencing expression perhaps exhibited a disturbing awareness among workers of their own instrumentalized, subordinated, and exploited condition. The image of *jhuk machine* also drew attention to the ways in which workers were expressing their agency in distorted ways, by bending, stooping, and submitting to managerial diktats and existing working conditions, selling their bodies and part of their *izzat*, in exchange for money. In the quest for the "loot" of wages, this *mazak* suggested, workers were being pounded into, and could behave like, *jhuk machines* for capital.[47]

Another word used in heteroerotic *mazak* is *mal*, meaning goods, materials, stocks, or stuff.[48] Unlike the word *machine*, which carries connotations of movement, activity, and energy, *mal* is generally used for static and inert objects. In the factory, *mal* was used to refer to raw (unpolished) pieces, finished pieces sent for checking, pieces designated for repairs, and pieces with defects that are set aside as "rejects." This language insidiously crept into the ratings system of the looks and beauty of women as seen in newspaper and magazine photos, and of women working in neighboring companies or walking along the roads of Okhla. "Raw," "repair," and "reject" became the terms of evaluation and adjudication of women in this *mazak*. One sometimes heard the lament, "In the industrial area, one can't find any 'raw' girls (*kora mal*),"[49] reflecting suspicions about the sexual character of women who work in factories, and also of the "modern"-dressed, educated women who work as clerical and technical staff in company offices.[50]

When this kind of talk occurred outside the gate or on the streets of the industrial area, as women passed by, it could come close to harassment, even if the women were not directly addressed. When female staff members arrived and exited from the companies near B156, one heard workers' comments such as, "Look, the stuff (*mal*) has come," "What a splendid thing (*mal*) is going by," or, "Will this machine work, brother?" followed by, "Oh, it won't just work, it'll run great!"[51] While these women, who walk by with eyes lowered, facing forward, not looking to either side, did not directly react to these comments, they did not appreciate them.[52] One morning, two male office workers from the company in the opposite shed, which distributed industrial irons to garment factories, came over and scolded the workers, as one of their female employees had just walked by and heard someone say, "Some fine *mal* has come."[53] Bhuvan, a helper, deployed an immediate defense that the word *mal*, if it had been heard, could have been used in reference to any of various objects, materials, and supplies at the factory. But the B156 workers, including those who were not present at the time, were embarrassed by the incident.

Amid the imagery of machines and things, workers also tease each other about the power and control of their wives. Amlakant's wife was rumored to be very thrifty and miserly, and kept a tight control on their finances.[54] Amlakant was also one of the most stingy of the workers, hesitant to loan money

Figure 2.2. An employee from a neighboring shed exiting the lane. Back, left to right: Narayan, Bhagvati, Govind, Ramji (guard).

or spend on others, asking for tobacco from others rather than offering his own, despite being one of the most senior, respected workers. So when Naresh was moving about the shop floor one day, asking for small loans in anticipation of a trip to the village, Varmaji, a worker on the other extreme from stinginess, advised Naresh aloud, stabbing at Amlakant's masculinity, "You won't get anything from Amlakant! Every day he goes home and has to give accounts of whatever he spent to his wife!"[55] When Bhagvati returned from the village, a few days before the end of his leave, while workers often stretch it and return late by a few days or weeks, others teased him, suggesting that his wife had had enough of him after ten days, kicked him in the *gand*, and told him to get back to the city and start earning again.[56] Anxieties of control are also expressed in stories of women who dupe their husbands and engage in sex with others, illustrating the wily, opaque, ever-suspect nature of women (*triya caritra*),[57] and in *mazak* on the allegedly compromised character of women workers, which partly reflects the troubling awareness of the ways in which women's wages might subvert domestic power equations. In these threads of *mazak*, women are evidently not machines or things, without mind, will, desire, or power, fully subordinate to and controlled by men. This humor partly emerges from the self-mockery of alleged male power.

Respect

When I asked workers how they felt about vulgar joking, I often got an embarrassed response. They felt that the *mazak* in the factory was as dirty (*ganda*) as the work. Some suggested that it was the by-product of the work, as so much debris and rubbish get stuffed and lodged in the head that it becomes difficult to express any clean, civilized thoughts. Because of the degeneracy of the *mazak*, it degraded the *izzat* of working in the metal factory.

Why then did vulgar *mazak* flourish? One reason workers gave was that unlike in their residences, there was some distance at B156 from close relations of family, kin, and village, that would place constraints on such *mazak*. In the absence of these checks, *mazak* was allowed to go to extremes.[58] Where there were close kin relations, as among the Jharkhandi brothers and other relatives, while they might sit close and eat together, they distributed themselves among the machines and at bathing time, according to relevant kin relations and age groups, so that *mazak* could be less constrained.[59] The *izzat* for elders also acted as a control on *mazak*, with younger workers censoring their speech and behavior, but when elder workers such as Rajender and Narayan engaged in vulgar *mazak* with them, such controls collapsed, permitting a downward spiral in conduct and civility. This became a symptom, for some, of the lack of proper *izzat* norms in the factory, and contributed to the substratum anxiety about the longer-term effects of inhabiting such an atmosphere for so many hours of the day.

The workers attempted to keep vulgar *mazak* within the factory and other discreet spaces, to maintain *izzat* in the social world of the residences. This required vigilant censoring of their thoughts and tongues, but leakages of vocabularies from the factory could occur unpredictably. Obscene words could slip out of Lallan's mouth while he was sleeping in his room in Tehkhand, causing his roommates to angrily rouse him and say, "What rubbish do you go on muttering?!"[60] One night, at a party for the son of Prakash, a helper, some polishers were drinking and joking loudly on the terrace of his tenement in Hari Nagar in southeast Delhi. At one point, an inebriated

Rajender said to Prakash, in earshot of his relatives and neighbors, "Hey, brother, show us your *mal*."[61] This was a disturbing violation of *izzat* considerations, which was embarrassing to Prakash, who regretted extending his invitation, graciously, to the entire factory.

Within the factory, some workers, such as Ramdev and Vinod, tried to keep a distance from vulgar *mazak*, out of practical concerns for safety at the machines and their own senses of *izzat* and proper conduct.[62] Some workers preferred to develop and deploy different *mazak* styles, such as *vyangya* (irony, sarcasm), which relied more on wit and mental alacrity than vulgarity and profanity. Some became very effective at turning *vyangya* into a ludic critique of the moves, deceptions, and stratagems of management in their ongoing efforts to tighten discipline and intensify production, while granting little by way of wage increases or other benefits. Expressions of the manager, such as, "My efforts are ongoing for you [at the head office] (*Koshish jari hai*)," in response to requests for wage increases and shift rotation became a sarcastic, circulating motto in workers' discussions about the company and its policies. Lallan developed an elaborate style of commentary about oppression and exploitation in the company, by drawing comparisons of work tasks, job titles, personalities, policies, and events at the factory to what life was allegedly once like within the ramparts of the Red Fort in Old Delhi. These bizarre analogies, often very cutting and incisive, would begin and end with, "This place is no less than the Red Fort."[63] The veiled, nondirect quality of *vyangya*, and its capacity to carry and convey "serious" feelings and meanings, made it a vital and useful mode of expression of workers' discontent, particularly given the omnipresence of collaborators in the factory. Workers' nonvulgar, witty, and sarcastic exchanges not only indicated the plurality of forms *mazak* might take, but also illuminated the importance of *izzat* within the factory, and the desires and aspirations of some workers to rise above the general styles and themes of vulgar *mazak*.

Qualities

Another genre of workers' humor revolves around regional origin and religious identity. In this *mazak*, deploying slurs for migrants from Bihar and Muslims,[64] workers draw upon negative stereotypes about these groups and also acknowledge the limits of generalizations in describing diverse, distinctive persons. Through this *mazak*, which expresses envy and hostility, an implicit auto-critique emerges of egoism, docility, and insularity among workers.

Bihari

As the B156 workers move about Okhla and the city, they might be derogatorily addressed as *Bihari*. When traveling on buses, conductors might shout, "Hey, Bihari, get on quickly! Bihari, move forward! Get down fast, Bihari!"[65] If a group of workers collects on the side of an Okhla road, and is discussing goings-on in the factory, a police officer might come over, with a bamboo staff (*lathi*), and angrily say, "Damn Biharis, why are you making a crowd here? You think this is your village? Come on, move!"[66] The word *Bihari* addresses migrant workers (*pravasi mazdurs*) in Delhi, who are recognizable by their thin bodies, clothing styles, and rustic gait, who might be from Bihar, but also from other states in north and eastern India. *Bihari*, qua migrant worker, is a figure at once necessary and unwanted in the city.

At the factory, the word *Bihari* is used to address workers from Bihar and Jharkhand (a state formed out of Bihar in 2000), comprising about 30 percent of the B156 workers, by the larger group of workers from Uttar Pradesh and Uttarakhand (a state formed from Uttar Pradesh in 2000), who comprise about 68 percent of the workers.[67] The word might be heard when polishers call out to helpers for materials, "Hey, Bihari, bring a polishing compound!"[68] Ramakant might shout across the shop floor, "Hey, Madan! Bihari! Can't you hear?"[69] One might also hear workers invoking the adage, "One Bihari causes a hundred diseases! (*Ek Bihari sau bimari!*)"[70] To which Lallan, who is from Bihar, gleefully responds, "If one Bihari comes, there will be a hundred diseases. All of you [Uttar Pradesh and Uttarakhand folks] will die from these diseases!"[71]

In interviews, workers shared negative generalizations about migrants from Bihar. "You'll get a hundred 'good' qualities (*gun*) inside a Bihari—thievery, dishonesty, wickedness, trickery, cleverness, political leader activity—you'll get everything inside him," says Varmaji.[72] Due to extreme poverty, the absence of jobs, recurring floods, high levels of criminality, and political corruption, Biharis are seen to migrate to cities in large numbers.[73] They crowd into rented rooms in Delhi, exceeding limits on numbers of tenants set by landlords, bring more migrants from the village, cook rice and *dal* in huge pots for ten people at a time, and subsist on meager diets, avoiding spending on meat, fish, liquor, and leaf-based intoxicants, so as to save and remit cash to the village home. Their rooms are dirty, with rice grains sticking to the floor, lingering garbage, and roaming cockroaches. They spread filth (*gandagi*) in the neighborhoods. They blast their radios and cassette decks at full volume, disturbing neighbors and provoking altercations. The Gujjar landlords in Tehkhand seem to share and vocalize such perceptions when they pass by the rooms of the Jharkhandis at night, count the pairs of slippers and shoes outside the door (necessitating the concealing of footwear inside the rooms), and angrily mutter, "All these Biharis, sister-*******, how many have packed in here! They've spoiled the rooms!"[74]

Further negative stereotypes pertain to the behavior of Biharis inside factories. They do hard work, but for lower wages, which depresses wage levels for others, prompting workers to complain, "All these Biharis have come and destroyed Delhi!"[75] They work quietly at the machines, without moving about, accept extra pieces, and avoid speaking up for legitimate demands, out of fears of losing jobs. They are egoistic, insular, and focused on their own advantage, regardless of *izzat* losses and adverse effects on others. They do not hesitate to inform on, deceive, or betray others, even close relatives, for the sake of their own slight monetary gain. "They have no loyalties to anyone," workers say.[76] Polishers gave voice to these negative feelings when they would say about Uday, Arun, and others who pursued speed, "The Biharis have screwed us all in the ass!"[77] Khan sahab seemed to regard Biharis as quiet, docile, and hardworking. "They only care about money," he said, making them easy to manipulate and control.[78] But he was not unaware of their other alleged qualities. They could make trouble, agitate for demands, form unions, access political leaders, and slow down production, inducing the closure of factories.[79] But he seemed to be gambling that through his managerial techniques, he could keep those qualities from manifesting at B156.

There was a play of repartee in *mazak* on *Bihari*. Once, during a break, Babloo Khan was teasing Arun, "Bihari! You probably came [to Delhi on a train] hiding in the latrine [without a ticket]!"[80] Arun replied, "OK, I came hiding in the latrine. And you must have come in on a plane. But you're still grinding away [at the machine]! What great thing have you achieved here?!"[81] In such *mazak*, Arun could sense currents of envy from Uttar Pradesh migrants, that so many Bihari fools (*murkhs, burbaks*) were coming to Delhi, earning wages, and advancing themselves. Babloo admits, "There are a lot of people from Bihar [in Delhi], and they've gotten into every line. They're dressing better than us, they're keeping better hairstyles too. They've outdone us Uttar Pradesh folks."[82]

But in interviews, the negative generalizations seemed to be only partly believed.[83] The purported Bihari qualities were also visible among migrants from Uttar Pradesh, who could be lousy (*bekar*), base (*ghatiya*), and dangerous (*khatarnak*).[84] Uttar Pradesh migrants could live with multiple migrants in rooms, to share costs and save earnings. When they were hired as casual workers in factories, including on the B156 night shift, they could work hard for long hours, at lower than minimum wages. "What will a desperate person not do [to survive]," Varmaji explains.[85] Uttar Pradesh migrants could also pursue speed (e.g., Naresh II) and become suspected collaborators (e.g., Babloo and Vijay II). Amlakant, a migrant from Ballia, on the eastern border of Uttar Pradesh, was skeptical that the qualities of persons could drastically change just by crossing the Ganga River into Bihar. He used *Bihari* in referencing migrants from both states, when they manifested so-called Bihari qualities. Uttar Pradesh migrants could also see that the negative stereotypes did not describe all Biharis and Jharkhandis at B156. Surinder avoided speed, moved about freely, and seemed concerned with the well-being of workers beyond the Jharkhandis. Umesh spoke up to Khan sahab to request rotation of the night shift. "Umesh regulates his work. He doesn't work like a Bihari. His way of doing things is different," Firoz observed.[86]

Among Biharis and Jharkhandis, there is also a play of *mazak* on *Bihari*, though with less envy and more friendly feeling. If Lallan does not promptly respond to Uday's requests for materials, Uday might wave his finger sternly and say, "Bihari, mend your ways!"[87] The Jharkhandis, who had been Biharis most of their lives, expressed pride in the new state, with its strong mining industries, and that, despite the activities of dacoits, gangsters, and Maoists, did not, as yet, have the ill repute of Bihar. When Arun addresses Uday as Bihari, he might respond, "We're not Biharis. We're Jharkhandis. Say 'Jharkhandi'!"[88] To which Arun replies, "You're a Jharkhand-variety Bihari."[89] The word *Bihari* can also convey close, friendly feeling, as when Naresh goes over to Arun's machine and gently asks, "What are you up to, Bihari?"[90]

The Jharkhandis are also addressed with the word *jangli*, meaning wild and uncivilized. While Amlakant is working intently at his machine, Surinder might come up from behind, unravel the *dhoti* fragment around Amlakant's head, pull off his goggles, and lightly swing a thin metal rod onto his back, saying that he is practicing cricket batting. Amlakant might get up, chase him around the floor, wrestle him to the ground, and shout to Naresh, "Hey, brother, will you control this *jangli*!"[91] *Jangli* conjures images of *adivasis*, seen as primitive, backward, naïve, and hardworking, who live in remote areas, close to forests, speak their own languages, and have yet to come into the mainstream (*mukhya dhara*) of society. (The Jharkhandis at B156 were Chero *adivasis*.) On the night shift, the young Jharkhandis could work silently in the back corner of the shop floor, not mixing much with others. Varmaji might say, "All these guys are *jangli*! They've lived close to the jungle, they've got jungle-like thinking!"[92] But the Jharkhandis spoke politely, with *izzat* and civility, to elders such as Varmaji, indicating a refined knowledge and experience of living in society. "The whole Jharkhandi group is very good (*sahi*). They're also from Bihar, but their way of speaking, conversing, and conducting themselves is good," Varmaji acknowledged.[93]

Alongside negative generalizations, there seemed to be a second, copresent discourse on the distinctiveness of persons. "All Biharis will not be alike. All persons from Uttar Pradesh will not be alike," says Ramakant, who engages in a good deal of *mazak* on *Bihari*.[94] "All persons are not the same. Differences exist between two brothers. One brother has one sort of nature, another brother has another, a sister has another. How to speak of [people from] a whole region," says Varmaji.[95] In this discourse, styles of working, living, and acting with others depended less on regional origin, and more on the complex specificities of the heart (*dil*), mind (*dimag*), nature (*svabhav*), character (*caritra*), society (*samaj*), and compelling difficulty (*majburi*) of persons. Ashis Nandy writes of "double ledgers," or the coexistence of negative prejudice and ambiguous openness in the psyche of persons in South Asia.[96] *Mazak* on *Bihari* seemed to derive fun and enjoyment (*maza*) from the coexistence of these two discourses, and the playing as if only the first discourse were true, that is, that negative generalizations properly described every person in the target group, as if they were rigid, uniform, predictable cogs, and that persons were not diverse, mysteriously constituted, and difficult to generally describe.

Muslim

Another word used in *mazak* is *katua*, for (circumcised) Muslims.[97] Polishers might greet Guddu Khan, a night worker from Prayagraj, Uttar Pradesh, by saying, "O brother, circumcised Khan, how are things?"[98] When Narayan wants to summon Babloo Khan, he might shout, "Circumcised one, come here!"[99] In interviews, Hindu workers amplified negative stereotypes. Muslims are untrustworthy, deceptive, and dangerous. Their hearts are cold, hard, and devoid of compassion. Just as they butcher buffaloes and cows, they can kill human beings.[100] But to fellow Muslims, they express remarkable solidarities, extending across national borders, and exhibit respect, compassion, and generosity, giving assistance to poorer Muslims in migrating, finding jobs, and managing wedding costs. At B156, these solidarities were visible in Khan sahab's perceived favoritism to Muslims, in giving them wage advances, jobs for relatives, and a long lunch break for Friday prayers at a nearby mosque, and in the suspected collaborative activities of Muslim workers (e.g., Babloo, Hanif, and Kalim). Muslims also purportedly had voracious sexual appetites, arising from excessive meat eating, and procreated without restraint, as a conscious strategy to expand their numbers, overtake Hindus, and exert dominance in India.[101]

In *mazak* on *katua*, workers draw attention to the circumcised phallus and its alleged potentialities. Once while in the bath, Rampal looked over to Babloo, who was standing outside, smoking a *biri*, and made a gesture of his right index finger cutting his left index finger, symbolizing a cut phallus, and said to Babloo, with a smile, "You're not capable [of pleasing your wife], your [phallus] is not intact. Mine is, send your wife to me, I'll fulfill her desires!"[102] Babloo calmly responded, "What have you seen of what a *katua* can do? Send your wife [to me] and see. She'll tell you what colors of ecstasy a *katua* will give her, how much vitality is inside a *katua*. What do you know?"[103] When there is a power cut, in the dark, quiet, eerie stillness on the shop floor, before the guard switches from the power line to the generator, Babloo might say, "Cut the line! My [phallus] is already cut, brother."[104] Muslims could also use *katua* among themselves. When Babloo was once rushing Firoz at the machine, near the shift end, he shouted, "*Katue* (Circumcised one), work fast!"[105] "*Katue*, you work fast too!" Firoz replied.[106] "No, [the manager] is my Muslim brother, so I don't have to," Babloo responded.[107] "So the *katua* will give you wages without you having to work? You're the *katua*'s damn collaborator!" shouted Firoz.[108]

At times, *mazak* makes reference to alleged Muslim solidarities across national borders. During the Cricket World Cup in 2003, in the days preceding the India-Pakistan match, workers would joke that Babloo, Hanif, and other Muslims, in their hearts, really wanted Pakistan to win, as they had love only for their religious community (*biradari*), not their country (*desh*).[109] Hanif would stoke this *mazak* by inquiring about how the feared Pakistani bowlers, Wasim Akram and Shoaib Akhtar, were performing in other matches. Babloo pledged to distribute sweets if Pakistan defeated India. One day, while standing by the machine of Babloo and Achaibar, Hanif explained that he saw India and Pakistan as brothers, did not wish ill against either of them, and would support both equally in the upcoming match. Achaibar (who identified as Buddhist) got agitated and shouted, "This guy's a Pakistani! He's getting his sustenance from India, and is singing the praises of Pakistan!"[110] Hanif shook his head and responded, "That's wrong. No one is giving me anything. I'm doing hard work, and thereby getting my sustenance."[111] "Who wins, who loses, I don't care. I'm concerned with my own work and life. What are we going to get from this that we should put in our energies?" Babloo interjected, with exasperation.[112] Achaibar laughed, as if momentarily realizing something, and said, "We'll be doing the same grinding that we're doing now!"[113] "Now you've understood!" Hanif replied, with a smile.[114] After India's victory, the *mazak* continued, with Rajender alleging that Babloo got angry on seeing the outcome, but instead of breaking his TV in his shanty, made love to his wife three times in the night to cool down.[115] Babloo expressed regret that he could not distribute *batashas* (sweet meringues) at B156. Hanif clarified that the Indian team won thanks only to the bowling and batting of its Muslim players, Zaheer Khan and Mohammad Kaif.[116]

But workers also seem to recognize limitations in these generalizations. In discussions about the alleged loyalties of Muslims in India, Babloo mentioned the importance of Maulana Azad, the Congress leader, in India's freedom struggle. Rajender brought up Abdul Hamid, a martyr of the India-Pakistan war in 1965, who was from his home district of Ghazipur, Uttar Pradesh, as an example of Muslims who had sacrificed (*qurbani dena*) their lives for India. "Don't speak of 'every' [Muslim]," he emphasized.[117] Sabbir says, "I was born here. Our lives are to be lived here. What do we have to do with Pakistan?"[118] The violence of the Ram temple movement and in Gujarat indicated that it is not only Muslims who are capable of coldly killing others. "When fights occur somewhere, do only Muslims kill Hindus? Hindus don't kill? Both will kill. Both will die," he says.[119]

A second discourse emerges here on Muslims as distinctive persons with diverse qualities.[120] The night polishers respect Sabbir over other helpers, as he speaks with *izzat*, stays awake, and attends to their requests. Guddu Khan criticizes the manager's manipulations, and does not get along with him, despite them being "Muslim brothers." Firoz voices criticisms of working

Figure 2.3. Achaibar and Firoz bantering with Babloo Khan.

conditions, speaks up to Khan sahab, and participates in protest activities, with more reliability than most Hindu workers.[121] "Firoz talks back because he doesn't tolerate oppression (*zulm*)," observes Varmaji.[122] "In going along (*sath calna*) with fellow workers, the best guy in the factory is Firoz," Amlakant acknowledges.[123]

In *mazak* on Biharis and Muslims, workers indirectly express envy and hostility toward one another. Uttar Pradesh migrants evince dislike and contempt toward migrants from Bihar. Hindus exhibit anxiety and resentment toward Muslims. But there is also a play of slurs in this *mazak*, for the purposes of fun, sport, and delight. For this play to thrive, one needs a "mixture" of persons from different regions and religions, as existed in B156, says Arun, so there can be an exchange of slurs.[124] This play also requires tolerance, in the context of familiar persons. If one wishes to deploy *Bihari* against others, Babloo says, one should be willing to be called *katua* and even call oneself *katua*. If Narayan taunts Babloo, referring to him as *katua*, he might respond, "I'll screw you in the ass so bad, Bihari, tears will flow, understand?!

Figure 2.4. The bath. Left to right: Pramod, Lallan, Narayan.

You won't be able to get medical treatment anywhere in Delhi. You'll flee back to Bihar, sob, and tell people, 'A *katua* buggered me!'"[125] Though one would take offense to such slurs from strangers in other settings, possibly leading to quarreling and fighting, "in the factory, these things are acceptable," Babloo says.[126] As in the multidirectional volleys of buff throwing, one might suggest, one wishes to target and be targeted, to provoke and be retaliated upon, and to put down and be put down, if there is to be widespread and mutual enjoyment from this *mazak*.

But along with this fun and entertainment, one could discern an implicit auto-critique of the undesirable qualities of workers, within the two coexistent discourses. A "bad" worker was one who was docile, submissive, and worked excessively, who was egoistic, insular, and exhibited enclosed solidarities, and who was untrustworthy, secretly collaborative, and dangerous to other workers. A "good" worker was one who regulated one's work, spoke up to the management, thought about the well-being of others (and not just one's relatives or religious community), mixed with others, and went along with fellow workers in protest activities.[127] These bad and good qualities were not seen to ultimately inhere in regional origin, caste-tribe, or religious community, despite the negative stereotypes about Biharis, *adivasis*, and Muslims. They were disclosures of the complex, diverse qualities of workers qua distinctive persons. The qualities that emerged in a given context such as B156 were also seen to be critically dependent on processes of divisiveness and collectivity among workers. The exhibition of bad qualities, nurtured by envy and hostility, could give way to the revelation of the good, if and when collectivity grew stronger.

Fate

Amid the dirty, difficult work of metal polishing, *mazak* was seen as a vital necessity.[128] *Mazak* enabled workers to get into the work, distract themselves from tensions, keep boredom, fatigue, and drowsiness at bay, and complete one's production.[129] In helping workers to work, *mazak* greased the cogs of production, not unlike the polishing compound that was dabbed into the buffing wheels as a lubricant, which made metal polishing possible. The management seemed to recognize this, which might partly explain why the manager stayed away from the shop floor and the supervisors did not try to stop *mazak*. In giving workers this space, the management, perhaps for its own ends, not only permitted *mazak* but tacitly encouraged it.

But while lubricating the work process, *mazak* also gave rise to a kind of autonomous, social, and critical theater at B156, whose workings were not clearly aligned to the imperatives of production. First, *mazak* exercised and regenerated workers' bodies and minds, in the relieving stimulations of wrestling and touching, in energizing mental faculties (e.g., of quickness, wordplay, and repartee), and in encouraging creative and imaginative powers (e.g., of inventing, implying, and insinuating). If the production process enforced monotonous repetition, cog-like discipline, and the commensurability and interchangeability of workers, *mazak* created spontaneity, unpredictability, and disorder, in which workers revealed themselves to be unique, distinctive, and nonexchangeable personalities. In the alchemy of *mazak*, blackened *jhuk machines* in the making transformed into animated, colorful, and diverse characters. Second, the theater of *mazak* was directed toward something other than the unrelenting drudgery of production, that is, the amusement and diversion of the *man* of workers.[130] In *mazak*, as workers described it, the revolving, direct participants were "actors," who were seeking to entertain not so much themselves, but the shifting audience of spectators.[131] In this theater, workers were attending to each other's tension, despair, and exhaustion. They were sustaining one another's lives. As Amlakant put it, "Only if we do *mazak* can we keep our spirits a bit up, otherwise it's just grind away [at the machine]!"[132] Third, *mazak*, as theater, worked to draw workers together amid competitive and divisive feelings. *Mazak* made workers want to come to B156, beyond the wages motive, so they could be with each other in an atmosphere of fun and conviviality (*raunak*), rather than remain in their rooms, with mental tensions as ever-present company. Unlike consuming liquor and leaf-based intoxicants, watching television, or simmering quietly in isolation, *mazak* was a social, dealienating treatment for tensions. *Mazak* required other people. And in *mazak*, workers observed, closeness (*ghanishta*, *nazdiqi*) developed in their relations. "Our *muhabbat* (close, affective feeling) increases," says Babloo Khan.[133] Fourth, an implicit subtext of this theater was an auto-critique of the injurious qualities of workers and a vision of what workers should be doing, with regard to production, sociality, and protest. While *mazak* could act as a conduit to express hostile feelings toward one another, it also seemed to call on workers to overcome ego and envy, and act together, in the face of oppressive managerial policies and working conditions. If *mazak* could oil the cogs of production, it could also be a spanner in the works.

On a winter night, after a long shift, Hanif was walking home, along with Uday, Naresh, and Surinder. He was discussing his persistent fever, which made him suspect the presence of some deeper illness. He hawked, spat, and shouted, with hands gesticulating to the sky, "Go on ingesting rubbish all day, son of a whore, don't know how I've gotten this kind of work in my life, mother-******?! Don't know, has my fate been written [by God] with a donkey's phallus or what?! What was the instrument [God] used for me?!"[134] The Jharkhandis broke into laughter. The fate of the metal workers indeed looked bleak, a dreary existence of strenuous work, black-gray dust, injury risks, and illnesses. The factory was akin to the image in *mazak* of Bhagvati's wife, a juice-extracting machine (*ras nikalnevali machine*), writ large, gradually squeezing, drawing out, and depleting the life energy of workers. Yet they could laugh, and vigorously, on acknowledging this fate.

But in *mazak*, they were opening spaces of life within that dark, grim fate. They revealed an unwillingness to completely put off the good life to a remote, hazy future in the village, as required by the migrant looting ethos. Instead, they seemed to be seeking, if not urgently demanding, some life within an austere, somber present. "Without *mazak*, life is worthless," says Amlakant.[135] In *mazak*, workers were defiantly holding onto some life energy from the deadly workings of the juice-extracting machine. They were attempting to realize a bit of fun, joy, and closeness, amid the vitality losses of the looting process. In so doing, the B156 workers were not only laughing at fate. They were altering the details of its script.

CHAPTER 3

Collectivity

The B156 workers confront multiple difficulties in the metal factory. The work is dirty, strenuous, and hazardous. The management exerts constant pressures to raise production and enhance quality. The workers respond with active collaboration, speed contests, surface-level respect, and valences of joking. In auto-regulated working, auto-critique, and conviviality, they attempt to cooperate less with the factory's thanatic process.

In this chapter, I explore developments in processes and activities at B156 over three years (2001–2004). A work-intensifying process arose at the factory through the interplay of managerial machinations and workers' loyalty and envy. This process gave rise to difficulty, disillusion, and discontent, due to job threats, wage stagnation, injuries, and illnesses. The workers resisted this interplay in the politics of collectivity. They engaged in unity politics, involving park meetings, refusals, unionization, and protests. They explored the politics of synchrony (*talmel*), in extreme auto-regulated working and a poster campaign, which contributed to the restoration of jobs.

In the process of developing collectivity, workers articulated understandings of themselves in terms of aggregate identities and the distinctiveness of persons. But they also exhibited a deeper self-understanding of being complex souls wrestling in decivilizing times. Souls, constituted by competing proclivities, were seen to be entangled in the present temporal context of the *Kalyug*, the fourth cosmic epoch in Hindu cosmology, characterized by the rise of forces that distort thoughts, actions, and dealings. A vision emerged of the ethico-political duty to resist the distorting interplay of souls and the *Kalyug*, and its manifestations in oppression, injustice, and wrongdoing.

Agitations

In the early phases of the factory's functioning, the workers got caught up in a work-intensifying process. This process began to unravel due to disillusion and discontent. The workers developed collectivity through unity politics, in which they sought regularization, wage increases, and overtime perquisites. Unity was vulnerable to disintegration due to managerial machinations, the reliance on worker-leaders, the strategy of refusal, the influence of associative circles, and the willingness to accommodate existing conditions.

Machinations, Loyalty, and Envy

When B156 began functioning in March 2001, metal workers flocked to the gate, seeking work, on hearing of an American-owned export company that hired legal, regular workers in an environment dominated by precarious casual and contract work. Khan sahab, the manager, stirred hopes in prospective workers by telling them that the company gave good wages and benefits, had abundant export orders, and retained its workers for the long term. Workers who were initially hired and kept on were regularized as Metal Artware Exports workers, and given minimum wage grades along with legal entitlements of state health insurance, provident fund, and bonuses. After a few months, additional workers were hired as casual workers of Artistic Goods, and paid less than minimum wages, without legal entitlements. Khan sahab cultivated a few active collaborators to raise production and give reports on goings-on in the factory. Vijay, the supervisor, in shop floor and offstage dealings, encouraged and enticed polishers to increase production and enhance quality. Out of hopes for advancement in the company, many polishers pursued speed and quality improvements.

Among those who harbored such hopes was Naresh Singh. Naresh came from a farming family in Palamu, Jharkhand. After failing his tenth standard exams, in the mid-nineties, he left with a relative to work on a farm in Panipat, Haryana. The next year, he came to Delhi to visit his younger brother, Madan, who was working in an Okhla dyeing factory. He stayed on and found work as a helper in a metal factory, working on a stone grinder machine. At that factory, he came to know Krishna and Sivam, who were earning high wages (Rs. 500 a day) on piece rates at the polishing machines. He learned metal polishing and worked in three factories (D45, F47, and T7)

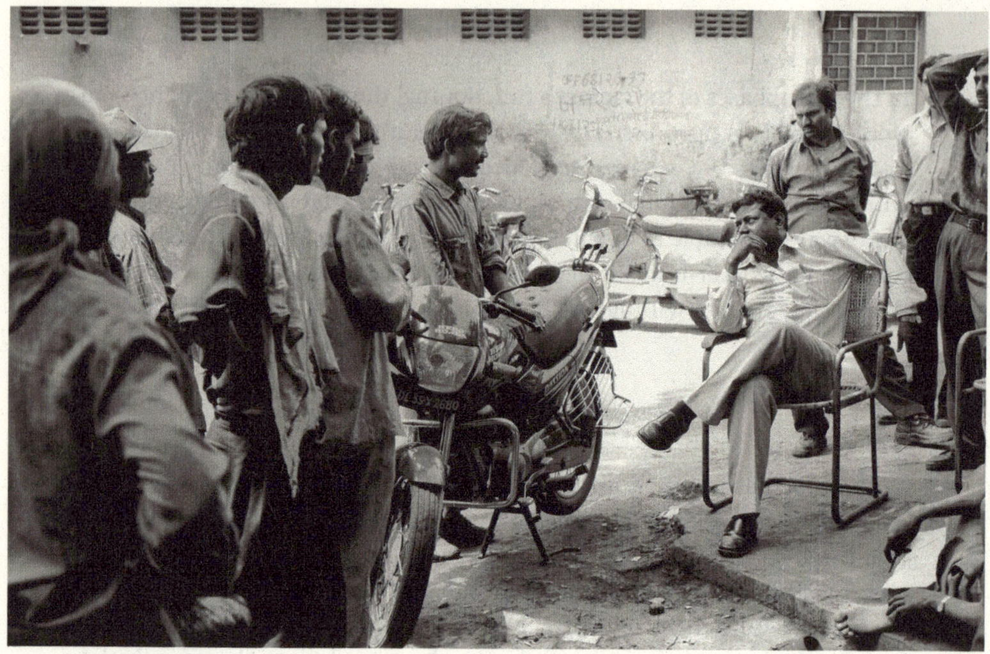

Figure 3.1. Polishers speaking to Khan sahab about unreceived provident fund slips.

over the next few years, making monthly earnings of Rs. 3,500–4,500. During this time, he trained his brothers, several relatives, including Uday, and others from Palamu in polishing workshops in Okhla.

In mid-2001, due to a decline in orders at T7, Naresh and Uday came to B156, and were hired as casual polishers. Once they learned to polish the steel pieces, with some difficulty, they began pursuing speed and modifications. At times, they completed their pieces by mid-afternoon, enabling production increases and engendering hostility from other polishers. By working quickly and diligently, and creating a good image, they hoped for regularization, wage increases, and jobs for their young relatives. Khan sahab gave continual, vague assurances of advancement, while hiring seven of Naresh's relatives as casual workers, who adopted similar working styles. Other polishers competed with them and one another for speed, quality, and good images. Machinations (*kutniti*), vertical loyalty (*vafadari*), and competitive envy (*jalan*) came together in a vigorous interplay of intensifying production.

This interplay generated production and quality increases of 20–25 percent within the first year, according to managerial estimates.[1] Its success owed a great deal to the gifts and talents of the manager. Khan sahab grew up in Budaun, Uttar Pradesh, as the son of a government clerk. After completing a degree in commerce in Ghaziabad, he worked as a typist, stenographer, and production supervisor, while developing his own metalware business. Along the way, he acquired a mastery in the arts of manipulating and controlling workers. At the factory, he conversed, drank tea, and joked with workers, and developed a close knowledge of their personalities, ways of thinking, domestic situations, and financial vulnerabilities. Through offstage dealings with his collaborators, he gained access to detailed information on workers' conversations, discussions, and work activities, though he was rarely visible in the factory. By speaking to workers in secluded, one-on-one conversations in a stroll down the lane, in his Maruti 800 car (which replaced his motorcycle), or in their shanties and rooms after hours, he could often persuade them to do his bidding, even when it was to their detriment. The supervisors marveled at his artistry, looked up to him as a *guru*, and tried to adopt his methods in their own dealings with workers.

Disillusion

By the next year, there were signs of discontent. The night workers faced difficulties due to the lack of sleep, weight losses, and low wages, exacerbated by multiple absences. Some of the night workers began holding meetings in the mornings, after the shift end, under the guidance of Rajender, an elder, articulate polisher, who had mysterious motives and ambitions. Rajender studied through the tenth standard in a village in Ghazipur, Uttar Pradesh, and came to Delhi in 1984. He learned to work a lathe machine in an Okhla factory, before shifting into metal polishing. He worked in numerous factories and workshops in Okhla and Noida, and gained knowledge and experience of managerial practices, labor laws, and industrial disputes. When the night shift began at B156, Rajender was hired as a casual worker, through his contacts with Bhagvati and Hanif, his neighbors in the Tata Steel shanty cluster in Okhla. He was about forty-four at the time, close to Khan sahab's age. Rajender began to emerge as an advisor and proto-leader of the night workers. In the spring of 2002, amid the exodus of some night polishers to other factories, due to persisting low wages, Khan sahab raised casual workers' wages, almost to the level of regular workers. To obstruct the night workers' collectivity, he brought Rajender to the day shift.

One morning, in June 2002, three officials of the Delhi labor department arrived at B156 for an unannounced inspection. They moved through the factory, asked questions to workers, and compiled a list of their names, posts, wages, and years of service. In this process of what was termed general checking, they found fifteen casual workers who were receiving less than Delhi minimum wages. They were also aware, they said, of a night shift that was operating illegally, without giving proper notification to the labor department. They left. That night, Khan sahab closed the night shift and told the night workers that he would contact them after sorting things out with the labor officials. They would not be paid wages during the shift closure. Some suspected that the closure signaled termination, without final settlements. On Rajender's advice, a group of night polishers engaged a union leader, Gupta, who was affiliated to the All India Trade Union Congress, the union wing of the Communist Party of India, and was known to a polisher in the group, Guddu Khan. Gupta submitted a complaint of illegal termination on behalf of ten polishers to the Delhi labor department's south Delhi office at Pushpa Bhawan (hereafter, the labor office), which compounded Khan sahab's legal problems. In response to the labor department difficulties, Khan sahab regularized the casual workers on the day shift, including Naresh and Uday.

On the date of the conciliation meeting at the labor office (in which the management and workers are given a chance to resolve the dispute, mediated by the labor officials, before advancing the case to the labor court), Khan sahab and the company's legal agent met with the night workers in Rajender's shanty, in the absence of the union leader. The polishers agreed to withdraw their complaint and their union membership, and the company regularized them. The shift restarted in late June, and other night workers were regularized.[2] Gupta was never heard of again. Khan sahab claimed victory, saying that he had "broken" the night workers' union. But many workers could see that this glimpse of unity, guided by Rajender and Gupta, had achieved more tangible gains than months of hard work and loyalty. Even Khan sahab later admitted that without this action, the company might never have regularized the night workers. In the aftermath of this turbulence, which equalized the day and night workers in wages and benefits, competition and hostilities increased, fueled by hopes for higher wages and shift rotation, and fears of Rajender's influence and ambitions. The work-intensifying process was reenergized.

During the winter months of high export orders, Khan sahab introduced an incentive to further promote competition. The machine with the highest production would be given a recognition (a *taj* [crown]), perhaps in the form of a higher wage increase. In offstage drinking sessions, Vijay suggested to Uday that the recognition could take the form of a promotion to supervisor in a proposed new unit in Okhla, and that Uday might get that post. Speed contests emerged between Uday and other polishers, including Arun, Guptaji, and Vijay II.

But Uday's working style caused difficulties for Naresh, his machine partner. Uday's speed generated tension with Naresh's friends, Krishna and Sivam, who engaged in auto-regulated working. Uday's practice of lifting and rocking the machine, kicking up dust and smoke, created hazards for Naresh when polishing the edges of pieces. For a year, Naresh had been experiencing disturbing chest pains, which would subside when he took days off. He suspected that the cause was the excessive force they were exerting at the machines to stay ahead of others. Though he was Uday's *guru* in polishing, and was a bit older than him, Naresh was his nephew in kin terms. Out of kin-based *izzat*, he avoided advising Uday, and adopted methods of resting and moving about, to regulate pace and conserve his body. Uday would learn his own lessons about polishing soon enough, Naresh felt.

One day in early 2003, when Uday was adjusting a cutting buff onto the machine shaft, the spinning metal tip caught his left glove, whipping his hand about vigorously, before he shut off the machine. He went to the Employees' State Insurance (ESI) Dispensary and was treated for a soft tissue injury. Other polishers were pleased about the injury. "The bloody Bihari is a fool. I told him so many times to work calmly and coolly," said Guptaji.[3] "He narrowly escaped. It would've been better if his hand got broken," others added.[4] But three days later, Uday was back at the machine, working at a furious pace.

Over the next weeks, Uday worked on pieces with complicated ring-based designs, whose holes and edges cut through the buffs, spewing fibers and debris. He began losing weight, coughing, and getting a fever in the evenings. His cheekbones poked out of his face. His voice became feeble. In March, he was admitted to the ESI Hospital for pneumonia, and was diagnosed with tuberculosis. The manager and supervisors did not visit him in the hospital. "So long as they need work from you, there's *izzat* for you. After that, who respects anybody," observed Uday.[5] The next month, he left for the village. When he returned in June, his outlook had changed. He took long rests at the machine, to the relief of Naresh, whose chest pains had receded in Uday's

Figure 3.2. The ESI Dispensary. Back, left: Naresh and Mithilesh.

absence. One morning, when Uday removed extra pieces put down by Vijay, he cried out, "Not so many pieces for me! I'm not going to the ESI Hospital again!"[6] "No, land up there again!" Achaibar shouted back cheerfully. "Don't let go of that place! ESI [health insurance] is being cut from our wages!"[7]

Uday was not the only one to experience disillusion. Before Uday's illness, when wages were increased for the night workers, the raises for the young Jharkhandi polishers were less than those of others, including those of shirking suspected collaborators. Naresh's younger brother, Vinod, a later hire, was still a casual polisher, despite Khan sahab's promises to regularize him. The Jharkhandis, whose working styles had assisted in driving the work-intensifying process, were angry and disgruntled. At B156, hard work did not seem to be generating good fruits. Instead, according to Naresh, it was giving rise to cheating, duping, and swindling (*thagna*) by the management. "They kept befooling us, giving us deceptive assurances, swindling us, and kept us working hard," he reflected.[8] The looters were being looted.

No recognition was ever given. On seeing the company's cold behavior to those who incurred injuries and illness, such as Uday, and a bit later, Guptaji, whose severe wrist injury forced him off the machine, polishers began rethinking their working styles.[9] More of them sought to regulate pace, conserve bodies from excessive looting, avoid competitive envy, and limit lateral *izzat* losses. Disillusion withdrew energy from the work-intensifying interplay and catalyzed processes of collectivity.

Refusals

In the factory's third year, managerial provocations gave a new impetus to collective politics. In June 2003, a new Okhla factory of the company group, operating under a different name, Dhatu Exports, was ready to begin production. C82, located a few blocks from B156, was a three-story building with twelve polishing machines in a large ground-floor room. According to rumors, some of the B156 workers would be shifted there, without a transfer letter guaranteeing continuity of service. This was a common managerial strategy in Okhla of terminating and rehiring workers, to reduce future gratuities. The rehired workers could also be terminated with relative ease during the probationary period of 240 days. For the first time, the day- and night-shift workers set aside their competitive and hostile feelings and met together in a park in Okhla.

Twenty-two workers gathered in this meeting to discuss the need for unity (*ekta*). Unity, symbolized by a hard fist, meant aggregation, solidarity, and collective action. If the management attempted to force a polisher out of the factory gate, for refusing to go to C82 without a transfer letter, other polishers should stop their machines, and if necessary, walk out of the gate. Unity also meant hierarchy and obedience. They needed to select persons among them to act as leaders, advisors, and spokesmen, whose decisions would be obeyed by everyone, without question. Rajender and Varmaji, due to their age, knowledge, and articulateness, were probable choices. Unity gestured toward the telos of unionization. By joining a union, they would gain access to a leader, with expertise in the labor laws and influence with the labor department, who could get labor inspectors to do general checking (the company was not giving current minimum wages or legal overtime rates), and who could pressure the management for better wages and benefits and proper documentation (such as appointment and transfer letters). But many were wary of unionization, and felt it could spoil their good images, antagonize the management, and provoke conflict, terminations, and closure of B156. To get unionized, as Mithilesh put it, offstage, was to axe one's own feet (*apne pair par kulhadi marna*). Only fourteen came to the next meeting.

At the end of June, Khan sahab abruptly closed the night shift, and instructed the night workers to begin duty the next day at C82. They would not be getting transfer letters. Seven of the polishers, including Varmaji, refused to go. The next day, six of this group came to B156 to meet with Khan sahab, who made them wait outside in the dry, burning heat for most of the day. Varmaji was missing. Rajender was absent from duty. When Khan sahab arrived, he ordered tea for the polishers, and quickly sorted things out. He sent two of them inside B156 to work on an empty machine. He told the other four that their employer would not change at C82, so there was no need for a transfer letter. Should they refuse to go, there would be adverse consequences for them. There were abundant stocks of pieces at C82, and they could begin extended overtime until 2 a.m., along with food allowances. He told Rambachan II to wipe down his Maruti. He caught hold of Ramakant and Umesh, with a half-jesting smile, pushed the three of them into the car, and drove them to C82, where they began work. Mohan lagged behind on foot, and bumped into Varmaji at a nearby workshop, who could not explain his absence. They drank together, and began work at C82 the next day. Over the next weeks, Khan sahab deftly shifted other polishers to C82, including Naresh and Uday, to fill the twelve machines. His machinations, through persuasion, enticements, division, and threats, exposed the fragility of workers' unity.[10]

Despite these victories, there were ominous beginnings at C82. One morning in late July, a group of three *hijras* came to C82 for a customary donation and blessing, at the starting of a new Okhla factory. Khan sahab was not present. He would give the *hijras* donations for Holi and Divali at B156, and even flirted with them on those occasions, but he had been eluding them at C82, and they were irritated. Varmaji came out and told them, in a rough tone, that Khan sahab was not there and to come back the next day. One *hijra* shouted back, with gesticulating arms, "Quiet! Ruin upon you! Watch this!"[11] She lifted her *sari*, squatted down at the gate, and passed water. This was a *hijra* curse on the new factory. They stormed off.

That evening, Varmaji drank with Vijay at a *pan* shop near B156. He had accepted extra pieces that morning, perhaps in exchange for this liquor session. After the rain subsided, he cycled home. As he approached the bridge to Hari Nagar, his cycle slipped off the road, hurling him headfirst into a rocky ditch. The jagged edges cut into his mouth and nose and split his tongue. His neighbors Rambhooan and Naresh II took him to a private clinic for stitches.[12] His face looked gruesome. The injury, other workers suggested, was the possible *karmic* consequence of Varmaji's recent activities, including his withdrawal during the C82 transfer, raising of production, and drinking, presaged by the *hijra*'s curse.

Varmaji had grown up in a village in Sant Kabir Nagar district, Uttar Pradesh. He studied through eighth standard, before coming to Delhi in 1980. After learning polishing in his village relative's Okhla shed, he worked in factories and workshops in Delhi, Noida, Faridabad, and Jalandhar, and spent a good deal of his earnings on drinking, pushing him into large, persisting debts. In April 2002, at the age of about thirty-eight, he came to work on the B156 night shift, with the hope of obtaining ESI health insurance, so as to get his three-year-old daughter treated for tuberculosis. In the wake of the injury, for the first time in two decades, Varmaji gave up drinking. The manager and supervisors could not control him as easily as before, through wage advances and liquor. He grew closer to the process of developing collectivity.

Managerial actions provoked further refusals. In August 2003, the polishers refused to accept wages on payday, as they were still receiving 2001 minimum wage grades, and were seeking raises above minimum wages. After a few days, with room rents and other monthly expenses to be paid, some polishers accepted Khan sahab's offer of wage advances, undermining the force of the refusal. A week after payday, other polishers accepted their existing wages, which were increased only the next month, and that too, only to current Delhi minimum wages. In late October, forty workers from both units refused their Divali bonuses, which had been decreased from one-and-a-half wage payments to the legal minimum of one monthly wage, allegedly due to reduced profits in Metal Artware Exports. It was a dull and dim Divali. Babloo Khan, Bhagvati, and Vijay II, suspected collaborators, began visiting workers in their rooms after hours, and encouraged them to accept the bonuses, rather than cause losses to their families. On the next payday, they were the first to take their bonus envelopes, inducing a domino-like process of capitulation by the others. Morale plunged again.

But amid the ebbs and flows of unity, there were currents of fellowship (*bhaicara*) among workers. Humor and joking, evincing affective feelings, thrived at B156. Workers exchanged loans when going to the village, and assisted each other in times of illness.[13] Friendships developed on the

Figure 3.3. Babloo Khan's family shifting from a demolished shanty cluster.

shifts, and significantly, between the Jharkhandis, once seen to be insular and uncivilized (*jangli*), and workers from other regions.[14] Workers visited one another's neighborhoods for birthday parties of small children, where they sat, conversed, and ate meals together. Despite ill feeling toward Babloo Khan after the bonus episode, a dozen workers came to his shanty near Mathura Road, a few weeks later, to celebrate Eid. In December, when Babloo's shanty cluster was demolished to make space for road construction,[15] Naresh II and Varmaji spent a day assisting Babloo in removing belongings, salvaging materials, and shifting Babloo's family to a rented room in their own lane in Hari Nagar.[16] One could see, in such interactions, currents of fellowship that were influenced, though not fully constrained, by goings-on in the factory. This fellowship could protect workers' relations, strained by factory dealings, and keep alive possibilities for future collectivity.

There were also provocations with regard to overtime perquisites. The management withdrew the provision of two *samosas*, along with a fifteen-minute break, during overtime. It was customary in many Okhla factories and workshops to provide tea and snacks in overtime, even for casual and contract workers. Restoring *samosas* was an issue of respect (*man-samman*), as Varmaji put it, given existing arrangements in Okhla. On the promise that Khan sahab would try at the head office to restore the *samosas*, workers continued to do overtime, and bought *samosas* with their own money (at Rs. 5 for two), as they would get hungry and fatigued by 7 p.m.[17] Khan sahab's promise did not materialize, and after Divali, workers refused to do overtime. The manager, in response, pressured polishers to increase production to make up for the overtime losses, discontinued wage advances, and floated rumors of impending terminations and factory closure. The polishers resumed their park meetings, reforged unity, and practiced auto-regulated working in larger numbers. Those who deviated from the refusal, they warned, would be met with verbal abuses and possible violence. To compensate for the withdrawal of advances, they began a loan society among themselves, which excluded the manager, supervisors, and suspected collaborators. At the end of December, three C82 polishers began overtime. In an evening park meeting, Babloo Khan advised others not to forsake extra earnings for the sake of two *samosas*. A few days later, he too began overtime. Others distanced themselves from Babloo, including in factory joking, in which he was previously a core instigator and participant.

By January 2004, workers were becoming agitated, restless, and impatient. In a meeting in the Sarita Vihar District Park, Rajender composed a letter of demands (*mang patr*) on behalf of the workers, demanding annual wage increments, legal overtime rates, restored bonuses, rent and transportation allowances, uniforms and shoes, better-quality bathing soap, clean drinking water, appointment letters, monthly pay slips, provident fund account slips (proving that wage deductions were being deposited and matched by company contributions), timely disbursement of leave pay, and provisions of advances and loans.[18] The list was long, Rajender admitted, but some demands could be conceded during negotiations. The letter was signed by forty-four workers and sent by post to the head office. Shortly thereafter, Khan sahab held a meeting at C82 with the workers of both units. He read off the list of demands in a humorous tone, and assured that a few of them, such as monthly pay slips, could be satisfied. For the others, he would make ongoing efforts at the head office ("*koshish jari rahegi*"). He was now willing to offer one *samosa* during overtime. Over the next weeks, through the workings of offstage machinations, involving words, advances, and liquor, polishers began to deviate and work overtime. Others uttered angry insults and abuses as they observed the capitulations, describing them as falling wickets in a cricket match. By the end of January, nearly all of the workers were doing overtime, and eating one *samosa*.[19]

The collapses of refusals often ended with feelings of embarrassment, disappointment, and defeat. But these episodes also revealed the company's intent to extract more production while deferring wage increases and reducing existing provisions. In so doing, these managerial victories seemed to promote, rather than prevent, growing disillusion and discontent. There were ominous feelings that more volatile disruptions might occur in the future. Amlakant said, with a sigh, "Now there's inevitably going to be a tumult in the company, a massive tumult."[20]

Vulnerability

The politics of unity confronted multiple vulnerabilities. First, managerial machinations could induce deviations. Khan sahab's activities of persuading, enticing, threatening, and dividing workers cultivated and capitalized on workers' egoism, fears, and hopes, within situations of compelling difficulty. His collaborators were adept at staying close to workers in joking, meetings, and drinking sessions, while obeying his bidding in deviating and convincing others to follow in their wake. Second, the hierarchies of unity politics created vulnerabilities to the actions of its proto-leaders. Workers vested authority and hope in a few persons, such as Rajender and Varmaji, who could speak in provocative, passionate, and militant tones in park meetings, calling for unity, violence against supervisors and collaborators, and tool-down strikes, but who might recede offstage in confrontations with the management. Workers spoke of the dangers of selecting a few persons as spokesmen. A small number of persons, Amlakant observed in one meeting, could be easily enticed or coerced into decisions detrimental to the larger group, as witnessed in films such as *Deewaar* (1975), in which a good, honest union leader of coal mine workers is isolated and threatened by the company boss into signing an unfavorable agreement. Perhaps this was why Khan sahab often advised workers to choose a few representatives, whom he could speak to separately, rather than having to engage with the entire group. Third, unity politics relied on refusals, a strategy with inherent vulnerabilities. Workers could boldly refuse wages, bonuses, and overtime, but with limited savings, persisting debts, and pressing cash needs for basic expenses, many could not hold out for long. They were refusing what they needed badly.

Unity politics also revealed workers' understandings of themselves, in the play of the discourses of generalizations and distinctiveness that were audible in humor practices. During upsurges and crescendos of refusals, workers seemed capable of suspending or setting aside negative stereotypes to do with regional origin, religion, and caste (e.g., Biharis and Muslims as egoistic, submissive, and untrustworthy). The politics of unity pushed aggregate identities, negatively understood, to the backstage. But when the deviations and decrescendos began, one could hear workers invoking identities in derogatory tones, as if these identities prefigured and causally explained the capitulations. The empirical picture, however, was complex. In the night workers' union action, Guddu Khan played a critical role in facilitating the connection to the union leader, contrary to suspicions that all Muslim workers at B156 were secretly aligned with Khan sahab. Umesh, from Bihar, was among those who held out the longest in the overtime refusal. Workers who deviated included non-Biharis and non-Muslims. The discourse on the distinctiveness of persons seemed more capable of accommodating this complexity. In discussions, workers spoke of the deeper, critical differences between persons, beyond aggregate identities. These were differences in thinking, feeling, attitudes, and intentions (*dimag* [mind], *buddhi* [intelligence], *vicar* [thought], and *dil* [heart]), which were visible in diverse working styles, comportment toward the management, and weaknesses (e.g., to liquor or verbal intimidation). Even two brothers, such as Naresh and Madan, could act quite differently in working styles and drinking habits. They also spoke of the importance of associative circles (*sangat*) that influenced thoughts, choices, and actions. These social circles of two to five workers comprised persons who might room together or live close by, share kin or village ties, or drink together after shifts. These circles partly explained why the dominoes or wickets tended to fall in groups.

A motive for unity, which could militate against vulnerabilities, was the striving for justice (*haq*). The category of *haq* has many valences of meaning, including right, justice, claim, due share, truth, and God.[21] In unity episodes, *haq* seemed to minimally mean legal rights (*kanuni adhikar*), though most workers had only a vague knowledge of the labor laws. But *haq* could also have contextual referents, including past practices at B156, customary practices in other Okhla factories, and more fluidly, what workers felt they were rightly and justly due in this context, from this company. In the night workers' union action, they were protesting against potential illegal terminations. The meetings and refusal of the C82 transfer were motivated by concerns of possible terminations and rehiring. *Haq* in these episodes gestured to the minimal valence of legal rights. In the wage and bonus refusals, workers were seeking more than current minimum wages and legal minimum bonuses, due to the production increases and quality improvements they had delivered at the machines, their time in the job, and past practices of giving higher bonuses. In the overtime refusal, Varmaji spoke of the *samosas* not only as bodily nourishment, but as their *haq*. The labor laws did not specify overtime food allowances, but they were customary in Okhla, and the company had given them in the past. Here, *haq* reached beyond legal rights to what workers perceived was their just due.

Rajender's letter of demands gave a sense of the horizon of *haq*, extending from minimal, legal rights (such as double overtime and legal documentation) to desired provisions unspecified by the laws (such as advances and loans). In interviews, Amlakant spoke of a further horizon of *haq*, in the ideal of true, just wages and working arrangements (*vastavik mazduri*), consisting of wages that were good enough to raise one's family with *izzat*,[22] good working arrangements (including pollution control systems, clean drinking water, proper bathing facilities, pollution masks, medicine, tea, overtime food provisions, uniforms, shoes, and access to advances), and good managerial conduct, in polite addressing (with *izzat*) and minimal tensions over production. True, just wages and working arrangements, which were bound up with desires for bodily, mental, and material well-being and respect in and beyond the workplace, seemed to be a distant, vague, outer horizon of *haq* in workers' visions.

The pursuit of *haq* enabled workers' struggles to be minimally bounded but not constricted by the existing content and implementation of labor laws and state policies.[23] *Haq* allowed workers to agitate for what they believed they were justly due from their employers, regardless of the specifications of the laws. *Haq* opened spaces for struggles.

But the quest for *haq* jostled with the desire to accommodate existing conditions, involving deprivations of *haq*. Some workers believed that agitating for *haq* was a losing battle. After deviating from the overtime refusal, Babloo Khan explained his rationale. "Workers can never put up a fight against the company owners. Wage workers everywhere are deprived of their *haq*. A wage worker has compelling difficulty, that's why he's doing wage work. I say, whatever the conditions are in the company, keep one's job going. I figure, let the company keep running, let one's job stay safe. Even if they're not bloody giving us hot *samosas*, consider that we're getting Rs. 1,000 of overtime!"[24] The willingness to survive amid existing conditions and deprivations contended with desires and passions to oppose further degradations.

Soul Politics

Along with unfolding processes of disillusion and unity politics, critical discourses arose on oppression. Workers articulated an implicit understanding of its deeper causes, in a distorting interplay of souls and the *Kalyug*. In cursing, sabotage, and restrained working, workers expressed discontent and sought ways to cooperate less with oppression and its underlying interplay.

Oppression

Workers deployed various categories to describe oppressive practices in the factory. The extraction and intensification of work, amid stagnant wages and reduced benefits and provisions, were spoken of as exploitation (*shoshan*, also meaning drying up, draining, sucking, absorbing). Oppression (*atyacar*, *zulm*), which conveyed a sense of egregious wrong, was exhibited in these exploitative processes, and also, in specific acts of force (*zabardasti*), such as shifting workers to C82 without transfer letters. Workers described the factory as a space of rule by thugs, goons, and gangsters (*gunda raj*).

When invoking these categories, the targets of critique were the factory manager and supervisors, seen to be the immediate, face-to-face perpetrators of oppression and exploitation.[25] While workers acknowledged that managerial posts were designed to conduct these activities, they also expressed desires that these particular persons, seen to be engaged in excessive oppression, be replaced. They hoped that the company directors might assist them in their difficulties, though some suspected that the senior managers at the head office might approve of Khan sahab's activities of intensifying production and defusing agitations. The American director, by contrast, was seen to be above culpability. He was a good, benevolent, but blind king (*andha raja*), who had been led to believe by his corrupt ministers that the workers were being given good wages and benefits, and were happy, while they secretly siphoned funds intended for workers and engaged in illegal practices. If the king had any fault, it was only his naïveté in believing his ministers, and his distance from the people (*praja*), as he did not often come to the Okhla units, ascertain their true conditions, and remedy their difficulties, as good kings would do in past ages.[26] Workers voiced hopes that he might come to know of their situation, and rescue them from the oppression and exploitation by his managers.[27]

The critique of oppressive practices at B156 did not suggest a critique of the necessity of companies, factories, managers, or wage labor. Companies were needed to invest capital, set up factories, procure orders, and market goods. Factories were necessary to make things, and gave vitally needed livelihoods to workers. Managers were required to supervise production. Poor people in compelling difficulty, willing to do wage work under others, were necessary for factories, and society more generally, to function.[28] Workers desired less oppressive and exploitative factories, not less factories. If companies provided true, just wages and working arrangements (*vastavik mazduri*, as described above), there would be no oppression or exploitation. But workers could not cite a factory in Okhla where such wages and arrangements were given.

Managers and supervisors were not the only perpetrators of exploitation. Working-class people were also exploited by state officials (in demolishing slum colonies and siphoning development funds), the police (in extracting bribes and brokering disputes), lawyers (in draining resources to fight long cases), private doctors (in charging large amounts to administer intravenous bottles), urban landlords (in charging high rents), shopkeepers, moneylenders, and private buyers of agricultural produce in the village. Workers also exploited one another in the village, they admitted, in giving low wages to workers (*mazdurs*) for agricultural operations, and in extracting dowries from one another's families. Workers confronted exploitation everywhere, they said, but not unlike others, they also perpetrated a bit of it, for advantage.

Soul and Epoch

Workers articulated ideas about the deeper causes of oppression that delved into understandings of souls and time. Once the polishers capitulated and accepted nonincreased wages in the August 2003 refusal, which were less than current minimum wages, an angry Sivam came out of the gate and said, "See,

Shankar-*bhai*, this is oppression. This is what's called the *Kalyug*. The deep, dense *Kalyug*!"[29] At tense junctures, Sivam would shake his head while polishing pieces, and mutter through the *dhoti* over his mouth, "There's so much injustice here, you tell me. What are these bloody times, what is this damn *Kalyug*?! Bravo, *Kalyug*!!"[30]

The *Kalyug* (or elsewhere, *Kaliyug* or *Kaliyuga*) is the fourth epoch in the cosmic cycle of time, and is referenced in the *Mahabharata*,[31] the *Puranas*,[32] the *Ramcaritmanas*,[33] political writings,[34] print literature,[35] novels,[36] Hindi films,[37] television serials,[38] spiritual discourses, and the news media. While textual traditions date its onset to 3102 BCE, workers gave varied estimates of its origins, from several years ago to a few decades, fifty years, one thousand years, a few thousand years, and twenty thousand years ago.[39] Along with these figures, they made references to the less distorted worlds of their grandparents or parents, and even of their own childhood in the village; events such as Independence or their migration to Delhi; varied images of Mughal and British rule; and Ram and Krishna, divine incarnations (*avatars*) of the *Treta* and *Dvapar* epochs preceding the *Kalyug*.

In workers' descriptions, the *Kalyug* is an epoch of ethical degeneration and the ascendancy of forces that corrupt and distort (or "decivilize") thoughts, feelings, actions, and dealings vis-à-vis human beings, nature, and the divine. It is characterized by the dominance and intensification of self-interest, avarice, material desires, tension, envy, enmity, thievery, dishonesty, deception, oppression, muscle force, and violence, and the decline and loss of morality, respect, compassion, mutual assistance, and truth in human dealings. The *Kalyug* is spoken of as an age of skills and artistry (*kala*), in speaking, behaving, and technologies, such as machines (*kal*, hence *kal-yug* or the machine age), which can be labor-easing, displacing, and hazardous,[40] and weaponry, which can be protective, dangerous, and destructive. As the distorted, wrongful actions (*gunah, pap*) of human beings intensify, the *Kalyug* is believed to progress toward catastrophic destruction, dissolution, and regeneration, with the probable intervention of a divine *avatar*.[41]

These distorted actions, in workers' implicit visions, as I have understood them, arise from an interplay of souls and time. Workers spoke of the soul (*atma*) as the deepest site of thought, feeling, and agency in human beings. The soul, located in the body, and sensitive to bodily experiences, does not bear markers of class, caste, gender, or religion, but rather, the marks of one's present and past actions (*karm*). The soul has dual, vying parts or shares (*hissas*), which represent the soul acting under the influences of two proclivities or tendencies (*sahi* and *rakshasi pravrttis*). These parts, or what might be called valences, of the soul, were described as the demonic soul-valence (*rakshasi atma*, also *pap atma*) and the true soul-valence (*sahi atma*, also *sacci, shuddh, punya atma*). The demonic soul-valence is driven largely by egoistic motives and passions such as self-interest, avarice, envy, arrogance, anger, fear, and cowardice. The true soul-valence evinces feelings of empathy, genuine respect, compassion, and devotion, and seeks truth, the good, and the divine. These soul-valences are involved, in varying degrees of influence, in thoughts, feelings, decisions, and actions, and in the shaping of a personality and character.

Epochal time intervenes in this struggle of soul-valences. The *Kalyug* is seen to enter souls, alter its internal balance of forces, arouse, activate, and bolster the soul's demonic valence, and encourage egoistic and wrongful actions in the world. Souls, acting on epochal influences and demonic proclivities, engage in distorted activities, and sustain and advance the progress of the *Kalyug*. Souls and the *Kalyug*, in this deep interplay, constitute and shape one another, and progress together toward a decivilizing, destructive telos.

The workers could see the workings of this deep interplay within the factory. The manager and supervisors, in manipulative dealings, deceptive assurances, divisive stratagems, and production pressures, were seen to be deploying methods expressive of the forces of the *Kalyug*. The epoch penetrated and pervaded the being of the manager, according to Firoz. In his actions and dealings, the manager was actively promoting the *Kalyug*. In the factory, as Firoz put it, "Khan sahab has deployed and diffused the whole formula of the *Kalyug*."[42] Workers too were caught up in the *Kalyug* formula. The *Kalyug* was visible in workers' collaboration and loyalty, in which they pursued egoistic interests and passions, at the expense of one another; in competition, speed, and looting mentalities, which exhibited the accelerating, destructive, and self-destructive dynamic of the *Kalyug*; in lateral relations of surface-level respect, envy, and hostility, depicted as *Kalyug*-like, distorted relations (*Kalyugi sambandh*); and in disintegrations of collectivity, due to self-interest, weakness, and fear. Given these activities of the management and workers, the factory could be seen to be a microcosm of the *Kalyug*. "It is a miniature world of the *Kalyug*. You get the whole *Kalyug* in that factory," Amlakant observed.[43] Oppression, in these implicit visions, arose from the initiatives and cooperation of distorted souls (of oppressors and the oppressed), acting on egoistic proclivities, encouraged by the *Kalyug*. The work-intensifying interplay of management and workers was an expression of a deeper interplay of souls and the *Kalyug.*

The awareness of this deeper interplay, and the agency that sustained it, was a source of anxiety and unease. "The one who endures oppression is more culpable than the one who perpetrates it (*Zulm sahnevala zulm karnevale se zyada gunahgar hota hai*)" was an oft-heard saying among workers.[44] "You're a human being, and you know how to live in a good and proper way," Varmaji reflected. "If someone is oppressing you, your duty is to oppose it. If you're not doing that, then you yourself are culpable."[45] They were doing wrong by permitting, tolerating, and withstanding oppression in the factory. In collective politics, one witnessed attempts to avoid such culpability, wrestle with demonic proclivities, and act on the felt, ethico-political duty to oppose oppression. To Khan sahab's expanding *Kalyug* formula in the factories, noncooperation was its emergent, contesting, disrupting counterformula.

Cursing

Workers' articulations of discontent in the factory revealed understandings of souls and the *Kalyug.* One way of expressing suffering and rage, silently or audibly, was in laments and curses (*hay, baddua*). These were seen to have potent, dangerous powers.[46]

The danger of laments and curses is an idea visible in poetry and literature. Kabir, the medieval poet-saint, warns, "Do not oppress the weak, whose cry of sigh is thick with curse / A lifeless hide blowing the fire [i.e., an ironsmith's bellows] doth burn iron to ashes."[47] In Premchand's story "The Power of a Curse (*Garib ki Hay*),"[48] an elderly Brahmin widow, Munga, discovers that a well-off man has consumed the pension she had entrusted to him, as he has done with many others' funds. She curses him incessantly, and goes mad, eventually dying at his door, causing him grave disgrace. Others refuse dealings with him. His wife dies from fearful visions. He leaves the village, returns, and dies in a burning house. His son is sent to a reformatory.

There were many Mungas at the machines. When the manager assured polishers of his ongoing efforts to raise wages, or when supervisors pressured them to take on extra pieces, they could utter curses that these persons be removed from the factory. As Sivam once put it, "If this bloody management goes from here, that'd be better! Even if worse people come in their place, we'd accept them!"[49] They might also voice ill wishes that the manager and supervisors be made to suffer like workers.[50] In meetings, Rajender and Bhagvati warned Khan sahab about the potency of their laments and curses, whose effects were dangerous, fearsome, and inescapable.[51] When Firoz was pulled from his machine and sent to C82, he said to Khan sahab, "If our curse reaches its target, no one can undo it."[52]

Curses could also be directed at one another. On seeing a polisher pursuing speed or taking on extra pieces, others might utter ill wishes that he incur an injury, suffer an illness, or worse. On returning to the factory after his illness, Uday moderated his speed, partly to avoid such curses. "A curse has taken effect," Varmaji reflected, on the night of his cycle accident, gesturing to curses that might have been directed at him by polishers, the *hijras*, or his wife.[53] In rage, on witnessing unfolding events, workers' curses at times could target the entire factory. "May such a factory be locked, closed, destroyed!" they might exclaim, indirectly cursing themselves, as they too would suffer from factory closure.[54] Curses could be destructive and self-destructive.

But there were uncertainties about the workings of curses. Curses were heard by the divine and could hasten and intensify *karmic* punishments to wrongdoers. But there was skepticism about the power of curses in the *Kalyug*, in which souls were weak and distorted, unlike in previous epochs, when sages and others possessed the soul strength (*atma shakti*) to utter effective curses. Workers' curses emerged only minimally from the soul's true, good valence, in voicing protest against oppression and injustice, and emanated largely from the egoism, rage, and vengeance of the soul's demonic valence. Such curses, said Uday, could take a very long time to reach their targeted wrongdoers. Varmaji was also doubtful of their powers. Given their experiences at B156, he observed, "This is the *Kalyug*. The more we curse the management, the more they get promoted!"[55] But these uncertainties did not prevent them from cursing.

Demonic Good

Workers also articulated discontent with their hands. Out of anger at production pressures, polishers could blow the motors of their machines, by mishandling the power switch or applying excessive force.[56] In January

2004, after the collapse of the overtime refusal, Vijay put down four large leaf-shaped trays, one more than the norm, at the machine of Uday and Naresh. These were difficult, unwieldy pieces, requiring strong exertions, multiple rotations, and careful movements. "Let it be three pieces, they'll get done calmly and carefully," said Uday.[57] "No, make four," Vijay replied curtly.[58] Uday and Naresh got angry. They skipped fine cutting and began with fiber buffing, pushing and pressing with extra force. After two hours, the motor blew. They shifted to another machine and kept working. Using force with the denim buffs, they heated up that machine, which began to secrete smoke, before shutting it off. Helpers brought a fan to cool down the machine. Other polishers watched and laughed. Two others who were making trays started applying pressure and heating up their machine. Khan sahab came by, saw the situation, and told Vijay, "Get the work done calmly."[59] Once the machines and tempers cooled, Uday and Naresh resumed working, and completed the trays in the evening.

Uday once spoke of the virtues of hard work, harbored hopes of advancement, and competed for the highest production. Now, he grumbled about the incessant pressures to increase production. Despite *izzat* for the machine and the divine Vishvakarma, a message had to be given to the supervisors. "To blow the machine is a wrongful act (*pap*). But in view of the oppression here, in compelling difficulty, one has to do this. It's not a wrongful act and it's also a wrongful act," he said.[60] Indeed, the machine was also suffering from the oppression, in the greater strain it was taking from the higher number of pieces. The demonic soul-valence (*rakshasi atma*) was behind the sabotage, but not completely. To fight oppression and wrongdoing, as called for by the true soul-valence, one had to engage in a bit of it. "To get rid of a gangster (*gunda*), you have to become a gangster. This is the *Kalyug*. The *Kalyug* can only be done away with by [the methods of] the *Kalyug*," he said.[61] The sabotage had its effects. Vijay did not give them trays the next day, and when he did, some weeks later, he put down only three pieces.[62]

Some polishers articulated discontent by pushing the limits of auto-regulated working to what might be called restrained working. In this working style, they regulated quantity and pace, but did not polish their pieces with complete diligence. Umesh and Rakesh acquired a negative image with the management for piece removals, speaking up often, giving their pieces close to the shift end, and allegedly, sending pieces of substandard quality. Early on, Umesh spoke of his high hopes for this foreign-owned company, and the duty to make their pieces well, so that the company and its workers would prosper. Rakesh was given the nickname *rakshas* (demon), as he worked quickly and vigorously during the night shift, at a time when demons are believed to grow stronger. After two years, their views had evolved. "If the company doesn't think about our well-being, why should we think about its well-being?" Umesh asked.[63] Rakesh cheerfully added, "The company is oppressing us so much, the day it mends its ways, we'll mend ours!"[64]

Restrained working emerged largely from the demonic soul-valence. The true valence wanted to accept pieces up to one's capacity, work honestly, utilize one's artistry, and finish them with high quality. But in the present context, hard work, along with open demands to the management, was not yielding tangible gains. One's hands were one's main weapons (*hathiyars*), they said. If polishers were to act more from the demonic soul-valence, and restrain quantity and quality, the company might begin to deliver on their needs and wants.[65] Where the true valence was failing, the demonic valence could bring about good, according to Umesh. "It's said that if by telling a lie, someone's life can be saved, then one should save that life. Sometimes, if something good can be gotten through the demonic soul-valence, one should do it. At that time, we won't think of our demonic soul-valence as wrong. Rather, it will prove that our demonic soul-valence is better than the true soul-valence, because *it* has done something good. If the demonic soul-valence does something good, we'll think of it as good!"[66] The demonic soul-valence, which collaborated with oppressive processes and epochal forces, could also evidently rebel against them.

Restrained working, unlike refusals, did not dissolve quickly. Rather, it drew in the occasional participation of other disgruntled polishers. As an extreme form of auto-regulated working, it was an instantiation of the politics of synchrony (*talmel*). But most polishers could not embrace this practice. They were not ready to be scolded for piece failures. They feared isolation, disciplinary action, and job loss. There were also deeper, ethical difficulties. "I cannot do it in good conscience (*Atma gavahi nahim deti hai*)," Amlakant said. The true soul-valence could not bear witness (*gavahi dena*) to this working style. To deliberately polish pieces of substandard quality was to dishonor one's artistry and betray implicit compacts to work properly. The dominant ethos was one of doing honest, high-quality work, not shirking, which they felt gave them the legitimate right to voice demands and agitate for justice.

Unity and Synchrony

Further threats to workers' livelihoods arose in 2004, which catalyzed escalations in collective politics. I examine a sequence of developments involving unionization, restrained working, disciplinary actions, and contestations. In these developments, one witnessed a confluence, amid differences, of the politics of unity and synchrony.

Union

In February 2004, the C82 workers were sent back to B156, allegedly due to difficulties in processing official paperwork for the new unit. These workers, who had been concerned about terminations and rehiring, since shifting there, were relieved to come back to B156. The manager arranged two shifts, beginning in the early morning and the afternoon, avoiding the hassles of restarting a night shift.

But by May, schemes to undermine jobs reemerged. Khan sahab visited polishers in their rooms, to persuade them to resign and work at C82 as contract workers. As piece-rate workers, he said, they could make much greater earnings. But they would not receive minimum wages, health insurance, or other benefits. A few polishers among his close circle seemed agreeable. Rumors circulated of other plans to shift workers to C82 without transfer letters and rehire them as casual workers of Dhatu Exports. During these machinations, Uday left for the village, extended his stay, and never came back to B156.

The workers resumed their park meetings. Rajender and Varmaji now emphatically advocated unionization. Given the past failures of refusals, many were agreeable to seeking outside assistance. Amid fears of job loss and lateral anxieties, one sensed the desire among workers for the "miracle, mystery, and authority" of a strong union leader, to draw on the discourse of Dostoevsky's Grand Inquisitor,[67] who would instruct, direct, and discipline them, bolster their unity, and protect them from aggressive managerial initiatives. But there were concerns about Rajender's true motives for pushing unionization. Some suspected that he was seeking to orchestrate a confrontation with the company, which could result in closure and lucrative settlements for proto-leaders.[68] Intriguingly, Bhagvati, a suspected collaborator, came to a meeting, apologized for subverting past refusals, and pledged his solidarity, given that their jobs, and not just *samosas*, were now at stake.

At a late-night park meeting in mid-May, workers gathered in a circle to discuss unionization. Bhagvati advised that they take a ritual oath of unity. From a nearby *dhaba*, Firoz brought a metal tumbler with water, to symbolize holy water of the Ganga (*Gangajal*). Workers in turn lifted the glass and pressed their hands together, sometimes dabbing some water on the head. Varmaji stood up with the glass and said, somewhat dramatically, "I take an oath on this holy water to struggle with loyalty and honesty. Whatever I lose, even if I lose my life, I can't break from you folks."[69] Others applauded vigorously. The motives for the ritual seemed to be the desire to raise collective confidence, test persons whose loyalties were suspect, and bind persons through fears of adverse consequences for sacral oath breaking.[70]

The workers proposed to become members of the Indian Federation of Trade Unions (IFTU), the trade union wing of the Communist Party of India (Marxist-Leninist)-New Democracy, a Naxalite political party (hereafter, the Party), which fought elections and engaged in armed struggle. The union, formed in 1978, currently had about 200,000 members, concentrated in Andhra Pradesh (with Telangana), West Bengal, and pockets of north India, including about 4,500 members in Delhi, largely in private industries and major hospitals. In Okhla, the union had a fluctuating membership of about 500 to 1,000, and was active in the engineering, electronics, and pharmaceutical industries. Some of the polishers had experiences of the union from struggles in other metal factories (e.g., D45, T7, A4). Varmaji had attended IFTU demonstrations against economic liberalization policies in the early nineties. Other workers had gone for medical treatment to Dr. Das, the Delhi union's general secretary, a lean, articulate, charismatic, buoyant, and poised gentleman in his forties, at a clinic in a shanty cluster in Govindpuri. I had known Dr. Das since the early stages of my work in Okhla and had brought several workers to the clinic.

IFTU had a militant image in the industrial area, and conducted demonstrations, processions, and strikes in protest against state policies to do with globalization and liberalization, Supreme Court judgments, the nonenforcement of labor laws, closures and retrenchments, and the growing usage of casual and contract workers. Unusually among unions in Okhla, IFTU was reputed to fight for the protection of jobs, rather than broker settlements for commissions.[71] In mid-May, after a park meeting with Dr. Das, forty workers became IFTU members. Over the next weeks, IFTU leaders came to

Figure 3.4. The IFTU office. Left to right: Sivam, Rajender, Dr. Das.

workers' meetings, and sought to cultivate and educate a small group of worker-leaders, accentuating the verticality of unity politics.[72] They advised workers to avoid immediate confrontations with the management (despite Rajender's eagerness), before strengthening their unity and understanding.

Later in May, Khan sahab's schemes began to unfold in opaque, perplexing ways. He shifted six polishers from his close circle to C82, with the promise of giving them transfer letters in a few days. The letters never materialized. Ten days later, in ostensible protest, four of the polishers, including Babloo Khan, resigned and accepted settlements.[73] Two others returned to B156. Polishing at C82 came to a halt.

In June, Rajender brought a metal pot of water to a Sunday park meeting, which now included workers who had not been present at the first holy water ritual. Workers took turns lifting the vessel, pledging solidarity, and vowing not to break from the group. Hanif refused this time, mysteriously, saying that he had already lifted the Ganga water at the first meeting. Others offered to substitute a Quran, but he said it would make no difference.[74] The refusal reinforced suspicions that Hanif might be a secret informer of Khan sahab. Some invoked negative stereotypes about the untrustworthiness of Muslims, while others contrasted the behavior of Firoz, who had eagerly contributed to the first ritual.[75] Hanif begrudgingly left the meeting. The next Sunday, after an ambiguous apology, he was allowed back into the meetings, though not without lingering doubts. At his machine, when drinking from a bottle of water, he would cry out, poking fun at these doubts, "All of you see! I'm lifting the holy water!"[76]

In the wake of unionization, workers became more emboldened and volatile in encounters with management. The day after the oath-taking ritual, when Achaibar reached the factory, after cycling from Faridabad in the midday heat of June, Khan sahab, who was sitting outside, said to him, "My mood gets spoiled on seeing your face."[77] Khan sahab could say such things before, in jest, but in the changed atmosphere, Achaibar lost his temper and shot back, "I also don't want to see your face."[78] "You want to see what a manager can do? I'll beat you up!" Khan sahab said.[79] "You can hit me, I can also hit back," Achaibar replied.[80] "I'm not going to let you work today," the manager said, and told Achaibar to stay outside.[81] The polishers tooled down. Fifteen tense minutes passed. After talks with Rajender and Varmaji, Khan sahab allowed Achaibar to go inside and start working at his machine. In the evening, he apologized to a still angry Achaibar.

Two days later, Govind instructed Guptaji, who was handling pieces downstairs, to go up and relay pieces to the office.[82] Guptaji refused, saying that a helper was already doing that job. "You don't do any work!" Govind shouted.[83] "If I don't do any work, then if you have the guts, give me my final settlement!" Guptaji retorted.[84] Govind grabbed Guptaji's shirt by the chest and started pushing him. Other polishers shut off their machines, came to the spot, and restrained Govind. He reached for a metal pipe on the ground. They threw punches at his body. The junior manager, Kaypiji, separated them and defused the situation. This was a glimpse, and a warning, of the possibilities of violence in the factory.

Over the next weeks, out of discontent with stagnant wages and working conditions, more polishers engaged in restrained working, by refusing extra pieces, regulating speed, and giving their pieces close to the shift end.[85] Production did not rise at previous rates. Higher percentages of pieces required repairs. This confluence of unity and synchrony seemed to disturb the company more than past, self-injuring refusals. Khan sahab made a surprise visit to a park meeting in Sarita Vihar, and amid tea, banter, and joking, emphasized the importance of restoring a peaceful atmosphere, raising production, and improving quality, for the sake of the factory's survival. But his words had little effect. There was a tinge of sadness on the manager's face.

Lockout

One morning in early August, four security guards appeared at the factory gate. A handwritten notice was posted, signed by Khan sahab, informing four workers (Achaibar, Bhagvati, Rajender, and Varmaji) of immediate termination. On the direction of Dr. Das, the polishers tooled down. The next day, they resumed work, while Dr. Das submitted a complaint of illegal termination at the labor office. Due to tensions and disturbed moods, many pieces failed. The dismissed polishers, who looked stunned and confused, sat outside, read newspapers, and played cards. The grouping was strange. The inclusion of Rajender and Varmaji, as proto-leaders, and perhaps Achaibar, due to the tense verbal exchange, was understandable. But it was unclear why Bhagvati, who had been close to Khan sahab, was on the notice.

A few days later, a second notice was put on the gate, signed by the Indian director, stating that the B156 polishers had been working slowly since the dismissals, causing production losses. They would be permitted to enter the factory only after signing a letter of undertaking promising to obey managerial orders and not commit such mistakes in the future. The text of the letter read, "I give assurance that I will give full production, follow appropriate orders of the management, and work with complete discipline."[86] If they signed the undertaking, the workers felt they would be bound to obey all managerial diktats, on the penalty of termination. They consulted Dr. Das, and did not sign the letters. Such "good conduct bonds" were deployed elsewhere by managements to divide workers, tighten discipline, or push workers outside of the gate in order to terminate them. The motive here was not clear.

The next day, workers were denied entry to the factory. Production halted. Dr. Das filed a complaint at the labor office, that they had been illegally refused duty through the imposition of a letter with illegal conditions.[87] Two days later, Dr. Das met with the deputy labour commissioner (DLC), the highest official in the labor office. The DLC sat at a large desk with piles of files with paperweights, in a dimly lit room with tube lights, off-white walls, metal closets, and a desert cooler. Dr. Das sat across from him, with workers standing behind him. After hearing the details of the case, the DLC phoned Khan sahab, and offered to send the workers back to B156 to resume duty. The manager was not agreeable. The DLC called him in for a conciliation date after four days.

At the factory, later that day, Khan sahab met with five polishers, and encouraged them to sign the letters and begin duty. Given the phone exchange at the labor office, in which the DLC seemed to be taking the workers' side, they were disinclined to sign the letters, that too, as the dismissed polishers would still be outside the gate. A few days later, a group of workers went to the head office to try to speak to the Indian director. (The American director was not in the country.) The guard outside the gate conveyed the Indian director's response. "Whatever talks are to take place will be done in Okhla, between you and the manager," was his message.[88] The workers dejectedly made their way back. The blind king's court seemed to offer little hope.

That night, a third notice was posted on the gate, suspending twelve polishers, including the four on the first dismissal notice.[89] The charges against them included slow working, instigating, threatening, and preventing other workers from working, rude behavior, and making threats to the management. The next day, the DLC phoned the manager, asked questions, and called him for another conciliation meeting the following week. Dr. Das filed a complaint of the illegal lockout of forty-six workers. Workers began to express doubts about the DLC's messianic powers.

In the evening, a thin, bespectacled IFTU leader arrived at B156. The workers hastily got up from their card-playing circles. Red union flags, with hammer-and-sickle symbols, were placed over the gate. A union banner, suspended on bamboo sticks, was set against the outside wall. No one was inside the factory. The IFTU leader led the workers in shouting militant slogans. "Long live the revolution![90] This illegal retrenchment will not be allowed! This lockout will not stand! Metal Artware management, come to your senses! Long live IFTU! Long live workers' unity! When the red flags flutter, they'll be brought to their senses! Those who won't agree through our flag, will comply through our bamboo stick! Those who don't agree through our words, will comply through our kicks!"[91] The workers looked unsure of what they were doing. They had awkward smiles on their faces, as if they were playacting to someone else's script. After some brief words from the leader, they dispersed for the evening.

The next day, at lunch time, flags were again put up over the gate. There were no union leaders present. Kaypiji and Govind were inside the factory.

Figure 3.5. The police summoned to B156.

Workers gathered near the gate to escape the rain. Varmaji led them in raising slogans, reading words from a piece of paper written by Rajender. "Long live the revolution! Despotism will not be allowed! Those who clash with us, will be smashed to pieces! What is the remedy for such a management? Beating and disgracing them with slippers and shoes!"[92] After a pause, they began to shout passionate abuses and curses at the manager, smiling, laughing, and clapping enthusiastically and rhythmically. "The jerk is dead! Curse on him *(Hay, hay)*! What a bastard! Take his corpse to the Yamuna River! Long live workers' unity!"[93] Cursing, in unity politics, could be public and collective. They dispersed after these gratifications.

A short while later, a Delhi police van arrived, with the slogan painted on its side, "With You For You Always." Two officers got out. An assistant sub-inspector (ASI) and constable drove up on a scooter from the Okhla police station. The stocky ASI spoke roughly, saying that he would rip up the red flags, and ordered workers to take them down. A call had been made to the police alleging that they were attempting forcible entry into B156. The ASI

Figure 3.6. An IFTU demonstration at Jantar Mantar.

made inquiries with the workers and with Dr. Das, by phone. The police van drove away. The ASI went inside, met with Kaypji and Govind, then came out and addressed the workers in a polite and gentle tone. He advised them not to engage in vandalism, arson, or violence, encouraged them to discuss matters with the management or go to the labor court, and clarified that the police were there to protect and assist both parties. For now, they were to leave and remain two hundred meters from the gate. The workers removed their cycles and left for the day. The company had not obtained a court stay order, but in its absence, the police could be mobilized to disperse agitating workers.[94]

The next day, Dr. Das came to B156. He sat quietly with the workers, to the side of the gate, then stood up and raised a few slogans, confidently, at a moderate volume, which seemed to instill courage in them. The police had no right to remove them, as the union had already given an information letter to the deputy commissioner of police, he said. The company was suffering from the work stoppage, and they would continue their sit-down protest (*dharna*). He spoke amicably with Govind, who remembered Dr. Das from his past union struggle at D45, about the company's production activities in Delhi, and encouraged the security guards, who were employed through contractors, to join the union, so they might avail of labor law provisions. The ASI drove up on his scooter, saw the assembled workers, and asked if their dispute had been resolved. On hearing the negative response, he muttered a vulgar abuse at the management, waved his hand, and drove off. He did not remove them again.[95]

The following afternoon, thirty B156 workers got into a truck in Okhla and rode forty minutes to the city's designated protest site at Jantar Mantar, for an IFTU demonstration against a proposed reduction in the provident fund interest rate. The workers looked weary, troubled, and disturbed as they shouted slogans against the government, along with thirty-five other union members from other industrial areas, and listened to speeches by union leaders on antilabor state policies and the complicities of Left political parties.[96] At times, they sat down in fatigue, got distracted by nearby, louder demonstrations, drifted away from the group, and needed to be roused and energized into slogan shouting by union leaders, with raised, gesticulating right hands, when press photographers came by. "When one is out of work, one doesn't feel good about anything," said Varmaji.[97] They had been shuttling between the factory and the labor office, where they were waiting, spectating, and feeling dependent on the power, will, and mercy of others (the management, the police, labor officials, and union leaders). Unity politics, in escalated conflict, seemed to be strangely disempowering. Some were growing anxious and panicky, and were rumored to be making discreet phone inquiries with the manager about final settlements.

Exodus

In late August, there were deeper revelations about the workings of managerial machinations, the facilitations of the labor department, and the limits of the union's strategic repertoire. On the August 24 conciliation date, Dr. Das opened the case folder at the labor office and saw a typed letter with the signatures and thumbprints of five workers—Bhagvati, Hanif, Krishna, Sabbir, and Sivam—along with the signatures of Khan sahab and a labor officer working under the DLC. The manager had evidently come to the labor office, the previous evening, and arranged these settlements, with the labor officer acting as witness.[98] The assembled workers were deeply disturbed. The deviations of Bhagvati, Hanif, and Sabbir were comprehensible. Bhagvati and Hanif had been close to Khan sahab in the past, and Sabbir was Hanif's relative. But the inclusion of Krishna and Sivam, who had been among the most vocal and oppositional polishers, was confusing. Khan sahab had evidently sent Raju, his close collaborator, terminated from C82, to persuade his friends to resign. Another conciliation date was given after three days.

At dawn the next morning, there was a knock on the door of Naresh's room in Tehkhand. It was Bhagvati. He came in, sat down, and spoke to a groggy Naresh. There was no point in fighting the legal case, he said. The company was giving good settlements and was setting up a new factory in Okhla. The Jharkhandis should take their settlements and form one shift, along with Bhagvati and other resignees, so the new unit could begin functioning. Bhagvati left and visited other workers' rooms in Okhla. At his shanty in the Tata Steel cluster, he set out a cot for prospective resignees and arranged conversations with Khan sahab at a nearby phone booth. Meat and liquor eased the work of persuasion. Within two days, a dozen workers were ready to resign. The union advised the worker-leaders to rough up Bhagvati, to deter his efforts, with an elder member giving precise, detailed instructions on where and how to do so. But the workers, despite their anger, wanted to avoid violence.

On the next conciliation date, Dr. Das led twenty B156 workers into the labor office with red flags and staffs, and shouted slogans against the labor officer, for allegedly taking commissions to broker the five workers' settlements. "The company owners' broker, come to your senses! Stop taking bribes!" they cried.[99] In the DLC's room, Dr. Das shouted at the silent labor officer, asking why he had agreed to witness the settlements, just before a conciliation date. The management, which was evading the conciliation process, would be encouraged by such actions, the DLC admitted, but stated that his office could not stop workers from seeking settlements. "Culturally, mentally, and economically, the labor department officials are associated with the management," Dr. Das said afterward. They often acted as discreet advisors to managements, worked to facilitate settlements, and rarely tried to enforce labor laws and restore jobs. Offstage, the labor officer told me that in witnessing the settlements, he had not done anything wrong. Such resignations were logical for workers, as they would otherwise have to fight a court case for five or more years, incur legal fees and other costs, and avoid working elsewhere, if they wished to claim back wages. Existing labor laws were obsolete, he felt, and such laws, along with union pressures, made it difficult for the economy to thrive, as in America, where companies could freely hire and fire workers.

Later that day, Bhagvati's group came to the labor office to withdraw from the legal case, as a prelude to resignation. They kept an awkward distance from the first group, in the hallways and outside the building, and seemed embarrassed to be deviating from the others. A few workers moved between the groups, uncertain of what to do, inquiring about Khan sahab's settlement offers. When asked why they were resigning, they spoke of mounting debts and apprehension about a long court case. Some said they wanted to extricate themselves from the excessive tensions of B156. Despite Dr. Das's eloquent attempts to persuade them to fight the legal case, twelve workers withdrew and took their settlements, this time, at the head office, in the presence of the labor officer.[100] A fifth conciliation date was given for the next week. Dr. Das instructed workers to maintain a vigil at the labor office, and deter the manager from entering the building and conducting settlements there. Ideally, they could shout abuses, create a ruckus, and rough up the labor officer. But such militancy, Dr. Das observed, was sorely lacking among these workers.

Moods were bleak at the factory gate. After a few days, Mithilesh and two relatives of Naresh took their settlements near the Okhla traffic circle. One could not say when others might join the exodus.

The exodus was revelatory. It seemed that Khan sahab had been operating from intricate, long-range plans, in possibly sending Bhagvati into the workers' meetings, months earlier, gaining reports, allowing him to regain others' trust, dismissing him, and getting him to resign and to persuade others to resign. It was also evident that the B156 workers were complex characters, whose thoughts, feelings, and actions were difficult to read, understand, and predict. They could take collective, sacral oaths, genuinely or otherwise, and then deviate en masse.[101] Rebellious workers could be among the first to deviate. Apparent well-wishers could advise resignations. The resignees were heterogenous, in regional origin, religion, and caste, as was the shrinking group that was fighting the legal case.

They could also see the limitations of the union's strategic repertoire, comprising slogan shouting, the sit-down protest, and the legal case. Much of their time was spent sitting restlessly at the gate, waiting for conciliation dates, speculating about dismal, future outcomes, and observing the attrition and departures of fellow workers. In the absence of alternatives, they realized that in time, they too might be compelled to join the ignominious procession of resignations.

Amplification

In late August, the workers sought alternative methods. Amlakant, Rakesh, and Varmaji went to the Workers Library (*Majdoor Library*), situated in a shanty cluster in Faridabad, to consult the advice of Sher Singh, the editor of the *Faridabad Workers Newspaper* (*FMS*). The Workers Library was a room with chairs, benches, a stove, dusty bundles of *FMS* issues, stacks of publications and correspondence, and a sitting area outside. Sher Singh, a thin, *kurta*-clad, articulate, sagacious person in his fifties, had worked closely with working people for about thirty years. At the time of the Emergency, in 1975, he left Jawaharlal Nehru University to become an activist of a Communist Party of India (Marxist-Leninist) faction. He worked in forest and hill areas of Rajasthan and Madhya Pradesh, with *adivasis*, students, and others, for four years, before moving to Gwalior, Indore, and Bhopal, to work with textile and engineering workers. In 1982, he settled in Faridabad, a large industrial center strategically proximate to the capital city, which had witnessed disturbances and unrest since the sixties, in the form of union politics, strikes, and police firings. He started *FMS* with a circle of activists and workers, as a Hindi monthly newspaper, with an initial distribution of one thousand copies, focusing on the workings of global capitalism, trade unionism, struggles in factories, and the possibilities for true, representative unions in Faridabad. The Workers Library was set up as a base for the newspaper, a meeting place, and a space for study and discussion of the writings of Marx and Lenin, among others.

Later in the eighties, with unfolding experiences in Faridabad factories, the *FMS* circle questioned and rethought its principles, stopped the paper for a time, engaged in readings of Marx and Luxemburg, and shifted its political perspective. In the nineties, when the distribution rose to five thousand copies, the paper drew closer attention to workers' own viewpoints, experiences, and activities, including collective resistance and coordination (described as *talmel*), in the context of automation, retrenchments, and closures. *FMS* developed connections with a range of political groups in Europe, America, and India, with ultra-left, autonomist Marxist, and anarchist tendencies, though *FMS* itself was difficult to classify into these categories. The *FMS* circle brought

Figure 3.7. The Workers Library. Left to right: Sher Singh, Bhupinder, Amlakant, Varmaji, Chintamani.

out booklets in English, articulating its understandings and critiques of modern work regimes, Marx's critique of political economy, and the autonomous activities of workers, and in particular, the innovative struggles of the Jhalani Tools workers in Faridabad.[102] The four-page paper was distributed for free and its operations were funded through donations from readers in and outside of India.

In the 2000s, the paper shifted emphasis away from regular workers, a small share of the present industrial workforce, to the vast numbers of casual, contract, and other precarious workers. In the next decade, *FMS* grew in visibility, due in part to the posting of English translations on websites (such as Gurgaon Workers News, Kafila, Radical Notes, and Libcom), its own blog,[103] reportage in the news media,[104] and the expansion of its distribution into the industrial regions southwest of Delhi. By 2020, its distribution had risen to thirty thousand copies. The paper was hand-distributed on the roadside by Sher Singh and elderly Faridabad workers, along with students, artists, journalists, young workers, and others, over about two weeks each month, in Faridabad, Okhla, Gurgaon, and Manesar.[105]

I met Sher Singh and the *FMS* circle in 1998, and got to know younger workers who distributed the paper in Okhla, in initial stages of my fieldwork. Through them, I met metal workers, who led me to B156. In the early 2000s, due to its growing connections in Okhla, the *FMS* group began distributing five hundred copies every month at the Okhla railway siding. A few polishers, including Amlakant, Ramakant, and Varmaji, read *FMS* and consulted Sher Singh's advice at critical junctures, such as the night-shift closure and the unionization decision. In August 2004, *FMS* carried a report on developing events at B156.

Amlakant, Rakesh, and Varmaji met with Sher Singh and two elderly Jhalani Tools workers, Bhupinder and Chintamani. The *FMS* circle had witnessed similar sequences of dismissals, good conduct bonds, gate protests, and terminations in other factories. Sher Singh gave a simple suggestion, to compose posters describing recent events at B156, and put them up across the Okhla Industrial Area, to create greater awareness, lateral exchanges, and potential pressures on the company. This way, their struggle would not remain confined to a single, silent factory gate. The polishers agreed to experiment with this method.

In early September, six B156 polishers met together in Tehkhand, in my room, which over time, had become an informal meeting place for workers. The room was about one hundred square feet in size, with gray plastic chairs, a wooden cot, gas stove, and ceiling fan, and was located on the second floor of a tenement, close to a cluster of rooms rented by Naresh and his relatives. They spent the day reflecting, discussing, and composing texts for the posters. Amlakant, Naresh, Naresh II, Rakesh, Ramakant, and Varmaji were involved in the activity, along with Lallan, Ramkumar, and others in the Jharkhandi circle who came by during the day. Rajender was not present. They exchanged critical remarks and sentiments about the resignees and those who were readying themselves for exodus, which included their own relatives, neighbors, and machine partners. But they also engaged in joking, which had been greatly subdued in the past weeks. As they engrossed themselves in the poster texts, their spirits and energies became more buoyant.

The poster texts described events at B156, the activities of the manager and workers, and experiences at the labor office. In contrast to the union's militant slogans, visible in graffiti on factory walls in Okhla, the poster texts were composed in workers' own language, with their own categories, idioms, and irony. The posters were addressed to other Okhla workers. They composed eleven texts and copied them onto recycled paper, using colored markers. Three of the poster texts were as follows:

Beware! (*Khabardar!*)
The illusory lures deployed by gangster rule (*gundaraj*)

> We permanent employees have been put out of the factory for one month. We are fighting a case in the labor department to protect our jobs and oppose *adharm* (ethical wrong, injustice). The manager says, to break us, "I'm opening a new unit in Okhla. If you fight the legal case, I won't hire you. If you don't fight the case, I'll arrange your final settlement."[106]

Be warned!
A labor official playing with workers' lives for cash

> To retain our jobs, we are contesting an illegal lockout. A day before every conciliation date, the management summons the labor officer, gets workers to sign papers, and arranges final settlements. Then the management doesn't appear on the conciliation date. Our dates keep advancing, the labor officer's earnings keep growing, but our struggle is also progressing.[107]

Be cautious!
Be careful of *Kalyug*-like brothers (*Kalyugi bhai*)

> A brother was put out of the factory on August 3. In the course of giving him support, we were all put out on August 10. Behind our backs, before anyone else, that brother took his final settlement and became an agent of the management. Nowadays, at six in the morning, he wakes up other worker-brothers (*mazdur bhai*), and to break them, advises them, "Take your settlement quickly, I'll arrange a conversation with the manager." Who is more dangerous to us? The management or our *Kalyug*-like brothers?[108]

The third poster text introduced a category, worker-brother (*mazdur bhai*), which brought together class identity, affective feeling, and ethical vision. They were identifying themselves as wage workers (*mazdurs*), a term used in union slogans, *FMS* discourse, and their own speech, despite its stigma.[109] The word *bhai* (brother) infused the category of *mazdur* with fellowship and a sense of coimbrication in oppression and suffering. The category of worker-brother seemed to imply ethical duties to avoid injuring and undermining one another. A *Kalyug*-like brother (*Kalyugi bhai*), by contrast, was one who posed as a good brother, but assisted in subverting workers' livelihoods. In the language of soul politics, a *Kalyugi bhai* was one who accepted, gave into, or perhaps embraced the interplay of the demonic soul-valence and the *Kalyug*. The posters in toto seemed to suggest that the dangers to workers emanated from the covert collaboration of the management, labor officials, and fellow workers, buttressed by deeper, covert compacts of souls and time.[110]

Over the next two days, the workers put up the posters outside B156, C82 (now operating with workers shifted from the head office factory), and other metal factories, and along the roads of Okhla. On the day of the next conciliation meeting, they put up posters about the activities of the labor officials outside the entrance and along the corridors of the labor office. Other workers gathered and read them, before staff persons removed them later in the day. It was not a secret that labor officials took commissions on settlements (indeed, union leaders spoke of their going rates), but they too had considerations of image, reputation, and *izzat*. While the workers could not say whether the posters would be effective, the activity of creating them and putting them up in and outside Okhla was revitalizing. The poster campaign militated against spectating, fatigue, defeatism, and disintegration.

In the following days, Khan sahab escalated his efforts to break the workers, with the assistance of Bhagvati. Rajender now got involved, making visits to the rooms of the Jharkhandis, to convince them to resign. A few days later, he took his settlement. Only seventeen were still fighting the case.

On the evening before the next conciliation date, Khan sahab appeared at Amlakant's shanty in a cluster near Mathura Road. I was inside, conducting an interview. Khan sahab had come, I suspect, to persuade him to resign, and given his constrained finances, without August wages, he was vulnerable. But in the course of the convoluted conversation and the walk back to his car, Khan sahab unexpectedly shifted his tone. If the workers had suffered in the past weeks, he said, the company had suffered even more, in production losses and damage to its reputation (*badnami*), due to the union flags and the posters. If they were willing to work properly, they could begin work again at B156. Amlakant was perplexed, but agreed. That night, the notices and undertaking were removed from the factory gate.

The following afternoon, at the labor office, Khan sahab, Dr. Das, and the workers signed a document, drawn up by a different labor officer, stating that the company was taking the workers back on duty. Outside the building, Khan sahab and Dr. Das had a cordial exchange. IFTU wanted industries to run, not close, Dr. Das said, and it respected disciplined workers. "See that production goes okay," Dr. Das told Amlakant, before leaving.[111] The workers were astonished by the outcome, and did not have a good explanation for it.

The next morning (September 17), they performed a *puja* at B156 for Vishvakarma. They cleaned the machines, set offerings before the posters of divinities, lit incense sticks, and cried out, "Hail God Vishvakarma!"[112] They distributed *laddus* to the managers, supervisors, guards, and one another. For the first time in six weeks, one could see bright, glowing faces at B156. "Come on, guys, sit down at your machines! Start them up!" urged Vijay.[113] They got back to work.

Given the production backlog, they began working seventeen-hour shifts, with dinner allowances. Khan sahab's presence became scarce, as he got busy setting up his own vendor unit in Ghaziabad. In October, he resigned from Metal Artware Exports. The company gave him machines and orders, and deputed Vijay as supervisor. Khan sahab rehired selected ex-B156 workers, paid them monthly wages (one third higher than at B156) with overtime, without health insurance and other benefits, and began raising production.[114] In Ghaziabad, another work-intensifying interplay was in the making.

At B156, Kaypiji and Govind made efforts to increase production. Some polishers pursued speed. But there were significantly reduced tensions. They were grateful for the overtime earnings and began to pay off debts. In November, the company paid back wages for the lockout period (an unusual gain) and a Divali bonus of one wage. No one refused. On Divali, they gathered and gave offerings at the shrine of a local Sufi saint, Pir Baba, on Mathura Road, in gratitude for the lockout resolution and the present good times.

The company's decision to restart B156 might have been induced by the backlog. The winter season of high export orders was quickly approaching.[115] A second cause was the union's contestations at the labor office.[116] But it was an unusual victory. Ninety-five percent of such struggles, Dr. Das said, concluded in settlements, not restored jobs. A third contributing factor was the

Figure 3.8. The shrine of Pir Baba.

workers' abilities to resist resignations and explore alternative methods. If they were able to hold out in the struggle, it was due to a range of motives. They wanted to protect their regular jobs, which were rare in Okhla metal factories. They also felt the will to oppose the perceived oppression and wrongdoing of the company, and to fight for justice. As Amlakant put it, "You can't oppress us like that. Sack someone whenever you feel like it. Put up some notice that no, sign this, then only you can work. Work overtime, but we won't give *samosas*. That they can go on oppressing us and we'll stay silent. Our fight was for a principle, for one's *haq* (justice), against *adharm* (injustice, ethical wrong)."[117] There were lateral bonds among them, as kin relatives, neighbors, friends, and worker-brothers (*mazdur bhai*), which worked against disintegrative forces. Within these relations, there were considerations of ethics and respect. They did not wish to be subject to critical judgments, offstage abuses, and *izzat* losses for deceiving, betraying, and deserting others. Fellow feeling, ethics, respect, and ideas of justice had sustaining and integrating effects.

In exploring alternative methods, the workers avoided waiting and spectating. In the poster campaign, they engaged in a second intimation of synchrony (*talmel*), away from the machines.[118] The activities of meeting, discussing, composing texts, and putting up the posters critically assisted in keeping the struggle alive. It also might have had other practical effects. The Indian director, in a later conversation, said that he decided to take the workers back as the matter had been "dragging on," and he did not wish it to "unnecessarily besmirch the reputation of the company." The posters amplified the protest beyond the factory gate, in and beyond Okhla. Production pressures, unity, and synchrony contributed to the resumption of work at B156.

Counterformulas

Over three years of the metal factory's functioning, one witnessed developments in the processes of entanglement and noncooperation. The management engaged in efforts to intensify production and precarity, through promises, transfers, job threats, and disciplinary actions. The workers responded with collaboration, loyalty, competition, and collectivity. Within these processes, one could see changes in persons and activities.

With experiences and reflections, workers' hopes could give way to disillusion, discontent, and shifts toward noncooperation. Naresh, who initially hoped that hard work would yield good fruits in this company, later felt that he had been duped, and made adjustments to limit bodily losses. Uday, once among the most loyal and ambitious polishers, was struck by illness, slowed down, engaged in sabotage, and left for the village. Umesh and Rakesh, who were once diligent, dedicated polishers on the night shift, discerned the motives of the management, and shifted into restrained working as quiet, stoic protest. During the lockout, workers harbored hopes of protection and justice from the DLC, which evolved into protests against the labor office's collusive, backstage activities. The workers' willingness to continue working at B156, and in the manager's new factory, suggests that disillusion never fully extinguished hopes. But those hopes, perhaps, became less naïve.

In time, two forms of collective politics emerged. Unity politics was structured around a vertical principle, in its reliance on proto-leaders and union leaders for advice, direction, and protection. It utilized a fixed repertoire of methods: refusals, tool downs, slogan shouting, gate protests, and legal contestations. It was animated by a passionate palette of rage, impatience, and violent proclivities. Synchrony politics was more horizontally structured, drawing on lateral connections and bonds, and did not seem to require leaders. Its methods were more flexible, context-sensitive, and improvised, in auto-regulated working and the poster campaign. It favored calmness, patience, and the evasion of violence. Amid these differences in structure, methods, and passions, unity and synchrony could work together in factory struggles. They flowed together in complementary, reinforcing ways, in the park meetings and restrained working prior to the dismissals, and in the union contestations and poster campaign during the lockout.

Within the unfolding conflicts and battles in the factory, one also encountered multiple forms of self-understanding. Workers could see themselves, at times, in terms of regional, religious, and class identifications, as Uttar Pradesh migrants, Biharis, Jharkhandis, Hindus, Muslims, and wage workers (*mazdurs*). They could also see one another as diverse persons, who had their own ways of thinking, feeling, and acting in the world. But a deeper, implicit vision of themselves emerged of being agentive souls wrestling in decivilizing times. In the context of the *Kalyug*, they confronted a range of distorted activities, emanating from their vertical oppressors and their lateral, *Kalyug*-like brothers. They contended with the seductive nudges of their own demonic soul-valences to give in, go along with, and even promote what Firoz described as the formula of the *Kalyug*.

But they also spoke of the injunction to resist and oppose these distorted activities and forces, in the world and in themselves. To not do so was to descend into a culpability greater than that of the active promoters of the *Kalyug*. If the factory could be viewed as a microcosm of the *Kalyug*, one could also see, within that world, the incubation of noncooperative activities in the present epoch, in unity and synchrony politics. While producing steel artware for export to the world, the B156 workers were also developing, experimentally, wittingly or otherwise, counterformulas to the *Kalyug*.

CHAPTER 4

Struggle Across Borders

Precarity and turbulence returned to B156, sooner than expected. The following year, a legal dispute between the company directors led to a stoppage of work across the company's factories, unpaid wages, terminations, and closures. Questions arose among the B156 workers as to how to respond to these developments. The union's protest strategy did not seem to be an adequate method in this context.

What alternative form of struggle was attempted by the B156 workers? What were its motives and methods? What kinds of linkages with others were catalyzed through the struggle? What were the effects of these linkages on the outcome of the struggle?

First, I describe the context in 2005 in which production ceased at B156; the union's contestations at the labor office; and the death of a worker in this process. Second, I discuss the workers' experiments with placard protests in Delhi, as an alternative to the union's protest formula and an attempt to expand synchrony politics; their motives of protecting jobs, pursuing justice, and keeping their microsociety (*samaj*) alive; and their adoption of methods of nonviolence (*ahimsa*). Third, I delve into the difficulties of sustaining the struggle amid strains and uncertainties, and the emergence of empathetic and practical bridges across boundaries and borders, including a grassroots boycott of the American company's goods. The struggle, I suggest, gave rise to truth forces that may, at times, pose challenges to the workings of global capital.

Precarity

After the turbulence of the work stoppage, retrenchments, and resumption of production in 2004, a strange calm came to B156. It was not to last long. I describe here the return of turbulence in 2005, involving the halting of production, delayed wages, and further contestations.

Dispute

When production restarted at the factory in September 2004, workers experienced relief, with the restoration of jobs, the exodus of collaborators, and the departure of the manager. Overtime began, initially, to 9 p.m., and later, to 2 a.m. Wages were raised in January 2005 by Rs. 100 and Rs. 83 for polishers and helpers, bringing monthly salaries to Rs. 3,387 and Rs. 2,950. With extended overtime, pay packets rose to as much as Rs. 5,500. Bodies became thin, with visible rib cages. Workers bought televisions on monthly installments, reduced accumulated debts, and took out new loans. Things had never been this good at B156.

But by the end of January, deliveries of raw pieces began to reduce in frequency. Rumors circulated that the American and Indian directors (hereafter, Directors I and II) were engaged in a legal dispute over alleged misappropriation of funds and other differences. Terminations of managers and workers ensued in the company's other factories.[1] In March, piece deliveries to B156 stopped. Workers sat idle. No advances were given for the festival of Holi. Workers had to manage the costs of colors, *pakoras*,[2] meat, and liquor through loans in the neighborhoods.

At the end of March, Director II, a lean, tall, articulate gentleman, unexpectedly came to B156 and addressed the workers. He told them of the court dispute and requested them to ask Director I, who was also the director of Metal Artware Co., the America-based company that bought and marketed the goods of Metal Artware Exports, to give work to the factory, or else company accounts would get depleted and B156 would be closed. He left. Fifteen minutes later, Director I, a tall, clean-shaven, well-built gentleman, arrived with a coterie of managers, and spoke to the workers, with one manager acting as translator. The legal dispute would be resolved quickly, he said, and workers would be paid wages during the work stoppage. There was ample work and funds, he assured them, and the factory would not be closed. Once the dispute was over, he would direct the company on a new basis, with transparency, equal regard, and understanding. The translator called for applause at this news. The confused workers obliged. The managers arranged for a round of double *samosas* before leaving. The words of Director I affirmed the existing image, in workers' perceptions, of a good, blind king who meant well for the workers, but was unaware of true conditions in the factories, due to the cleverness and cunning of his managers. But the workers were also cautious. The senior managers were not unaware of the turbulent episodes the workers had endured at B156, including the efforts to terminate them in 2004.

It was difficult for the workers to sit idle at the factory. They chatted, played cards, and slept. Appetites reduced in the absence of work. Tensions brewed among those carrying debts. Tempers flared and quarrels broke out. For those accustomed to exhausting work, forced inactivity was not easy.

In May, June, and July, there were ominous developments. Director I set up a new factory at C109, under a different company name, Metal Innovations, with selected managers from Metal Artware Exports. About sixty workers from idle units were shifted there, on assurances of wage increases and other benefits. Once there, they were told to give resignation letters and were hired as new workers of Metal Innovations, with health insurance and provident fund benefits.[3] The managers also recruited new hires, including for the polishing department, bringing the C109 workforce to over one hundred workers. The dispute was dragging on, but Director I's production was back online.

In early June, when wages were delayed, a group of B156 workers went to the C109 gate to speak to the senior manager, Jacob sahab, who looked after dealings in Metal Artware Exports. He assured them that wages would be paid the next day. He then called Amlakant, Naresh II, and Ramakant inside the gate, gave them a tour of the factory, and said they could come to work there, for better wages than at Metal Artware Exports, though they would have to give resignation letters. The polishers did not accept the offers. The news of these offers created doubts among others at B156 that they might exit at any time.[4] The next day, when workers returned to the C109 gate, Director I told them that the company accounts were lacking in funds. If they wished, he could give them final settlements with an extra month's wages. Jacob sahab came to B156 that evening and the next day, with a list of calculated settlements, but the workers replied that they were seeking work, not final settlements. A few weeks later, Naresh and Surinder stopped by the C109 gate to speak to a junior manager, Manoj, whom they knew from T7, about hiring a relative. He brought them inside, put them on a machine, and asked them to demonstrate to untrained polishers how to polish certain items. They did so, creating anxieties at B156 about their intentions and loyalties. In July, an illegal night shift was started at C109, under the charge of a contractor, with ex-B156 workers (including Babloo, Hanif, and Sabbir) at the polishing machines. Metal Innovations was getting high-quality work done by its own trained ex-workers, without having to directly employ them. Given the managers' overtures to distributing settlements, about forty workers at C82 (including Vijay) met Dr. Das and became members of IFTU. With their fragile unity, there would be uncertainty about their future actions.

Death of a Wage Worker

In July, when wages were delayed, Dr. Das submitted a complaint to the labor office. That evening, two labor officers went to C109 and met with the managers. The next day, Dr. Das called the workers to the labor office to inquire about the complaint and exert pressure on the labor officials. They packed into the small office of the labor officer, who told Dr. Das that the C109 managers had requested four or five days more to pay wages. Outside, Dr. Das and others expressed suspicions that the company had given bribes to the labor officials the previous evening. The next step, Dr. Das said, would be to conduct a gate demonstration to pressure the management.

As workers cycled out of the labor office that afternoon, in drizzling rain, a sedan hit one of the cycles from behind. Vinod, who was driving the cycle, was thrown over the handlebars and incurred gashes to his forehead. Ramdev, who was sitting on the carrier, rubbing tobacco in his palm, fell backward, and suffered head injuries. Workers took them by autorickshaw to Okhla. Ramdev was brought to the ESI Hospital, while Vinod, who did not have an ESI card, was taken to a private clinic in Tehkhand, and then to Safdarjung Hospital. Due to the seriousness of the injuries, Ramdev was also sent to Safdarjung. After processing paperwork for medicolegal cases, they were admitted to the surgical emergency ward.

The air in the ward was pungent with the smells of medicine, urine, and chemical disinfectant used by the masked hospital workers who periodically swabbed the floors. One could hear sounds of hawking, vomiting, wheezing, and weeping at the beds, which sometimes accommodated two patients. Patient attendants walked silently in and out of the ward emptying spittoons

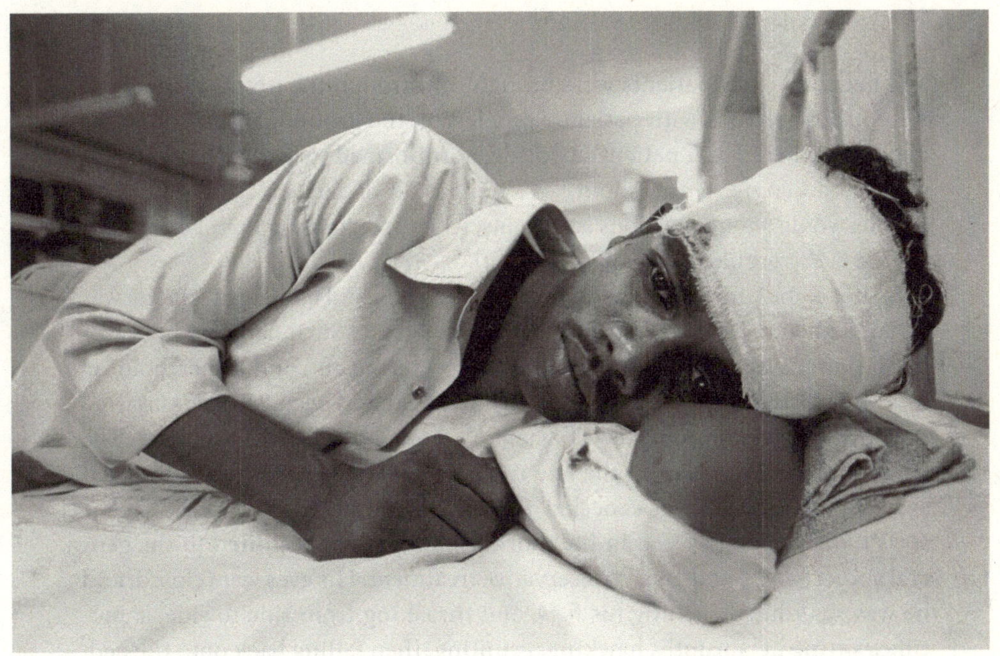

Figure 4.1. Vinod at Safdarjung Hospital.

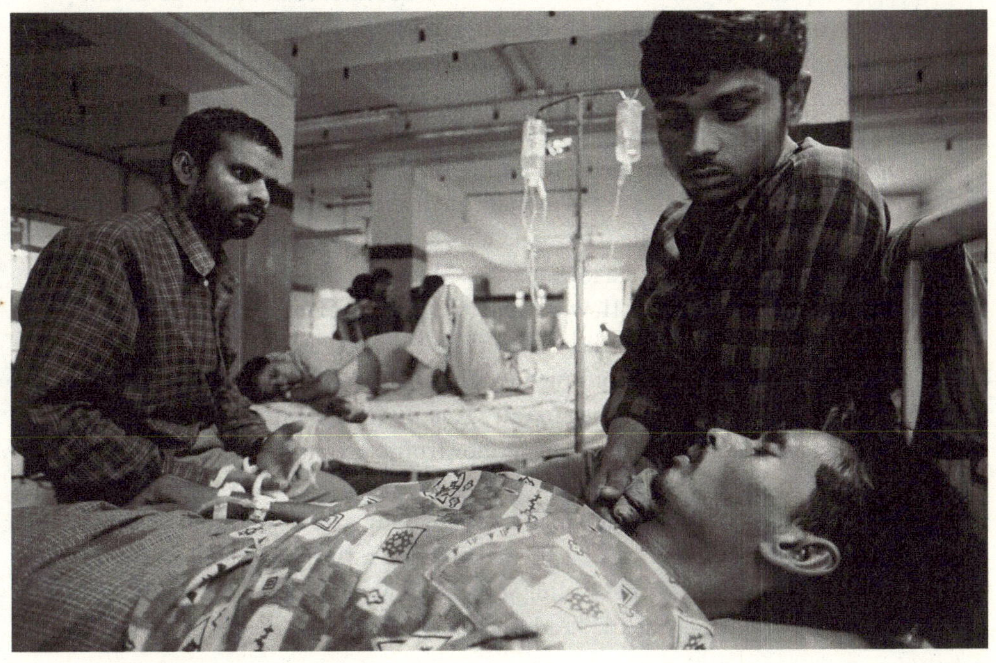

Figure 4.2. Ramdev.

and bedpans. New patients were brought in through the night. When beds were full, stretchers with patients were left on the ground. When too many persons gathered at a patient's bedside, a uniformed guard with a bamboo staff would come in and shout, "Go on, go out of the ward!"[5] Doctors on rounds would shout questions at patients, when ascertaining their conditions, "What is the problem-difficulty (*taklif*)?!"[6]

After some time, Vinod's forehead was stitched and bandaged, and he was given medicine. He rested on a bed, with Naresh and Surinder close by. Ramdev lay on his side on another bed, near a sputtering air conditioner, holding his head in his hands, as blood oozed from his ear and head. Workers assisted in getting his tests done. His CT scan indicated multiple brain injuries. The neurosurgeons saw him in the late night. While one doctor recommended surgery, the decision was canceled, for reasons not noted on the case sheet.

Vinod was discharged in the morning. Ramdev was shifted to the general surgery ward and given conservative treatment. His eyes were closed, and he was shaking, clenching his fists, and thrashing from side to side, sometimes sitting up abruptly, hawking, grunting, then falling back onto the bed. Opender, a cousin-brother, sat by his side and wiped the perspiration from his face. His wife and siblings were in the village in north Bihar. Dr. Das came to the hospital and made inquiries with the doctors. A neurosurgeon saw Ramdev once, but afterward, he was largely left alone by the neurosurgery and surgery doctors, a casualty of the hospital's triage system.[7]

Back in Okhla, the company paid wages. Dr. Das called for a gate demonstration at C109, to charge the company with responsibility for the accident and demand commitments to Ramdev's family. The B156 workers were wary of a confrontation with the management at this time, which could provide a pretense to close idle units, and aborted the demonstration. The next day, the C109 managers put a lock on C82. The union filed a complaint at the labor office, as did Director II, who went to Okhla and had the lock removed. The directors and managers did not come to the hospital.

Ramdev was gradually coming out of his grogginess, saying a few words, and recognizing persons. He began eating again. On the fifth night at Safdarjung, he stayed up talking with a neighbor from Sangam Vihar. He slept off around 3 a.m. He never woke up.

Force, writes Weil, "is that *x* that turns anybody who is subjected to it into a *thing*. Exercised to the limit, it turns man into a thing in the most literal sense: it makes a corpse out of him. Somebody was here, and the next minute there is nobody here at all."[8] A development process that uproots persons and induces migrations of workers to cities, companies that exploit them and do not pay wages on time, a labor office that permits them to do so, government hospital doctors who leave poor patients to die—these were all the workings and manifestations of force. Force made a corpse of Ramdev. "There's no telling when something can happen to a wage worker," observed Achaibar, when he got the news, intimating an awareness that workers' lives and existences are fragile, uncertain, and vulnerable to the will and ravages of force.[9] "It's a government hospital. The patient is a poor person," said Dr. Das. "They die." Wage workers live and die in worlds of precarity.

In the early morning, the body was taken to the morgue for an autopsy. Two managers, the B156 workers, and Ramdev's relatives and neighbors, including his uncle, wife, and five-year-old son, who had arrived from the village in the night, came to the hospital. Kaypiji and Manoj, from B156 and C109, informed the relatives that the company would give Rs. 5,000 for cremation expenses, a job for Ramdev's widow, Shibbo Devi, and a future ex gratia amount to be deposited in her bank account. Manoj left quickly. Kaypiji went to the local market with a few workers to purchase materials for the last rites. Shibbo Devi sat on the sidewalk, sobbing. Her son sat nearby, with a blank, empty look on his face.

Dr. Das advised workers, by phone, not to cremate the body. The union would hold a gate demonstration in the evening to demand firm commitments from the management for a job and compensation for Ramdev's widow. The workers resisted the idea of bringing the body to the gate, seeing it as a strategy of playing politics (*rajniti khelna*) with Ramdev's body, in which there would be a dramatic amassing of crowds, road blockages, and possible violence. "The IFTU leaders wanted to use Ramdev's corpse to bolster the union's image and power in the industrial area," Amlakant observed.[10] Instead of carrying the body through the lanes of Okhla, with drums and slogans, exposing it to dishonor (*beizzati*), Varmaji felt, they should be trying to bring peace (*shanti*) to Ramdev's soul (*atma*) by arranging for the funeral rites. The workers were also concerned about provoking the management, which was already trying to close C82. As the body was being taken to the Kalkaji cremation ground, Dr. Das conveyed to Panditji, Ramdev's elder village relative staying in Delhi, who was making decisions, that it would be difficult to exert pressure on the company once the cremation was done. Panditji agreed to wait.

The workers and relatives waited restlessly at the cremation ground, in the July afternoon heat, for three hours. The atmosphere was tense. Ice was brought to slow the body's decomposition, which melted quickly. Some of Ramdev's relatives speculated about how much compensation the union leaders might be able to obtain from the company. A few opposed the idea of allowing Shibbo Devi to work in the factory. Kaypiji circulated among the conversations and spoke discreetly on his mobile, which kept getting calls.

At quarter past six in the evening, about fifty workers from C82, B156, and other unionized factories gathered at the C109 gate, with red flags and banners, and shouted slogans. "There is an outcry across Okhla! Director I is a swindler! Beat the jerk with shoes! Long live comrade Ramdev! Who is responsible for his death? Directors I and II, answer! Give his wife employment!"[11] Workers pounded on the bolted gate and deflated the tires of management vehicles. Dr. Das sent in a letter demanding compensation, a job for Shibbo Devi, and the issuing of ESI cards for all workers at C109. A crowd collected in the street. A police officer arrived on a motorcycle, spoke to Dr. Das, and instructed the guard to summon the management. A few managers came out and brought Dr. Das, along with two workers, to an upstairs conference room, where they met with Director I. After expressing dislike at the language of demands, Director I gave a verbal promise to give Shibbo Devi a job at C109, but did not put it in writing. Dr. Das gave word, by phone, for the last rites to proceed.

It was already dark, and the caretakers were eager to close the cremation ground. The workers rapidly gathered wood. Four of them, with Varmaji at the front, hoisted the bier onto their shoulders and brought the body to the cremation pit, chanting, "God is truth (*Ram nam satya hai*)!"[12] They lifted the body out of the polythene bag and placed it on the pyre. Amid the tensions and confusions of the day, they had neglected to bathe, anoint, and dress the body. Seeing this, a priest sprinkled a few drops of Ganga water as a purification. Workers wrapped a fresh shroud (*kafan*) around the body. A cremation ground worker, with alcohol on his breath, tried to pull out the used shroud, but Naresh packed it underneath the body. The priest rapidly chanted verses. The workers and relatives cast ritual essences and set wood over the body. Kailash, Ramdev's younger brother, who was confused, weeping, and distraught, circled the body, pouring water from a clay pot, and let it drop and shatter. He circled the body, with his uncle steadying him, and lit the pyre. The workers and relatives dispersed from the ground. A few B156 workers lingered near the gate, discussing the day's events, but were ushered out by the cries of the caretakers, "Go on, guys, leave the ground!"[13] At the factory, labor office, hospital, or cremation ground, workers were always getting pushed around.

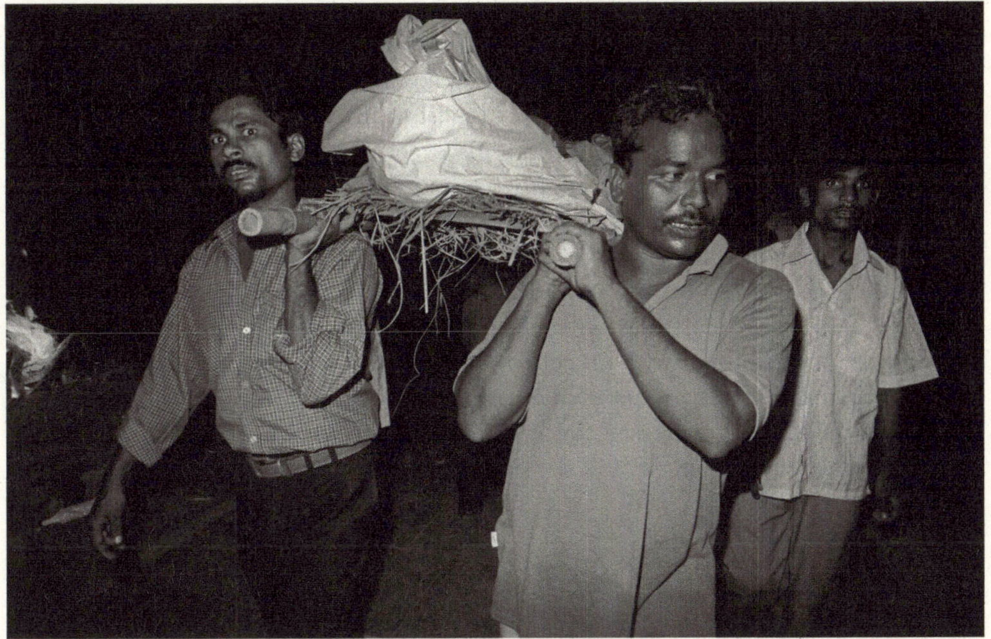

Figure 4.3. Ramdev's funeral.

The next day, the C109 managers put a lock on C82, and posted notices on the gate of the transfer of workers of Metal Artware Exports to an idle unit in Sahibabad, Uttar Pradesh, and the terminations of Dhatu Exports workers, who were also sent closure notices by speed post. Ramdev's relatives came to the union office to request funds for the journey to the village and the final rites to be done there. They were seeking at least Rs. 10,000, one elder relative said, and seemed ready to accept a final settlement from the company. Shibbo Devi sat under a tree some distance away. The union would arrange a modest collection from workers, Dr. Das told them, but would not negotiate a settlement at this time. He advised them of the importance of a job for Shibbo Devi, so that she would be able to raise her children. The next evening, the relatives were given a collection from B156 and C82 of Rs. 3,350.[14] They left for the village.

In meetings in the Sarita Vihar park, the B156 workers expressed regret about the rough language they had used with Ramdev, a thin, polite, soft-spoken helper in his mid-thirties.[15] On the night shift, Ramdev set out pieces, modified buffs, and watched over the shop floor, rousing polishers when they got drowsy. When polishers removed pieces, they shouted, "Who put this many pieces out?! Hey, jerk! Don't you know how many are normally made?!"[16] They had addressed him as *mariyal* (quasi-dead), due to his thin, bony body, and hurled abuses at him for his exacting checking. He took the rough language and abuses, calmly, without answering back, sometimes gently smiling, seeing it as part of the job. Despite his work efforts, the management did not elevate his post or raise his wages. This gradually eroded his feelings of loyalty and his willingness to work hard. He was made to sit at the machines, where he grew closer to the polishers, and contributed to the humor with his subtle, laconic irony, at times directed at the management. Amid anxieties about the trajectory of Metal Artware Exports, the workers expressed concern about the precarious future of Shibbo Devi and her children, should she succumb to pressures and not become a factory worker.

Averting Sacrifice

In the wake of Ramdev's death, a disturbing image arose in the union's discourse. At a public program attended by about sixty workers in Okhla, the union leaders spoke of the historical gains of the Indian working class, such as legal rights to health insurance and provident fund benefits, which were not gifts by the state or capital, but were won through struggle and sacrifice (*qurbani*). The deaths of striking workers by police firing in Haymarket Square in Chicago in May 1886 were cited as a great historical instance of sacrifice for the cause of the eight-hour working day. In the present, when rights were being taken away from the working class, Dr. Das said, "There is need for more sacrifice."[17] In the coming weeks, through pamphlet distribution, wall writing, processions, and demonstrations, the union would seek to "heat up" the atmosphere in the industrial area.[18]

In late July, workers saw images in newspapers of the police assaulting Honda workers in Gurgaon with bamboo staffs, who were waiting to meet with state officials, after a procession involving violence and the beating of police officers. Hundreds of workers were hospitalized with head injuries, broken limbs, and fractures. Sixty-three workers were charged, some with attempted murder.[19] "The workers fought bravely," said Dr. Das, in a meeting with the Okhla workers. But they did not seem eager for such sacrifice.

The next month, wages were withheld from the Dhatu Exports workers. At the labor office, the DLC directed the labor officers to pursue the union's complaint. As the factory was not functioning, he instructed them to ask the managers about the final settlements they were offering. The dispute in the Company Law Board restricted the directors from unilaterally closing units and terminating workers, but the DLC seemed agreeable to allowing settlements. Director II filed a complaint at the labor office against the activities of Director I, and arranged the wage payments. In September, wages were again not paid to Dhatu Exports workers, and before the union could organize a gate protest, they took their settlements. Dr. Das met with the labour commissioner, the head of the Labour Department of the Delhi government, and informed him that the management was keeping its workers idle and pursuing terminations and closure, while getting identical work done in a new factory (violating the spirit of the labor laws), that too, utilizing an illegal night shift of contract workers, and was also not appearing for the labor office conciliation dates. While the Labour Department could not legally force the company to give work to the idle units, the labour commissioner responded, it could take action against the illegal night shift. Before inspectors came to C109 (in late October), the company sent the night shift back to the contractor's workshop in Ali Vihar, and continued to get its polishing work done there.

In early October, the B156 workers wrote a letter to the management, communicating the desire for work, in any functioning unit, for themselves and Shibbo Devi. The C109 managers refused to accept the letter by post, but the workers handed them a copy at the gate. They chuckled as they read it. When wages were delayed in October, the union filed a complaint. The festival of Dussehra, celebrating the victory of truth and goodness over distortion and wickedness, was observed with constrained finances. When workers went to the C109 gate to inquire about their wages, the managers informed them that Director I had left India, and the accounts of Metal Artware Exports were depleted. They could shout slogans, burn effigies, and hurl vulgar abuses, Jacob sahab said, but it would make no difference.

The union organized a procession in Okhla in mid-October to inaugurate a metal workers' organization under its auspices. About fifty workers, mostly from B156 and C82, stood in two lines in front of B156, with red union flags and placards with messages such as, "Implement ESI and PF provisions in the metal polish industry," "Guarantee the health protection of metal polish workers," "Give everyone masks, gloves, jaggery, and clean drinking water," "Contract work on per kilo rates will not be accepted," and, "Organize. Struggle."[20] Madan and Surinder, who were in the front of the line, were smiling vaguely, with watery eyes. They had been drinking. Vijay, standing at the back of the line, was in a similar state. "B156 is like one's mother," he said. "I can't bear to see the hoisting of union flags here."[21] As a non-B156 worker explained, one needed to drink to get into the mood for such events. Indeed, once the leaders arrived and the slogan shouting began, these unsteady workers were the most audible and energetic. The procession moved through Okhla, pausing to raise slogans at factory gates where the union had members. At one point, when the procession was obstructing traffic, a small goods truck nudged Vijay. The young driver, who was also under the influence, said to him, "Sister-******, move to the side and shout your slogans!"[22] A scuffle broke out. Rambachan II, Mohan, and Surinder joined in. Tapesvar's punch to the driver's face drew blood. Others tried to separate them. A crowd collected. The procession was falling apart. Dr. Das rushed over, broke up the fight, promised to give treatment to the driver at his clinic, and shouted to the workers to keep moving. The driver swore to retaliate. The procession continued, stopping at the C109 gate, where Vijay took the lead in shouting slogans, such as, "Swindler owner of Metal Artware Exports, come to your senses! The C109 proprietor is a thief! The company will have to pay wages!"[23] The loudest voices were of the C82 workers, motivated possibly by desires for quick, favorable settlements. The procession concluded at Tehkhand Mor, and the workers dispersed, just as the truck driver arrived on a motorcycle with three muscular men riding pillion, hurling angry abuses and ready to settle scores with Rambachan II, who wisely fled after the fight. The incident was a reminder that workers, when provoked, could easily descend into violence.[24]

In late October, two labor officers went to C109, and emerged after a half hour to tell Dr. Das, along with the assembled workers, that according to the management, there were no funds in the Metal Artware Exports accounts to pay wages. The labor officers would prepare a case against the company on the nonpayment of wages. Dr. Das asked the workers if they were ready for a militant gate struggle to create immediate pressure (which would involve slogan shouting, a sit-down protest, and possible damage to the factory, vehicles, and managers), or if they only wished to pursue a legal battle, which in his view, was not a real struggle. "To fight and die is better than a long, drawn-out death. In two, four, or five days of struggle, we should achieve a conclusive outcome," he told them.[25] Given the experiences of the aborted gate demonstration and the rapid flight of the Dhatu Exports workers, he allowed

Figure 4.4. IFTU procession. Slogan shouting at the C109 gate.

them to decide. Some C82 workers, who seemed nervous, restless, and impatient, and were potentially readying themselves for exodus, did not favor a gate struggle. Others advocated pursuing the court case. After a few attempts to convince them otherwise, Dr. Das accepted the workers' decision.

The B156 workers had reasons for refusing the gate struggle. First, they were wary of getting entangled in possible violence (including police beatings) and police cases, which could be used to pressure workers into taking final settlements. Second, there were doubts about the efficacy of a gate struggle, which could fix workers in a single place and lead to rapid disintegration, as witnessed in 2004. Third, there was growing unease among some workers about the union's method of functioning. Amlakant described the union's style as that of dictatorship (*Hitler shahi*), in which only the leaders, not workers, were presumed to possess minds (*dimag*) and the abilities to decide right courses of action, and whose orders had to be obeyed without question, as if they were lines of fate written by God (*Brahma rekha*). Varmaji suspected that the militant protest formula was a deliberate way of pushing

Figure 4.5. Naresh and Ramakant distributing the *Faridabad Workers Newspaper.*

workers out of jobs, so they would become captive, dependent cadres for the programs of the union and Party, for as long as the court cases lasted. "We'll struggle as we think appropriate, as we ought to," he said.[26] The B156 workers sought alternatives to the sacrifice (*qurbani*), by managerial actions or militant formulas, of their quasi-legal livelihoods and the descent into more precarious worlds of work.

Truth Experiments

As an alternative to militancy, the B156 workers composed placards and engaged in street protests in Okhla and other parts of the city. I discuss the origins of the idea and workers' motives of pursuing justice and keeping their microsociety from dispersing. The method of nonviolence, I suggest, allowed them to sustain a visible, disturbing presence in multiple locations of the city.

Theaters of Protest

In a park meeting in October, Sher Singh, the editor of the *Faridabad Workers Newspaper*, discussed the need to avoid getting confined to a single place and to adopt a means of generating visibility and exchanges about their situation, which could build pressures on the company. He conveyed the story of the experiences of the Jhalani Tools workers in Faridabad. The company had gone through episodes of turbulence, strikes, and retrenchments in the eighties, and stopped paying wages to its two thousand workers in the mid-nineties. In August 1997, a group of twenty to twenty-five workers stood silently with placards, describing ongoing events, along the sides of roads, at intersections, and at railway crossings. A few months later, the management began paying partial wages. The placard holders eventually became targets of physical attacks, and in December 1998, discontinued the protests.[27]

The placards idea was intriguing to the B156 workers. They could make placards at low cost, change the texts with developing events, and transport them by cycle to different places. By standing several yards apart from one another along the sides of roads, they could create visibility across a large area, and evade Section 144 of the Criminal Procedure Code, restricting gatherings that might cause "disturbance of the public tranquility." They bought recycled cardboard, paper, and colored markers and made twenty-two-by-twenty-six-inch placards with texts describing events to date (the directors' dispute, work stoppage, delayed wages, labor office complaints, death of Ramdev, and cessation of wages), with headings such as, "Workers ground between two company directors," "Wages discontinued, directors disappeared," and, "Dussehra was lackluster, Divali will be pitch dark."[28] One placard, with the heading, "Working for the government, service for capitalists," described the capital-friendly activities of state labor department officials.[29] At the bottom of the placards, the workers identified themselves as "Metal Artware Exports workers."[30] The C82 workers began taking their settlements.[31]

In the early mornings, in late October, the B156 workers stood with the placards along the congested path of the Okhla railway siding. Persons briskly walked by, glancing at them curiously, sometimes pausing to read the texts and crowding around the placard holders. The workers felt awkward and embarrassed to stand in front of others with placards, and were not sure of what they were doing. Amlakant held his placard high to obscure his face. Vinod stood several paces back from the footpath, such that few persons could read the text, and after some time, crouched on the ground, hiding his

Figure 4.6. Madan holding a placard in Okhla.

face and body behind the placard. A few mornings later, they stood along a main road in Okhla Phase I. Crowds gathered around the placards. Buses slowed down, with conductors and passengers peering out of the windows to read the texts. Rakesh propped his placard on a cycle and stood nearby, making it seem like he was a street vendor of sexual potency medicine. Others placed placards at their feet and stood casually, rubbing tobacco in their hands, or rested placards against nearby walls and moved a few paces away, or left placards with another worker and disappeared. They could sense that persons were looking at them as fools (*buddhu*), idiots (*bevkuf*), madmen (*pagal*), or beggars (*bhikhari*). It was not easy to stand on the roads, out of work, watching others rushing purposefully to their jobs. Okhla workers asked why they were doing this, whether the company was giving settlements, and if they were unionized. They advised them to go to union leaders, lawyers, political leaders, and the news media. Some stood by the placards, reading and lingering, without speaking. Others hurled abuses at the directors and suggested that the workers beat up the managers. A group of women workers asked

Mohan if they were advertising for a job vacancy. "This is not an ad for a vacancy," he replied. "This is about vacancies [job losses] across Okhla!"[32] The remaining C82 and Sahibabad workers took their settlements. The B156 workers, the managers told them, were the last ones left in Metal Artware Exports.

The next week, at lunchtime, from 1 to 2 p.m., they stood with placards along the two lanes outside C109. Workers from neighboring factories crowded around them, especially those near the street vendors selling *rotis*, rice, vegetable curries, and lentils. The C109 workers came out of the gate and milled about close to the placards, reading, and speaking to one another in hushed tones. The C109 polishers, with gray-black *dhoti* fragments over their heads, peered down from the factory roof. The managers came out, read the texts, chuckled, and gathered at a vendor's cart. They called the C109 workers inside, five minutes before the end of the lunch break, and instructed them not to fraternize with the placard holders.

On the day before Divali, they distributed themselves along the Okhla traffic circle and the main road leading to the ESI Hospital. Cyclists and pedestrians collected near the placards. "What's going on, brother?" a worker asked.[33] "Hey, brother, 'Wages discontinued, directors disappeared!'" another shouted, with a laugh, and crossed the road.[34] Seeing the crowds, a police officer with a bamboo staff walked over to Firoz and Vinod, and told them to move. They shifted a few yards down the road and backed into the grass. The officer stood by for a time, read the texts, and watched the crowds, before returning to his post. An IFTU leader also appeared, paused at one of the placards, and walked away, without saying a word. No Divali bonuses or sweets were given to the B156 workers.

In November, the workers made forays into other parts of the city. On Divali, they stood with placards at Connaught Place, in the center of Delhi. They felt anxious, insecure, and out of place in such an area, but in the evening, they were encouraged by supportive exchanges with shopkeepers and journalists in the busy and festive Janpath market. They were relieved to be back in Okhla the next week, among other workers, and were more confident standing with the placards, as this was their own area (*apna ilaka*). A few days later, Kaypiji, who had expressed solidarity with the workers and had briefly joined the protests, took his final settlement, leaving no manager at B156. The next week, they brought the placards to the commercial complex of Nehru Place. During lunchtime, people flowed out of the multistory buildings and formed thick crowds around the placards. They read the texts and asked questions. Police officers tried to remove the placard holders, but after a few tense exchanges, in which the workers agreed to come to the police station, they left them alone. The next day, they returned to Connaught Place, standing near the *India Today* and *Hindustan Times* offices and interacting with photographers and journalists. The following morning, a short article appeared in the *Hindu* describing the dispute and the protests, based on a press release I had circulated to journalists, activists, and others in Delhi, which boosted workers' spirits.

A few days later, in the morning, they stood in front of the registered head office of Metal Artware Exports in the elite colony of Sujan Singh Park (the Delhi residence of Director I, who was not in India). No managers were present. Two journalists from *Today*, a tabloid of the *India Today* group, took photographs and interviewed workers. After an hour, an elderly resident came out of the building and told Firoz, who was standing in the driveway, that if they didn't leave, he would call the police, who would give them a few blows with bamboo staffs and get rid of them. He went back inside the building. The drivers in the colony brought them drinking water and advised them to stay, but they thought it wise to leave. As they packed up the placards, two police officers arrived on scooter, asked questions, and told them of Section 144, enforced in this part of the city, before letting them go.

After resting at India Gate, they brought the placards to Shastri Bhavan, where the directors' dispute was being adjudicated, and to the Press Club of India. As they walked along Rajpath, carrying the stack of placards wrapped in blue tarpaulin, some workers joked that they should be careful, as it looked as if they were carrying a dead body to Rashtrapati Bhavan (the president's residence). Lallan maintained that they were only carrying their main weapons (*hathiyars*).[35] A few stayed on to attend a meeting at Mandi House with the activist group, the People's Union for Democratic Rights, to discuss methods of struggle. While proceeding along the clean, wide roads of New Delhi, lush with greenery, the otherwise open, sauntering, village-style gaits of workers became more controlled and restrained. "It's a VIP area. They can take action at any time and ask, 'What's a fellow like you doing here?'" Varmaji said.[36] The *Today* piece, with photographs of the workers at Sujan Singh Park, appeared three days later.

The workers also approached political leaders, though without great expectations. They met Sunil Bidhuri, the municipal councillor in Tehkhand, who apparently tried to phone Jacob sahab on his mobile, but could not reach him. He advised them to stop doing the placard protests, which would not

Figure 4.7. Mohan at Sujan Singh Park.

be of any benefit, and to focus on the court case. "There's no higher authority than the court," he told them.[37] The councillor might have feared, Naresh suspected, that the workers might bring the placards to his own office. At a public function in Indira Camp, Naresh and Surinder listened to speeches of local leaders, so as to briefly meet Ramvir Singh Bidhuri, the local member of Legislative Assembly, afterward onstage, and pass him documents about the court case and placards struggle. His office sent a letter to the labor office two days later, requesting that action be taken on the unpaid wages, which prompted the DLC to send a letter to the management the following week. They made unsuccessful attempts to meet Sajjan Kumar, member of Parliament of outer Delhi. Just as Naresh was about to visit the office of Manoj Kumar, member of Parliament from Palamu, Jharkhand, the latter's photo appeared on the front pages of newspapers as a minister caught in the "Operation Duryodhana" exposé for accepting money to table questions in Parliament. Political leaders did not offer much hope for the workers' struggle.

Figure 4.8. Crossing India Gate.

Motives

The struggle was motivated by a mélange of interests, strivings, and feelings. First, there was the motive of self-interest (*svarth*), in the desire to retain quasi-legal livelihoods (i.e., with minimum wages, health insurance, and provident fund, despite working conditions that violated labor laws), amid a sea of precarious, illegal, invisible casual and contract work situations in other metal factories and workshops in the Delhi region. Self-interest could sometimes seem to be the dominant motive for the struggle, and was admitted, in part-jest, by Naresh II.

A second palpable motive was the striving for justice (*haq*). Over the past four years, the B156 workers had engaged in tussles, contestations, and struggles for *haq*, for example, against the night-shift closure and for wage hikes, transfer letters, better bonuses, *samosas*, and the restoration of work. Though they had lost many of these contestations, they had managed to gain and retain quasi-legal jobs, with difficulty, amid ongoing efforts to terminate them. Given these experiences, they were not so willing to give in, or bend or submit (*jhukna*), to the present deprivations of *haq*. Workers' ideas of *haq* could be informed by existing laws and rights (e.g., tussles to do with minimum wages and illegal terminations), but were not limited by them (e.g., contestations for restored bonuses and *samosas*, the horizon of just wages and working arrangements [*vastavik mazduri*]). At the present juncture, when they would say, "We're fighting for our *haq*,"[38] *haq* meant what they felt they were legitimately or justly due in this context. They were fighting a court case for the *haq* (and legal right) of the payment of wages. If C109 was getting polishing work done through new hires and contract workers, *haq* also meant giving the idle B156 workers a due share of this work. It was uncertain if the labor court could restore work to them, given the possible winding up of Metal Artware Exports, the different ownership structure of Metal Innovations, and present, unfavorable trends in court judgments. But this did not constrain their sense of *haq*. *Haq* did not gesture to an ideal work situation, with drastic improvements in working conditions, or a return to a legitimate status quo. *Haq* meant only the restoration of quasi-legal work and wages. After this, there could be struggles for other aspects of *haq*. The struggle was also implicitly questioning the deprivation of the *haq* of other workers in Okhla and elsewhere. "We're fighting our struggle [for our own *haq*]. But we're opposing contract work. ESI and PF provisions should be implemented in other companies too. All these things are not just matters for me, but for other workers too," said Amlakant, in the meeting with the People's Union for Democratic Rights.[39] By standing up for *haq*, they were protesting against oppressive and exploitative practices that were inducing the dispossession of quasi-legal work at B156 and in Delhi factories more generally.

A third, less audible motive was the desire to keep alive the workers' nascent microsociety (*samaj*). In the course of working, associating, struggling, and surviving at B156, workers could sense that their relations had evolved from the dominance of self-interest, competitiveness, envy, surface-level *izzat*, and divisiveness to the beginnings of a sense of a microsociety, in which there was critical sensitivity, synchrony, and deeper qualities of *izzat*. In meetings, rather than depending on decisions of dubious proto-leaders, as in past episodes of unity politics, they could discuss, debate, argue, quarrel, advise, criticize, correct one another, and also create laughter, while deliberating and deciding on courses of action. They developed affective feelings, understanding, and friendships. As Varmaji put it, "When one lives in any place, even if he constructs a shanty . . . I know B156 is not heaven. But one's love is not for the factory, it's for the microsociety (*samaj*). Our microsociety will get dispersed. We'll be able to find many other jobs, we'll find a better factory, a better garbage dump than this. But we won't find a microsociety like this one."[40] If workers were fighting for the chance to do polishing work in Metal Artware Exports or Metal Innovations, it was partly due to the existence of this fragile, shanty-like microsociety, and the importance of a space of meeting and struggling, to keep it alive and growing. Along with protecting quasi-legal jobs and fighting for *haq*, they wanted to avert the sacrifice of this microsociety.

In November, citizens in America began to get involved in the struggle. A scientist and close friend in New Jersey, Fred, with whom I was in close contact, organized an online petition under the auspices of a new entity, Justice for Workers, calling for the restoration of work, payment of wages, and a job for Shibbo Devi, and initiating a boycott of the company's goods.[41] The petition read as follows:

> Great art should not be created at the expense of human dignity.
> It has come to our attention that a dispute within your company's management has caused an unfair work stoppage, non-payment of wages, and denial of legal bonuses for at least eighteen of your workers at Metal Artware Exports, Okhla Industrial Area, New Delhi, India. We therefore call upon you to immediately:
>
> - Pay these workers all wages and other payments they are due.
> - Let them get back to work: re-absorb these workers immediately at any of your operating production units of your existing companies in India.
> - Honor your verbal promise to offer work to the wife of your former worker Ramdev, who as you know was killed while in transit from the labor department to your site as a result of the non-payment of wages.
>
> Until these conditions are met to the satisfaction of these workers, we shall promulgate a grassroots boycott of Metal Artware Co. goods in the United States and elsewhere, effective immediately, through a campaign of discussing this issue with all of your US-based retail distributors, demonstrating in person at selected locations and events, and spreading the word to media outlets and your prospective customers.
> We ask that you show your integrity as an artist and as an employer, and treat your workers with dignity and fairness.

The petition and a description of events were circulated across email networks and blogs. Citizens (and potential consumers) in America began writing messages to the company's website. One person wrote, "As a worker myself, I am concerned about the welfare of my brother and sister workers. When I purchase an item, I am respectful of the fact that I am paying for the sweat and toil of others. I am honored to pay a fair price for their efforts. I have no wish to profit by their misery and degradation. If the account referenced above is substantially correct, I must conclude that to purchase an item from you is to make a dishonorable purchase. However, I wish to give you the opportunity to provide me with your perspective on these events before finalizing my conclusion." Others were less reserved. Another wrote, "I have read about your exploitation of artisans in India. I will be telling my friends about you, notifying my local Macy's and organizing a boycott of your products this holiday season. Shame on you. Your karma is about to manifest in a big way."

In the petition and subsequent messages, one could see bridges between ideas of justice and dignity among citizens in America and workers' ideas of *haq* and *izzat*, and also, between protest methods of direct action and synchrony (*talmel*). In his responses to these messages, Director I affirmed the American company's humane image, spoke of the strength of democracy, human rights, and labor laws in India, and suggested that the B156 workers were seeking to "extort large amounts of money" in settlements. But the boycott could cause difficulties, especially during the impending gift-buying season.

Methods

In November, the workers began to have closer encounters with the police. On November 23, to escalate pressure, they attempted a sit-down protest (*dharna*) at C109. They stood with placards in the lanes until the beginning of the shift, then sat down close to the gate. A manager asked them to move across the road, so they could park their vehicles. They moved, stayed until 3 p.m., and returned to B156. The next morning, they sat across the road again. After a half hour, two police officers arrived on motorcycle, and told them that they needed to get permission for a sit-down protest from the assistant commissioner of police. But if they wanted to take settlements, one officer offered to arrange a meeting with the managers. A worker asked if they could just arrange their back wages. "Don't talk of your wages!" he said, and ordered them to leave the area. "You shouldn't be seen here! Or I'll crack your skull with my bamboo staff!"[42] But the other officer said, in a soft tone, "Brother, move from here, come back after some time."[43] The police would likely receive cash from the management to remove them, as in the 2004 work stoppage, workers suspected. They went back to B156, returned at lunchtime, and stood with the placards in the lanes. The police did not return. It was wise to stand, stay dispersed, and keep moving (deviating from the sit-down protest formula), if they wished to avoid such encounters.

Before returning to Sujan Singh Park, workers gave an information letter to the Tughlak Road police station, describing the cause and nature of the protests. The station house officer reader spoke roughly, citing Section 144, and asked Amlakant who were the leaders and organizers behind the protests, before reluctantly receiving the letter. The next day, in the late morning, the workers dispersed along the main road at Sujan Singh Park, avoiding the driveway. The deputed police officer advised that they go to Jantar Mantar, where they could shout slogans, seek media coverage, and submit letters to state authorities. At about 2:45 p.m., as they were ending the protest, a tall woman in a red *sari* emerged from the driveway, shouting, "You can't stand here!" She moved toward Varmaji, raised her hand as if to slap him, seized his placard, and gave it to a male domestic worker with her, who tore it, threw it to the ground, and stomped on it. She crossed the driveway, took Rampal's placard, flung it on the ground, and began hurling abuses. "Bastard dogs! Why are you standing here?!" she shouted.[44] The other workers gathered at the driveway. The woman made a call on her mobile, ostensibly to the police, as she walked back into the building. In a few moments, she reemerged with an entourage of the C109 managers. They stood in a semicircle facing the workers (a *gherav* [encirclement], ironically, by the management) and shouted abuses, insinuations, and accusations. A crowd collected to witness the drama. The police officer encouraged workers to respond, saying, "Speak up for your *haq*!"[45] They stayed quiet, out of pragmatic concerns and fear, except for Rambachan II, who agitatedly asked the managers why they were not paying their wages. A jeep arrived with more police officers, who asked questions, took notes, and allowed the workers to leave. The woman and a few managers left in a vehicle and filed a complaint at the police station, alleging that the workers were carrying banners, shouting slogans, and trying to forcibly enter the building (the militant protest formula). The police were aware of the nature of the protests, and after taking some workers' written statements at the police station, let them return with the placards the next day.[46] Journalists from *Tehelka* and *Jansatta* came to the protest, partly due to the disturbance, and wrote stories on the struggle. In America, Justice for Workers sent the petition with 250 signatures to the head office of Metal Artware Co. The Okhla managers told the C109 workers that if the protests continued, the factory could close and they could lose their jobs. The next time they saw the B156 workers on the roadside, the managers said, they should be beaten and made to flee.[47]

In the refusals of militancy, the silence of the protests, and the resistances to provocations, one could discern an implicit nonviolence (*ahimsa*) in the methods of the struggle. This nonviolence arose less from a Gandhian ideology, and more from wisdom and necessity, given the aims of sustaining a presence on the roads, avoiding police encounters, and keeping alive possibilities for employment under the existing managers, which might have been foreclosed by rough speech, abuses, or beatings.[48] Workers adopted nonviolence as an experimental method, without knowing what its consequences might be.[49]

Maintaining nonviolence would not be easy, given the rumors of an impending, management-orchestrated assault and the growing impatience of other Okhla workers. "Hey, you guys give us a date and time! Let's go! We'll set fire to the whole bloody factory [C109], blow it up!" other workers would say on the roads of Okhla.[50] Workers from neighboring factories advised them to wait and watch for the managers to arrive at the gate, catch hold of them, and beat them. Some seemed to be desiring a provocation, muttering, "Sister-******, let them come, we'll kill the jerks and lay out their corpses right here."[51] The B156 workers felt protected by the presence of these workers, but also vulnerable to what they might do. "There's no telling what workers can do [in such a situation]," Amlakant noted.[52] The precarity in workers' worlds was exacerbated by volatile passions.

The methods of the protests generated unexpected effects. The silence, the speaking of truth on the placards, and the dispersal of workers across large areas created a chilling, disturbing gravitas, demanding attention. The police were aware of this. "This method is wrong!" one police officer said at Sujan Singh Park. "This protest is not appropriate in this sort of area."[53] They were not disturbing the peace, he agreed, "but it looks bad, as per my opinion." Factory workers were visible in industrial areas of the city, not on roads

Figure 4.9. Shibbo Devi.

of elite colonies. Their difficulties were camouflaged behind closed factory gates and company advertising images. The silent theaters of protest—these proletarian truth experiments—were disturbing the social-psychic peace. In December, a female face added to the disturbance. Shibbo Devi, in a white *sari* and purple shawl, who was yet to be given a factory job, now sat with a placard on the footpath.[54]

Vortex

While the managers made attempts to end the protests, empathetic linkages developed with Okhla workers and others in the city. Workers confronted anxiety, fatigue, and uncertainty about the struggle, and difficulties and tensions in residences. With meetings, sustained protests, and boycott activities, openings developed out of the struggle's vortex.

Bridges

As the struggle progressed, interactions on Okhla roads began to evolve. The placards became less of a novelty for curious crowds, and more of a catalyst for lateral exchanges. Workers paused to ask how the struggle was progressing, what were the responses of the management, and what they were planning to do next. They shared experiences of factories, terminations, union dealings, and settlements. The C109 workers also began to express new sentiments toward the B156 workers. They had their own sources of discontent, as they had resigned from Metal Artware Exports without settlements, and had not been given promised wage hikes and other benefits. Outside the gate, when the managers were not looking, they would whisper, "You guys are doing the right thing."[55]

Drivers and conductors on private Blueline buses plying from Okhla also began exhibiting interest in the struggle. Buses would slow down, and conductors would stick their heads out and ask the workers when they were going to Sujan Singh Park, insisting that they go in their bus. There was a monetary incentive, as one trip meant ten to fifteen tickets, but conductors gave them discounts, not without affective feelings.[56] When a drunk worker got into a scuffle with the B156 workers in Okhla, and pursued them onto a bus, a conductor intervened, roughed him up, and pushed him out, referring to the workers as "our own people (*apne admi*)." Empathetic linkages also developed with drivers, security guards, tea stall workers, and others at Sujan Singh Park. "It's a good thing you're doing, keep standing!" a traffic policeman, who had worked in a factory in Faridabad, would say to them.[57] Professors, students, journalists, activists, and others from India, Europe, and America visited the protests, listened to workers, and gave reactions and advice. Through these linkages, the Sujan Singh Park footpath, which once evoked feelings of strangeness, anxiety, and fear, became a partly habitable space.

To draw upon a Platonic idea in Weil's thought, one might read these exchanges, gestures, and sentiments as the work of *metaxu*, or bridges, intermediaries, and links among human beings, and between souls and the divine. "Two prisoners whose cells adjoin communicate with each other by knocking on the wall. The wall is the thing which separates them but it is also their means of communication. It is the same with us and God. Every separation is a link," she writes.[58] The street exchanges might be seen as efforts of workers and others, in attention and affliction, to communicate across the adjoining, prison-like walls of factory gates, class differences, and city spaces. In workers' understandings of the soul, *metaxu* might be viewed as bridges between the true soul-valences (*sahi atma*) of human beings, exhibiting and drawing one another toward the immanent divine within souls.

There were also counter-*metaxu*. The managers would try to discourage the B156 workers, when they passed them at the siding, telling them that they were creating such negative publicity for the company that they would never get jobs again in Okhla. At the C109 gate, staff persons and collaborative workers would mutter taunting words in earshot of the workers, such as, "If I get the chance, I'll rip up the placards and take care of two or four of the jerks myself."[59] On a night in December, the managers sent a few polishers to the Tehkhand room of a Jharkhandi polisher at C109, with meat and liquor. While the food was being prepared, they tried to persuade Naresh, Madan, and Surinder, as "old workmates (*purane sathi log*)," to stop the protests and accept settlements. "We're just asking for Rs. 3,000–3,500, what we're getting as wages. What will we do with all that settlement money? It'll get spent so fast, you won't even know how," Naresh replied.[60] The caste relatives of Ramdev tried to pressure Shibbo Devi to stop attending the protests, as she was causing them dishonor (*beizzati*) by mixing with other men. She heard them, but did not comply. The managers could also engage in joking as a way of making light of the protests. One day, Lallan was holding a placard outside C109 that read, "We don't want final settlements. We want work and wages." "Just remove the word 'don't,' then I'll take a photo of you with the placard," Jacob sahab said to him.[61]

But all was not humor and joking. In mid-December, despite legal constraints of the directors' dispute, a closure notice was put up on the B156 gate, listing the names of the workers, and signed by Director I.

CLOSURE NOTICE

As you are aware that there is no production activity in the unit, B156, Okhla Industrial Area, Phase I, New Delhi, since April 2005.
Due to certain administrative reasons and paucity of work the operations of this unit has come to a complete stop.
In such circumstance it has been decided to close the unit at B156.
Accordingly by reason of the aforesaid closure your services stand terminated w.e.f. December 14, 2005. You are requested to collect your full and final dues from the unit during official hours on any working day.
We wish you all best for the future.

The security guard was instructed by the managers to stop marking attendance at the B156 gate. The workers brought a register and took attendance themselves. The next evening, a company vehicle pulled up behind the Jharkhandis at Tehkhand Mor. The driver asked how long they were going to continue the protests, and told them that the company was giving good settlements. As they were leaving the C109 gate, the next week, Jacob sahab and a few managers pursued them on foot and let them know that he was going on holiday leave, hinting that they should speak to him soon if they wanted to take settlements. To the managers' surprise, they responded that they were seeking work and wages. There was no exodus.

Darkness

As the winter deepened, anxieties grew more intense. Numbers lessened for protests in the cold and fog of the early mornings. A few times, due to low numbers, the protests were aborted. Okhla workers still asked about the progress of the struggle. But some would say that nothing would come of the protests,[62] and that they were suffering in the cold for no reason. At one point at Sujan Singh Park, an entire line of workers set their placards on the ground and sat on the footpath, due to fatigue and depressed spirits. Amlakant undertook a strange, impromptu survey, asking each worker if he thought that the protests were having any effect, and in the process, created more uncertainties. At the edges of the group, a few were considering accepting settlements.

Workers were also confronting tensions, illnesses, and deaths in residences and the village. Wives and children were beset with colds, fever, and jaundice in the winter months. Tapesvar's younger brother, Varmaji's uncle, and Rampal's father and five-day-old child passed away, calling them away from the protests for some days. Debts were mounting for rent, rations, and children's tuitions. Cash was lacking for milk and vegetables. Strains entered relations with wives. I describe here some of these experiences, unfolding behind the scenes of the street protests.

Naresh lived in a rented room in Tehkhand with his younger brother, Vinod, and brother-in-law, Hans Raj. His wife and child were in the village, attending to illnesses. The Gujjar landlords demanded the rent on time, which was managed through Hans Raj's polishing wages. Due to their past good record, the Gujjar shopkeeper allowed their ration bills to accumulate. But as the struggle continued, he would get anxious and ask them to settle their accounts. As three of the brothers were not getting wages, their relatives in the neighborhood were wary of offering them loans, as they did not know when they might be repaid. "Others are just looking after their own, what else, what help will they give. They're just with us, they're listening to our problems. They're not about to give practical assistance," Naresh said.[63] Some advised them to take settlements. No such pressure came from his family members in the village, who followed the struggle with great interest.[64]

Rakesh, who lived in a shanty in Faridabad with his wife and small son, managed expenses with savings and small loans from his sister who lived across the lane. When the struggle began, his wife thought it best to go back to the village, to reduce expenses, but he asked her to stay, so he would not be alone, and so she too could partake of the enjoyment (*maza*) of the struggle. She managed the household matters, allowing him to focus on the protests. "She took care of all problems. I didn't have to bother about anything. I just had to pick up my cycle and reach whatever locations for the struggle," he recounted.[65] When his spirits would flag, she would tell him to keep fighting, and offered to work in an export factory to cover expenses. "But don't quit the struggle," she told him.[66]

Rambachan II resided with his wife and four children in a small, partly built house in Faridabad. Due to growing debts, he would sometimes miss protests to do wage work of brick loading for Rs. 80–90 a day. When the shopkeepers discontinued their rations, his wife borrowed food items from neighbors. Sometimes there were lentils but no vegetables, or vice versa. He would often ask for a bit of vegetables from other workers at lunchtime. His children's tuitions had to be discontinued. Despite the strains, his wife did not ask him to abandon the struggle. When his morale would plunge, his school-going daughter, Anita, would say, "Papa, don't do anything such that people will accuse you of acting wrongly."[67]

Firoz stayed in a small rented room with his younger brother, Pappu, in Hari Nagar. They managed expenses through Pappu's wages from thread cutting for a contractor in an Okhla export factory. In August, Firoz's wife, Asma Begam, came from the village, a month after giving birth, to bring their two-year-old son, Sahil, to the ESI Hospital, where he was diagnosed with tuberculosis. While at the hospital, the infant, Sohail, contracted pneumonia, and Asma Begam also fell ill, requiring a night's stay in the emergency ward. She stayed on in Delhi to continue the child's six-month tuberculosis treatment. The children needed two liters of milk each day. After wages were discontinued, they could buy only one liter, which she would secretly dilute with water, though the children were aware of the difference. Bills with the shopkeeper rose to Rs. 8,000, and their rations were suspended twice. A loan from Firoz's aunt, who stayed nearby, helped to pay two months of rent. Others in the colony, with whom he had previous borrowing and lending relations, would avoid speaking to him or even extending greetings, thinking he would only wish to ask for loans. Between cooking and looking after the children, Asma Begam did home-based hand stitching of clothing embellishments for a contractor on piece rates, earning about Rs. 10–20 a day. Her eyesight suffered from working into the late night under the light of a single bulb, that too, when her landlord was not scolding her to reduce their electricity usage. A payment from the contractor, a few days before Eid, got them through the festival. She recounted, "I could not understand anything at that time, there were so many difficulties. Neither any essential things nor money in the house. There was a lot of tension as to what will happen, how are the children to be kept alive, where is the milk to be brought from, how are the expenses to be met. I felt like crying, that's all."[68] She would ask Firoz how they were going to go on like this. He didn't have good answers, except that they were making efforts every day. Each evening, he would discuss in detail what had transpired that day at the protests. "OK, no matter, whatever happens, we'll see," she'd say.[69] They buoyed one another's spirits. But tensions could sometimes get the better of them. If Sahil asked for toffees and other things, which they could not afford, she occasionally raised a hand to him. One morning, when she was rushing to finish stitching pieces for a deadline, and there was confusion about the children's medicine dosages, Firoz slapped her, causing her cheek to impact with the edge of the wooden bed, leading to swelling and discoloration, a trip to the ESI Dispensary, several days of pain and anger, and contrition in Firoz. Nonviolence on the streets did not rule out lapses in close quarters.

Amlakant lived with his wife, son, and two daughters in a shanty in Rajiv Camp near Mathura Road. As they had a BPL (Below Poverty Line) card, they could avail of subsidized rations. They rarely ate meat, and vegetable curries were mostly prepared for Amlakant, whose appetite reduced after the work stoppage. Shveta, his elder daughter, had gotten accustomed to Amlakant's earnings with extended overtime, the previous winter, and was disappointed when they decreased to basic wages. "This much money will not do," she said, and advised him to leave the job and find work elsewhere.[70] He gave her a copy of the *Faridabad Workers Newspaper* and told her to read about the general situation in factories. When his daughters came to him with their torn shoes and book bags, he asked them to be patient. They did what they could to restrain their demands. Amlakant's wife, Dulari, was opposed to the struggle. She was fearful of a prolonged court case, given the experience of Amlakant's elder brother, a polisher who had been fighting a case against illegal termination for the past twelve years. She did not understand the strategy of the placards struggle, and advised Amlakant to accept a settlement. He could not do so while the others were fighting, he replied. He resisted her suggestions to pursue night work, as it would affect his attendance at the protests. When food items dwindled, she would get angry and say that he was gone all day but did not bring home any earnings. "What do you do all day? Nothing is happening!" she might shout, as he got ready to leave in the morning.[71] "Papa, don't say anything. Go, just go," Shveta would quietly advise.[72] Amlakant cycled home in the evenings, in fear of her rage.

Ramakant stayed in a rented room in Tehkhand with his wife, Shivpati, and small son. They met the expenses for rent, rations, and private school fees through Shivpati's export factory wages. She had been supportive during the lockout contestation, but now, given the absence of tangible progress in the struggle, wanted him to take a settlement. On a morning in December, Naresh came by before the protests and stumbled into a tense exchange. "How long will you keep doing this?! Nothing will come of it! Take your settlement! Whatever they're giving, take it!" Shivpati shouted at Ramakant.[73] "If they give Rs. 200,000, then I'll take it," he responded.[74] "Will they give Rs. 200,000?" she asked Naresh.[75] They were trying to secure jobs, Naresh gently replied. "Who knows if they'll give you jobs or not! Nothing is happening!" she ex-

Figure 4.10. Placards at the Okhla railway siding.

claimed.[76] "Look, something is happening, we're not able to see it, but on the inside, something is definitely happening. Now see, they're coming after us in a vehicle to Tehkhand Mor [to get us to take settlements]," Naresh explained.[77] "Come on, Naresh, let's go," Ramakant muttered, not wishing to prolong the discussion.[78] They left quickly. The city streets, for all the difficulties, could be a refuge from such exchanges.

The questions they were being asked, and which they were asking themselves, about the effectivity of the protests, did not have clear answers. The managers did not disclose information on the impact of the protests and boycott. The struggle was one in darkness (*andhkar*), as Varmaji put it, in which gains or losses were not and would not be easily visible. "We can't measure the effects of the struggle," admitted Amlakant, in a meeting after his troubling survey.[79] Workers began to reconcile themselves to this uncertainty. They needed to keep making efforts, with calmness and patience, in a context of increasing financial difficulties.[80] To draw on an image from *Aaghat* (1985), a film on factory workers in Mumbai, this was the vortex of struggle (*sangharsh ka bhamvar*), of dark currents, eddies, and gyrations, in the psyche and in practice, in which openings were not immediately discernible. If workers were able to resist exodus, it was partly due to the weekly meetings and discussions, lasting many hours, in which there was conviviality, joking, passionate criticism of one another's conduct, lateness, and absences, deliberations about possible next steps, and provisional commitments (rather than holy water dramas or abusive threats) to continue the struggle for a few more weeks.[81] The meetings were critical in mitigating tensions, bolstering courage, and averting exodus.[82] The microsociety, which workers were fighting to hold together, also held workers together. When workers would sit at B156, modifying the placards, rewriting texts, affixing press clippings, and discussing ongoing events, the darkness could temporarily recede. To avoid anxieties of inactivity, they began going for the afternoon tea break at the C109 gate, and stood with the placards from 4 to 4:45 p.m. A struggle fund, cobbled together by students, activists, and others in India and America, coordinated by Justice for Workers, providing loans of Rs. 1,000 per worker in December and January, extended critically sustaining support. The workers attempted to focus on present tasks amid tensions and difficulties, cultivated patience, which troubled the management, and hosted vague hopes of emerging from the vortex's gyrations.

Openings

In January 2006, pressures on the company escalated. Justice for Workers, now a coalition of citizens in America and India, set up a website on the struggle (designed by a musician and close friend from New Jersey, Matt, along with his associates), including a chronology of events, the petition, press reports, legal documents, and photographs of the B156 workers on the streets, at the factory, and in residences. More messages were written to Metal Artware Co. One person wrote, "You have shown nothing but disregard and disrespect for the 'hands' and heads and souls—the humanity—that produce your products. How can this be justified?" "The Dickensian scenes from which your fortune arises may not yet be visible to your buyers, but they cannot be hidden forever," another person wrote. A woman who had worked in a store selling Metal Artware Co. goods wrote, "[I]t was with great disappointment and sadness that I learned of the deplorable working conditions your factory workers must endure to create these pieces of 'art-

Figure 4.11. Filming the protests. Front, left to right: Rahul Roy, Asheesh Pandya. Back, left to right, with placards: Varmaji, Firoz.

Figure 4.12. The placards in Okhla. Left to right: Amlakant, Madan, Surinder, Rambachan II, Mohan.

work,' and worse yet that many have been deprived of these very jobs due to a dispute. . . . Every object has a story, and when the truth about how your pieces were created comes to light, people will no longer regard them as beautiful." A crew from the CNN-IBN news channel filmed the protests at the Okhla siding and at the C109 gate, generating crowds, and conducted interviews with managers and workers. A CNN-IBN reporter also interviewed Director I in New York, who said, "We work very closely with all the Indian agencies and are in constant touch with all the union officials in India, to make sure that we run a beautiful, safe, respectful, absolutely legal, and productive environment for everyone." Rahul Roy, the documentary filmmaker, filmed the protests in Okhla and at the C109 gate, drawing more crowds. This time, the management bolted the gate. Arundhati Roy, the writer, spoke with workers at Sujan Singh Park, expressed doubts about the effectivity of the nonviolent protests, but offered creative ideas and practical support.[83] An Indian labor activist from Los Angeles suggested connections with organizations involved in global antisweatshop and boycott campaigns.

On the streets of Okhla, workers expressed more impatience and rage. "Nothing is going to get resolved this way. You've shown the placards for many days. You've become Gandhians, but you're not going to win Independence (*azadi*). Now tell us, when do we get together [to attack the factory]," a group of workers agitatedly said to them.[84] At the C109 gate, others would shout, in earshot of the managers, "Stand firm! If not today, they'll concede tomorrow!"[85] Workers inside C109, whose spirits were bolstered by the protests, urged them not to give up the struggle.

But there was disquiet among the union leaders. Dr. Das saw the protests as a struggle of the weak, oriented toward publicity, with Trotskyist and anarchistic tendencies, contrary to the militant revolutionary ideology and politics of the union and Party.[86] On an evening in early January, Dr. Das scolded the workers in the IFTU office, that despite participating in numerous meetings and demonstrations since 2004, they still had not understood the basics of communist trade union struggle. He advised them to find work elsewhere and pursue the legal case, but gave interviews to reporters and observed the struggle from a distance, not without solidaristic feelings.

In mid-January, Director I came to Delhi and called a meeting with the B156 workers. As they stood inside the C82 gate, the managers explained that the accounts of Metal Artware Exports were depleted, and that Metal Innovations did not have the finances, space, or work to give them jobs.

However, if they wanted to set up a workshop, with one of them acting as contractor, Metal Innovations could give them orders. The workers were perplexed. They reiterated their request for jobs, politely left the meeting, picked up the placards, and went as scheduled to Sujan Singh Park. Though the meeting was disappointing, they could now perceive the effects of the protests and boycott. Hopes within families were renewed. Wives changed their minds. "Don't quit this," Dulari instructed Amlakant.[87] "Brother, stand firm!" Shivpati told Naresh.[88] Justice for Workers posted letters to 350 retailers of Metal Artware Co. in America.

A few days later, Director I held another meeting at C82, and told the workers that he was offering double the legal settlements, until 2 p.m. the next day. After this, he would divert funds to his lawyers to fight a prolonged court case, which could last several years. They were not seeking exaggerated "multinational company settlements (*bahurashtriya hisab*)," but only work, said Varmaji. Director I quickly ended the meeting. Despite a night of tense anxiety, there was no exodus.

The following week, Director I called a third meeting. As the *hijras* had cursed C82, and they had already had two failed meetings there, Rampal suggested that they meet in a different location. Director I brought them to C109, apologized for the events that had occurred, and promised to give the workers and Shibbo Devi jobs in Metal Innovations. Two days later, at the end of January, in a meeting room in C109, Director I, the managers, the B156 workers, and I finalized the details and documents of the resolution. Director I handed appointment letters, as permanent workers, to the B156 workers and Shibbo Devi, and issued checks for back wages and other dues for the struggle period. Justice for Workers discontinued the boycott.

B156 was vacated the next month. The workers were shifted to C82, where after a *puja*, attended by Director I and the managers, and the blessings of the *hijras* (and an apology from Varmaji for his earlier rough speech), they began production. They packed the placards into the blue tarpaulin covering, which was never opened again. Their park meetings continued, as did their struggles for transport (to a new factory in Noida), pollution controls, and better wages. At the time of writing, nine of the workers, along with Shibbo Devi, were still working for the company group.

Forces of Truth

"The strong are, as a matter of fact, never absolutely strong, nor are the weak absolutely weak, but neither is aware of this," Weil writes.[89] At B156, it could often seem as if the managers could do as they pleased, in utilizing casual, invisible workers, intensifying production, giving stagnant wages, and shifting, dismissing, and retrenching workers. The workers could feel a sense of grave weakness, amid the directors' legal dispute (which did not directly involve them), the cessation of work and wages, and the large-scale exodus of workers from other units. They were left alone and isolated at B156.

But within that vulnerability, they sought ways to fight back against the perceived injustice and ethical wrong of the management's activities. They wanted to avoid the potential hazards and weaknesses of the union's militant formula, which might have propelled them into violence and long court cases. They were willing to experiment with protest methods, drawing upon the insights of the *Faridabad Workers Newspaper* and the past experiences of other factory workers.

In engaging in placard protests across Delhi, they expanded synchrony politics, far beyond B156. The motives and methods of the struggle were vital to its longevity and outcome. The striving for the just due of quasi-legal work and the survival of their nascent microsociety critically assisted in contending with financial inducements and the dark uncertainties regarding the effects of the struggle. By adopting nonviolence, they were able to maintain a continuing, uncomfortable presence on the streets of Okhla and Delhi.

The resolution suggests the possibility of an alternative protest formula to militant unity politics. The pursuit of justice (*haq*), the method of nonviolence (*ahimsa*), and a microsociety (*samaj*) to hold persons together can, under certain conditions, catalyze practical and empathetic linkages (or bridges [*metaxu*] in Weil) across boundaries and borders of factory gates, city spaces, and global geographies. In the truthful texts of the placards, the nonviolent methods, the linkages across Delhi, and the global grassroots boycott of the company's goods, the struggle seemed to give rise to what might be termed, following Gandhi, as forces of truth.[90] These truth forces can at times exert counterforce and pressure on the precarity-inducing force of global capital, delivering provisional degrees of justice for workers.[91] The struggle offered a glimpse of the nonabsolute weakness of migrant workers, when acting together with others in the world.

In this struggle, there was no mention of the *Kalyug* on the placards. In part, this was because the collaborative, *Kalyug*-like brothers (*Kalyugi bhai*) had left B156. But on the streets of Okhla and Delhi, on the buses, in dealings with the police, in park meetings, and in connections with working people and others beyond India, one could witness the emergence of currents, flows, and energies of non-*Kalyug*-like fellowship (*bhaicara*) between the B156 workers and many, diverse others. In the attempt to work out an alternative protest formula, the workers, it would seem, were further developing counterformulas to the *Kalyug*, across the vast spaces and prison walls separating B156 from the rest of the world.

CHAPTER 5

Warp and Weft

In the metal factory, migrant workers get caught up in machinations, efforts to undermine livelihoods, mental tensions, and lateral divisiveness. They noncooperate with these entanglements in auto-regulated working, joking, and the politics of unity and synchrony. In these activities, a self-understanding emerges of being souls struggling with distortive forces in the present, decivilizing epoch of the *Kalyug.*

This chapter explores migrant workers' experiences in the sphere of the city and the village. Migrants get entangled in accumulation efforts, tensions, illnesses, excessive usage of intoxicants, discord within the family, and insularities to do with boundaries of caste and religion. They noncooperate with these processes in empathetic closeness in families, assistance in times of illness, and fellowship, involving the loosening of village norms in caste dealings and close relations among Hindus and Muslims. One might see these noncooperative activities as the work of weaving integrative filaments in the social fabric (*tana bana* [warp and weft]) of migrant worlds, drawing people together, against the disintegrative forces of egoism and hostility, and enabling them to survive, forge fragile dwellings, and experience elements of a good life.

I focus here on the worlds of two B156 workers, Naresh and Varmaji. I begin by describing Naresh's experiences of childhood, migration, mental tensions, family dealings, and illnesses, including the attempts to get his aunt treated for cancer in Delhi. I discuss Varmaji's experiences of the village home, his drinking, his vision of the family as a circular maze (*cakravyuh*) of tensions, duties, and attachments, and the discord and struggles with his wife, Durgawati. I then examine Naresh's social dealings within and beyond his *adivasi* relatives, Varmaji's views on religion and his relations with

Muslims, and migrant experiences of the festivals of Holi, Muharram, and Eid.

Travails

In his school days, Naresh dreamt of working in Delhi, earning money, and gaining *izzat*. Once he got to Okhla, and began working in metal factories, he confronted the realities of precarious work, constrained earnings, bodily losses, and illnesses. Amid mental tensions, he sought solace and refuge in being with his close relatives and family members. Despite disillusion, he did not give up hope in the possibilities of earning, accumulating, and returning, with *izzat*, to the village.

Dreams

Naresh grew up in a farming family in the villages of Sua and Soko, near Medininagar in Palamu district, Jharkhand. They cultivated about seven acres of land, jointly with Naresh's father's two brothers (whose sons included the B156 polishers, Tapesvar and Jitender). They grew rice, wheat, lentils, sesame, mustard, and vegetables. They rented a tractor for plowing, utilized chemical fertilizers, and irrigated the fields from open wells, using diesel engines. They kept six cows, bullocks, and buffaloes. Most of the harvest was consumed at home. Naresh's elder sister, Chano Devi, lived in her marital home in Madhi village, across the North Koel River, close to Uday's home. He had three younger brothers. Madan and Vinod were metal polishers in Okhla. Sarju looked after the fields and livestock. They were Chero *adivasis*, a Scheduled Tribe in Jharkhand. Cheros were kings in medieval Palamu, with military land grants. Naresh spoke with pride about being descended from kings, such as Raja Medini Rai, who ruled from the old Palamu Fort. Over time, the wealth and holdings of the Cheros declined, and they eventually became cultivators.[1]

In middle school, to raise cash for books and tuition classes, Naresh began doing wage work. He worked on night shifts in nearby factories that produced talc and dolomite powders, lifting stones into a crushing machine and loading bags of powder onto trucks for Rs. 15 a night. In the mornings, after bathing, white powder marks remained on his body, which he would try to hide under his clothes, so that his teachers would not know that he was working nights and lose confidence in his abilities in school. When he was ten years old, he got married to Anita Devi, though it would be several years before she moved to his home.

Since his early teens, Naresh dreamt of going to Delhi. Groups of elder boys, working in garment factories in Delhi, would come home for Chath festival, wearing colorful long-sleeve shirts, tericot slacks, and white sneakers, speaking in Hindi, and bringing boxes of sweets, new clothes, and cash for their families. Crowds of young boys would follow them around the village. Large groups of family members would accompany them to the bus stop when they left. They boasted of the wages they were getting in Delhi, which were five times the wages in the stone-crushing factories. One day, after his studies, he thought, he too would make it to Delhi, earn good wages, bring money home, gain the respect these boys enjoyed, and someday, start a small business in the village.[2] After failing his tenth grade exam, Naresh left the village in 1996, along with his brother-in-law, to work on a farm in Panipat, Haryana. The next year, he came to meet Madan, who was living in Tehkhand and working in a dyeing factory. Naresh began working in Okhla metal factories.

Tehkhand village is located in the southeast of the Okhla Industrial Area. At one corner of the village is Tehkhand Mor, a busy intersection with a bus stand, in front of the massive grain godown of the Food Corporation of India (FCI). In the evenings, one sees large numbers of workers coming and going through this crossing. They mill about in the market along the sides of the wide road, at the vendors of fruits, sugarcane juice, batter-fried boiled eggs, and *gulab jamuns*, the vegetable sellers along the pavement, the carts with belts, wallets, mufflers, and handkerchiefs, the stalls selling clothes and duffle bags, and the tea shop, amid blaring film music and the bustle of autorickshaws, motorcycles, buses, and trucks. Along the road bordering Okhla, there are eateries and sweet shops, general stores, shops selling *saris* and televisions, doctors' clinics, and a private hospital. As one enters Tehkhand, one encounters a maze of congested lanes, with open gutters and piles of dung of roaming cows and buffaloes. Sometimes there is space for only two bodies to pass. Elsewhere, the lanes accommodate goods carriers and trucks. Along the lanes, one sees provision stores, tea stalls, phone booths, barber shops, chemist shops, and doctors' clinics. One finds workshops engaged in multiple industries, including metalworking (with about twenty polishing machines in the village) and garment stitching.

Figure 5.1. New Delhi railway station before Eid and Chath Puja.

In the eighties and nineties, with the growth of the Okhla Industrial Area, there was expanded construction of residential buildings in Tehkhand, with rooms given on rent to migrant workers. By the mid-2000s, there were an estimated 15,000–20,000 migrants living in about 5,000 rooms in Tehkhand.[3] The landlords of the tenements were mostly Gujjars, a Backward Class in Delhi. The Gujjars held government jobs in the Delhi Police, the Delhi Transport Corporation, and the Delhi Jal Board, were labor and transport contractors for Okhla factories, and managed general stores, dairies, and other businesses in the village. They were dominant figures in electoral politics in Okhla and southeast Delhi.

In Naresh's early days in Delhi, he stayed with ten Chero migrants in a ten-by-ten-foot room in Tehkhand. They had two kerosene stoves, some vessels for preparing lentils and vegetables, and one large pot for cooking rice. They would get up at 3 a.m., begin working the stoves, cutting vegetables, and washing vessels, prepare breakfast, and pack lunchboxes, before leaving for 9 a.m. shifts. On Sundays, the stoves would be working all day, with roommates

Figure 5.2. Tehkhand village.

cooking, eating, going out, coming back hungry, and cooking again. Two to four Cheros at a time would eat in one round metal plate. They were young migrants, living like close female friends (*saheli log*), without tension or envy, Naresh says. But such proximities created difficulties. In the nights, bodies would be tightly packed on the floor, wall to wall, pressed up against one another, with legs extending onto other legs, and little room to turn one's body. Naresh slept on his side, with both hands tightly covering his ears, due to the loud snoring. He was anxious that he might fall ill by living close to so many people. But he thought to endure the hardship (*kasht*), learn a skill like metal polishing, and try to earn better wages. Once Naresh got into D45, the next year, and was making Rs. 4,500 a month with overtime, he moved to another room with Madan and one other Chero, where they could eat, sleep, and breathe more easily.

While working at T7, after D45, Naresh shifted to a room on the ground floor of a two-story tenement. Over the next years, fifteen of his kin and village relatives took five more of the seventeen rooms in his tenement and the adjacent three-story building. The rooms were eighty to one hundred square feet in size, with three to four persons staying in each room. There was one latrine on each floor. The room rents were Rs. 600–800. They referred to these two buildings as the "boundary."

To get to Naresh's room, one had to step gingerly through stagnant puddles of water that collected on the ground floor, where tenants bathed and washed their vessels and clothes. Shoes and sandals, sometimes accumulating into piles, were kept outside the room. Naresh's room was ten-by-ten feet, with a thin wooden door and a window with a metal grill. Inside, behind a curtain, there was a wooden bed, plastic chairs, water containers, a ceiling fan, and a desert cooler. Jackets, shirts, pants, undergarments, shoulder bags, satchels, and plastic bags hung on nails on the walls. On the back wall above the bed, there were calendars, a clock, a photograph of Naresh's son, Guddu, and images and posters of gods and goddesses, including Lakshmi, Saraswati, Ganesh, Ram, Lakshman, Hanuman, Shiva, Parvati, and Durga. On the left wall, there was a clothesline, a shelf of toiletries, a mirror, a tube light, and posters of film actors and actresses, including Bobby Deol, Kareena Kapoor, Shilpa Shetty, and Amisha Patel. On the right side of the room, there was a kerosene stove, pressure cookers, metal vessels, a clay water pot, canisters of rice and wheat flour, and a high shelf behind curtains, with a suitcase and a wooden box containing documents, medical reports, and X-rays. Naresh lived in this room for over fifteen years. The room became an anchor during the 2000s, amid the precarity at B156.

In the boundary, there were multiple activities of mutual assistance among Naresh and his Chero relatives. They helped to fill each other's water containers when the landlords activated the motor pump for the water supply (from borewells and the Municipal Corporation of Delhi [MCD]), including when others were away in the factories. They borrowed small quantities of rice, lentils, vegetables, spices, oil, and other cooking ingredients from each other. They exchanged cash loans (Rs. 500–1,000), especially before trips to the village. For a time, they operated a savings committee, in which a monthly pool of Rs. 10,000 was given to members by drawing lots, not by competitive bidding (as in the committee at B156, which could engender hostilities). When a person fell ill, others would go along to the doctor's clinic to give support and strength, while receiving injections or intravenous glucose bottles. Naresh also developed friendships with non-Chero neighbors, Bhasu and Sitaram, who were from Patna, Bihar. They worked with Naresh's uncle at the FCI godown and respected the Jharkhandis. They too exchanged loans. In

2001, Naresh and Madan went with Bhasu and a dozen others to the Okhla Barrage, at the Yamuna River, to celebrate the final morning of Chath festival.

In the 2000s, once Naresh came to B156, he began to have difficulties saving and remitting to the village home. His wages stayed close to Delhi minimum wages (Rs. 2,400–3,319 from 2001 to 2005), and overtime was unpredictable. He could sometimes make Rs. 5,000 in the winters, with higher overtime hours. But after covering the costs of rent, rations, vegetables, doctors' visits, savings committee contributions, life insurance premiums, and a few evenings of meat and liquor, he could often only save his overtime earnings. He could also go into debt when Anita Devi and Guddu, who was born in 2000, were visiting from the village. During these stays of six months at a time, he would spend more on milk, rations, medicine, clothes, cosmetics, and occasional trips to the Kalkaji and Chattarpur temples.[4]

In his childhood, to Naresh, the *Kalyug* also seemed to be only a child (*bacca*), in its nascent stages of development. There was deprivation, hardship, and work, but also the joys of grazing the buffaloes in the forest, plowing the fields in the monsoon rains, bathing the bullocks in the pond, playing soccer with schoolmates, singing devotional songs (*kirtans*) in a village group, attending music programs at Ramnavami festival, and going for fairs (*melas*) at Holi and Chath. After migrating to Delhi, and encountering the travails of providing for his family, "The *Kalyug* grew into adulthood," he says.[5] The progress of the *Kalyug* seemed to be moving in tandem with his own descent into intense work, growing tensions, and expanding responsibilities.

Hollowing

In the 2000s, Naresh could see that wages and working conditions seemed to be deteriorating for metal polishers across the Okhla Industrial Area. Many companies were closing their factories or shifting them to Noida, Faridabad, Gurgaon, and Bhiwadi, seeking lower land costs, taxes, and wage levels. In Okhla, he could see the greater prevalence of contract workers, higher production quotas, and reductions in overtime hours. The days seemed long gone when Okhla factories, in metal polishing, garment exports, and dyeing, were running around the clock, like violent storms (*tufan*), with companies keeping workers inside the gate for consecutive nights, providing food allowances and blankets to sleep on the shop floor, in order to complete export orders. In those days, one could see masses of workers walking on the roads of Okhla at 3 a.m., coming home from long shifts at the factories. Now, at nighttime, the streets were quiet and empty. "Okhla has become hollow (*Okhla khokhla ho gaya*)," he says, in a rhyming phrase, as a space to rapidly accumulate and "loot" earnings.

Through his wages in Delhi, Naresh had contributed to farming expenses in the village, the costs of two diesel pumps for irrigating the fields, the purchase of livestock, and the weddings of two brothers and his sister's daughter. But he had not been able to accumulate enough to begin some business activity in the village, such as a general store or a vehicle for hire. He was just passing time (*timepass karna*), or worse, wasting time (*samay barbad karna*), in Delhi, he felt, rather than spending it well, in activities that could enable a life of greater ease in the village. He thought of shifting, along with some Chero relatives and ex-B156 workers (including Bhagvati and Manoj), to the polishing factories in Rajasthan.

The myriad tensions of working at B156, managing his living costs in Tehkhand, and attending to the ongoing needs in the village home could sometimes feel crushing. The illness of thinking excessively about things (*socnevali bimari*), as he put it, could have deleterious bodily effects. As Satish, a B156 helper, once said, "Tension hollows you out from inside (*Tension admi ko andar se khokhla karti jati hai*)."[6] Along with Okhla, migrant bodies were becoming hollow, through this hosting of tension.

Outside the factory, one could see Naresh's attempts to mitigate this hollowing process, through social dealings with his kin and village relatives. After shifts, on the way home, he would sit and chat at the carts of leather goods operated by his relatives in the Tehkhand market.[7] Once he got to his room, he would not sit there for long, but moved among several rooms in the boundary and proximate tenements. At nights and on Sundays, in the absence of extended overtime, one would see fluid movements in the buildings, as Naresh and other Jharkhandis would gather in rooms with televisions (up to twenty people at a time, violating the restrictions of the landlords), engage in vigorous joking (without the vulgarity of factory humor, and with considerations of *izzat* for kin elders), play with the children, cook and eat together, recline, and doze off. Being with others helped keep tensions at bay. The presence of many Jharkhandis also made Tehkhand feel like his own village (*apna gamv*) and home (*apna ghar*), despite the poor water quality, congested buildings, and disease.

After long shifts and on paydays, Naresh sometimes got together in a room with Uday, Surinder, and others, to drink liquor. During these gatherings (or *parties*), they would speak to one another with less inhibition about

Figure 5.3. Naresh's room. Front, left to right: Uday, Madan, Deepak (B. K. Singh's son), Lilesvar. Back, left to right: Naresh, Jitender, Tapesvar, Vinod.

goings-on in their lives and village homes. For Naresh, the liquor made him feel like he was getting a good massage after exhausting work, and he would sleep well, though he would wake up with a splitting headache. Surinder tried to get him to come more frequently to parties. But Naresh restrained his drinking, due to the costs and the hangovers, and to set an example for his younger brothers in the boundary (even when it was not effective, as wit-

Figure 5.4. Madan's room.

nessed in Madan's excessive drinking). He also had unpleasant memories of the consequences of drinking in his village home. After long, tiring days in the fields, his father, Kailash Singh, would come home drunk, and get into heated quarrels with his mother, Patiya Devi, explaining that he drank out of extreme fatigue. Naresh did not wish to re-create such routines and pass them on to his son. He also avoided the palette of leaf-based intoxicants (*nashapatti*), of tobacco, *gutkha*, *biris*, and *ganja*,[8] that were close companions of metal workers.

Naresh's tensions were also mitigated by the visits of Anita Devi and Guddu to Delhi. They would come due to recurring illnesses of headaches, stomach disorders, and fevers. These ailments were induced, Anita Devi believed, by the sorcery activities of close kin and shamans (*ojhas, bhagats*) in the village. "Our own people feel envious. They think, how is it that you are living in Delhi, earning, eating well, dressing nicely, and getting ahead. There are so many of you. We'll do something so that you won't be able to eat properly, and you'll be distressed," she says.[9] The shamans could foist spirits

Figure 5.5. Anita Devi and Guddu.

(*bhuts, pret atmas*) into others' bodies, where they could cause dizziness, fainting, body aches, digestive problems, and fever, which could escalate into fatal illnesses, if they were not exorcised (*jhar phumk*) by another shaman.[10] Anita Devi visited multiple shamans in Palamu and in Delhi, spending Rs. 10–1,000 each time.[11] She also went to allopathic doctors. By coming to Delhi, Anita Devi's and Guddu's health would improve, she felt, due to the long distance from her ill-wishing relatives in the village.[12]

When Anita Devi and Guddu were in Delhi, Naresh seemed to feel more vitality, courage, and hope, despite the higher living costs and tensions of their illnesses. He delighted in the company of his small son. In the mornings, Guddu would stand eagerly by Naresh's bicycle, holding Naresh's lunchbox, insisting that he also was going along for "*duty*." He probably thought Naresh was going to some carnival (*mela*), like at the Dussehra festival in Okhla. "He has no idea what we're doing at B156. That our minds are ruined there," Naresh says.[13] On Sundays, he would take Guddu to the Tehkhand market for small glasses of sweet lime and sugarcane juice that would fill his stomach, after which he would say, with a smile, "That was good (*Maza a gaya*)."

But Anita Devi did not wish to stay too long in Delhi. She did not like being constricted in a small room in Tehkhand. She missed the good air, clean water, and open space of the village. She liked mixing with a larger circle in Sua and Soko. She felt the duty to go back, as her cooking, cleaning, and farming work were needed in the village home. She also worried about the hollowing of migrant bodies in Delhi. Naresh was bulky and muscular in the village. In his early days in Okhla factories, he was nicknamed Sher Singh (Lion), due to his build. "Not even half his body is left," she observed, after five years.[14] There were also multiple cases of tuberculosis in the boundary. During times of turbulence at B156, when prospects for good, future earnings looked bleak to Naresh, she would assure him that they could go back to the village. "Everyone is surviving there and looking after their families, we can't do so?" she would say.[15] Earning and accumulating seemed less important to Anita Devi than conserving bodies and being together.

Naresh tried to visit the village a few times a year, for health emergencies, weddings, and festivals. But such trips were costly. He required cash for train and auto fares, purchases of clothing, shampoo, cosmetics, and biscuits, spending money for food and liquor for his relatives, and a lump sum for the village home.[16] Over time, his parents asked that he not bring clothes or other gifts, but just cash, which they could spend on farming costs, medical bills, and debts in the village. On these visits, he got some respite from the factory clock. He would sleep in, work in the fields, and visit relatives in Palamu. When his leave got over, his parents did not pressure him to extend his stay. They began to regard him as not just their son, but as the company's son (*company ka beta*), with obligations to get back on time. Naresh wanted to live together with all of his people (*apne admi*) in the village. But he could not go back without sufficient savings, or he would have to return to the difficult, low-wage work of stone crushing and the loading and unloading of construction trucks. This would cause embarrassment (*beizzati*) in the village. Others would laugh, after he had spent so many years working as a craftsman (*karigar*) in Delhi.

So Naresh kept at it, working in metal factories and seeking other sources of income in Delhi. In the early mornings, he rode a bicycle around Okhla delivering magazines and newspapers to factories.[17] He invested and lost money, along with other Cheros, in a multilevel marketing scheme called Future Zone. Once he got his final settlement from B156 in 2006, he bought a sewing machine, to learn tailoring in the nights. When I noticed it one day

Figure 5.6. Naresh's village home, Palamu, Jharkhand. Left to right: Kailash Singh, Naresh, Patiya Devi, Anita Devi.

Figure 5.7. Chath Puja, Palamu, Jharkhand. Right: Uday.

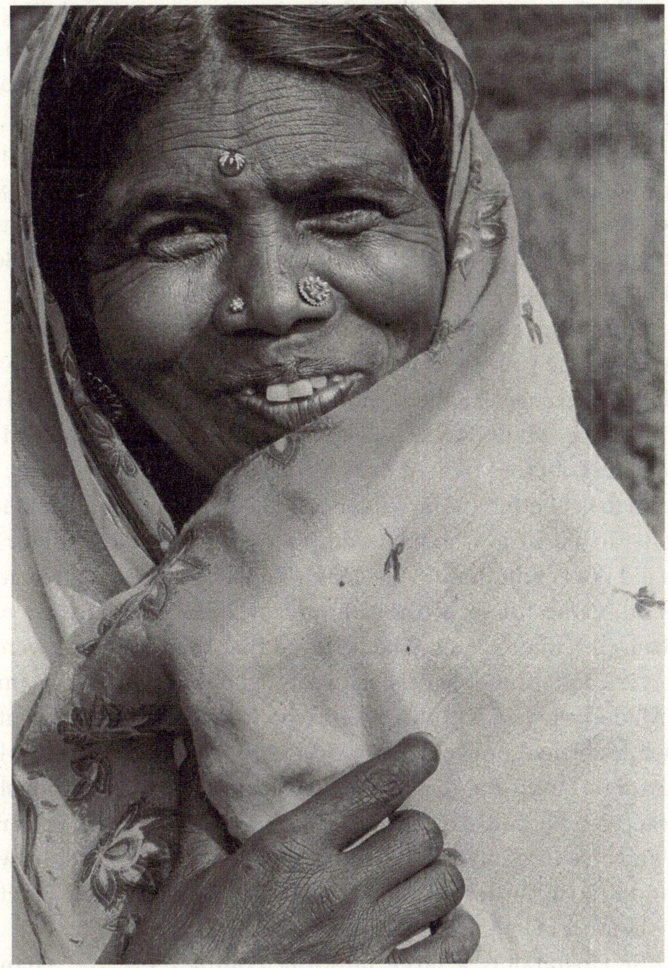

Figure 5.8. Patiya Devi.

in his room, he laughed. He might not have prospered in metal polishing. But his ambitions of accumulation were still unvanquished.[18]

Illness

At times, Naresh got involved in the medical treatments of ailing relatives. In 2006, Tapesvar, Naresh's cousin-brother, brought his mother, Madodari

Devi, to Delhi. I describe here their difficulties in navigating through hospitals, the actions of doctors and relatives, and her journey to death. In this episode, one witnessed the jostling of negligence and triage with empathetic assistance, among doctors and the Jharkhandis.

Madodari Devi was a tall, thin, and frail Chero woman in her forties, with high cheekbones, deep wrinkles, graying hair, and dark-green tattoos on her arms and legs. Her husband, Naresh's paternal uncle, had died from an epileptic seizure seven years earlier. She had six children. Bajrang, the eldest son, in his mid-twenties at the time, looked after the fields. Tapesvar was in his early twenties. Dukh Raj, about twenty, was a casual worker in a water-bottling company in Okhla. Anil, a teenage son, did construction wage work in Medininagar. Matva, a teenage daughter, and Lagni, a girl of ten years, stayed at home.

In the village, Madodari Devi experienced stomach pains and vaginal bleeding. Local doctors treated her with medicine and injections, and she would seem to get better. In the winter of 2004, her bleeding increased. Dukh Raj took her to a doctor, who advised him to take her to Ranchi for surgery. The sons did not act on this advice. Dukh Raj, who was being treated for polio in Delhi, came home in the summer of 2005, and tried to bring his mother to Delhi. She resisted. She believed that their ailments were caused by the sorcery activities of her sister-in-law, who was allegedly burning with envy, as Madodari Devi had three sons who were earning wages outside the village, while she had only one son working for a time in Delhi.[19] Madodari Devi pressured Dukh Raj to stay back to pursue treatment from shamans. He contracted tuberculosis. In the autumn of 2005, he died. In early 2006, her pain and bleeding intensified. The family quickly arranged the weddings of Anil and Matva. Under pressure from Naresh and his brothers, Tapesvar brought Madodari Devi to Delhi in the summer of 2006.

The ESI Hospital is a large building complex on Ma Anandmayee Marg, on the southwest corner of the Okhla Industrial Area. As one enters the hospital, one sees queues and clusters of patients and their relatives almost everywhere, at the registration counter, outpatient departments, and investigation rooms, in the lobby and hallways, outside the wards, and in the courtyard, standing, sitting, waiting, sometimes sleeping. They carry their ESI cards, hospital papers, and plastic bags of X-rays and other documents. Inside the wards, patients are at times doubled or tripled on a single bed. They share these beds with flies, bugs, and cockroaches, amid noxious odors, blown in by noisy desert coolers, of a massive MCD landfill of the city's garbage, adjacent to the hospital. It is not uncommon to see doctors and other staff persons speaking roughly with workers, scolding and shouting at them, for not bringing proper hospital papers (on which notes are written in English, which many cannot read), not following instructions, going to the wrong rooms, bringing their uneducated, pregnant wives to Delhi (as occurred with Naresh, when Anita Devi miscarried), and having excessive numbers of children.

Tapesvar brought his mother to the emergency room of the ESI Hospital, due to her extreme abdominal pain and bleeding, in May 2006. The doctor referred her to a gynecologist in the labor room, who prescribed medicine for the bleeding, and referred her to the gynecology and surgery outpatient departments (OPDs) for the next day, possibly without doing a pelvic examination. Tapesvar took her home, but she was soon in agony again. He brought her back to the hospital in the night. She was admitted to the emergency ward and treated by a medicine specialist for colitis and anemia. Her bleeding symptom was not recorded this time. She was referred the next day to the orthopedic OPD for her lumbar pain. Three days later, she followed up at the medicine OPD, where she was given injections and prescribed medicine for anemia and abdominal pain. Four days later, given her extreme pain, she came back to the emergency ward in the night, where she was treated by medicine doctors for pain and vomiting. She was given injections, and an X-ray and blood tests were done. The doctors seemed to have lost track of the initial complaint of bleeding. They wrote, "Pain relieved," and referred her to the medicine and surgery OPDs. Two days later, the surgery doctors recorded her symptoms in detail, and referred her to the gynecology OPD. The next day, the gynecology doctor noted her symptoms of discharge, not bleeding, and prescribed medicine given for infections. There were no notes indicating a pelvic exam. An ultrasound was also requested, but as the radiology doctor was on leave, she was told to return in ten or twelve days.

Her pain was getting more severe. When she returned to the gynecology OPD, ten days later, the doctor recorded a symptom of swelling on her face and legs, and strangely wrote, "No gyne problem at present." There were no examination notes. She was referred again to the medicine OPD for anemia treatment, from where she was directed to the emergency room, due to her serious condition. She was given medicine and sent home.

Seven visits, eleven doctors, eighteen encounters, twenty-three days, and no proper diagnosis. She had gone repeatedly to the emergency room and the medicine, surgery, and gynecology departments, with specialized doctors treating particular symptoms and fractions of the body, without identifying the underlying cause of her pain and bleeding. Tapesvar came to feel that the doctors were not interested in curing her illness, only in shuttling them to different queues, departments, testing rooms, and the ESI Dispensary.[20] "She was getting very agitated. And they were just making us run here and there, saying do this, then do that. Her pain was intense. No doctor would promptly see her. No one was attending to us," he said.[21] Tapesvar might not have always followed instructions properly, sometimes going to the wrong place or aborting tasks. But as the ESI doctors admitted, patients often do not know where to go. Given mistakes, queues, and lags in getting tests done, it can take many visits to make progress in one's treatment.

In mid-June, Naresh and Tapesvar brought Madodari Devi to Dr. Das's clinic in Govindpuri. She was now emaciated, bony, and pale. Her face, hands, and ankles were swollen. A few days later, the clinic's gynecologist examined her, ordered an ultrasound, and diagnosed her ailment as cervical cancer. "This is criminal," Dr. Das said, with anger. He referred her to the All India Institute of Medical Sciences (AIIMS), a large, well-regarded government hospital in south Delhi, and wrote a note for an oncology doctor there who was connected to the Party.

The All India Institute of Medical Sciences is a vast and complicated maze of buildings and passageways. The cancer hospital is a dark-red-and-beige multistory building with waiting areas of tightly arrayed black metal chairs and wooden benches, lined with patients, many middle-aged, but sometimes also children. They sit quietly and stare ahead with solemn and somber faces, waiting to see doctors, get tests done, and undergo treatments, their stoic stillness contrasting with the hustle and bustle of the passages crossing through the hospital. In shadowy spaces along the walls, patients lie on metal stretchers, with attendants close by, clutching bags of documents, medicine, food, and spare clothes. Men in dark-blue uniforms and pale-green masks move about the passages, eyes down, swabbing the floors with disinfectant. It was an arduous walk for Madodari Devi, along lanes, passages, and detours around construction work, to reach the cancer hospital from the AIIMS entrance on Aurobindo Marg. She hobbled slowly, leaning on Tapesvar's shoulder, sometimes pausing and resting on the ground.

The oncologist known to Dr. Das, who was a young, calm, and concise doctor, ordered a biopsy from the gynecology department, which was done the next day. But due to a doctors' strike over the attempted dismissal of the AIIMS director, it took two weeks to obtain the report. After the biopsy, Madodari Devi was referred to a second oncology unit in another building, giving rise to confusion, mistakes, and delays. Her condition abruptly worsened, and she spent a night in the AIIMS emergency room, where she was given a blood transfusion and medicine. The oncology doctors examined her in the OPD, diagnosed her cancer at stage IIIB, and ordered further investigations, which were done at AIIMS over two difficult weeks.

Madodari Devi was withering. She would rest on the floor in the waiting areas and hallways of the hospital. Her pain, vomiting, and bleeding persisted. She became anxious, tense, and distressed, as she lay in Tapesvar's room in Tehkhand, on the ground floor of the boundary, in the heat of July. The lost wages, costs of traveling to the hospital, and difficulties of the OPD process were also disturbing Tapesvar. Instead of going to AIIMS in the early mornings, to get into queues, he would show up for duty at the factory. "It's useless now, she's not going to get better," he would say.[22] In the nights, when she would cry out in pain, he would vent his rage for the difficulties and costs of her treatments to date, saying, "You've ruined our entire home, from having to get you medicine for two–three years! You're causing so much trouble in the room! You're not even dying quickly!"[23] Before the doctors gave their assessments, Tapesvar seemed to want to triage Madodari Devi.[24] He thought to send her back to the village, while she was well enough to travel, but given the pressures from Naresh and his brothers, did not do so. Tapesvar's behavior was deeply baffling to his relatives and coworkers.

Naresh felt a sense of duty (*farz*) to Madodari Devi, and also compassion. But he was concerned that if he took a more active role in her treatment, and she were to die, others in the envy-infused atmosphere of the village would raise questions about his possible hand in her death, given that the two families had existing disputes over land and the division of their houses. The desire to help Madodari Devi could be interpreted as deep, camouflaged self-interest (*gahra svarth*). He seemed to be unsure, hesitant, and paralyzed into partial spectatorship.

Once the AIIMS doctors saw the test reports, at the end of July, they gave a grim prognosis. The disease had advanced considerably. Her kidneys were close to failure. They referred her to the palliative care department. But in early August, the oncology doctor connected to the Party reviewed her reports, discussed the case with other doctors, and admitted her to the radiotherapy ward.

She was settled into a clean room with six beds and large windows. The nurses gave her intravenous drips and injections. Dialysis began the next evening. As fluid flowed into her body, and was retained there, she would feel pain, cry out, toss and turn, and grab at the tubes. A thin, gray-haired woman

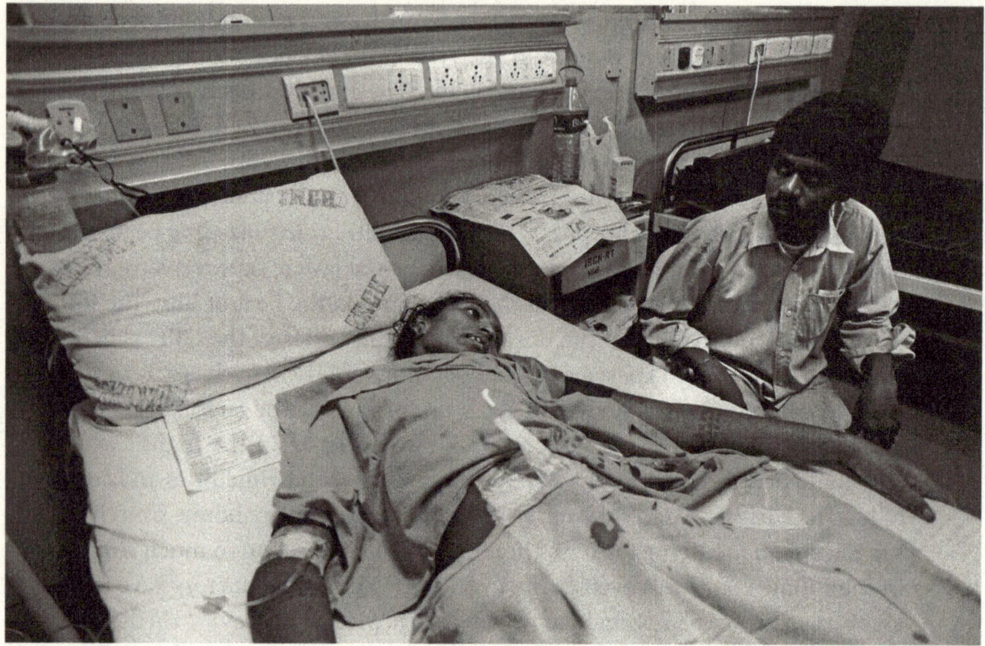

Figure 5.9. The AIIMS ward.

from Patna woke up in the next bed and consoled her, explaining that the fluid was medicine, and that she would soon feel better. As the fluid drained out of her body, she would become calm and quiet. Tapesvar, Naresh, and a distant nephew, Anil, looked after the dialysis through the night. By dawn, her agitations subsided. The swelling on her hands and legs reduced. Two days later, the doctors performed a nephrostomy, inserting a catheter into the kidney, with a bag to collect fluid. The dialysis continued. After a few days, she began eating the watery rice with lentils and vegetables given in the hospital. When doctors came on rounds, she would move her legs to one side, under the blankets, to give them a place, saying, "Please sit."[25] She would gaze bewilderedly at the many tubes coming out of her body. She did not understand what her ailment was.

The doctors wanted to give her blood, and asked her relatives to donate to the blood bank. No one from the Jharkhandi group was eager to do so, out of fears that blood donation could result in bodily weakness, illness, and death.[26] Her brother, who was her only sibling, and his son, who had come from the village, were rarely visible in the ward. They would sit in the hallway, roam about the hospital grounds, and drink liquor in Tehkhand. Her youngest son, who had come with them, eventually gave blood. Her brother did not believe that she would live for long. He advised Naresh to have her funeral rites done in Delhi, and avoid the difficulties of bringing her home. They caught a train back to the village, without seeing Madodari Devi. "My brother just left. He didn't even meet me," she said in the hospital bed, with perplexity.[27]

In mid-August, the doctors began radiotherapy. Her white blood count dropped, and she developed fever. After the third session, she was discharged. As she was leaving the ward, she approached the doctors and nurses at the desk, and put her hands together in a gesture of gratitude. She perhaps thought that she had been cured.

The AIIMS doctors referred her to Shanti Avedna Sadan, a nearby cancer hospice, managed by Catholic nuns of the Sisters of the Holy Cross. The hospice, which charged no fees, had twenty beds, a prayer room, and a serene garden with green lawns and trees. In the dimly lit ward, patients with bandages on their cheeks, throats, and extremities silently lay in beds, occasionally clearing throats, coughing, and vomiting. Another patient from the AIIMS ward lay in the next bed to Madodari Devi, panting and wheezing. Her husband, a migrant worker from Bihar, sat at her side, holding her hand. She died that night. The nurses came to Madodari Devi's bed frequently to bring her food and tea, give her medicine, change her clothes, wash and rub oil on her body, and walk with her in the garden. She did not know what a hospice was. But as she saw patients disappear from the beds, she gradually realized that she was not there to be cured.

After a week, Tapesvar went back to the factory. She would be left alone during the day. She grew more anxious, nervous, and fearful. The catheter slipped out of her back. The swelling returned. She could not digest food or swallow medicine. She lost the ability to recognize persons. She asked for her mother, who was in the village. A few days later, Bajrang, her eldest son, Kavita Devi, his wife, and Matva, her daughter, came to Delhi. She could recognize people again. That Sunday, she had many visitors. Anita Devi and Anil's wife (also named Kavita) sat with her, combed her hair, and pressed her legs. She sensed that she did not have much time left. She still believed that her ailment had been induced by her sister-in-law's witchcraft. "She didn't even let me live with some disability. She's taken my very life," she said.[28] She asked Naresh, Madan, and Anil to look after her children,

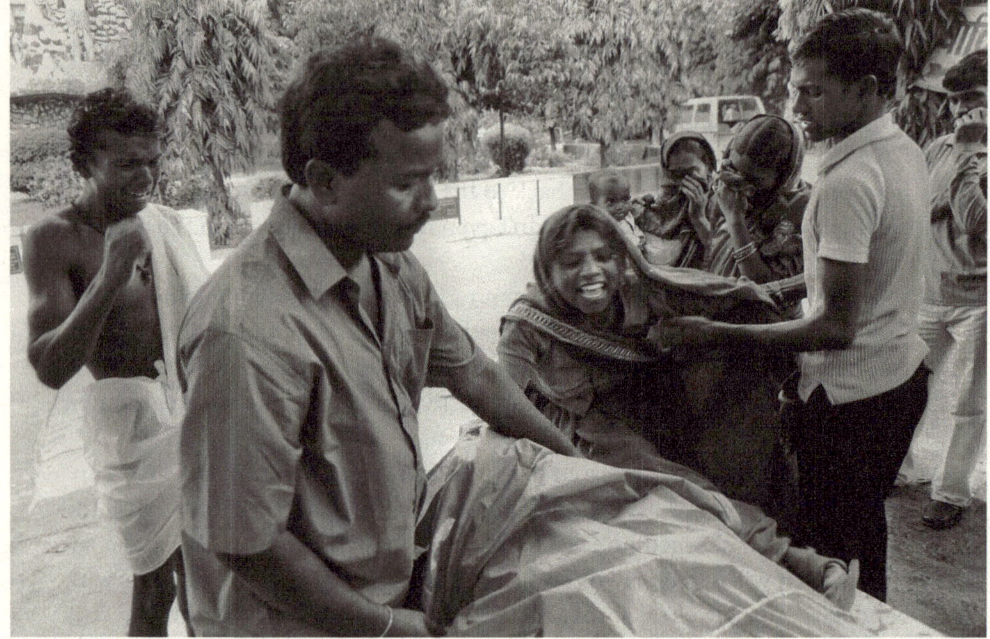

Figure 5.10. Madodari Devi's funeral.

and to avoid envy and hostility, saying, "Live harmoniously with each other, don't fight among yourselves."[29]

Two nights later, her condition deteriorated. She was restless and agitated, and had breathing difficulties. A nurse's injection calmed her down. Her breathing slowed. Naresh, Anil, and Bajrang gave her spoons of holy water. She became quiet.

In the morning, her body was brought to the Kalkaji cremation ground, and set on a stone platform near a large tree, close to where Ramdev's body had rested one year earlier. Thirty of Naresh's relatives and coworkers came there from Okhla. The gathering included about fifteen Jharkhandis who had refused to give blood for Madodari Devi's treatment. Kavita Devi, Matva, and Tapesvar's wife, Pushpa Devi, approached the body, weeping, wailing, and lamenting. Bajrang, who was otherwise silent, broke into tears. The women exited the ground.

Bajrang circled the body, pouring water from a clay pot, as a priest chanted *mantras.* Bajrang, Madan, Vinod, and Tapesvar hoisted the bier and brought it to the cremation pit. The body was draped with two new *saris* and a red cloth.[30] They cast ritual essences and placed logs and branches over the body. Bajrang circled the body, along with Naresh, Madan, Vinod, Rambachan II, and Varmaji, and lit the pyre. The assembled persons dispersed and went back to their factories.

The next day, Bajrang gathered the bones and ashes from the pit and brought them to the Yamuna River, near the Okhla Barrage. He watched as handfuls of ashes sifted through his fingers into the frothy, flowing water. He tossed the cloth bundle of bones. He gazed for a few moments at the river, then bent down and washed his hands and arms. With a small bag of Madodari Devi's ashes, Bajrang returned to the village.

Given such close encounters with illness and death in Delhi, it is understandable that Naresh was not content to defer the good life to a distant, uncertain future. One might not be "living life" (*zindagi jina*) in the city, as he once put it. But one need not completely forfeit life to the accumulation (and hollowing) process. In inhabiting close, affective bonds with his family and relatives, with their attendant duties, Naresh could be seen to be claiming a bit of life, and joy (*maza* in Guddu's language), in the present.

Circular Maze

After coming to Delhi, Varmaji spent a good deal of his time and earnings in drinking. This gave rise to discord with his wife, Durgawati, and distance from his family in the village home. He spoke of feeling caught in a *cakravyuh* (circular maze) of tensions, duties, and attachments, from which exit was not ethically possible. In closeness and struggles with Durgawati, they sought ways to build a dwelling within the maze.

Drinking

Varmaji grew up in Rupin village in Sant Kabir Nagar district, Uttar Pradesh. His father, Muneshwar, worked as a fitter in a paper mill in Kolkata, along with other relatives from the village, before retiring in the late eighties. The family cultivated two acres, on which they grew wheat, rice, millets, chickpeas, sugarcane, peas, and mustard. Varmaji's elder sister, Hausla Devi, married and shifted to Delhi, and his elder brother, Ramprasad, looked after the fields with their parents. Varmaji's family were Rajbhars, a Backward Class in

Uttar Pradesh, believed to be descended from medieval kings, including, in some accounts, Raja Suheldev.[31] Over time, the caste devolved into cultivators.

In school, Varmaji was good in Hindi, and was encouraged to pursue a college degree. He wrestled, as his father had done, and played *kabaddi*.[32] He sat with elders and listened to their stories from the *Ramayana* and the poetry of Kabir, Rahim, and Surdas. He attended spiritual discourses in the winters on the *Bhagavat Purana* and the *Bhagavad Gita*. In eighth standard, he began drinking toddy (palm wine), and moving in a circle of drinking friends.[33] When he began secretively selling wheat and rice from home to finance his drinking, his mother and brother asked him to leave. In 1980, at age sixteen, he got on a train for Delhi.

While staying with his sister in northeast Delhi, he began working at a metal polishing workshop, where the piece rate earnings were high (Rs. 100 a day). Ramjit, his elder brother in village kin relations, was running an Okhla workshop, and invited him to learn polishing and stay with him in Harkesh Nagar. Varmaji began as a helper, got trained as a polisher, and then pursued work in other factories. In the eighties, and until the mid-nineties, there was a high demand for metal polishers, and managers gave them a good deal of *izzat*, he recalls. Over two decades, he worked in twenty factories and workshops in Delhi (Okhla, Harkesh Nagar, Khanpur, Sant Nagar), Mumbai, Gurgaon, Jalandhar, Noida, and Faridabad, shifting due to vicissitudes in orders, better earnings, desires to enhance his skills, and factory closures. He sometimes worked on wages, other times on piece rates, taking contracts for multiple polishers. His earnings were often Rs. 5,000 a month, and sometimes twice this amount.

Much of these earnings dissolved in drinking. He also went into debt. He roamed about Delhi, going for films in cinema halls, often dozing off in drunkenness. He loved spectacles like the Jumbo Circus. In the late eighties, he avidly watched the *Ramayana* and *Mahabharata* serials on television in Harkesh Nagar. He would cover his mouth with a muffler, after drinking, and attend spiritual discourses at the Sant Nirankari Mission in north Delhi. He liked reading the *Shuksagar* (*Bhagavat Purana*). His desire for intoxicants (*nasha*) seemed to coexist with his quest for spiritual wisdom (*gyan*). But the drinking created distance with his family in the village. For many years, his brother did not speak to him. In the mid-nineties, his father passed away, with grief about his son's lifestyle in Delhi.

In 1995, Varmaji got married to Durgawati in the village. Five years later, he brought her and their two small children, Amit and Priti, to Hari Nagar

Figure 5.11. Hari Nagar.

in southeast Delhi. The houses in Hari Nagar were mostly constructed by migrants from Uttar Pradesh and Bihar. Migrants were visible in large numbers not only in markets, but in cultural and religious activities, such as Bhojpuri music programs, Muslim religious gatherings (*jalsas*), Ramzan prayers at mosques, and Chath celebrations on the banks of the Agra Canal. Rambhooan, Ramjit's younger brother, and Naresh II stayed in their built houses. Firoz and Manoj lived close by. Mohan and Prakash lived in proximate neighborhoods.

In the mid-2000s, Varmaji stayed in the first-floor room of Naresh II's house. The room was eight-by-ten feet, with a wooden door, brick walls, and an asbestos roof. The walls had hooks with clothes and plastic bags, a clock, calendars, including one with a photo of the politician Ramvir Singh Bidhuri, and a poster of Rani Mukherji. On a high shelf in the back-right corner was a suitcase, documents, and a stack of books, including the *Shiv Puran*, the *Bhagavad Gita*, and Renu's short stories. In the back-left corner was a gas cylinder with a stovetop, metal vessels, pressure cookers, and containers of

Figure 5.12. Varmaji's room. Left to right: Sohbatti Devi, Durgawati, Priyanka.

flour and rice. Milk powder, spices, and mustard oil were kept on a shelf above the stove. Bedding, pillows, and a quilt were rolled up in the front-left corner near the desert cooler. There was no ceiling fan. Outside the room, there was a terrace with clotheslines, a plastic chair, potted plants, a latrine, and a staircase to the ground floor.

Varmaji came to B156 in 2002, with the hope of getting regularized and obtaining ESI health insurance so that his daughter, Priti, could be treated for tuberculosis. A few months later, after the night workers' union action, he got an ESI card, and Priti got better. His basic wages were Rs. 90–100 a day, of which he was spending Rs. 70, and sometimes more, on intoxicants, including 500 mL of country liquor and 250 mL of Scotch (mixed with sweet lime juice or lemon soda, accompanied with snacks), *pans*, *gutkhas*, and *biris*. He worked extra hours in Tehkhand workshops and took on debts, but still had cash shortages, so took most of his wages as advances. On paydays, Khan sahab began sending his light pay packets to Durgawati, through Firoz, instead of handing them to Varmaji.

The cash scarcities gave rise to discord (*klesh*) with Durgawati. She needed money for milk, vegetables, and transport to the ESI Hospital. The children pestered Varmaji for coins to buy toffees from the corner shop. "I've got nothing," he would say.[34] "You've got money for liquor, but not for us," Amit would respond.[35] Sometimes, Durgawati would angrily say, "You're not capable of anything! You can't provide properly for the children's upbringing! You're worse than even a beggar!"[36] If he was drunk, he might unleash abuses, saying, "Shut up, sister's ****, whore's daughter, you're ruining my mood!"[37] The abuses could extend to divinities. When she was fasting for Durga Puja, he might kick over the flickering earthen lamps, and shout, "Get rid of this! There's no so-called Durga! It's all a deception!"[38] Durgawati uttered curses that his mouth and limbs be broken, as punishment for the drinking and abuses. She also went to a Muslim healer in Jamia Nagar, with the assistance of Firoz, to get a protective amulet, in case a neighbor had inflicted a malevolent spirit onto Varmaji, which was causing his extreme drinking.[39]

The children were disturbed in this atmosphere. Amit did not like the drinking, quarreling, and abuses. At night, while others slept, he could sometimes be found in the corner of the room, sitting up quietly. He became thin and frail. He left for the village with Durgawati's mother, Sohbatti Devi, joined school, and assisted in the fields. He did not come back. Priti could not tolerate the smell of liquor. When Varmaji opened a bottle, she would hold her nose and leave the room. But she was attached to him. At night, she slept close by, with her small fingers holding onto his shirt buttons, so that he would not run off somewhere to his drinking companions in Hari Nagar. When he got up to go to the latrine, she would ask where he was going, then only let him go.

In 2003, after his cycle accident, which cut his nose, mouth, and tongue, he gave up drinking. Durgawati took the injury as a blessing.[40] The next year, he visited the village home. His thin mother, Phoola Devi, who worked in the fields, was relieved to see a sober Varmaji. After years of silence, he spoke at length with his brother. Amit, Priti, and Priyanka (born in 2002) delighted in his presence.

Though Varmaji recognized the influence of associative circles (*sangat*) in his getting into drinking, he did not blame others. Rather, he attributed his actions to the destructive desires of the demonic soul-valence (*rakshasi atma*), which sought the mental escape and arrogant pride (*ahamkar*) that came with drinking, even at the cost of wages, respect, and the well-being of others. Varmaji was not unaware of the hazards of drinking. But destruction could

Figure 5.13. Varmaji's village home, Sant Kabir Nagar, Uttar Pradesh. Left to right: Phoola Devi, Ramprasad, Varmaji.

be inviting. "There is some delight in danger, and in pursuing a bit of that delight, a guy goes on sinking into a quagmire, plunges his future into darkness, and invites ethical wrong (*adharm*) to 'come, rule over me.' That's how I sunk," he said.[41] In the next years, Varmaji worked to recover his finances, repair his relations with Durgawati, and rebuild his *izzat* in the social world.

Desires

Varmaji was plagued by mental tensions, of how to settle his drinking-induced debts with shopkeepers, moneylenders, and workers, while trying to cover the family's living expenses in Delhi, including the costs of the children's medicine, clothes, and tuitions. He often felt lost in mental turmoil (*uljhan*), and now, without the solace, fog, and escape of liquor. Mental peace was elusive for a sober Varmaji.

These tensions were exacerbated by quarrels with Durgawati. They had met when he was visiting her aunt's village in Sant Kabir Nagar. He camouflaged his drinking. They got to know each other over three years, and when she was in her late teens, they married. "If I had known he was such a drinker, I would not have agreed to the marriage. I never thought I would get someone like that in my life," she said.[42] She should have judged more carefully, she felt, though at times, she would say, "It's all the play of fate."[43]

Durgawati, like Varmaji, felt the tensions of wanting to settle debts. But she also harbored desires to acquire "*hi-fi*" things, of a better consumption standard, like a television, cassette deck, and jewelry. She wanted to construct their own house, so they would not have to live under the rule of landlords. "Do something with dedication!" she urged Varmaji. "We've got to visibly achieve something!"[44] These desires were not devoid of competitive envy. She wanted to look after the family, but also to catch up to and impress more prosperous neighbors, such as Naresh II and Rambhooan, in the city and village.

During Varmaji's years of drinking, Durgawati had to suppress these desires. Now, it seemed, she was trying to make up for lost time. To Varmaji, she was like Zeenat Aman's character in *Roti Kapada Aur Makaan* (1974). She had big dreams (*hi-fi sapne*). She wanted speed (*raftar*) in getting ahead in life. She wanted to reach greater heights (*uncai*) in the world.[45] Varmaji did not feel he could ever match her desired speed. But he was disturbed by her discontent and sadness. Due to cash shortages, he could not even do modest things with her, like go to the Kalkaji temple or the Delhi Zoo.

When Durgawati was in Hari Nagar, she spent her days cooking, cleaning, filling water from the hand pump, washing clothes,[46] going to the market, and looking after the children. She liked to sit and talk with Firoz's wife, Asma Begam, and other female neighbors. In the village, she was often working all day, like a machine, she felt, doing domestic chores under the direction of Varmaji's mother. She could not roam about freely. She was told to speak softly at home. She did not like the feelings of suffocation (*ghutan*) and confinement (*bandish*). In Hari Nagar, she controlled her own work. She moved about as she pleased. She did not lower her voice. When Varmaji was home, he assisted in cutting vegetables, grinding spices, cooking fish curry, and making *rotis*. He helped with bathing, feeding, and holding the children, which allowed her to do other tasks. But he was admittedly not so good at handling their scattered movements and multiple demands for salty snacks, toffees, and biscuits. Polishing four steel platters in eight hours at B156 was easy, he said, compared to looking after his two small girls on a Sunday morning.

Durgawati understood that Varmaji's wages and debts made it difficult to pursue her desires. She was willing to do wage work to augment their earnings. Along with Asma Begam, she did stitching work at home for a contractor, but developed headaches and eyesight problems, and quit after a few months. She wanted to learn decorative designs (*mehndi*) at a beauty parlor in Jaitpur village. She was ready to work in garment factories. But Varmaji would not allow it.[47] He would lose *izzat*, in its patriarchal valences, in the eyes of his family and others, if he were no longer the sole provider for his family.[48] If she began working, he also felt she might one day say, "I'm earning! You depend on me!"[49] He was not ready to hear such things. But nor was he able to figure out how to satiate her *hi-fi* desires on his wages alone.

Allies

In Varmaji's descriptions of his life as a migrant, an image arises of the *cakravyuh*, a military formation that appears in the *Mahabharata*. The *cakravyuh* has complex, mysterious, and labyrinthine qualities. The formation resembles a rotating wheel with spiraling layers, and great warriors posted at its inner gates. Only some know how to enter and exit the deadly, encircling maze. The image of the *cakravyuh* has resonances in Hindi cinema (as a depiction of the workings of criminality, politics, the police, and the media), poetry, plays, folk dance, and the news media.[50]

In the epic, Abhimanyu is the son of Arjun, the Pandava, and Subhadra, the half-sister of Krishna. When he is in the womb, Arjun describes the intricacies of military formations and the strategies of defeating them to Subhadra.[51] He listens carefully and masters these formations. But when Arjun explains how to exit the *cakravyuh*, Subhadra dozes off, so Abhimanyu learns how to enter the maze, but not how to escape it. At the time of the war between the Pandavas and the Kauravas, on the battlefield of Kurukshetra, Abhimanyu is a young, bold, and fierce warrior. On the war's thirteenth day, the Kaurava army forms the *cakravyuh*. Krishna and Arjun are drawn to a distant part of the battlefield, and it falls on the sixteen-year-old Abhimanyu to lead the Pandavas into the *cakravyuh*, which he does valiantly. Jayadratha, on the Kaurava side, prevents the Pandavas from following him inside for vital support. Though Abhimanyu defeats many great warriors, and gets

Figure 5.14. Varmaji and Durgawati.

through six of the seven gates of the maze, the Kauravas break the rules of combat, gang up on him, and destroy his weapons. Abhimanyu keeps fighting on foot, wielding the wheel of his broken chariot, but is eventually slain.

The family sphere, for Varmaji, was akin to this *cakravyuh*. There were mental tensions to do with material needs, domestic quarrels, Durgawati's desires, the children's illnesses, and requirements in the village home. There were duties (*kartavya*), responsibilities (*zimmedari*), and affective attachments (*maya, moh, lagav*) with regard to his wife, children, mother, and brother. Like in the epic, the *parivarik cakravyuh* (circular maze of the family), as he called it, was inescapable.[52] But it was ethically wrong to seek to extricate oneself from this maze, as to do so would be to abandon one's duties in the world. Unlike in the epic, women too were caught in the *cakravyuh*. Through the clever concealment of Varmaji's drinking before the marriage, Durgawati felt she had gotten ensnared. She too was struggling with constrained finances, illnesses, duties, deferred desires, and attachments, from which she could not get free. "I got caught in the *cakravyuh*," she said. "The marriage took place. Now I can't leave."[53]

But the *cakravyuh* was not only a path to impending doom. There were also possibilities for closeness and common struggle.[54] Varmaji admired Durgawati's strong will, courage, and patience in negotiating the crowds and multiple tasks at the ESI Hospital and AIIMS, when seeking treatment for the children, which he was unable to do. Durgawati appreciated his knowledge, generosity, and resolve to not resume drinking. In 2004, she was preparing to go to the village for an indefinitely long stay, and asked Varmaji for Rs. 10,000 for the trip, through advances and loans. He could not raise this amount. "You're incapable!" she shouted, and angrily left.[55] But after a few weeks, they began to miss each other's presence. "When you stay alone, it feels very strange," said Varmaji. "Married life is such that once you've spent seven or eight years together, and then have to be apart, life looks very burdensome."[56] She asked him to come to the village, and he went. A few months later, she came back to Delhi.

In the placards struggle, they would quarrel in the winter mornings, when Varmaji asked for breakfast and Rs. 10 for transport to go to Okhla (she held the wages of her two younger brothers, who were staying with them). "It's cold," she'd say from under the covers. "What job are you going to? How much cash did you bring home last night to be asking for food so early?"[57] She got pregnant, and experienced lethargy, nausea, and fever. But she never asked Varmaji to take a settlement and leave the struggle. She did not say he was incapable. "During the struggle, she assisted me a lot," admitted Varmaji.[58]

In these empathetic struggles, to attend to the family and to one another, amid disturbances at B156, Varmaji and Durgawati seemed to recognize that they were allies in the *cakravyuh* (albeit quarreling ones), not adversaries.[59] They were not alone, unlike Abhimanyu, and they were not seeking escape. They seemed to be seeking a hospitable dwelling, however precarious, within the *cakravyuh*.

Fellowship

Amid insularities and aversions to do with caste and religion, one could see practices of fellowship in migrant milieus in Delhi. Naresh loosened his observances of village norms of caste dealings, hosted non-Cheros in

Tehkhand, and developed friendships with non-Jharkhandis at B156. Despite past associations with communal politics, Varmaji engaged in close dealings of exchange and assistance with Firoz, and they exhibited respect for one another's religion. In festive times, one witnessed the vitalities of fellowship in more intense forms, in revelry, the giving of *izzat*, and the expression of affective feelings in neighborhoods of Delhi.

Loosening

Naresh and his Chero relatives sometimes hosted non-Cheros in their rooms in Tehkhand. The Cheros claimed Rajput status in the village, and practiced untouchability with regard to Scheduled Castes and Muslims. Careful rules were to be observed when giving food and water to these groups at Chero homes, and Cheros were not to eat or drink in the homes of these groups. Violations of these rules could be met with questioning, censure, and expulsion by other Cheros. But social norms were different in Delhi, and Naresh felt he should adjust to them, invoking the saying, "Do as the people of that place do (*Jaisa des, vaisa bhes*)."

In Naresh's early days in Tehkhand, when he was living in a room with three Cheros, one brought a Scheduled Caste (Dusadh) and two Muslim migrants from Palamu. They lived, cooked, and ate together in one room, setting aside village rules. Naresh assisted in finding them work in garment factories. After some months of earning wages, the new migrants dispersed and took their own rooms.[60] When Naresh visited Palamu, he would bring cash, clothes, and messages from non-Chero migrants to their families, as they did for him.[61] The families would give him *izzat* and blessings, some of whom lived in Chando, Anita Devi's village, and regarded him as their son-in-law in village relations. Naresh's parents, when they learned of his close dealings with non-Chero migrants, felt a sense of relief, that if their son fell ill or got injured in Delhi, there were others to look after him.

There were motives for this loosening in caste dealings. First, there were the compulsions (*majburi*) of survival in Delhi. To access drinking water, Naresh had to set aside village norms. In the boundary, tenants touched a common hose when filling their water containers, but Naresh did not know the castes of one quarter of the tenants, who were also continually shifting. Second, there were the duties of village relations. Naresh had to give *izzat* and look after non-Chero migrants, if he wanted *izzat* and a good name in

Palamu.[62] Third, there was the ethos of fellowship (*bhaicara*), which involved a commingling of survival motives, understandings of mutual assistance and interdependence, and affective feelings. "We're living like brothers, distant from home. One becomes the support of one another," he says. "Live together, share what you've got, earn wages. If one follows village untouchability rules too much, one won't be able to get on here."[63] From living in Delhi, Naresh's views on the legitimacy of these rules were relaxing, he felt. But he did not overtly challenge these practices in the village.[64]

The easing of village norms coexisted with insularities. At B156, workers were generally believed, by one another, to be from Backward Class, Scheduled Caste, Scheduled Tribe, and Muslim backgrounds.[65] The Jharkhandis and Muslims were clearly identified.[66] A few workers used surnames indicating Backward Class origins (e.g., Maurya, Yadav). Some identified as Scheduled Caste and were involved in the political activities of the Bahujan Samaj Party (e.g., Bhagvati, who self-reported as Raidas). But for many, who did not use revealing surnames, caste backgrounds could be ambiguous.[67] Identifications, when audible, could conflict with others' guesses, rumors, and reports.

At lunch at the factory, Naresh and other Jharkhandis sat outside, among other workers, amid these caste ambiguities. Before eating, they exchanged vegetables with migrants from Uttar Pradesh and Bihar, according to machine partner relations, friendships, perceptions of cleanliness, and suspicions of illnesses. After beginning eating, they would freely go into the containers of other Jharkhandis, with saliva transfers (*jutha*), but sat in a tight circle, to deter the eager, roving hands of others from reaching in, not always successfully.[68] At roadside eateries, in a more public setting, they ate and drank without difficulties, as the vessels, glasses, and teacups (including those brought to B156 at tea breaks) were washed after usage. But Naresh avoided going to Muslim-managed eateries, due to aversions to beef eating.

In 2003, Prakash, a helper, invited the B156 workers to his room in Hari Nagar to celebrate his son's birthday. One day, when Naresh was surreptitiously taking vegetables from Prakash's lunchbox in the storeroom (without knowing his caste), while Prakash was sweeping the shop floor, Rajender, the proto-leader, who took keen interest in ascertaining caste identities (and self-reported as Yadav), asked him in a scolding tone why he was taking food from a Chamar (Scheduled Caste).[69] "That's OK, it's the city, such things are alright here," Naresh replied.[70] But he put the vegetables back. Now, he felt hesitation about going to eat at Prakash's home. But as many were going, including other Jharkhandis, and they had good dealings with Prakash, he did go.[71] The B156 workers sat on the terrace of Prakash's building and ate *puris*,[72] chickpea and potato curry, and *laddus*. Thoughts of caste pollution came into Naresh's mind, but he attempted to push them aside.[73]

In factory struggles, negative generalizations about Scheduled Castes were at times audible. In the lockout exodus, during the poster writing in Tehkhand, Naresh and others sought to connect the resignations of certain workers to their suspected Scheduled Caste backgrounds. According to the negative generalizations, Chamars were self-seeking, submissive, and untrustworthy. Amlakant invoked a village saying, in an interview, "Chamar-jackals are very clever / Where there is loot, they pounce / Where there is danger, they flee."[74] But such connections were also contested. As they speculated about the caste identities of the resignees in the poster meeting, Varmaji brusquely intervened, "Leave it, what does caste have to do with it?! Ravidasji [the poet-saint] was a Chamar by caste, he stitched shoes. But see what a great thinker he was."[75] Among those who exited and those who remained in struggles, they also seemed to recognize, there were possible Scheduled Caste workers, and indeed, all caste groups in the factory.

Through dealings at B156, Naresh developed friendships (qua more close and deep variants of fellowship) with non-Jharkhandis in Delhi. In the early days of the factory, he mixed with Arun and Mithilesh, but with the progress of struggles, grew close to Amlakant, Naresh II, and Ramakant.[76] He became friends with Mithilesh at D45, in the late nineties (without knowing his caste). They met again at B156 in 2001. They joked on the shop floor, they walked back to Tehkhand in the nights, they went together to the ESI Dispensary, and they took part in a savings committee in Mithilesh's boundary. Only in 2004, when Mithilesh resigned, Naresh came to know that he was from a Scheduled Caste, with whom he had sometimes spoken, in part-jest, of feeling surrounded by camouflaged "Chamar-jackals" at B156. Friendships could exist amid caste ambiguities, but did not always silence caste aversions.

In later years, Naresh developed a close, deep friendship with Varmaji, after Varmaji quit drinking. They would sit together in Tehkhand and have calm, detailed conversations about the factory, their families, illnesses and remedies, and goings-on in the village. Durgawati had a fiery temper (*ulti khopdi*), as Naresh once witnessed at the ESI Hospital, when she was trying to get Varmaji treated for his accident injuries. But in Hari Nagar, where Naresh and Anita Devi stayed one night in 2004, after going to a shaman in

Faridabad, she was a warm and generous host, who showed them *izzat*, spoke openly, with a sense of humor and without envy, and gave one a feeling of being in one's own home (*apna ghar*). In 2006, when Madodari Devi passed away, Naresh immediately summoned Varmaji to advise and assist them with the multiple steps of the funeral rites. In 2007, when Varmaji suffered a lower back injury (a prolapsed disc) and was admitted to the ESI Hospital, the Jharkhandis took turns looking after him, dealing with the nurses, and staying in the ward in the nights. Surinder's concern about Varmaji's deteriorating condition, amid the lack of attention by the ESI doctors, led to a critically missed diagnosis of nerve root compression (cauda equina syndrome) and his transfer to AIIMS for urgent surgery, which enabled him to escape paraplegia.[77]

In building such friendships, beyond the circle of Jharkhandis, Naresh seemed to look less at caste identities (though aversions of caste and religion persisted), and more at the qualities, actions, and character of persons. These attributes were revealed in factory dealings and in times of crisis, illness, and death. Such friendships, in their deeper forms, seemed to be guided less by egoistic motives, and more by ethico-political alignments, respect, and emerging, strong affective feelings for others in the city.

Hindu-Muslim

In the nineties, Varmaji would go back to the village at election times, and campaign for political leaders of the Bahujan Samaj Party, the Janata Dal, and the Bharatiya Janata Party (BJP).[78] Varmaji's extended family were supporters of the BJP and its predecessor, the Bharatiya Jana Sangh.[79] While campaigning for the BJP in the late nineties, Varmaji would shout the slogan in processions, "Say with pride, we are Hindus, Hindustan is ours!"[80] Other slogans mobilized for the Ram temple in Ayodhya, such as, "The divine infant Ram, we'll come and build a temple right there [at the disputed site]!" and, "The circumcised ones (*katue* [Muslims]) will be cut down, they'll shout the name of Ram!"[81]

In interviews, Varmaji could at times speak in Hindu nationalist language, of Muslim invaders who deceptively killed Raja Suheldev, destroyed temples, and engaged in forced conversions; Gandhi's mistake of not allowing Muslims to leave India at Partition; the coldness, untrustworthiness, arrogance, excessive sexuality, and exploding population of Muslims; the speading of terrorism by Muslims; and the need to declare India as a Hindu nation. But at other times, Varmaji articulated different views. Though he had gotten caught up in communal politics in election campaigns, he said, he did not harbor desires to destroy mosques to build temples. The demolition of the Babri mosque was illegitimate and wrong (*najayaz*). The communal tensions, riots, and deaths, for the sake of building one temple, could not have pleased God. "Lord Ram was born in *Tretayug* (two epochs ago), and you're fighting about it today, in *Kalyug*," he observed.[82] "The God I believe in is also the God Muslims believe in. Or what, has God come specially for them, or specially for us? No. God is one, but we see Him in one way, they see Him in another."[83] Just as the Ganga had multiple places of worship along its riverbanks, God was worshipped in different ways in diverse religions. "All religions, in their own beliefs and practices, are true and legitimate (*Sab dharm apni jagah par sahi haim*)," he said. The core message of religions, as given in holy books such as the *Bhagavad Gita*, Bible, Quran, and Guru Granth Sahib, was one, which was to engage in ethical action (*accha karm*) and seek the divine. No religion sanctioned illegitimate violence (*najayaz himsa*).

The violence of the Ram temple movement, to Varmaji, emerged through the activities of political leaders (*netas*), along with spokespersons, representatives, and "contractors" of religion (*dharm ke thekedar*),[84] who were able to arouse, provoke, and mobilize egoistic interests, fears, and hostilities among the short-sighted, foolish demos. Unlike true religious teachers who preached nonviolence (*ahimsa*), these political and religious leaders would seek to keep the Ram temple issue alive, so that a violent *Mahabharata* would erupt across Uttar Pradesh and India, allowing them to expand and consolidate their political power.[85] These leaders, regardless of party affiliations, were only variations of the clever politician Chaurangilal Domukhiya, played by Kader Khan in *Insaaf ki Awaaz* (1986), who gave the definition of *rajniti* (politics), a word in the "devil's dictionary," as, "R means like a *rakshas* (demon), J means to the *janta* (demos), N means causing *nuksan* (loss, damage), and T means doing *tikrambazi* (stratagems)."[86] Alongside the Hindu nationalist idioms in his discourse, Varmaji seemed to seek a distance from this politics. In 2006, local activists of the Rashtriya Swayamsevak Sangh, in black caps, white shirts, and khaki shorts, were moving through the lanes of Hari Nagar, promoting an upcoming convention celebrating the birth centenary of M. S. Golwalkar. "I don't have any interest in that convention," Varmaji said. "I'm a Hindu. But I don't believe in this, getting all Hindus together and killing Muslims. No."[87]

Political leaders were not always like Chaurangilal Domukhiya. During the freedom struggle, Varmaji observed, Gandhi engaged in campaigns against untouchability. Ambedkar sought to remove caste discrimination and drafted laws to ameliorate the conditions of lower castes.[88] Gandhi, along with Muslim leaders like Maulana Azad and Abdul Ghaffar Khan, attempted to foster fellowship (*bhaicara*) among Hindus and Muslims. He questioned why Muslims should leave India, at Partition, after they had fought and sacrificed themselves (*qurbani dena*), along with Hindus, Sikhs, and other communities, for India's freedom. Gandhi, a god-like person in the *Kalyug* (*Kalyug ka devta*), lost his life for opposing this exodus. If Hindu-Muslim fellowship was strong before Independence, it had severely eroded in recent decades, as seen in the Ram temple movement, the Gujarat violence, and terror attacks in India. The fellowship that existed in Gandhi's time, which helped to free India from British rule, Varmaji felt, would not return in our times.

Yet, in Varmaji's life, one could see practices of fellowship with Muslims. When he came to Delhi, he stayed with Aminuddin, a close friend from the village, in Harkesh Nagar. They learned polishing, cooked and ate together, and lived like brothers (*bhais*), until they got caught up in their own *cakravyuhs*, after marriage. In Hari Nagar, Varmaji and Firoz lived in close proximity. They exchanged spices, sugar, and other cooking ingredients. When Firoz was staying alone, Durgawati would at times make tea for him, or give him *pakoras* and *halva*.[89] She would serve them in separate vessels that she kept for Muslims and Scheduled Castes, or in Firoz's own glass and bowls, to avoid caste pollution.[90] Firoz and Asma Begam also gave assistance to Varmaji's family in times of illness.[91] In 2006, when Varmaji's infant son, Hari Om, required surgery at AIIMS for a hole in his heart, Varmaji asked his relatives, and Firoz, to give blood. Firoz did so without hesitation.[92] During Ramzan in 2007, when Varmaji was on his back at home, recovering from spinal surgery, Asma Begam would bring *pakoras*, and sometimes, *papad*,[93] chickpeas, dates, and sweets, for Varmaji and Durgawati, before breaking her fast in the evenings.

Varmaji and Firoz did not always get along, due to the ebb and flow of factory turbulence, Varmaji's volatile temper, and Firoz's blunt speech. But Varmaji valued Firoz. In 2006, when Firoz's family shifted to Saurabh Vihar, after a falling-out with their Muslim landlord, Varmaji called them back, after five days, and settled them into a room in the house where his own family was staying. The Saurabh Vihar room was too high in the building, and Firoz's small sons, Sahil and Sohail, were badly missing the children in Hari Nagar.

But Varmaji also said to Firoz, "Don't go that far away. It causes a lot of difficulty for me."[94]

When Firoz spoke about religion, he sounded like Varmaji. "God is one. People have different beliefs and practices and call Him by different names. We address Him as Allah, some call Him Ram, others call Him Jesus," he said. "To say our God is good and their God is worthless, that's wrong. All religions, in their own tenets and practices, are true."[95] When starting the machine at the factory, Firoz would say, "In the name of Allah, the greatest."[96] But he also distributed the offerings of the Tuesday *puja*. To Firoz, Vishvakarma was akin to a Pir (Sufi saint). In Hari Nagar, Firoz went for prayers in the morning and evening, when possible, at nearby mosques. This sometimes meant abruptly leaving conversations in the rooms of Varmaji and Naresh II. "Okay, go, pray and come," Varmaji would say.[97] Firoz would pray, return, and seamlessly reenter the discussion.

Lal Das, the temple priest at the disputed site in Ayodhya in the eighties and early nineties, opposed the destruction of the Babri mosque, arguing that Hindus and Muslims had lived there together in relative peace for generations, before the communal politics and violence of the Ram temple movement. "[W]e should not hurt the religious sentiments of others," he said. "Our religion does not permit this, ever."[98] Shortly after the Babri mosque demolition, he was murdered. But in Delhi, some years later, one could see surviving elements of the ethos of Lal Das. Varmaji and Firoz seemed to find messages, from within their own religious inheritances, that allowed them to respect, if not encourage, the other's beliefs and practices. The fellowship of Hindus and Muslims might have been gravely deteriorating, in Varmaji's eyes, but it was not yet dead.

Festivity

Migrants did not wish to let go of the convivialities of festivity, even when cash was scarce. At festive times, one could see the less ordinary, more intense energies of fellowship in migrant milieus. At Holi, Muharram, and Eid, migrants reveled, explored unfamiliar religious practices, and gave *izzat* to one another, within and across boundaries.

On Holi, the festival of colors, there was play, revelry, and the crossing of boundaries in the factory and neighborhood. At B156, several days before Holi, there were heightened activities of horseplay and joking, as workers would throw buffs across the ducts with increasing frequency, hurl handfuls of white powder, pour kerosene down the backs of shirts, and wrestle one another to the ground. On the eve of Holi, workers would come up behind one another at the machines, rub colored powder across cheeks, foreheads, and beards, and dump mugs of colored water onto heads and into clothes. The colors created bright, stark contrasts with the gray, brown, and black of work clothes. While special attention was given to favorite targets of humor and joking in these attacks and ambushes, all got involved in this play, including active collaborators. Some observed *izzat* to elders, by applying only a vertical, colored mark to the forehead (*tika*) and warmly shaking hands. After bathing, there was more play of colors on faces, heads, and clothes outside the gate, along with handshakes and embraces. There was also play across boundaries of posts. Helpers threw colors on polishers and vice versa. Workers embraced Vijay and Govind, the supervisors, from behind, rubbing colors on their faces and pinching their cheeks, to the laughter of others. They also did not spare the checker, the junior manager, and the head office cashier who came to distribute much-needed wage advances for the festival. *Hijras*, who came to the gate for customary donations for Holi, took the chance to rub colors on the faces of the supervisors. When Khan sahab arrived, he might insist in a stern tone that workers apply only a single mark to the forehead, but polishers would smear colors on his face and clothes, as he protested, "Enough, enough!"[99] and laughed along with the drama. The management was subtly aware that this was one chance for workers to exact a bit of friendly revenge on those who gave them difficulty all year round.[100] After the play of colors, many would head to the liquor shops with their advances, to continue the festival celebrations.

But the true revelry would begin the next morning in the neighborhoods. On Holi in 2005, Madan and Surinder began drinking early in Tehkhand, prepared *pakoras*, and ate a meal of chicken curry and rice, before setting off to various buildings, meeting relatives, friends, and coworkers, applying colors, eating *gujiyas*,[101] drinking liquor, and watching cricket on televisions. In the rooms, male migrants might put colored marks on the forehead or swipe colors on the faces of others' wives, depending on the degree of familiarity, a rare instance of permissible touching across genders, and sometimes expressing flirtatious energies.[102] In the tenements, the Jharkhandis gathered in groups, singing, dancing, playing with hands and sticks on metal vessels and plastic containers, sometimes accompanied by harmonium, hand drum (*dholak*), and hand cymbals. One could see arms flailing and inebriated heads shaking furiously with the accelerating tempos, ascending volume, and in-

Figure 5.15. Holi in Hari Nagar.

Figure 5.16. Chath Puja, Hari Nagar.

Figure 5.17. Muharram in Old Delhi. Left to right: Naresh, Babloo Khan, Sabbir.

Figure 5.18. Eid prayers, Saurabh Vihar. Front, center: Firoz.

tensifying moods of these songs. As the Jharkhandis moved in groups through the lanes of Tehkhand, they had to negotiate their way past clusters of well-built, muscular Gujjar boys, who might douse them with colors or try to rip their clothes. They would move to the edge of the lane, close to the flowing rivulets of multicolored water, to avoid passing Gujjar women, who might strike them with sticks on the knees, legs, or torso, in the practice of *latth mar* (stick beating). They applied colored marks to Gujjar shopkeepers, landlords, and womenfolk, followed by the respectful touching of feet. On this Holi, the landlord invited Madan and other tenants into his flat for drinks. In these interactions, one saw glimpses of affective feelings and respect, not only fear and dislike, between landlords and tenants. By the late afternoon, the play of colors diminished, but there was more drinking, eating of chicken curry, and mixing with one another into the night. In this festivity, one could see an ephemeral crossing of boundaries. The play of colors could take place across distinctions of job, class, and gender. Handshakes, embraces, eating, and drinking occurred with persons whom one might otherwise not strongly like, if only for this day.[103]

At Muharram, in 2004, the festival commemorating the martyrdom of Imam Hussain and his companions in the battle of Karbala, Babloo and Sabbir took the day off to go to the Jama Masjid in Old Delhi to watch the procession of *taziyas* (representations of Imam Hussain's mausoleum). At the time, closer relations were developing between Babloo and the Jharkhandis. Naresh was curious to see the festival at Jama Masjid, and came along, though he was nervous about going to a Muslim area of Delhi.[104] As they sat together at the water tank in the courtyard of the Jama Masjid, Babloo explained aspects of the mosque's design to a quiet and uneasy Naresh, who was entering a mosque for the first time. They moved among the crowds outside, observing the large, tall, colorful *taziyas*, and walked down the lanes, occasionally holding onto each other's fingers, with Babloo describing the geography and narrating past experiences of living with relatives and working in factories in the area. Recognizing (without any discussion) that Naresh might feel uncomfortable eating at a Muslim restaurant, where beef might be served, Babloo brought him to a Hindu-managed hotel for a vegetarian lunch of *chole bhature*.[105] After following the processions through the lanes, they walked on to the red light district of G. B. Road, then came to India Gate, where Naresh felt at ease again, before returning to Okhla. In this experience, Babloo acted as a guide, narrator, and host, introducing Naresh to the Jama Masjid and surrounding area, allowing him to partly overcome anxieties of nonfamil-

Figure 5.19. Eid at Varmaji's. Left to right: Amlakant, Rampal, Naresh II, Varmaji, Firoz, Gulshan (Naresh II's son).

iarity and difference. They grew closer not only as friends, but as friends of distinctive faiths.

On Eid, in 2003, one observed affective, integrative tendencies in the neighborhoods. As Firoz was staying alone at the time, he asked Varmaji and Durgawati to prepare the customary *sevaiyam* (sweet dish with vermicelli) in their room and assist in hosting others who would visit that day. That morning, Amlakant, Rampal, and neighbors Naresh II and Manoj came over and sat on a woven cot in the lane, along with Firoz. Durgawati brought out the sweet vermicelli in metal bowls and served it to the guests and to Firoz. After fifteen minutes, Firoz got up and left, as he had to visit relatives elsewhere in Delhi for Eid. The others sat and discussed various things, including metal pieces at the factory, political parties, India-Pakistan relations, and Karna and Draupadi of the *Mahabharata*, agreeing, when conversation drifted in that direction, to avoid talking about the company. As it was Amlakant's first visit to Varmaji's room, Varmaji and Durgawati got to work preparing a sumptuous lunch of chicken curry, lentils, *rotis*, and rice (and no liquor), as a way of showing *izzat* to him. Though their daughter Priti was sick with a bout of recurring pneumonia, Durgawati was delighted to be hosting persons without serious drinking habits. Amlakant, who had not had good things to say about Varmaji in the past, due to his drinking and other activities, and was seemingly always in a hurry, stayed for a few hours, as a gesture of *izzat*. After lunch, in the late afternoon, Amlakant, Rampal, and a reluctant Varmaji cycled to Babloo's shanty, amid tensions after the Divali bonus episode. Babloo smiled warmly on seeing them. They sat on the floor, chatted, ate flaky pastry, chickpeas, and vermicelli, and drank tea, occasionally glancing at a fuzzy image of a Hindi film on a black-and-white television.[106] Amlakant and Rampal shortly left. Varmaji, who had ceased speaking to Babloo in the past weeks, relaxed, put his feet up on the cot, and talked with him and his children, taking it as a chance to thaw relations. They did not discuss the factory. That evening, once Firoz returned, Durgawati served sweet vermicelli to his Muslim friends living close by, and gave a bowl of chicken curry to Firoz.[107] In these experiences, one could see the integrative work of festivity, in the activities of assisting, hosting, visiting, and giving respect to one another, which could vitally nurture possibilities for closer relations between and among Hindus and Muslims.

In the 2004 struggle, one of the posters composed by the B156 workers advised Okhla workers to be wary of *Kalyug*-like brothers (*Kalyugi bhai*), who might collaborate with managements to undermine the livelihoods of other worker-brothers (*mazdur bhai*). In the activities of Naresh and Varmaji in the city and village, one could also see an implicit message to avoid acting like distorted brothers, expressing a *Kalyug*-like brotherliness (*Kalyugi bhaicara*), by adhering to insularities and evincing hostilities to do with identities of caste and religion. In deviating from village norms, assisting and hosting other migrants, and building friendships, within and beyond caste and religious boundaries, they were attempting, imperfectly and incompletely, to practice a less distorted, more integrative form of fellowship (a less *Kalyugi bhaicara*) among migrants in Delhi.

Filaments

"[F]actory workers are, in a sense, truly uprooted beings, exiles in their own land," writes Weil.[108] In Varmaji's early peregrinations around Delhi, when he ventured into elite localities like Defence Colony, he would feel apprehensive, that he might be asked at any time, by security guards or residents, what he was doing there, given his revealing garb and gait of a migrant worker. At such times, he realized that he was in the city, not the village, in a space distant from home (*pardes*), a space that was not one's own (*paraya des*).

But in that uprootedness, migrant workers work to weave a complex social fabric, spanning across the city and village. I invoke here the image of warp and weft (*tana bana*), the cross-weaving pattern of handloom textiles, to describe this social fabric.[109] The warp and weft might be seen to be constituted partly, and perhaps dominantly, through disintegrative forces, which include large-scale processes of development, inducing deprivation, low-wage work, and ecological vulnerabilities in villages, and pushing migrants to cities; inherited ideas and practices in the village to do with untouchability, patriarchal controls over women's lives, and communal politics; and difficult and hazardous working and living conditions in the city, contributing to bodily losses and illnesses. Augmenting the disintegrative forces are migrants' own looting strategies, excessive intoxicant usage, domestic discord, and insularities to do with caste and religious identities. These disintegrative forces stretch, pull apart, weaken, and rupture the social fabric. They contribute to the hollowing of bodies, destructive experiences of the *cakravyuh*, and more egoistic forms of fellowship.

Against these disintegrative forces, one sees the workings of integrative filaments in the warp and weft.[110] These filaments include empathetic closeness and common struggle in families, whereby migrants attempt to forge less tumultuous habitations within the *cakravyuh*. These filaments involve deviations from caste insularities, distancing from the violent politics of religion, and the building of more close and deep forms of fellowship. Integrative filaments work to attend to bodily losses, resist isolation, and mitigate the hollowing process. They interconnect multiple Abhimanyus, across boundaries, in their struggles with disintegrating forces.

Given the difficulties of accumulation in the city, migrants are often not able to return quickly to the village, with their *izzat* intact. They find themselves caught in an indefinite exile in an inhospitable city. Through the weaving of integrative filaments, migrants build a fragile dwelling, not only in their city rooms and village homes, but within the warp and weft of connections among family members, relatives, neighbors, coworkers, friends, and others, across spaces of the city and village. This fragile dwelling not only keeps migrants alive. It allows them to realize a bit of the good life, in affective bonds, *izzat*, and conviviality, during exile, not in a vague future.

CHAPTER 6

Churning

Migrant workers confront a multitude of difficulties in their lives. They contend with deprivation in the village, congested living conditions in urban neighborhoods, dirty and dangerous work processes in factories, mental tensions, envy, illnesses, accidents, work stoppages, terminations, familial discord, doctors' negligence, deaths, and exile in the city. This chapter explores migrant workers' understandings of the causes of these difficulties and the proper responses to suffering in the world.

Why is there such suffering in migrant workers' lives? Is the world just? What should they be doing in the present world? What future might they hope for? I begin by describing workers' discourses on the sources of difficulties in their lives, with reference to ideas of fate, action, and God. I then discuss views of the contributions to suffering of the present, decivilizing epoch of the *Kalyug*, which promotes distortions in societies and souls, and possibly, in God. The noncooperative and integrative activities of migrant workers, outlined in the previous chapters, I suggest, might be interpreted as efforts to decelerate the progress of the *Kalyug*, through a process of churning (*manthan*) in souls and time. In pursuing these activities, migrants articulate hope in the possible effectivity of resistances to the decivilizing process, which might defer and alleviate the destructiveness of the future dissolution of the world.

Difficulty

In discussions with migrant workers about difficult experiences in their milieus, such as injuries, illnesses, or deaths, one often hears references to the workings of fate (*qismat*). Fate is understood as a written narrative of the course of one's life, including its most significant events, and also, potentially, the microdetails of one's thoughts, feelings, relations, and activities. Though fate is written by God, it is shaped by one's actions (*karm*), which give rise to consequences.[1] "As you sow, so shall you reap (*Jaisa karm vaisa phal*)" is a saying articulated in conversations (among Hindu and Muslim workers), films, songs, and the news media. One's actions in previous lives shape one's fate, but as these actions are unknown, they provide little assistance in making sense of present experiences. Rather, workers invoke proximate, imprudent actions in this life, such as leaving school, falling into drinking circles, and entering the metal polishing line, when giving causes for their present, difficult conditions.[2] The fate narrative of one's future can also be altered by one's present actions.[3]

While a predominant tendency is to seek causes for difficulties in one's own acts, narratives also draw in the actions of proximate and remote others as contributing causes. For example, difficulties in the village might be attributed to the actions of ancestors, for not educating children enough or not getting them into government jobs; envy, ill-wishing, and spirit affliction practices of relatives, which can induce illnesses and deaths; and the actions of political leaders, governments, and state officials in failing to bring about employment-generating development, forcing persons to migrate for work. In discussing the causes of Uday's tuberculosis, workers spoke of his arrogant pursuit of speed, the excessive debris emanating from the buffs, and the curses of other polishers. Varmaji's cycle accident was brought about by his dubious allegiances in the factory, his drinking practices, and the curses of Durgawati and the *hijra*. Ramdev's death was induced by the company's delaying of wages, a driver's recklessness, and triage by the Safdarjung Hospital doctors. A causal role is also left for the mysterious workings of fate. Rather than seek a single cause for conditions or events involving difficulty or suffering, workers gather multiple causes, and attribute varying degrees of innocence and culpability to suffering persons.[4] As workers say, "In one event, many things are causally involved."[5]

As one acts within a complex field of causes (fate, one's actions, others' actions) only partly amenable to one's control, migrants advocate focusing on one's own right conduct or good actions (*accha karm*), for example, doing hard work, avoiding lying, deceiving, cheating, and stealing, respecting elders, and praying to God, which can generate good consequences (*acche phal*). Though workers confront oppression and injustice in their lives, they articulate beliefs in a deeper, *karmic* justice in the world. Images emerge of a just, benevolent, and fearsome God, who might permit oppressors to engage in wicked activities for a time, before administering punishment. At a time when the B156 managers were intensifying work and being rewarded with salary hikes, Uday invoked a village saying, "God gives abundantly but takes terrifyingly."[6] "God is aware of all the oppression that is going on in our company, and thinks, 'I will certainly take revenge,'" said Firoz.[7] Within this scheme of justice, workers' difficult existences could also be viewed as possible *karmic* punishment for actions as past oppressors. "Who knows, those who are oppressing us, it might be a story carrying on from a past birth, and we're suffering the punishment. In our past birth, we oppressed them, today they are oppressing us," Amlakant reflects.[8] This does not excuse present oppressors, whose actions provoke resistances and future punishments, including possible rebirth as wage workers.

There might be other divine purposes for the difficult lives of wage workers, aside from *karmic* punishment. For Babloo, God (*Allah*) constructs an unequal world, with wealthy and poor people (*amir garib*), so that these classes become the means (*vasila, zariya*) for one another's livelihoods. The wealthy create companies, establish factories, earn incomes, and give employment to others. The poor, due to deprivation, are driven into servitude (*gulami*) and wage work for the wealthy, which give them livelihoods and allow them to survive. The functioning of the world, as arranged by God, requires unequal classes, deprivation, and suffering.[9] The suffering of the poor, Hanif says, may be a test (*pariksha*) given by Allah, within a context of multiple births in diverse circumstances. Good kings might be reborn as beggars, so God can see if they choose ethical paths within conditions of deprivation, not luxury. God creates difficulties in the lives of working people as part of a divine, inscrutable design (*uparvala ki maya*), Firoz says, so that they will be induced to pray to God for assistance in their struggles. "God figures, 'The wealthy will stay busy with their money matters, when will they think of God. The poor will take God's name,'" he says.[10] Deprivation has diverse, divine purposes.

In seeking to explain the difficulties in migrant workers' lives, Amlakant offers an image of the world as an unfolding, divine drama (*lila*). In one version of this drama, God is all-controlling, manipulates human beings like puppets, decides what actions they will do, and dispenses rewards and punishments.[11] "God is writing a drama, and we act as its characters. Like in films, a writer writes the story, on that basis they make a film, and the director makes all of them dance according to that story. We're marionettes. We dance as we are made to dance," he suggests.[12] God observes from above and manipulates characters, but is also immanent and indwelling within living beings and feels their experiences and emotions in the world. The purpose of this *lila* is God's amusement. "He's putting on his own drama," Amlakant says. "He makes someone do wrong, makes another deliver the punishment, gets someone killed, gives birth to another. By lifting and moving us about, He's entertaining Himself."[13] Given the densities of difficulties in the lives of the poor, and the apparent absence of deep contentment (*atma ki santushti*) even for the wealthy, this entertainment seems to be only for God. "If one looks at the whole *lila*, it is without any substantive enjoyment (*niras*). There's nothing joyful in it at all," he observes. "And *Ram Rajya* (the ideal society of Ram's rule) is not on the horizon."[14]

But Amlakant also gives a different reading of the *lila*, in which there is freedom, a benevolent God, and *karmic* justice. God constructs the *lila* to show the workings of *karm*, that good actions generate beneficial consequences, and wrong deeds (such as the arrogant, oppressive activities of Hiranyakashipu in the *Puranas* and Ravan in the *Ramayana*) bring about destruction. By beholding the *lila*, human beings, who are autonomous (not automatons), gain knowledge of *karm*, and decide how they wish to act in this drama, with attendant consequences. "There are many ways to dance [in God's *lila*]," says Varmaji. "One can dance a dance of devotion (*bhakti*) or of ethical deviation (*adharm*)."[15] Action in the world becomes an acquired artistic activity.

A ground-level view of the divine drama, which draws in elements of the above narratives, is that of the world as *mela* (festive gathering). *Melas* are fairs or carnivals, in villages and cities, which conjure images of festivity, crowds, markets, street food, music, dance, folk theater, livestock, circuses, amusement rides, spiritual discourses, and worship activities. "In a *mela*, one gets everything," migrants say.[16] God sends human beings into the *mela* to experience many things. "Like one's parents send one, saying, 'go for the *mela*,' God is like that. He's sent us into a *mela*, 'Go, have a good time, undergo difficulties and hardships, and return. To play, go through travails, for everything, go. Then I'll take you back,'" Naresh says.[17] All of these things should be experienced in some measure, if one is to avert arrogance that comes from enjoying too many comforts; develop empathy for others who are suffering; recognize joy and the good, which requires knowledge of their opposites, sorrow and wrongdoing; and understand the diversity of life.[18]

There is dynamic flux in the *mela*, in changes to one's finances, bodily health, character, and respect, and in processes of meeting, mixing, separating, exiting, and reentering the world. While this flux can take on precarious forms for migrant workers, such that one's existence becomes fragile, unpredictable, and vulnerable to force, it keeps alive hopes and possibilities for changes in fortunes and well-being.[19] The poor are sent into the *mela* with the constraints of material deprivation and *karm*-generated fate. But it is for them to utilize their God-given minds and bodies, acquire knowledge and artistry (*kalakari*) to survive and earn livelihoods, understand the workings of *karm*, and decide how to live in the world. Naresh says, "In the *mela*, how one is to do things, what to eat, what work to do, that's in our hands. How to go about things to survive, or to stay hungry, what skills to learn so as to earn more. If one does wrong, one will get bad fruits, if one does right, one will get good fruits. God is seeing how folks are doing things, how they're going about things."[20] In the world as *mela*, there is agency, artistry, *karmic* justice, a present, witnessing God, and diverse and dynamic possibilities.

Justice

But why do migrant workers confront such a magnitude of difficulties and hardship in the world as *mela*? Alongside the gathering of causes (one's own actions and fate, others' actions, divine purposes), narratives suggest a deeper cause—the temporal context of the *Kalyug*. The *Kalyug*, whose origins are given by migrants as several years to twenty thousand years ago (texts date its beginnings to 3102 BCE), is an epoch that distorts thoughts, feelings, motives, actions, and dealings. Human relations become increasingly dominated by self-interest, avarice, envy, deception, muscle force, and violence, and less guided by truth, respect, and compassion. The *Kalyug* is spoken of as a wicked agent that draws and pulls persons toward it, enters minds and souls, and gets persons to engage in ethically wrong actions, such as deceiving, lying, stealing, and murdering. Rather than God as puppeteer, "The *Kalyug* makes us dance," says Varmaji.[21]

The *Kalyug* does this through a deep interplay. The epoch distorts the souls of human beings by activating, encouraging, and bolstering the dominance of the soul's demonic valence over the soul's true, good valence, and nudging souls to engage in egoistic, deviant, and wicked activities. Distorted souls, propelled by demonic proclivities, engage in deviant activities, which contribute further to the distortions of the *Kalyug*. In this interplay of souls and the *Kalyug*, souls collaborate in decivilizing activities, give momentum to the *Kalyug*, and advance its progress toward destructive dissolution. The magnitude of difficulties in migrant workers' lives could be seen to arise from this interplay.[22] Fields of causes become dominated by distorted activities—by others and by migrant workers—giving rise to a multitude of suffering caused by others' deviant actions and by *karmic* punishments due to one's own past and present wrongful actions.[23] "The *mela* is unfolding according to the ways of the epoch," says Naresh.[24] The world becomes a *Kalyug*-like *mela* (*Kalyugi mela*), a nonfestive gathering of agency, distortion, and suffering.

The workings of the *Kalyug*-like *mela*, driven by an intimately distorting interplay, were visible in the multiple contexts of migrant workers' lives. First, at the factory, the management engaged in manipulations, deceptions, and divisive dealings, kept invisible workers, gave depressed wages, eroded existing benefits, and made efforts to terminate workers due to desires for work increases, cost reductions, and greater control, egoistic ambitions, and managerial conflicts. These activities could be assisted by workers' collaboration, loyalty, envy, looting mentalities, spectatorship, and acquiescence, driven by egoistic interests, passions, fears, weaknesses, and compelling difficulties, despite beliefs in the ethical wrongness of assenting to oppression. This field of distorted activities of the management and workers could generate myriad forms of suffering, in work intensification, tensions, bodily losses, injuries, illnesses, deprivations, capitulations, and terminations of managers and workers.

Second, migrants confronted distorted activities in diverse spaces of the city. In dealings with the labor office, they witnessed the slow, tedious progress of complaints and the offstage, collusive activities of labor officials in legal violations and the terminations of workers. On the streets of Delhi, they encountered police officers who spoke rudely, threatened them with beatings with bamboo staffs, and removed them from protest sites, as desired by the management. At government hospitals, they experienced brusque, callous speech, negligence, and triage by doctors, nurses, and staff persons, exacerbating the hardships and vulnerabilities of injuries and illnesses. In neighborhoods, amid congested space, limited water supplies, and poor sanitation facilities, migrants contended with the rough speech, intimidating presence, and restrictive controls of Gujjar landlords. They could engage in excessive intoxicant usage, giving rise to mounting debts, mental tensions, and discord in families. They could exhibit insularities to do with caste and religious boundaries, in accordance with village norms.

Third, in the village, large-scale development processes were not generating adequate, proximate livelihoods to meet the cash requirements of farming, medical costs, and the servicing of debts, inducing migration to distant cities and separation from families. Migrants speak of the seepage of the *Kalyug* into social relations in the village, in the loss of *izzat* for elders, the absence of time for social dealings, the rising importance of money and its display (e.g., in house building and weddings), and intensified tensions and hostilities to do with caste and religious identifications and competitive envy. The *Kalyug* also influences changes in ecologies, in the increasing use of soil-enervating chemical fertilizers and pesticides, depleting of groundwater supplies, rapid deforestation, and polluting of rivers, guided by development policies, short-sighted visions, and compulsions, inducing suffering for present and future generations.[25]

It was not just B156 that was a microcosm of the *Kalyug*. The labor office, city streets, government hospitals, neighborhoods, the family, and the village were microworlds of egoistic, disintegrative, and destructive activities characteristic of the *Kalyug*. These pervasive, distorted activities could be seen to arise from an intimate interplay of the *Kalyug* and the souls of managers, workers, state officials, police officers, doctors, landlords, neighbors, family members, political leaders, and many others. These diverse human beings, acting on demonic proclivities, were promoting the *Kalyug* across the world-*mela,* inducing difficulty and suffering for migrant workers and damage to the ecological world.

Given the distorted nature of the world-*mela*, questions arose about *karmic* laws and justice. Did hard work really generate good fruits? Many migrants had been doing hard work since their days in the village—in schools, fields, factories, brick kilns, construction, streetside eateries, and other wage work. Yet they found themselves caught in precarious, low-wage, dirty, and dangerous work in Delhi. At B156, they could see that hard work in naïve and reckless forms could be exploited and could eventuate in illnesses, *izzat* losses, *haq* deprivations, retrenchments, and death. Hard work could give rise to bodily decline, swindling, and exodus. Some expressed doubts about whether the alleged good fruits of hard work were realizable in workers' lives. Others wondered if the good fruits might accrue to one's descendants. They also observed that persons engaging in ethically distorted activities seemed to be receiving good fruits of comforts, power, and longevity, not *karmic* punishments. *Karmic* laws seemed to be inverted (*ulta*) in the *Kalyug*. One could not always see the workings of a deeper justice.[26]

These apparent inversions might arise, Amlakant suggests, because God is disappointed at the distorted activities of his own rebellious marionettes. "God too must feel saddened about his own creation, that 'what I created is doing such things,'" he says. "The Maker just made human beings. But when doing so, He probably didn't think, 'The toy I am making will also be explosive.'"[27] God might also be saddened and disturbed by the decline in *izzat* for the divine in the *Kalyug*. "Everyone wants *izzat*, whether one is a human or an animal. All things seek *izzat*," says Uday.[28] As God cannot endure these *izzat* losses, He retreats from the world, enters into objects such as stones, and dwells there until the end of the *Kalyug*.[29] Distortions are allowed to continue without obstruction. Apparent inversions of *karmic* laws can make it seem as if God too has been corrupted by the *Kalyug*. "Even God has not remained good. God is going along with the ways of the *Kalyug*," Naresh suggests.[30] But he admits that there could be a deeper vision and design at work. The *Kalyug*, as one of four epochs in the unfolding structure of time, cannot be restrained or reversed, even by God, and must be allowed to complete its course before regeneration can take place.[31] God might permit distortions to intensify and accumulate, rather than intervene to set things right, so as to allow the *Kalyug* to quickly progress toward its telos of creative-destructive dissolution (*pralay*).

There is ambiguity and uncertainty as to how dissolution is to occur, but narratives suggest that it might involve the escalation of ethical deviations;[32] violent conflicts, wars, and the possible use of nuclear weapons; ecological disruptions such as landslides, cyclones, earthquakes, and tsunamis (as reactions of the earth to alleviate the excessive, accumulating weight of the oppression of human beings and violence to nature); the leveling of the earth's surface (in the transitional period of the *Bhatyug* [age of leveling] prior to the *Satyug* [epoch of truth]);[33] and the descent of the incarnate divine (*avatar*) to mediate the destruction and regeneration of the world. But alongside these views of distortion, inversion, and a grim temporal telos, workers also articulate beliefs that hard work does generate good fruits (at some point of time); there can be limited justice (e.g., punishments of wrongdoers, restorations of livelihoods) in the present, administered by an observing God; and God is immanently, intimately present in human beings, even within the *Kalyug*. Narratives suggest that an *avatar* may descend not just due to intensifying degeneration, but also in response to the accumulating devotion of human beings.

Among Muslim workers, cognate and distinctive discourses arise on agency, soul distortion, decivilization, and a destructive telos of time. As a cognate discourse to the contest of true and distorted tendencies within the soul, Firoz speaks of the efforts of the Devil (*Shaitan*) to capture souls (*atma*, *ruh*) and turn them away from Allah, the omnipresent and immanent divine. The success of the Devil is manifested in wicked activities of human beings and resulting decivilizing processes, which are propelling the world toward the *Qayamat* (doomsday).[34] Signs of the impending *Qayamat* are visible in the world, says Babloo, in technologies such as television, fashions of women's clothing, pornographic films, disobedience to one's parents, love marriages, the loss of closeness among siblings, and the decline in the reading of the Quran. In the progress toward doomsday, says Firoz, the world will witness intensifying oppression, muscle force, rioting, wars, climate change, and natural disasters. In this process, the *Kalyug* acts as a devil (*shaitan*), luring souls into distorted activities (such as the manager's *Kalyug*-promoting actions at B156) and bringing the world closer to doomsday. "The *Kalyug* is drawing us toward the *Qayamat* (*Qayamat ki taraf khimcta a raha hai Kalyug*)," he says, offering a glimpse of the interweaving of categories and understandings in Muslim workers' narratives.[35]

The magnitude of difficulty and suffering that migrant workers confront in the world-*mela* seems to arise from the distorted activities of many agents (including themselves) in multiple spaces, intimately encouraged by the *Kalyug*, and permitted by a witnessing, possibly *Kalyug*-like God. In the immediate, visible world, actions do not necessarily yield just consequences, though there might be intermittent glimpses of justice. But beyond the immediate and visible, with a longer time horizon, perhaps extending beyond one's death, migrants seem to affirm the possibility of a deeper, opaque, and just world, in which *karmic* justice is upheld by a non-*Kalyug*-distorted God.[36]

Artistry

Given the destructive telos of time, what do migrants believe they should be doing with their agency in the present world? Despite the awareness of being caught up in distorting entanglements in the factory, city, and village, they do not offer ethical justifications for their collaboration. They are also aware that these distorted activities incur costs, in losses to bodily health, *izzat*, *haq*, and togetherness. They do not defend a stance of allowing the *Kalyug* to intensify without obstructions, as some suspect God might be doing. Rather, they argue that persons should try to act ethically, change present society, and restrain the accelerating distortions of the *Kalyug*. Amlakant says, "One should keep making efforts. One shouldn't think to let things go as they're going. One should try to change society, bring about a good society, bring a wrongdoing person onto the right path. It's not certain how successful one will be, but one should try, everyone should try—me, you, anyone—to bring change. Because the present low speed—destruction is occurring slowly, morality is declining slowly—its reason is that we're making efforts now to change this society. The speed is increasing slowly. But if those efforts cease, the speed will suddenly increase many times."[37] Through ethical efforts, Uday suggests, we should try to slow down the acceleration of the *Kalyug*. As polishers regulate speed to conserve bodies and resist work intensification, and apply excessive force to blow the motors of machines, human beings should attempt to restrain or arrest the gyrations of the *Kalyug* qua age of machines (*machini yug*). But the gyrations will continue toward an apocalyptic telos. "We know that things are not going to change, and someday in the future, it's all going to be destroyed, and then the *Bhatyug* (earth-leveling age) will come," admits Amlakant.[38] "We know that the *Kalyug* won't stop, it has to go forward," says Uday.[39] Still, one attempts to limit the suffering and damage generated by progressively distorted fields of activities, despite the catastrophic telos of time. One attempts to slow down time, and defer the dissolution of the world.[40]

Yet migrants do not clearly outline the ways in which social change is to be brought about. They might refer to the need for better governments, honest political leaders, revolution,[41] or the descent of an *avatar*. They also emphasize the measures that all persons can take to act in less distorted ways, by avoiding deception, lying, stealing, and doing harm to others, and trying to get others in one's milieus to do the same. But in workers' lives, one observes actions and dealings that might be interpreted as attempts and efforts, conscious or otherwise, at what might be termed anti-decivilizing activities in the *Kalyug*, in noncooperation, integrative filaments, and devotion.[42]

First, anti-decivilizing activities are discernible in the factory, in noncooperative and integrative processes. In auto-regulated working, workers engage in hard work, in less naïve, reckless, and egoistic forms, by adjusting workloads, speed, and quality to conserve bodies, avoid harming others, and protect livelihoods. In expressing lateral *izzat* to one another, they resist the divisiveness of competitive envy, encouraged by managerial machinations. In humor, in certain valences, migrants affirm the desire to live, draw closer together, and articulate auto-critiques of excessive work, submission, and insularity. In forging collectivity, through unity and synchrony politics, they engage in meetings, deliberations, and refusals, practice restrained working, and pursue struggles for the *haq* of better wages, perquisites, and job restoration. In a nonviolent struggle for the *haq* of quasi-legal work and the sustenance of an ethico-political microsociety, they experience empathetic bridges with others in the industrial area, on city roads, in their own families, and across distant borders.

Second, in the social fabric of spaces of the city and village, migrants engage in affective, integrative activities. In neighborhoods, they assist one another in exchanging loans, looking after new migrants, finding jobs, and attending to relatives in times of illness. They move among the rooms, joke and laugh, and eat and relax together, mitigating the hollowing effects of exhaustion, tension, and isolation. In empathetic exchanges and common struggles, they grow closer to their spouses, amid tension, discord, differing ambitions, and restrictive valences of *izzat*. In developing friendships within and across boundaries of caste, region, and religion, they forge fragile dwellings and closer, deeper varieties of fellowship, in spaces of prolonged exile, distant from the village.

Third, in practices of devotion, migrants weave integrative filaments to the divine, and seek assistance in travails and struggles. In prayer and worship, to Vishvakarma, Hanuman, Durga, Allah, the Buddha, Ravidas, Sufi saints, and others, they ask for protection and blessings in negotiating bodily hazards and distorted *karmic* fields. Though Naresh expresses doubts about *karmic* laws and the existence of a just God in the *Kalyug*, he goes to the Kalkaji temple and participates in Chath Puja, with the hope that God exists, and that the good fruits of hard work will one day be realized. Through devotion and good actions (e.g., avoiding causing harm to others, assisting others in need, speaking truth, and not submitting to oppression), says Firoz, the *Kalyug*, qua a devil, can be kept at a distance from minds and souls. On his own efforts, he says, "I am firmly taking on the *Kalyug*, to the best of my abilities."[43] If prayer at temples and mosques and other good actions were to increase in the world, says Babloo, "The *Qayamat* will recede further into the future."[44] The deep purpose within the divine drama, Varmaji suggests, is for human beings to adopt and practice nonegoistic devotion (*nisvarth bhakti*), rather than ethical deviation, which involves prayer, service to others, and empathetic concern for the well-being of other souls, as sites of the indwelling divine.[45] These devotional activities, while restraining accelerating distortions in the *Kalyug*, can also invite divine interventions that deliver *karmic* justice, in limited degrees, within the present world.

Though migrant workers become enmeshed in distorting and disintegrative processes, they articulate aspirations to collaborate less with them. They attempt to survive and get ahead, but also to oppose oppression, give and earn *izzat*, forge closer relations, and seek the divine. One might read these activities as a kind of deeper artistry, drawing on Naresh's imagery, not just of acquiring skills to earn wages, but of pursuing good actions (*acche karm*) in the *Kalyug*, that seek to sustain and promote life within one's diverse milieus. In developing counterformulas to the *Kalyug*, migrants attempt to make the world-*mela* less oppressive and isolating, and more life enhancing. The world becomes not only a Kurukshetra-like battleground of combat, *cakravyuhs*, death, and destruction. It becomes a space of possible respect, humor, friendship, intimacy, and glimpses of joy, a less distorted, more festive *mela* of existence.[46]

While it might be difficult to say how effective anti-decivilizing activities might be against the accelerating speed of the *Kalyug*, this uncertainty (or darkness [*andhkar*]) should not impede efforts to bring about transformations, as Amlakant observes. One attends, with duty and compassion, as Uday suggests, to fragile, precarious, and possibly doomed lives. While migrants seem to undertake these activities so as to not endure ethical wrongdoing, alleviate difficulties in their milieus, and realize a bit of life in the present, anti-decivilizing activities also seem to aspire, wittingly or otherwise, to longer-term visions of possible *karmic* justice, prolonged life for human society, and a less cataclysmic passage out of the *Kalyug*.

In the final days of his life, Gandhi offered a talisman to guide persons through difficult decisions and dilemmas. "Recall the face of the poorest and the weakest man whom you may have seen, and ask yourself, if the step you contemplate is going to be of any use to him? Will he gain anything by it? Will it restore him to a control over his own life and destiny? In other words, will it lead to Swaraj for the hungry and spiritually starving millions?"[47] Migrant workers, caught in oppressive, difficult contexts, seem to live by an implicit, modified talisman.[48] Act so as to slow down the pace of the *Kalyug* and defer the *Qayamat*, their words and activities seem to be suggesting. Do not grease the cogs of the machine age. In this struggle, draw on what is best within one's soul and within the *Kalyug*.[49]

Temporal Agitation

To understand the possible relations of entangling, decivilizing processes and noncooperative, anti-decivilizing activities in migrant workers' worlds, I suggest the integral image of churning (*manthan*).[50] In the *Puranas*, the gods and demons come together, with the aid of Vishnu in the tortoise *avatar*, to churn the ocean of milk, which brings forth many things, including poison, a gem, a tree, animals, celestial nymphs, goddesses, the moon, and the nectar of immortality. In the factory, one witnesses the gyrations of the entangling interplay of the management and workers, along with its buttressing interplay of the demonic soul-valence and the *Kalyug*, confronted by the countergyrations of noncooperative attempts to conserve bodies and forge collectivity, drawing on proclivities of the true, good soul-valence.[51] In the city and village, one sees the gyrations of disintegrative, destructive forces opposed by the countergyrations of the weaving of integrative filaments to other human beings and the divine, exhibiting the life-promoting capacities of the true soul-valence. These gyrations and countergyrations might be seen to create churnings in the factory, social worlds, and souls, generating many things, such as ambitions, envy, illnesses, deaths, terminations, struggles for *izzat* and *haq*, empathy, fellowship, and festivity.[52]

The countergyrations of anti-decivilizing activities need not be seen, as workers at times suggest, as futile, doomed efforts to be engulfed by the progress of the epoch to its inevitable telos. They might be read as vital efforts to restrain decivilizing gyrations and slow down time, making the world-*mela* less precarious and more inhabitable in the present, and creating *karmic* possibilities for future, less distorted societies and souls. One might hope, in darkness, without evidence, that this churning might give rise not only to poisons, but also to transformative processes that can bring about better worlds for migrant workers and others, well before the finality of the *Kalyug* and the *Qayamat*.

POSTSCRIPT

There have been many developments in the lives of the B156 workers since the fieldwork for this book. I give here a sketch of the trajectories of their work lives, after the struggle across borders. The story is a grim one, recalling elements witnessed in the fieldwork, of machinations, resistances, injuries, terminations, and exodus.

In 2006, after the resolution of the placards struggle, the B156 workers shifted to C82. Panditji, the elder checker, who was respected by the workers, was given charge of the unit. Shibbo Devi worked alongside him in the office, packing pieces. The C109 management left them alone. There was little pressure to increase production or quality. Some of the workers began to feel a sense of safety. Instead of working to strengthen and expand their linkages beyond the factory, in good times, before a possible crisis, they abruptly discontinued their park meetings.

Over the next years, the company resumed its machinations to enhance discipline and control. In 2007, the C109 and B156 workers were shifted to a multistory factory in Noida, Uttar Pradesh, eighteen kilometers from Okhla, with transfer letters and notices giving assurances of bus transport, continuity of wages (i.e., Delhi wage levels, which were higher than those in neighboring states), and continuity of service. When Khan sahab shifted workers from B156 to C82 in 2003–2004, transfer letters were not given, so this might have been an effect of the 2005 struggle. In the Noida factory, the managers worked to create microdivisions, by giving higher wages, bonuses, overtime earnings, and other perquisites to the C109 workers, while hiring contract workers through a security agency at Uttar Pradesh wage levels. They stopped the bus service for a time, and attempted to get workers to shift residence to Noida. They allowed the B156 workers' wages to drop below Delhi wage levels. In 2011, they shifted workers to a second Noida factory, without giving transfer letters. When Rambachan II suffered a serious injury to his leg at the machine, he was taken to a private hospital, not the ESI Hospital, and only after his insistence, was given an accident report, vital for obtaining ESI benefits.

There were also workers' efforts at resistance and collectivity, through auto-regulated working, intermittent park meetings, and writing letters to the management. These letters, signed by the B156 workers and varying sections of the C109 workers, made requests for the resumption of the bus service, restoration of Delhi wages, better pollution controls, transfer letters, and more decent managerial behavior inside the factory. Justice for Workers, which was aware of the developments in Noida, also wrote letters to the American company, inquiring about the workers' requests. Due perhaps to these combined actions, the management restarted the bus service, gave pollution masks and backdated transfer letters, and provided monthly rations, in lieu of raising wages. But the company seemed adamant about not giving Delhi wages, though they were transporting the workers from Delhi, where the costs of living were higher. The C109 workers were generally earning more than Delhi wages, with incentive payments and overtime earnings. It was not clear how Justice for Workers, a loose assemblage that coalesced during the struggle across borders, could agitate on behalf of the B156 workers, who were working in a larger unit of 150 workers, with differences in wages, terms of hire, and grievances, and who were inside the gate, not protesting on the streets.

In 2012, to tighten discipline and control, the management suspended three B156 polishers (Firoz, Rakesh, and Ramakant), with strange charges, such as inciting others to stop work, verbally abusing the managers, and shouting slogans outside the gate. After a long, convoluted legal process of inquiry, they were terminated. With the assistance of a Delhi-based lawyer, they contested the terminations in the labor court.[1] Perhaps not wishing to provoke a rekindling of the assemblage that occurred in the 2005 struggle, the management did not terminate more of the B156 workers. They tolerated them, perhaps unwillingly and uncomfortably.

Over the next years, the Jharkhandis, recognizing that the company was committed to keeping their wages depressed, drifted away from the factory. In the mid-2010s, Madan and Surinder migrated to polishing factories in Rajasthan, where their earnings were higher. In 2020, amid the mass exodus of workers from Delhi and other cities due to Covid, the B156 workers stayed in the Delhi region. The company gave partial wage advances during the lockdown, and after two months, the factory resumed production. In 2014, Naresh was gravely injured when a photo frame with a complex design got caught in the machine, shattering the bones of his left thumb. He had an operation at Safdarjung Hospital, and after his medical leave, shifted to the finishing department, where his etching work was highly regarded. During the pandemic, he left the factory to develop his own polishing and etching workshop in Noida, which grew to accommodate five polishing machines, and took orders from Metal Innovations and other companies. In 2023, Vinod returned to the village to focus on his wedding decorations business. Tapesvar shifted to polishing workshops in Tehkhand, where he continued to reside, close to the boundary. Rambachan left to run his welding workshop in Noida, along with his two sons. Amid this turbulence and exodus, Shibbo Devi, the sole woman worker in the factory, stayed on in Delhi, worked in the finishing department on helpers' wages, did sewing work at home for a contractor in the evenings, managed the weddings of her two daughters, and constructed a house in southeast Delhi, where she lived with her son.

In 2024, there were nine B156 workers still working in the factory, at wages of Rs. 12,154–14,779 (about $5–6 a day), with Amlakant approaching retirement, and Guptaji, Rambachan II, and Varmaji with long-term injuries. Rakesh and Ramakant, after six years of pursuing the labor court case, accepted settlements. Firoz still fought the case. Durgawati passed away, unexpectedly, from a heart attack in the village.

If one considers the strivings for a good life, with which this book began, it would be difficult to suggest that I have witnessed more than fragmentary, ephemeral glimpses of progress toward the realization of those elements in the B156 workers' lives. Yet I would wish to affirm their ongoing efforts toward that implicit vision, in trying to look after their bodies, resist wrongdoing, come closer to one another, and seek the divine. I would also wish to join in their implicit hope that through these efforts, the visible deprivations and injustices in their social worlds can possibly resolve into *karmic* and divine justice, in a perhaps distant, only vaguely visible future.

When one looks at other developments in India, it can certainly seem as if time is accelerating into deeper phases of the *Kalyug*, heading toward the *Qayamat*. One is witnessing growth without adequate employment generation, agrarian distress, pressures to migrate to cities (including after the Covid exodus), displacement and dispossession for development projects, ecological destruction in villages and cities, and the expansion of Hindu nationalist politics, as visible in the militant rhetoric of political leaders, violence to Muslims and lower castes in riots and lynchings, the construction of the Ram temple, and the demolition of mosques and dargahs. But alongside these processes, one has witnessed large-scale, noncooperative agitations.

Auto workers of the Maruti Suzuki factory in Manesar engaged in strikes and occupations in 2011–2012, in resistance to managerial practices and the activities of the company union, exhibiting vertical politics and horizontal energies, and developing solidarities between regular and contract workers, and with other workers, unions, students, and activists in the Delhi region, before the factory violence and during the long court cases. In 2019–2020, Muslim women anchored a sit-down protest in Shaheen Bagh, southeast Delhi, against state efforts to alter citizenship eligibility laws, in which empathetic linkages emerged with denizens of the locality, students, activists, artists, journalists, and many others in and beyond Delhi. In this protest, one could see the workings of autonomous, improvisatory politics, without visible leaders, the invoking of ideals of democracy, justice, nonviolence, and fellowship, drawing upon Gandhi, Ambedkar, Azad, and Abdul Ghaffar Khan, among others, and a grounding of resistance in legal understandings and religious practices.[2] During Covid, in 2020–2021, farmers in vast numbers gathered at the borders of Delhi, blocking and occupying roads, in protest against laws facilitating greater corporate control over agriculture, in which one observed the organizational politics of unions and the vibrant, autonomous energies at the protest sites (e.g., kitchens, libraries, a newspaper), and widening solidarities with workers, students, activists, and others in Delhi and India, extending to citizens and farmers in North America and elsewhere. These protests, attempting to improve the conditions for farming, were also questioning a development model that views large-scale migration from the countryside to cities as necessary and desirable for progress. If this book has sought to draw attention to the B156 workers' efforts to resist oppressive, disintegrative, and distortive forces, promote life, and slow down the *Kalyug*, these and other agitations, in India and the world, suggest that they are not alone in their struggles.

APPENDIX

Diagrams

This appendix offers a set of diagrams to give a visual image of the contrary processes of entanglement and noncooperation described in this book, which has assisted in my own understandings.

In Diagram 1, on the factory, the dominant trajectory is the entangling interplay of management and workers. The management deals in machinations of conciliatory speaking, enticing, punishing, and dividing (see the downward, counterclockwise arrow), while workers engage in active collaborating, loyalty, speed, modifications (for speed and quality), looting, envy, and valences of humor (as assisting work and expressing envy and hostility) (upward, counterclockwise arrow). A noncooperative trajectory emerges in which workers engage in modifications for safety and ease, resting, auto-regulated working, lateral respect (*izzat*), and valences of humor (as vital, integrative play and auto-critique) (clockwise, spiraling arrow). Along this trajectory, there are unity episodes motivated by discontent and the striving for justice (*haq*), which collapse due to machinations and vulnerabilities; restrained working (as extreme auto-regulated working); and a resurgence of unity (with Ganga water oaths), unionization, and work stoppages, eventuating in terminations, legal contestations, and the resumption of work. This trajectory culminates in a struggle across borders, which gives rise to widening linkages and restores livelihoods. In these noncooperative activities, there is the substratum presence of synchrony (*talmel*), as thoughts, feelings, methods, and energies, which infuses auto-regulated working, lateral *izzat*, unity actions, and protests.

Diagram 2 depicts the warp and weft (*tana bana*) of the city and village. The social fabric is partly constituted through the workings of disintegrative forces. Development processes push migrants to cities, where they confront difficult and hazardous working and living conditions. In their social dealings, migrants draw on village inheritances to do with caste practices (e.g., untouchability), envy (e.g., among kin relations), patriarchy (e.g., *izzat* as control over women), and communal politics (e.g., electoral politics, ground-level Hindu-Muslim tensions) (downward, counterclockwise arrow). In pursuing rapid accumulation and deferring proper life to an indefinite future, migrants become vulnerable to tensions, injuries, and illnesses, or the hollowing of minds and bodies. They can descend into excessive intoxicant usage and discord in the family, which can be experienced as a circular maze (*cakravyuh*), and they can exhibit insularity and hostility in caste dealings and Hindu-Muslim relations. These activities contribute further to the isolating, weakening tendencies in the social fabric (upward, counterclockwise arrow). Against these disintegrative gyrations, migrants weave integrative filaments to one another, drawing on concepts of duty and *izzat*, in empathetic costruggle in families and deeper varieties of fellowship, witnessed in the loosening in dealings among diverse castes, closer relations among Hindus and Muslims, and friendships. Through these activities, migrants forge

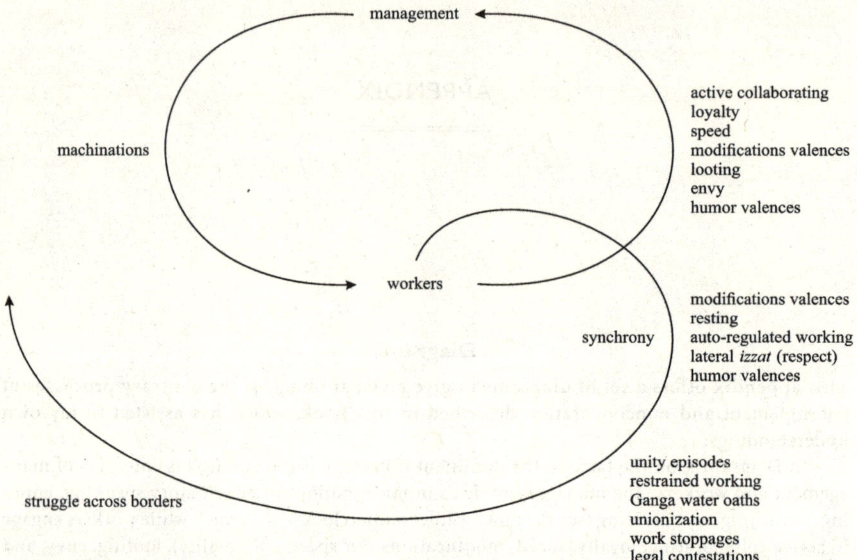

Diagram 1. The Factory.

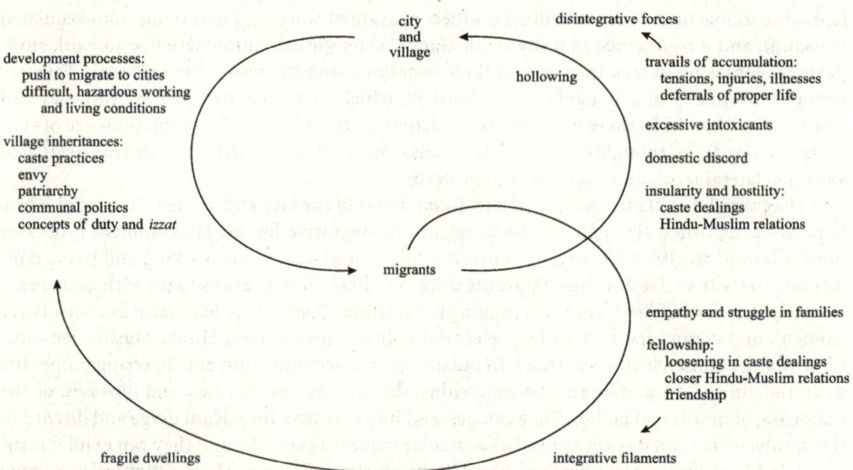

Diagram 2. Warp and Weft.

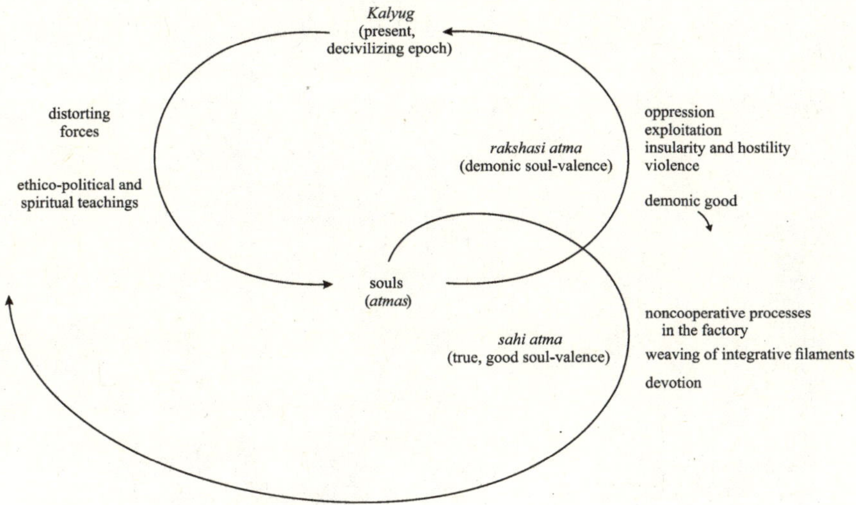

Diagram 3. Souls in the *Kalyug*.

fragile dwellings within these interconnections, and attempt to realize a bit of the good life in the present, prolonged exile from the village (clockwise, spiraling arrow).

In Diagram 3, on souls in the *Kalyug*, the present, decivilizing epoch can be seen to exert distorting forces on souls (downward, counterclockwise arrow), while souls acting on demonic proclivities (the demonic soul-valence [*rakshasi atma*]) engage in distorted activities, furthering the progress of the *Kalyug* (upward, counterclockwise arrow). These activities, guided by motives such as egoism and envy, give rise to and sustain oppression, exploitation, insularity, hostility, and violence to others and nature, but also include noncooperative demonic good (e.g., sabotage and restrained working). In the *Kalyug*, ethico-political and spiritual teachings (e.g., on the wrongness of enduring oppression) also become available as vital resources. Souls acting on truth-seeking tendencies (the true, good soul-valence [*sahi atma*]) engage in the artistry of anti-decivilizing activities, which includes noncooperative processes in the factory, the weaving of integrative filaments, and devotion (clockwise, spiraling arrow). One might understand the relations of the gyrations and countergyrations in these diagrams as processes of churning (*manthan*), within the factory, social worlds, and souls in the *Kalyug*, leading toward *pralay* (dissolution) and *Qayamat* (doomsday).

GLOSSARY

adivasi: original inhabitant
biri: leaf-wrapped cigarette
cakravyuh: circular maze
dhaba: streetside eatery
dhoti: cotton *sari* fragments used as face masks in the factory
guru: mentor, teacher
gutkha: a mix of tobacco, betel nut, and other ingredients
haq: right, just due; justice
hijra: third gender
izzat: respect
jhuk machine: bending, stooping machine
Kalyug: present, decivilizing epoch
karm: action
lila: play, drama
mal: goods, materials, stocks, stuff
man: mind, heart
mazak: humor, joking
mazdur: wage worker
mela: festive gathering
pan: betel leaf with areca nut and other ingredients
puja: worship ritual, festival
Qayamat: doomsday
talmel: synchrony in thought, feeling, or activity; autonomous collectivity

NOTES

Introduction

1. The numbers of migrant workers in India in the past two decades have been estimated to be 50 million to 175 million (Breman 2009:9; Deshingkar and Akter 2009:28; Mazumdar et al. 2013:55; Misra and Gupta 2021:733).

2. The vast majority of the workforce are informal workers, who work without legal provisions such as minimum wages, health insurance, provident fund (state-managed accounts into which deductions from workers' wages and employer contributions are deposited), annual bonus, and recourse against illegal terminations. Estimates from the period 1999–2012 suggest that informal workers constitute over 90 percent of the workforce (Mehrotra et al. 2014:52; NCEUS 2007:4). India's development process has been described as one of "jobless growth" due to the low levels of noninformal job creation (Drèze and Sen 2013:32, 340; Shrivastava and Kothari 2012:60–63).

3. These figures were given in company documents filed for a legal case in 2005.

4. Okhla factories were often referenced by managers, workers, and others by their plot numbers (e.g., B156), rather than by company names.

5. During the fieldwork, in the early 2000s, according to official figures, Okhla had 1,354 registered factories, employing 102,213 workers (Delhi Labour Department, Chief Inspector of Factories, July 2004; 19,016 of these workers were working in engineering industries, which included metal polishing factories). According to a survey conducted by the Indian Federation of Trade Unions in 2002–2003, there were 300,000 workers in Okhla, of whom only 15 percent were regular workers. News reports in the 2010s give figures of 3,000–4,500 Okhla factories (Yadav 2016; 2019).

6. For documentation of these processes in Okhla in the mid-nineties, see Lal Das (1997:38–45).

7. On the rise and workings of these unions in post-Emergency Delhi, see Mazumdar (2001:46–47). On the predominance of such unions in Okhla, see Lal Das (1997:36–37, 49).

8. As was common in Okhla, they were asked to sign appointment letters with extra pages that could be later utilized as resignation letters. Copies of these documents were not given to the workers.

9. The B156 workers were from Uttarakhand (6), Uttar Pradesh (38), Bihar (10), and Jharkhand (9), with one each from Madhya Pradesh and Kerala (considering 65 who worked at the factory). They identified as Hindu (56), Muslim (6), Buddhist (2), and Christian (1).

10. *Biri*: leaf-wrapped cigarette. *Pan*: betel leaf with areca nut and other ingredients.

11. On the importance of studying and giving space to diverse visions of the good life in the world, see Appadurai (2013:290–293, 299–300).

12. The words that indicate these strivings (e.g., *paisa*, *izzat*, *haq*, *samaj*, *bhaicara*) will be discussed in the book.

13. The category of entanglement also arises in Abdul Bismillah's novel *The Song of the Loom*, on handloom weavers in Benaras, in gesturing to the social and existential conditions of being caught up in exploitative economic dealings, financial difficulties, mental tensions, and illnesses (Bismillah 1996:87).

14. See Hardiman (2021).

15. A brief word might be given here on my own background. I grew up in New Jersey, raised by Tamil scientist parents from Kerala, who came to America for doctoral studies and postdoctoral work in the 1960s. Prior to college, my connections with India were mostly through food, language, childhood visits to India, Carnatic and Hindustani classical music, Hindi films, and my mother's devotional Hinduism. As a student of economics at Harvard College, I took courses on international development, the history of capitalism and work organization, and modern Indian history, and wrote a thesis on the development visions of Gandhi and Nehru, development economics, and emerging critiques of development in India. I later spent a year at the Centre for the Study of Developing Societies in Delhi, conducting a project on the politics and ideologies that animated the architects of the Green Revolution strategy in agriculture. I then went to graduate school in anthropology at the University of Chicago, where I took courses on the history and anthropology of modern India, and began exploring philosophy and theology (e.g., Kierkegaard, Nietzsche, Dostoevsky, and Weil). I also took part in study circles on Hegel and Marx, where I became acquainted with nonvanguardist and autonomist strands of Marxism. Through these experiences, I decided to work on migrant workers in Delhi for my doctoral fieldwork.

16. See Cleaver (1979), Edwards (1979), Guha (1983; 1989), Hardiman (2013; 2018; 2021), Kelley (1996), Ness (2016), Ngai (2005; 2016), Peña (1997), Scott (1990; 2012), and Thompson (1966; 1993).

17. See Graeber (2013), Peña (1997), Sitrin (2012), and Sitrin and Azzellini (2014).

18. See Desmond (2016) and Duneier (1992; 1999).

19. See Breman (1996; 2013), Chakrabarty (1989; 2008), Chandavarkar (1991; 1994), Joshi (2003), Parry (2020), and Parry et al. (1999).

20. In cinema, see *Do Bigha Zamin* (1953), *Gaman* (1978), *Aaghat* (1985), *Disha* (1990), and *Dharavi* (1991). In documentaries, see Rahul Roy's *When Four Friends Meet* (2001), *The City Beautiful* (2003), and *The Factory* (2015).

21. Majdoor Samachar-Kamunist Kranti (1996; 1998; 2020; 2021).

22. See R. Gandhi (1984; 2015), Hardiman (2021:292–302), Nandy (2013), Tracy (2020a; 2020b), Unger (1984; 2001; 2014), and West (1999a; 1999b; 1999c).

23. See Gooptu (2001:143–184, 263–286), Guha (1983:112, 294–297), Hardiman (1987; 2021:65–87, 274–275, 283), and Lutgendorf (1991:374–378).

24. See Agrawal (1994), R. Gandhi (1992; 2007), Nandy (2001; 2002), Nandy et al. (1995), and Naqvi (2012). In documentaries, see Anand Patwardhan's *Ram ke Naam* (1992), *Father, Son and Holy War* (1995), and *Reason* (2018). In literature, see Premchand (2017) and Reza (2008).

25. See Marx (1963; 1977) and Anderson (2010).

26. Dostoevsky (1956; 1983; 1992; 1994).

27. Weil (1951; 1952a; 1952b; 1977; 1986a; 1986b; 1986c).

28. M. Gandhi (1999; 2010).

29. These workers were Amlakant, Arun, Babloo, Bhagvati, Firoz, Jitender, Madan, Mahesh, Mathew, Mithilesh, Naresh, Rajender, Ramakant, Sabbir, Sivam, Sundar, Surinder, Uday, Umesh, and Varmaji.

30. My residence during the fieldwork was in south Delhi, about seven kilometers from Okhla.

31. For instructive works that attend to the language of working people, see Duneier (1999) and Willis (1977).

32. By retaining certain Hindi categories (e.g., *izzat*, *haq*, *Kalyug*), one hopes to avoid the potential distortions of erasing nuances through rough translation and exaggerating differences

through italicization. Rather, one wishes to locate such words in social contexts, describe their usage and importance, and convey their conceptual and political commonalities and distinctiveness vis-à-vis conventional English categories used in describing the lives and ideals of working people in the world (e.g., respect, dignity, rights, justice, democracy, revolution).

33. McGregor (1997). For Hindi words drawn from English, I retain the English spellings (e.g., *company, machine, tension*). I use *sh* rather than *s* without diacritics (e.g., *koshish*).

34. Duneier (1999:347–348).

35. The flame was shifted to a nearby site in 2022.

Chapter 1. Factory Work

1. These are Power Master machines manufactured by Prem Brothers in Delhi, which has been producing metal polishing and belt grinder machines since the early fifties and late sixties, respectively, drawing on German technologies and designs.

2. "*Jaldi karo, yar! Kya kar rahe ho, tum log?! Calu karo machine!*"

3. Weil (1977:54). The noise levels at the polishing and belt grinder machines during the workday, as measured with a decibel meter, are 79 to 107 decibels.

4. "*O haramkhorom! Chai pi lo!*"

5. "*Calo bhai, time ho gaya.*"

6. In the demographics of the factory, "young" refers to workers in their late teens to mid-twenties, while "elder" refers to those in their mid-thirties to mid-forties.

7. "*Tum log ghar par meat khate ho, vo to isse bahut bara hai. Yah bhi kha lo.*"

8. For an evocative and resonant account of the bathing rituals of prisoners in nineteenth-century Siberia, see Dostoevsky (1983:136–147).

9. "*Ram, Ram, Ram, Ram! Duhai Ganga Mai ki!*"

10. "*Eh tu kitna ganda kar raha hai! Tu ganda karne aya hai ki nahane aya hai?!*"

11. "*Kaham ja rahe ho?! Are do minat ruko bhai! Dekh le, jagah nahim hai, bhai!*"

12. "*Calo bhai, bahar nikal! Kya kar raha hai re? Bahut time laga diya! Khali tum log nahaoge, ham nahim nahaemge?! Aurom ko nahane de!*"

13. "*Calo bhai.*"

14. During the first year, the night shift began at 10 or 11 p.m., to give some rest to the machines.

15. "*Calo utho! Kya kar raha hai tum log?! Calo calo!*"

16. Khan sahab transferred Ramesh to the night shift for only three nights, he was told, due to a shortage of polishers, but he was never brought back.

17. "*Larakpan khel mem khoya, javani nind bhar soya, burhapa dekhkar roya.*"

18. "*Phataphat camak kholo!*"

19. "*Are sale mariyal, tune mera mal fail kar diya?! Upar se khecke phemk demge nice! Le a to idhar!*"

20. *Samosas*: deep-fried, triangular pastries filled with potatoes, peas, onions, and chilis. Bread *pakoras*: batter-fried, triangular sandwiches with spicy potato filling.

21. "*Us din samajh lo chutti hai.*" When there are two persons with the same first name, the second one to be hired (usually a night worker) is referenced with a "II" in addressing practices.

22. "*Rat sone ke lie bani hai, kam karne ke lie nahim bani hai.*"

23. *Bhang*: cannabis.

24. Legally, wages should be paid by the seventh of the month for companies of this size.

25. The polishers and helpers, therefore, are making $1–2 a day.

26. Overtime payments of about $10–31 (Rs. 500–1,500) are disbursed along with wages to casual workers, and separately to regular workers after the twenty-second of the month. Overtime is paid at one-and-a-half times the hourly wage, though the legal rate is double.

27. "*Hamji ki naukri, naji ka ghar.*"

28. "*Dekho, unka mal jaldi ban gaya! Tumhara nahim bana abhi tak! Calo camak kholo!*"

29. "*Tumhara mal pass nahim hua. Kya karte ho yar? Kya karigar ho tum? Batao kya production likhum? Aj kuch kam nahim hua!*"

30. On the phenomenon of active collaboration (*camcagiri*) in Indian politics, history, and literature, see M. Gupta (2016).

31. "*Subah subah admi ka dimag kharab ho jata hai.*"

32. The junior manager and checker once told me that in the absence of the supervisor, polishers might complete their production more quickly. They would feel less tense and agitated, and would make the pieces more carefully, necessitating less repairs, saving materials and time.

33. "*Bahut sirdardi hai yaham par. Production bhi nikalna hai. Mal bhi pass karana hai. Time bhi dekhna hai. Utne mem sab kuch bhi karna hai. Sabki batem bhi sunni hai. Majburi sab karati hai!*" "A wage worker means one who is compelled (*Mazdur ka matlab majbur*)," is a saying one hears among Okhla workers, meaning that migrants engage in and endure wage work out of compulsion in their lives, especially, economic needs in the village home.

34. "*Dimag kharab ho jata hai. Yahi hal hai ki kam karo aur bad mem lat bhi gand pe khao.*"

35. On the tension of getting others to work, Frederick Taylor writes, "After about three years of this kind of struggling, the output of the machines had been materially increased, in many cases doubled, and as a result the writer had been promoted from one gang-boss-ship to another until he became foreman of the shop. For any right-minded man, however, this success is in no sense a recompense for the bitter relations which he is forced to maintain with all of those around him. Life which is one continuous struggle with other men is hardly worth living" (Taylor 1998:24).

36. Weil (1977:59).

37. To describe this sought-after good image, workers used words such as *nam* (good name, fame), *chavi* (image), and *superhit* (referencing successful films and songs).

38. There are partial resonances here with Michael Burawoy's study of factory work, in which workers pursue speed for incentive pay, status, autonomy, satisfaction, and relief from boredom and fatigue (Burawoy 1979). At B156, speed could generate a good image, material advantages, ego satisfactions, and spaces of rest, but also, respect losses and lateral hostilities.

39. "*Sala aj dekhta hum Jharkhandi kaise bhagta hai!*"

40. "*Aj isko cot khiyaumga.*"

41. "*Apas mem log khud ko marna cahta hai.*"

42. Modified buffs require time, effort, and hardship to prepare. One must slowly and patiently cut and level a carefully selected buff with a blade at the machine, while spewing and ingesting fibers. Such buffs are highly valued, and polishers try to hide and protect them in one's workspace, stashing them in one's storage crate or under the ducts. Despite these efforts, they are pilfered, sometimes under one's nose, as when Varmaji comes over to one's workspace, and while chatting and examining one's pieces, subtly drags a modified buff out from under one's stool with his toes, and gently kicks it over to his machine. When a buff is stolen, a polisher might get up in a rage, shout abuses, and storm over to other machines, searching and pulling out things, hurling accusations at everyone. To guard against pilfering, when a polisher comes over and starts eyeing his crate (where he too keeps pilfered buffs), Amlakant shouts, "What are you looking at over here?! Don't touch that! (*Kya dekh rahe ho yaham?! Usmem hath mat lagao!*)" He grabs the other's shoulders, turns him around, and pushes him away. Polishers also share modified buffs, allow others to sit and use them at one's machine, and observe, discuss, and exchange methods and techniques.

43. On efforts of managements to acquire and exploit workers' knowledge in the history of the industrial workplace, see Edwards (1979), Marglin (1990), and Montgomery (1979).

44. "*Kuch isse khimcne ke lie bharti karte haim.*"

45. Maquila workers engage in modifications for safety, speed, and job protection (Peña 1997:177–212). They resist doing unpaid skilled work, by feigning ignorance or asking for higher wages, but the B156 polishers expect themselves, qua craftsmen, to continually come up with modifications.

46. While the business media often extols the innovative *jugad* practices of farmers, workers, and others, it does not necessarily emphasize their risks and hazards (Birtchnell 2011).

47. The value of hard work, migrants say, was taught in their village homes and schools. Children are told that if one does hard work, with dedication and diligence, in plowing the fields, seeding, irrigating, and other tasks, the yields will be good. In village schools, teachers advise them to work intently in their studies, if they want better futures.

48. "*Mehnat manav jivan ka mukhya adhar hai. Mehnat se admi ko sab kuch mil sakta hai. Bagair mehnat kuch nahim mil sakta hai.*"

49. "*Private naukri ka koi bharosa nahim hai. Aj hai, kal nahim.*" Government jobs, though rare, difficult, and costly to get, are viewed as more secure.

50. "*Ham log ko to ciriya ka ghomsla hai yah company. Jaise hava ata hai, andhi ata hai, vo ghomsla khatm ho jata hai. Phir kahim dusre jagah laga lemge jake. Yaham nahim to vaham, vaham nahim to vaham.*" Such workers, even when regularized, see themselves as "footloose" (see Breman 1996).

51. "*Admi socta hai ki calo, kamane aya hai. Ek sal ya do sal kasht sahna hai. Bardasht karemge. Jaldi jaldi kamao, punji banao. Lutne jaise admi kar raha hai, kisi tarah paise luto! Jab tak mauqa hai, mil raha hai, tab tak lut rahe haim. Pata nahim kal kya ho jaega, jaisin yaham ko sthiti dekh rahe haim.*" The word *loot* in the *Oxford English Dictionary* derives from the Hindi word *lut* (plunder). While looting is often used to describe the illegitimate activities of dacoits, thieves, political leaders who siphon funds, and factory managers who embezzle from companies, it is invoked here, with some amusement, to depict (legitimate) hard work for wages.

52. One sees glimpses of such cycles in the lives of auto workers in America (Hamper 1992). For a cinematic rendering, without intoxicants, see the frenzied work routine of Vasant, a migrant working in a textile mill and other jobs in Mumbai to rapidly accumulate savings, in *Disha* (1990).

53. "*[Yaham] admi zindagi thode hi ji raha hai. Bas kamaya hai, phir cal jaemge, sab apne admi ke sath rahemge. Udhar hi to jina hai zindagi. Bahut zindagi hai.*"

54. "*Sare din to ap khud kam karvate ho apni marzi se. Ek din to hamari Sunday chutti hai, bhaiyya, hamari marzi hai.*"

55. Weil (1952a:236).

56. The altered numbering can create bizarre, volatile situations, as when polishers are engrossed in final polishing at a machine and have not yet sent any of their pieces for checking, but suddenly get a piece "returned" to them with red marks all over it. This can generate outbursts of vulgar abuses. Once the numbering system has been put into doubt, Narayan and Kalim also capitalize on it. When they get their own shoddy pieces back for repairs, they might angrily object that they have been mistakenly sent someone else's pieces, and thrust them back into the helper's hands. To avoid the extra, tedious work of repairing such pieces, polishers prefer Narayan and Kalim to stick to collaborative activities, and shirk, sleep, and shout, rather than sit at the machines.

57. "*Kamcor! Do paise ka kam kar le!*"

58. "*Aisa nahim calega! Agar kam nahim karna hai to helperi kar lo!*"

59. "*Agar piece mem ek minat ka samay hai to Khan sahab ke samne to usmem car minat lagaumga. Sale ko ragarta rahumga, ulta sidha ragarta rahumga. Lo ap dekhte raho ap, meri bhi kalakari. Yah socemge ki ham, is piece mem bahut time lag raha hai. Ve cale jaemge, turant bhaga dumga us piece ko.*"

60. "*Ab dekho hoshiyar chand! Abhi tak ghum raha tha! Ab laga raha hai lancer!*"

61. "*Har admi kahta hai mehnat ka phal mitha hota hai. Thik hai, samajhte haim. Uska phal milte milte, pata nahim, ho sakta hai admi ka antim sanskar tak pahumc jae.*"

62. "*Manager-supervisor-malik ke lie, kabhi kam hi rahega, zyada nahim ho sakta hai production.*"

63. Auto-regulated working is distinct from work-to-rule in that it involves giving high-quality production, which requires much more than minimal observance of rules.

64. Eight of seventeen day-shift polishers and twelve of twenty-five night polishers, in the initial years, practiced auto-regulated working.

65. On craftsmen's practices of output regulation ("soldiering") in the history of America, see Edwards (1979), Montgomery (1979), and Taylor (1998).

66. If a polisher is seen counting pieces or discussing quantities at another machine, the supervisor can make a complaint to the manager, who might reprimand the polisher for interfering with the work of others.

67. "*Pamcom ungliyam barabar nahim hotim!*"

68. "*Usne gand marvaya to maim bhi gand marvaum?! Jao, banva lo usse!*"

69. Maquila workers adopt the practice of working "at a turtle's pace" (or *tortuguismo*) to avert workload increases (Peña 1997:112–121).

70. "*Kisi bhi karigar ki jan pyari hai, kam pyara nahim hai.*" Firoz sticks to his pace regardless of the styles of his partners. "Whoever sits with me, I first tell him, brother, however fast you want to go, if you want to work hastily and break your hands and legs, it doesn't matter to me. I am going to regulate my work (*Mere sath jo baithta hai maim usse pahle kah deta hum, bhai sahab apko kitna bhi tez kam karna hai, ap cahe jaldibazi karke usse apne hath per tor lo, hamse koi matlab nahim. Maim apne hisab se kam karumga*)."

71. Work ethics, amid other motives, guide styles of working slowly and diligently. Amlakant works this way, he says, due to a principle imbibed in childhood teachings that, "Whatever work you do, do it with hard effort and dedication. Whatever task you take up, do it properly and completely (*Jo bhi kam ap kijie, usko mehnat se, lagan se kijie. Jis kam mem hath lagao, use pura karke choro*)." Other factors also play a role. Sundar, an elder polisher, works slowly and thoroughly, going over areas of pieces extra times to be safe, as he cannot always see fine imperfections, due to weakened eyesight.

72. A strange exception is Surinder, a soft-spoken polisher from Uday's village in Jharkhand. He gets up many times and takes rounds to the storage ledge, rummaging for buffs he does not need, joking with helpers outside, or chatting with other polishers at their workspaces, while rubbing tobacco. The supervisor makes complaints and the manager scolds him, but Surinder does not change. If the manager does not take disciplinary action, it might be because Surinder is polite and pleasant, is close to Uday and Naresh, and his pieces pass. Even if the manager took action, it might not make much difference to Surinder. He is something of a free, looting bird, moving through many factories, leaving precarious nests on his own, and trying different lines of work. As with Madan (and often along with Madan), much of his loot disappears at the liquor shop.

73. "*Ham kam karte hue rest karte haim.*"

74. Calmness and discipline are required to not hasten one's pace as others send their pieces early and the supervisor rushes everyone else along. When Varmaji gets nervous on seeing the flurry of activity, Mohan, his machine partner, coolly says to him, "Let them complete their pieces, Varmaji. Let them rush ahead. Ours is not one day's work, that we do it today, and we'll get to rest from tomorrow. We have to do it every day. We'll work, but in a regulated way. We'll give our production at the proper time (*Taiyar karne do, Varmaji. Bhagne do. Ek din to hai nahim, ki ham aj kar lemge, kal se ham baithe rahemge. Roz karna hai. Ham kam karemge, magar hisab se. Jitna hamari production hai, ham apne samay par de demge*)."

75. Within the ambit of auto-regulated working, when there is excessive pressure to not remove pieces, polishers might accept them, but make a few pieces poorly or deliberately damage pieces. After a few days of this, the supervisor might restore the previous norm.

76. "*Paristhiti ke anusar, sara nap tol karke.*"

77. *Talmel* brings together senses of *tal* (beat, rhythm) and *mel* (meeting, mixing, connecting, concord), and roughly translates as thinking, feeling, or acting in synchrony with one another. I adopt this category from the *Faridabad Workers Newspaper*, which has worked on the concept and documented its practice among factory workers in Faridabad, Delhi, and elsewhere since the nineties (Majdoor Samachar-Kamunist Kranti 1998).

78. See McGregor (1997:104) and the *Oxford English Dictionary*. For discussions of valences of *izzat* in modern India, see Chakravarti (2005), Chowdhry (2007), Khan (2016), Reddy (2005), and Shah (2014). Sethi (2012a) references *izzat* in the lives of migrant construction workers in Old Delhi.

79. "*Bahut bura lagta hai.*"

80. "*Hay sale qismat! Aisi zindagi se mar jana behtar hai.*"

81. "*Langur lagte haim.*"

82. "*Lekin garib admi hai, kya karem. Factory mem dhul ganda hota hai.*"

83. "*Nikalte haim to koi pata nahim, pahcan nahim hai ki export mem karke a raha hai ki kahum yah supervisor hai ki manager hai ki computere cala raha hai. Aisin aisin badal jata hai turant.*"

84. Once the bathing area was removed, due to a government demolition drive, workers had to bathe outside in their underwear, causing more public exposure. Even the recovery of *izzat* came at the cost of some embarrassment (*beizzati*).

85. "*Dekhna, thoda saf dho dena.*"

86. "*Lo apni vardi dhote raho! Maimne bis bar kaha ki aisa kam mat karo! Aur tumko koi kam nahim milta puri Dilli mem?! Kyom kura chantte ho?!*"

87. "*Kya fayda dhone se.*"

88. "*Angrez ki factory hai, aur mal banke sidha America jata hai!*"

89. Family farming is seen to have high *izzat* as there is autonomy from the direction and control of others. Amlakant invokes a saying of the medieval poet Ghagh, "*Uttam kheti, madhyam ban / Nishiddh cakri, bhik nidan* (Farming is the best, business is of medium value / one must not take up employment, begging is worthless)" (Jha 2001:107). On the desire for the autonomy, independence, and respect that comes with working one's own land, among peasants, workers, and others in history, see Scott (2012:89–92). On alterations of Ghagh's ordering in recent times, in which employment has changed places with farming, see Gidwani and Sivaramakrishnan (2003:195) and D. Gupta (2005:755). One might see migrants simultaneously pursuing a range of activities (farming, wage work, small businesses), seeking spaces of autonomy and *izzat* in each activity.

90. The repair machine is an exception, where polishers must endure frequent coaxing by the supervisor, who gives them pieces throughout the day.

91. "*Utna bhar, apna raj samajhta hum. Yaham koi hamko ankh dikha nahim sakta hai. Apna machine, apna adda, apna peti, yah sab ke lie sher hum.*"

92. Naresh feels anxiety at his machine as the main electric switch, meter, and circuit breaker are located only two feet from his head. But as he is settled in his workspace, he does not shift.

93. "*Apna machine bahut pyara hota hai.*"

94. "*Vishvakarmaji Bhagvan ki jai.*"

95. "Vishvakarma is giving us livelihoods and sustenance (*Vishvakarma ham log ke khana khila rahe haim*)," Madan says.

96. "*Bismillah Allahu Akbar.*"

97. Ironically, workers who describe their dirty appearances, pejoratively, as those of monkeys (*bandar*) worship the monkey god, Hanuman.

98. *Bundis*: small, fried sweets.

99. The company gives Rs. 25 to buy the sweets from the Tehkhand market.

100. For discussions of Vishvakarma *puja* in the jute mills of Calcutta, among artisans and workers in Benaras, and in other work sites in India, see Bear (2015:169–172, 182–185), Chakrabarty (1989:89–90), Fernandes (1997:102–105), George and Narayan (2022:5–7), and Kumar (1988:203–208).

101. *Laddus*: sphere-shaped sweets.

102. "*Jab cot lagni hogi, jo hona hoga, vo ho jaega, cahe kiska bhi nam le lo.*"

103. "*Tumhara maza hai, bhai, tum aish kar rahe ho!*"

104. "What enmity do we have with the machine? Our antagonism is with the management (*Machine se hamse kya dushmani hai? Dushmani hamse management se hai*)," says Varmaji. According to Prem Brothers, the machine manufacturer, in 2017, automation was present in only 20–30 percent of polishing processes.

105. The craftsman works the machine, and the machine works the craftsman, making the latter adjust and exert according to its position and speed. "The two are 'working' each other (*Donom ek dusre ko cala rahe haim*)," says Ramakant.

106. "*Bas kam ke calte. Kam hai to sahi hai na to kam dhila ho gaya to vo kuch samjhemge nahim. Badal jaemge turant.*"

107. "'*Pyar ka nagma' karemge to phir company calegi hi nahim. Company dub jaegi.*"

108. "*Ghora ghas se yari karega to khaega kya?*"

109. Five of the polishers had worked under Panditji at D45, a decade earlier, where he had looked after multiple activities, including production, checking, and packing, without the tensions of B156.

110. "*Oye helper, buff le a!*"

111. "*Tumhi to puri company ki gand marke rakhe ho. Tu jayega to koi nahim tumko bacane ayega.*"

112. "*Vo maut ki kothri hai. Jab ham log baithte haim machine pe, to sir pe kafan bandh karke baithte haim.*"

113. Khan sahab too was aware of the hazards of the polishing process. Once, on seeing Surinder leveling a buff at his machine, scattering fibers across the shop floor, he said, "Before his time, a guy will die right here (*Apne samay se pahle, admi yahim mar jaega*)."

114. "*Admi mehnat karta jaega aur company shoshan karti jaegi aur usko phal milnevala nahim hai, aur vo phamsta cale jaega. Ek din uska sharir nasht ho jaega, aur har man karke, apna hisab le kar kinara ho jaega.*"

115. A wholesale dealer of these *dhotis*, based in Faridabad, admitted that funeral shrouds might enter the used cloth supply. These might include extra shrouds set on or beside the body at the last rites, and shrouds on bodies that are submerged into rivers.

116. "*Are sala kaham se le aya yah?! Shmashan ghat ka kapda le ake de diya sala muh par bandhne ke liye! Sali kaisi company hai yah?*"

Chapter 2. Humor

1. "*Dimag idhar udhar palatta rahta hai. Bivi, bacce, mata, pita, bhai, bahn, ghar, ristedari, nanihal, koi na koi batem, kuch acchi cizem, kuch kharab cizem. Socte rahte haim. Kya kaise zindagi calegi, kya karna hai, kaise hamari musibat dur ho sakti hai? Man hai. Daurta rahta hai.*"

2. "*Ene kamo cal raha hai, ene nino ke mane jagal hai, onhom gharo denhem ke samacar a raha hai ja raha hai. Socat rahte haim, ghare kaise kar raha hoga. Ene piece ekdam cal raha hai danadan, au udhar bhi cal raha hai.*"

3. "*Cal gae the ghare yar. Bat kar rahe the sabse.*"

4. "*Ab tak kitna din Dilli mem ho gaya, kuch abhi tak ghar mem kuch kiye nahim haim. Kitna din aur mehnat karna parega? Kitna din aur kamaemge ki paisa hoga? Yah sab socte rahte haim, yah sab ke lie cinta karte haim.*"

5. "*Bhai sahab, aise koi rasta bataie hamko ki aram se apna do roti kama kha sakem, aur koi tension na ho. Dimag aisa bataie ki ham ghar mem aram cain se kha sakte haim, sab parivar ke sath rahem. Aisa maim cahta hum.*"

6. "*Free mem raho to tension rahta hi hai. Idhar udhar ki batem kuch na kuch dimag mem aya karti haim. Matlab ki apne ghar pe hote, apne parivar ke sath hote. Ya yah kam accha nahim hai. Free rahte haim to sari batem a jati haim.*"

7. On the fluidity and interchangeability of aggressors and targets in the horse play of German factory workers at the turn of the twentieth century, see Luedtke (1986).

8. "*Kabhi kabhi Mithilesh ko ham pakar lete haim, lagta hai ki ham gharvali ko pakar rakhe haim.*"

9. "*Jab puri bhukh ho, to vo samose ka kam karta hai, bas itna hi hota hai.*" Amlakant migrated to Delhi from a village in Ballia district, Uttar Pradesh. In the mid-eighties, he studied political science, sociology, and Hindi for two years toward a bachelor's degree at a college in Mau. When his father retired from the railways and acquired one-and-a-half hectares of land, Amlakant left his studies and looked after the fields. During college and afterward, he got involved in politics, working for a Congress leader in elections and other activities. As cash was needed for farming, he left the village and came to his elder brother's shanty in southeast Delhi in 1992. Due to his education, he got work as a helper in a lottery ticket-printing factory in Okhla, under a contractor, for Rs. 1,200 monthly wages, for a year, and then as a machine opera-tor in another unit, for two years, earning Rs. 1,800. In 1995, due to a decline in work, he shifted into polishing. He began as a helper in a Tehkhand workshop, at Rs. 1,200 plus overtime, then learned polishing, and worked in three Okhla factories, before Bhagvati and Vijay II called him to B156 in 2001. He was about thirty-four years old. Though he had grown distant from village politics, he took an active role in deliberations and activities in his shanty colony.

10. Babloo Khan grew up in his grandmother's house in Budaun, Uttar Pradesh. After learning shoemaking in his early teens, his aunt brought him to Old Delhi, where he learned polishing from her son-in-law. He shifted to a factory in Seelampur, east Delhi, where he polished brass pieces for a contractor. After his marriage, he returned to Budaun, and began learning his father's business of the street hawking of clothes. For several years, he traveled to towns of Uttar Pradesh, selling women's suits, and also in Delhi and Faridabad for a year, making Rs. 200–500 a day, depending on seasons and locations. After his father's death, Babloo returned to polishing, working on piece rates in a factory in Moradabad, before coming back to Delhi. He found work in D45 in Okhla, for six months, but was terminated for damaging some pieces, and then worked for a contractor at D8/3 for a year, at Rs. 2,500 plus overtime, until the factory closed. He worked for short periods in polishing factories in Faridabad, Noida, and Badarpur, and in Hanif's Tehkhand workshop, before coming to B156 in 2001, at age thirty-three. After a few nights on the aborted night shift, he met Khan sahab, who recognized from his speech that he also was from Budaun. Babloo was brought onto the day shift and regularized.

11. "*Are time lagta hai, yar, muth mar raha tha!*"

12. "*Calo, nikal lo khamba bacake.*"

13. "*Ap log zara bacaie.*"

14. "*Thik hai, baca hi rahe haim.*"

15. "*Are teri gand mem dal do.*" Exchanges of tobacco and *biris* are accompanied by this directive.

16. "*Are bas ek bar de do yar.*"

17. "*Bhai sahab, maim uski mang raha hum, magar de nahim raha hai. Ap zara usse bat kar lo.*"

18. "*Rampal ki gand compani mem sabse pyari hai.*"

19. "*Rampal ki gand maro! Rampal ki gand ki sale lagi hai! Bolī lagao!*"

20. "*Teri hazri lag gai. Tu ek bar de de!*"

21. "*Land pe rakhke aise uchalumga sidha Bihar nazar ayega!*"

22. "*Kaise haim Shankarji? Atthanni abhi tak piti ya baci?*"

23. "*Aie Shankarji is par baitho!*"

24. "*Kis par baithem?!*"

25. "*Are kursi par yar.*"

26. "*Namaste Shankarji aie is par baitho!*" Horseplay, touching, and *mazak* on buggery were described by workers as quite distinct from homosexuality, which was often spoken of in unfavorable terms, as wrong (*galat*) and against nature (*prakriti ke khilaf*). "The fun in joking [about buggery] is not [going to be] there in actually doing it (*Vo ciz mazak karne mem hai maza, vo karne mem nahim hai*)," says Uday. It was otherwise common to see male migrants holding hands, with arms around each other, lying down with limbs on each other's bodies, and sleeping close together in rooms. In David Halle's ethnography of workers in a chemical plant in New Jersey, he observes, "Men are often physically intimate in a nonsexual way. They put their arms around each other and touch each other in genuine gestures of affection" (Halle 1984:182).

27. "*Iske bad yah upar jake gand marvaega.*"

28. Bhagvati was from Sultanpur district, Uttar Pradesh. In the mid-eighties, he worked as a helper, conductor, and driver on trucks plying on the Delhi–Kolkata route, at Rs. 150–500 monthly wages. Through a friend in Delhi, he found work as a helper in a brass factory in Okhla, and learned polishing. In the nineties, Bhagvati worked at two other Okhla factories, earning Rs. 3,500–5,000 a month with overtime. He set up two polishing machines, hired polishers, and began doing job work. Due to electricity problems and noise disturbances to neighbors, he sold the machines and went back to his village. In 2001, he returned to Delhi, at about thirty years of age, and resumed polishing in a Faridabad workshop, before coming to B156.

29. Many things in workers' discourses get buggered, such as metal pieces, work clothes, and bicycles. When Mithilesh sat down at Arun's machine to help him finish some steel bowls, he directed him, "I'll get the outer portion of the piece screwed in the ass, you get the inside of it screwed in the ass (*Maim upar ki gand marvaumga, tum andar ki gand marvao*)." On images of buggery to depict relations between political parties, religious groups, the police, and the demos, in pamphlets circulating at Holi in Varanasi, see Cohen (1995).

30. "*Kam lena rahta hai to itna pyar se bolega ki ekdam inkar karne ke lie dil nahim karega. Vo andar andar aisa gand marta hai ki koi ke pata nahim calega.*"

31. "*Calo, gand marao!*" When Tulsi was hired as a casual welder for the night shift, Premchand, a regular day-shift welder, observed, "Now I'm not entirely certain whether he'll get buggered for Rs. 3,300 or Rs. 3,500 wages, but he'll surely get buggered (*Abhi mere ko pura confirm nahim hai ki tentis sau ya paimtis sau ke lie marvaemge, par zarur marvaemge*)."

32. "*Sari rat gand cudana.*"

33. "*Are vo siding gaya, ajkal uski double kamai ho rahi hai!*"

34. "*Abhi time hai. Siding jao, paisa kamao, apna balance banake ghar jao!*"

35. "*Paise nahim dega to teri gand bahut marumga Hanifa!*" The *hijras* were also a referent in *mazak* directed at me. Once at a tea break, Rajender advised me, in a serious tone, "In the dark, don't ever go toward the siding with Babloo Khan. Take this much care (*Babloo Khan ke sath kabhi andhere mem siding ki taraf se hoke mat jana. Itna dhyan rakhna*)." "I'll get him buggered by the *hijras* (*Maim to cakkom se gand marva dumga inki*)," Babloo responded. "They stand in the cargo containers. I'll shove him into one and say to all the *hijras*, you take Rs. 30 each from me and bugger him! I haven't come to bugger anyone! (*Containerom mem khare rahte haim. Ek*

container mem guser dumga, sab cakkom ko kahumga, tis-tis rupaiya mujhse lo, tum inki gand mar do! Maim marne nahim aya hum!)" Rajender offered to take me to the siding, given my curiosity, but could not promise that once we got there, my *gand* would be safe from my escort, let alone the *hijras*, especially during the erotic, lunar month of Phagun.

36. "*Siding jao, gand marao, paisa kamao, tabhi to apni bivi cavanni de degi!*"

37. "*Yah gand marvane vala kam hai.*"

38. "*Ham khud hi apni gand marva rahe haim.*"

39. "*Tumhare se nahim hoga. Shankarji ko sath le calo.*"

40. "*Ek bar mera nam le lo!*"

41. "*Bhagvati ki machine a gai hai!*"

42. "*Ganne ka ras nikalnevali machine mere pas ai hai.*"

43. "*Barhiya machine cal rahi hai,*" "*Mujhe machine cahie,*" "*Machine to lani paregi.*"

44. "*Ab batao, kis machine mem dal dum, is mem ya us mem?*"

45. "*Apni garmi nikalo. Jao, jugad dhumdho, mobilail change kar lo.*" Just as polishers needed to find *jugads* (modified methods and implements) to polish the metal pieces properly, they needed to find *jugads* to maintain their bodies qua machines. For a rich, evocative account of language, ideas, and experiences within truck drivers' milieus in north India, with specific reference to *mobilail change* (motor oil change) as sexual metaphor, see Simeon (1997).

46. "*Admi ko bhi jhuk machine banna parta hai!*" *Jhuk machine* could also be invoked to insinuate buggery, as when Uday pointed to gaping holes in the *gand* area of Hanif's baggy trousers, and explained to others, "Every day he becomes a *jhuk machine* [at the siding]! (*Yah roz jhuk machine banta hai!*)" Hanif migrated from Barabanki, Uttar Pradesh, in the early nineties, after working in a biscuit factory in Lucknow in his mid-teens. He learned polishing in an Okhla factory, and worked in contractors' workshops in Harkesh Nagar and Tehkhand, and in two Okhla factories, at monthly earnings of Rs. 3,500–4,000. He set up a few machines in a Tehkhand workshop, but vacated it due to a government drive to close nonconforming industries. After brief stints in other factories, he came to B156 in 2001, when he was in his mid-twenties.

47. The comic derives, Henri Bergson suggests, from "something mechanical encrusted on the living" (Bergson 1999:39). One laughs when human beings act in rigid, repetitive, absent-minded, machine-like ways, deviating from their true nature as fluid, creative, living beings with vitality (for a cinematic illustration of Bergson's insight, see *Modern Times* [1936]). Part of the humor in *mazak* on *jhuk machine*, one might suggest, is in the awareness of workers' naïve, pathetic, and futile attempts to emulate machines, by pushing their bodies to work longer and harder, forgetting, absent-mindedly, that machines have fixed capacities. If polishers overwork or manhandle the machine, it might react unexpectedly and induce an injury, overheat, or break down. In the pursuit of wages and advancement, workers can forget that their machine-like bodies too have limits that should be respected, if they wish to avoid breakdowns and the difficulties that arise from excessive submission (*jhukna*) to managerial power.

48. In the village, *mal* might refer to livestock, wage earnings, and purchases of grains and pulses.

49. "*Industrial area mem kora mal kaham milta hai.*"

50. "If you want 'raw' girls, you have to go to the countryside (*Kora mal cahie to dehat hi jana parega*)," workers would say, sometimes in desirous reference to the young wives of co-workers. As with *machine*, *mal* could also be invoked in reference to the male body. At the shift end, Babloo would sit in his underwear, with arms crossed, at Amlakant's machine, and pass detailed commentary on the quality of the *gands* of those exiting the bath. When he would see the stocky Achaibar's rear end, he might say, "This is the only [good] *mal* in our factory (*Hamari compani mem yahi mal hai bas*)."

51. "*Dekho, mal a gaya,*" "*Kya gajab mal ja raha hai,*" "*Machine calega bhaiya?*" "*Are calega nahim, daurega!*" Some workers leave their rooms early in the morning, so as to be able to walk

and look at women on the roads of Okhla with ease, sometimes taking circuitous routes that pass by garment factories. The wives of Ramakant and Vijay II (who engaged in this *mazak* at B156) were workers in such garment factories.

52. "Women don't want to come and work in this area," says the director of the neighboring shed, which dealt in computer hardware. A young, female employee working in that office admitted, "The way they stare at me, it feels a little strange."

53. "*Mal a gaya barhiya.*"

54. For a comic depiction of such control, see *Pay Day* (1922).

55. "*Amlakant se kuch nahim milega! Har din ghar jake uski bivi ko hisab kitab dena parta hai!*" On joking on the power, control, and influence of women in rural Haryana, see Chowdhry (2015:9–10).

56. Naresh II pontificates that men migrate to the city, do difficult work, and earn wages, only to please their wives (by attending to their demands for clothing, cosmetics, and other goods), so as to get access to their genitalia. All male ambitions in the world, including the setting up of companies like Metal Artware Exports, he says, are for this sexual end. He once said, during a break, "It's for this [showing curved fingers to indicate a vagina] that I've left home and come this far. It's for this that I'm earning a living. I remove imperfections, get my pieces passed, and do overtime just for this. It's the same for me, you, and everyone. It's for this that Shankarji too is doing all of this study! (*Isi ke piche to itna dur chorkar aya hum. Isi ke lie maim kama kha raha hum. Dana sori nikalta hum, mal pass karvata hum, overtime lagata hum isi ke calte. Hamari apki sabki yahi bat hai. Usi ke piche Shankarji bhi yah sab kuch parhai likhai kar rahe haim!*)"

57. A saying conveying these anxieties is, "*Triya caritra devo na janam* (Even the gods do not know the *caritra* [mind, character, nature] of a woman)."

58. The manager could occasionally participate in nonvulgar *mazak* with workers during breaks, creating an awkward, uneasy sense of levity across hierarchical divisions. But *mazak* took on a different, somewhat humiliating tone when he would prod and tease workers about their wives, and watch as they grew embarrassed and silent, unable to fully answer back as they would among each other.

59. In the cluster of rented rooms of the Jharkhandis in Tehkhand, one might see brothers sharing a room and eating meals together, but splitting up into different rooms for conversation, nonvulgar *mazak*, and sleeping, along with others in their age group. By staying in separate spaces, they maintain the *izzat* of kin and age, avoid awkwardness, and enjoy more freedom. This separation might be seen as avoidance within kin joking relationships (Apte 1985:37–38, 51), which preserves certain aspects of social order (e.g., kin hierarchies). But this practice also creates more free and anarchic spaces of *mazak* that seem to reveal desires for less hierarchical and less ordered sociality.

60. "*Yah kya ulte sidhe batem karte rahte haim?*" Lapses in censoring could also occur in the village, as when Mithilesh's father directed him to do a task in the fields, and he blurted out, as he might do when given an unwelcome task by Vijay, "Screw it, I'm not going to do this work! (*Land pe jae yah kam nahim karumga!*)"

61. "*Are bhai, tum apne mal ko dikhao.*"

62. When Babloo's *mazak* becomes excessive, Hanif might wave his hands in the air and walk away, shouting, "I don't want to hear such dirty things! (*Gandi bat maim sunna nahim cahta hum!*)"

63. "*Yah Lal Qila se kam nahim.*"

64. I did not hear exchanges of slurs in *mazak* on the castes of workers.

65. "*O Bihari, jaldi jaldi carh! Bihari, cal age cal! Jaldi utar le Bihari!*"

66. "*Bihari sale kaise bhir laga rakhe ho? Gamv samajh rakha hai kya yaham pe? Cal hat!*"

67. Of 65 workers who worked at B156 at various times, 10 (15 percent) were from Bihar, 9 (14 percent) were from Jharkhand, 38 (58 percent) were from Uttar Pradesh, and 6 (9 percent) were from Uttarakhand.

68. "*Eh Bihari, masala le a!*"

69. "*O Madan! Bihari! Sunta nahim hai?*"

70. Bal Thackeray, the Shiv Sena leader in Mumbai, wrote an editorial with this title (*Saamna*, March 6, 2008).

71. "*Ek agar Bihari cala aya, to sau bimari ho gaya. Mar jaega sab bimari se!*" "*Ek Bihari Sau Pe Bhari* (One Bihari is greater than a hundred others)" was the title of a Bhojpuri film in 2012.

72. "*Sau gun ek Bihari ke andar milemge—cori, beimani, shaitani, hera pheri, calamki, netagiri—sab kuch milega uske andar.*"

73. According to migration data, migrants from Bihar increased from 11 percent to 23 percent of in-migrants to Delhi from 1981–1991 to 1991–2001; migrants from Uttar Pradesh declined from 50 percent to 46 percent of in-migrants to Delhi (Government of NCT of Delhi 2006:42).

74. "*Yah sare Bihari, bahn ke laure, itne itne bhar gaye haim! Quarter kharab karke rakhe haim!*"

75. "*Sare Bihari akar Dilli ko barbad kar diye!*"

76. "*Yah log kisi ke nahim hote.*"

77. "*Bihariyom ne is compani ki gand mar rakhi hai!*" When Arun accepts extra pieces, and then sends them upstairs early, Mithilesh might shake his head and exclaim, "The Bihari has gone mad! (*Bihari pagal ho gaya!*)"

78. "*Unko sirf paisa cahie.*"

79. On negative stereotypes about Bihari workers (as feisty, insular, and not hardworking) in the discourse of a manager in a Tata Motors factory in Jharkhand, see Sanchez (2012:819–820).

80. "*Bihari! Latrine mem baithke aya hoga!*" Ironically, when Babloo Khan came to Delhi, from Uttar Pradesh, he too was called Bihari by local residents in the Jama Masjid area of Old Delhi, where he lived with his relatives, due to differences in his appearance, clothing, and language.

81. "*Ham latrine mem baithke ae. Aur tu havai jahaz mem baithke aya hoga. Tabhi tu ragar raha hai! Kaun se land par tir mar diya yaham?!*"

82. "*Bihar ke log bahut haim, aur har line mem ghuse pare haim. Hamse accha pahn bhi rahe haim, hamse accha bal bhi rakh rahe haim. UP valom ko fail kar diya inhomne.*"

83. "Individuals and groups who narrate ethnic jokes do not necessarily accept the negative or pejorative stereotypes of the target groups," observes Apte (Apte 1985:141).

84. On the alleged quality of engaging excessively in political activities, Varmaji explains, "Persons from Uttar Pradesh and Bihar learn politics in the mother's womb (*UP aur Bihar ke admi ma ke pet mem hi rajniti sikh lete haim*)."

85. "*Marta kya nahim karta.*"

86. "*Umesh apne hisab se kam karte haim. Vo Bihari jaise kam nahim karte haim. Unko kuch hisab kitab aur kism ka hai.*"

87. "*Bihari, tu sudhar ja!*"

88. "*Ham Bihari nahim haim. Jharkhandi haim. 'Jharkhandi' bolo!*"

89. "*Tu Jharkhand vala Bihari hai.*" Despite this *mazak* with Arun, Surinder admits, "We are Biharis (*Bihari hi haim*)."

90. "*Kya kar raha hai, Bihari?*"

91. "*Are bhai is jangli ko sambhalo yar!*" The Jharkhandis did not use the word *jangli* in *mazak* among themselves.

92. "*Yah sab jangli haim! Jangal ke pas rah cuke haim, jangal jaisi buddhi hai!*" Varmaji might also use the word *jangli* for Naresh II, an Uttar Pradesh migrant, when he would speak desirously, in *mazak*, about dogs moving about outside the factory gate.

93. "*Yah sab to bahut sahi haim. Haim to yah bhi Bihar ke, baki dekho bolne calne mem bhi sahi haim, bat karne mem sahi haim, vyavahar mem bhi sahi haim.*"

94. "*Sare Bihari ek jaise nahim homge. Sare UP vale ek jaise nahim homge.*"

95. "*Sabhi log ek saman nahim hai. Farq to do bhaiyom mem par jata hai. Koi bhai kisi svabhav ka rahta hai, koi bhai kisi svabhav ka rahta hai, koi bahn kisi svabhav ki rahti hai. Khair prant to bahut dur hai.*" Varmaji could see a vast difference (*zamin asman ka farq*) between the Jharkhandi brothers, Naresh and Madan. For a deep exploration of this insight, see Dostoevsky (1992).

96. Nandy (2002:8).

97. Six of the 65 B156 workers (9 percent) were Muslims, who were all migrants from Uttar Pradesh. On usages of *katua* and references to circumcision in Hindu nationalist discourse and contexts of Hindu-Muslim violence, see Chatterjee and Mehta (2007:71–72, 106–107), Mehta (2000), and Nandy et al. (1995:29).

98. "*Aur bhai, kate Khan, kya hal hai?*"

99. "*Katue idhar ao!*"

100. Stereotypes about the alleged ability to coldly kill animals and human beings also appear in an ethnography of Ahmedabad (Ghassem-Fachandi 2012:127, 135–137).

101. One could see in these negative stereotypes the "mix of paranoia and admiration" that inheres, Ashis Nandy observes, in India's ambivalent feelings toward Pakistan (Nandy 2007:30). On stereotypes about excessive procreation among Muslims, in an ethnography of Old Delhi, see A. Gandhi (2013:197, 199).

102. "*Tere bas ki bat nahim, tera salamat nahim hai. Mera salamat hai, mere pas apni bivi bhej de, maim uski icchaom ko pura kar dumga!*"

103. "*Abhi katue ka dekha kya hai? Apni bivi ko bhejke dekh. Katua kya rang layega, teri bivi tere se bataegi, katue ke andar kitna jan hai. Tere ko kya pata hai?*"

104. "*Are line kato! Hamara to kata hua, bhai.*"

105. "*Katue jaldi jaldi kam kar le!*"

106. "*Katue, tu bhi to jaldi jaldi kam kar le!*"

107. "*Nahim, mera biradar bhai hai, islie maim nahim karumga.*"

108. "*To tere ko katua baithake paisa de dega? Sala tu katue ka camca hai!*"

109. On suspicions about Muslim loyalties, which could become visible at the time of India-Pakistan cricket matches, in an ethnography of Zakir Nagar in Delhi, see Kirmani (2013:124–126).

110. "*Pakistani hai yah! Dana Hindustan ka kha raha hai aur gun ga raha hai Pakistan ka!*"

111. "*Galat bat. Koi hamko khila nahim raha hai. Maim mehnat kar raha hum to kha raha hum.*"

112. "*Koi jite koi mare mujhe koi matlab nahim. Mujhe apne kam se kam hai. Hamem kya milega jo gand ka jor lagaem?*"

113. "*Ham jo ragar rahe haim, vahi ragaremge phir!*"

114. "*Ab samajh mem aya hai!*"

115. Once the match got over, there were fireworks, the shouting of slogans, "Long live India! Down with Pakistan! (*Hindustan zindabad! Pakistan murdabad!*)," and the distribution of sweets in Tehkhand, shanty clusters in Okhla, and other working-class colonies of the city.

116. The victory was costly for Surinder, who made a bet on Pakistan, and had to provide chicken and liquor for his Jharkhandi neighbors in Tehkhand.

117. "*Har ek ki bat mat kahie.*" If the Pakistani government acted in crooked, deceptive ways (*kutniti*) toward India, Rajender said, that did not mean that the ordinary citizens of Pakistan were enemies of India.

118. "*Maim yahim pe janam liya hum. Yahim pe zindagi hamari guzarni hai. Hamko Pakistan se kya lena dena hai?*" After the cricket match, in reflecting on suspicions about Muslims in India, Firoz mentioned that it was very wrong to have ever divided the country into India and Pakistan.

119. "*Kya kahim jhagre hote haim, to kya khali Mohammadan hi maarte haim Hindu ko? Hindu nahim maarte haim? Maaremge donom. Donom maremge.*" Sabbir left Mumbai a day before the demolition of the Babri mosque in December 1992 and lost a relative in the Gujarat violence of 2002. Babloo cites the killings of Muslims by Police Armed Constabulary forces in Moradabad in 1980, among other incidents, to question the view that only Muslims do not have compassion.

120. "All Muslims are not alike (*Sab Musalman ek saman nahim hote haim*)," workers say. A Muslim woman in Zakir Nagar recounts her past experiences of Hindus in Old Delhi, who protected her and her sibling during a curfew, by saying, "'There are all types of people amongst Muslims, and there are all types of people amongst Hindus'" (Kirmani 2013:122).

121. Firoz came to Delhi in his late teens, in 1997, from a village in Jaunpur district, Uttar Pradesh, after failing high school. With the assistance of his cousin-brother, he learned polishing in Tehkhand, then worked in six metal factories in Okhla, Faridabad, and Noida, before coming to the B156 night shift in 2001.

122. "*Firoz akharta hai kyomki vo zulm bardasht nahim karta hai.*"

123. "*Worker ke sath calne mem, company ke andar sabse best larka hai Firoz.*" "Firoz, as a worker, wants to be with and go along with other workers (*Firoz ek mazdur rah karke ek mazdur ke sath rahna cahta hai*)," says Varmaji.

124. If everyone in the factory is from Bihar, Arun says, one will not get the fun of the word *Bihari*. On exchanges of joking insults among diverse workers in an auto plant in Jharkhand, see Sanchez (2016:298–299).

125. "*Teri gand aisi marumga, Bihari, amsu aegi tere ko, samjha?! Puri Dilli mem ilaj nahim hoga! Bihar bhagke jayega, royega, kahega, katue ne gand mar diya!*"

126. "*Company mem cal jata hai.*" Radcliffe-Brown writes, "Any serious hostility is prevented by the playful antagonism of teasing" (Radcliffe-Brown 1952:92; for a resonant view, see Halle 1984:183–184). At B156, it is unclear that *mazak* averted feelings of serious hostility.

127. Laughter, as Bergson suggests, might be seen as a "corrective" gesture (though here, not by humiliating, but by teasing and chiding one another in contexts of familiarity), although it is difficult to say to what extent *mazak*, on its own, "corrects" working styles or solidarities (Bergson 1999:82, 176–177). At B156, those who engaged in *mazak* (and indeed, most actively, such as Babloo Khan) did not necessarily follow its corrective messages.

128. "Doing *mazak* is very necessary (*Mazak karna bahut zaruri hai*)," says Uday.

129. "Time passes with *mazak*, one feels like working, one doesn't feel sleepy (*Hamsi mazak se timepass ho jata hai, kam bhi man lagega, nind nahim lagega*)," says Rampal.

130. Sivam angrily says, "Production, production, production! Is there anything else but production or not?! Do a little *mazak* too! (*Production, production, production! Are production ke alava kuch aur bhi hai ya nahim hai? Hamsi mazak bhi thodi karo!*)"

131. "[I]t is not the person who makes the joke who laughs at it and who therefore enjoys its pleasurable effect, but the inactive listener," Freud observes (Freud 1960:118–119).

132. "*Hamsi mazak karemge, tabhi to ham thoda apne ap ko khush rakh paemge nahim to bas ragaro ragaro!*"

133. "*Hamari muhabbat barhti hai.*"

134. "*Sara din kura khate raho bhosrivala, pata nahim kaisa kam zindagi mem mil gaya hai madarcod?! Pata nahim gaddhe ke land se likhi gai hai nasib, kahe se likhi gai hai?! Kaun sa qalam tha hamara?!*" In workers' discourses, the fatter the pen used by God to write one's fate, the worse that fate will be.

135. "*Bina hamsi mazak, zindagi bekar hai.*"

Chapter 3. Collectivity

1. Changes in quantity norms of regular items, for example, from three to six large round platters in a twelve-hour shift, with quality improvements, suggest greater increases.

2. The night shift still operated without legal paperwork, according to the manager.

3. "*Bihari sala cutiya hai. Kai bar samjha diya ki aram se karo.*"

4. "*Bac gaya. Hath tut jata to aur accha hota.*"

5. "*Kam lena rahta tab tak izzat hai. Uske bad kaun izzat kisko karta hai.*"

6. "*Itna piece nahim banana hai! Ab ESI mem jana nahim hai!*"

7. "*Nahim! Ek bar phir pahumco! ESI choro mat! Hamari ESI kat rahi hai!*"

8. "*Ham log ko to cutiya bana banake kah kahke thag thagke rakh diye.*"

9. While Guptaji was denim buffing the inside corners of a small tray, and subtly trying to race with Firoz, the buff caught his glove and pulled his left hand into the machine, fracturing his wrist. A metal plate and screws were placed into his arm at Safdarjung Hospital, a large government hospital in south Delhi. The following year, Guptaji began to receive an ESI monthly pension of Rs. 87.

10. Amlakant described these practices as the political techniques of *sam, dam, dand,* and *bhed* (verbal persuasion, enticement, threats and punishments, and division), as he had witnessed in electoral strategies of political parties in his home district of Ballia, Uttar Pradesh. The terms (which are discussed in the *Mahabharata, Arthashastra*, and the *Bhagavat Purana*) are also audible in cinema and other media.

11. "*Cup kar! Tera satyanash ho jae! Le, dekh le!*"

12. The ESI Hospital referred Varmaji to Safdarjung Hospital. They came back instead to a local clinic.

13. Polishers came down with persistent coughs, fever, pneumonia, and jaundice.

14. The Jharkhandis developed friendships, for example, with Amlakant, Arun, Lallan, Mithilesh, Naresh II, Ramakant, Rambachan II, and Varmaji.

15. An estimated sixty thousand families in shanty clusters in Delhi were evicted between 1990 and 2007 (Bhan and Shivanand 2013:54).

16. The room was above Varmaji's rented quarters and next to Naresh II's house.

17. "No poetry concerning the people is authentic if fatigue does not figure in it, and the hunger and thirst which come from fatigue," writes Weil (Weil 1952a:236).

18. Elder polishers had experienced such working conditions in Okhla metal factories in the early nineties.

19. Only five polishers (Amlakant, Rajender [who went to the village], Rakesh, Umesh, and Varmaji) held out and refused overtime.

20. "*Ab company mem baval to hona hi hona hai. Bahut zabardast baval hoga.*"

21. McGregor (1997:1054). For ethnographic research on meanings of *haq* in north India and Pakistan, which acknowledges the divergence of *haq* from laws, see Madhok (2021).

22. Amlakant and others spoke of a good, living wage as Rs. 5,000 in 2003, when Delhi minimum wages were Rs. 2,784–3,208.

23. Migrant workers' agitations in China also seem to be guided by perceptions of what is just, fair, and right, not only by legal rights (Ngai 2016:138–161).

24. "*Worker aur malik ki kabhi larai nahim ho sakti. Har jagah ke mazdur ka haq to mara hi jata hai. Mazdur ki majburi hai, isilie mazduri kar raha hai. Maim kahta hum company mem jaisi naukri cal rahi hai, calao. Ham to yah soc rahe haim company calti rahe, naukri salamat rahe. Bhale hi sala nahim de raha hai garam samosa. Lekin hamara Rs. 1,000 ka overtime to lag raha hai!*"

25. Along with stagnant wages and reductions in bonuses and overtime provisions, which were allegedly due to financial losses in the company, workers were aware that the manager and supervisors were receiving raises. On seeing Khan sahab upgrade from a motorcycle to a Maruti,

workers joked that the new vehicle had been bought with the earnings from exploitation (*shoshan ki kamai*).

26. On practices among peasants in colonial India of holding local landlords and officials responsible for oppression, and looking to the alleged good ruler for justice, see Hardiman (2018:112, 116, 156). In ethnographies of development in Uttar Pradesh, villagers attribute blame for corruption on the activities of local leaders and intermediary officials, not the good, well-meaning chief minister (Narayan 2011:137, 141–142, 146) or government (A. Gupta 2012:101). On the idea of *rajdharma* (the duty of rulers) in premodern and colonial India, which involves the ruler's obligation to protect his subjects, see Guha (1989:244, 268). For discourses on good, just rulers among subordinate groups in Russia, Europe, and Southeast Asia, see Scott (1990:96–103).

27. This image of the American director might partly derive from a reverence for foreign, fair-complexioned, wealthy persons in India. But the generous attribution of qualities of goodness, innocence, and unawareness, without confirming evidence (workers too were "blind" with respect to the king), might have been a way to maintain a space for redeeming good, at the apex of power in the company, and therefore, for messianic hope, amid feelings of powerlessness and hopelessness.

28. Though workers could be resentful about microdifferences in wages among themselves, they seemed to defend the necessity of larger wealth inequalities between rich and poor classes, for the good of society. They spoke of the desire for equal *izzat* across diverse occupations in society, rather than class equality.

29. "*Dekhie, Shankar-bhai, yah hai atyacar. Ise kahte haim Kalyug. Ghor Kalyug!*"

30. "*Yah kitna anyay hai bahncod yaham bataie. Kya sala zamana hai, kya Kalyug hai sala yah. Vah vah Kalyug!*"

31. Smith (2009:200–201, 339, 555, 639, 665).

32. Dimmitt and van Buitenen (1978:37–41).

33. Tulasidasa (1999:632–637).

34. Gandhi characterizes modern civilization as the Black Age (*Kaliyuga*) in *Hind Swaraj* (M. Gandhi 2010:32).

35. For rich explorations of discourses on the *Kaliyug* in print cultures in colonial Bengal, see Sarkar (1989; 1997a; 1997b; 2002).

36. See Ananthamurthy (2012:20, 102), Premchand (2002:268–269, 302), and Reza (2008:182).

37. See *Kalyug* (1981), *Kalyug Aur Ramayan* (1987), and *Kalyug* (2005).

38. See *Sacred Games* (2018–2019).

39. For vast variations in the temporal location of the *Kalyug*, among denizens of Himachal Pradesh, see Halperin (2014:50–51).

40. On the technology of the polishing machine, Varmaji says, "This is a *kala* (art) which ends the *lila* (play, drama) of life. We're putting our lives into the clutches of death (*Yah to jivan lila samapt karne vali kala hai. Ham apni zindagi ko maut ke muh mem dal rahe haim*)."

41. For illuminating ethnographic accounts of narratives on the *Kalyug/Kaliyug* in north India, see Gold (1998), Halperin (2014; 2020), and Pinney (1999). For other references, see Agrawal (2019:173–176), Alter (1992:241), Arumugam (2015:786), Banerjee (2006:40–81), Bate (2009:177), Cohen (1998:119, 171–173), Daniel (1983:56), Guha (1983:30, 294–297), Hardiman (2021:280), Kishwar (2000:286), Lamb (2000:94, 96–99), Nandy (1995), Omvedt (2008:36–38), Ponniah (2014), Ramanujan (1990:51), Reddy (2005:223), Roy (2014:140), and Van Hollen (2022).

42. "*Khan sahab Kalyug ka pura formula apna faila rakhe haim.*" Firoz, a Muslim polisher, seemed to use the category of the *Kalyug* with ease, and that too, to critique the activities of Khan sahab, a Muslim manager.

43. "*Kalyugi ki duniya hai, choti si. Us company ke andar pura Kalyug samaya hua hai.*"

44. In *Nishant* (1975), a priest says to villagers, who are suffering under the oppressive practices of the landlords, "If you continue to endure injustice, the oppressors' injustice will not lessen. Rather, they will do more of it. Don't forget that in every epoch, to fight against injustice is a good thing. . . . [I]f it's a wrong to perpetrate oppression, it's an even greater wrong to tolerate it (*Anyay sahte rahoge to anyay karnevalom ka anyay kam nahim hoga. Ulta barhega vo. Yah mat bhulo ki har yug mem anyay ke khilaf larna bhala hai. . . . [A]gar atyacar karna pap hai to atyacar sahna usse bhi bara pap hai*)."

45. "*Ap manav ho aur acche tariqe se apna jivan nirvah karne ki buddhi jante ho. Tum par koi zulm kare to apka kam hai zulm ko rokna. Aur nahim rok rahe ho to apne ap gunahgar ho.*"

46. To inflect Marx's thoughts on religion, laments and curses might be seen as the potent, even deadly "sigh of the oppressed creature." "*Religious* suffering is at the same time an *expression* of real suffering and a *protest* against real suffering. Religion is the sigh of the oppressed creature, the sentiment of a heartless world, and the soul of soulless conditions," Marx writes (Marx 1978:54).

47. "*Durbal ko na sataiye, jaki moti hay / Bina jiv ki sams som, lau bhasm huvai jay*" (Karki 2001:68–69).

48. Premchand (1969a).

49. "*Sala yah management hat jae to hi behtar hai! Isse aur kharab bhi a jae, na, to phir bhi ham log svikar kar lem!*"

50. Cursing emerges in the discourses of oppressed groups elsewhere. "At a more cosmic level we have the effort of subordinate groups to call down a curse on the heads of their aggressors. . . . The curse is an open prayer—even if confined to the backstage audience—embodying an intricate and lovingly ornate vision of revenge," writes James Scott (Scott 1990:42).

51. "These men, wielding power, have no suspicion of the fact that the consequences of their deeds will at length come home to them—they too will bow the neck in their turn," Weil writes, on the heroes of *The Iliad*. The Greek understanding of "retribution . . . which operates automatically to penalize the abuse of force," she writes, has been forgotten in the Occident (Weil 1986b:174–175).

52. "*Hamara baddua kahim lag jaega to usko koi nahim mitha sakta hai.*"

53. "*Baddua lag gai.*"

54. "*Aisi factory ko tala lag jae, band ho jae, nash ho jae!*"

55. "*Yah Kalyug hai. Jitna management ko ham log baddua dete haim, utna unka promotion hota ja raha hai!*"

56. According to polishers' estimates, about one machine would blow each month due to sabotage. Sometimes, on seeing one another's example, they could blow two or three machines in succession.

57. "*Tin piece rahne do, aram aram se ban jaega.*"

58. "*Nahim, car banao.*"

59. "*Aram se kam karvao.*"

60. "*Machine ko phumkna pap hai. Lekin atyacar dekhke majburi mem karna par raha hai. Pap bhi nahim hai aur pap bhi hai.*"

61. "*Gunda ko mitane ke lie gunda banna parta hai. Ab Kalyug hai. Kalyug ke Kalyug e se mitaya ja sakta hai.*"

62. On sabotage activities in the maquilas to regulate quantities, pace, and quality, see Peña (1997).

63. "*Yadi company hamare bare nahim socta hai, to ham company ke bare kyom socem?*"

64. "*Company itna atyacar kar rahi hai, jis din vo sudharegi, ham bhi sudhar jaemge!*"

65. Sabotage and restrained working might be viewed as experiments with *apaddharm* (ethics in adversity or emergency). According to this concept, which appears in the *Mahabharata*, temporary, provisional engagements in ethically distorted activity may be permissible

under mitigating, adverse conditions, for the sake of the good. For evocations and explorations of the concept, see Bowles (2007), Dhand (2008:181–198), Nandy (1983:108), and Ramanujan (1990:48).

66. "*Kahta hai ki agar jhuth bolne se agar kisi ka jan bacta hai to baca lena cahie. Kabhi kabhi admi ko, yadi rakshasi atma se hi agar koi ciz prapt hota hai, to use kar lena cahie. To us vaqt yah nahim shamil karemge ki yah rakshasi atma hamara ganda hai. Us vaqt yah sabit hoga ki yah atma hamare us atma se barhiya hai kyomki isne hi accha kam kiya hai. Agar rakshasi atma hi agar koi kam sahi kar leta hai, to ham usko hi sahi manemge!*" On the idea of demonic good in Hindu mythology, see O'Flaherty (1976). Among the good demons (*asuras, rakshasas*) in contemporary imaginaries are Prahlad, Ghatotkach, and Mahabali. The demon (*rakshas*) or devil (*shaitan*) within the soul (*atma*) is also a god (*devta*), says Firoz.

67. Dostoevsky (1992:255).

68. Offstage, Rajender said to Varmaji, "This company is a foreign hen. She'll give a golden egg (*Yah videshi murgi hai. Sone ka anda degi*)."

69. "*Maim Gangaji ko uthake kasam kha raha hum ki maim apke sath vafadari aur imandari ke sath sangharsh karumga. Cahe kuch bhi jae, meri jan cali jae, baki maim ap logom ka sath nahim chor sakta hum.*"

70. The workers spoke of experiences in the village of oath-taking rituals with Ganga water, to test a person's claims of innocence against charges of theft, or to pledge group solidarity in land disputes or village council politics. In colonial north India, textile workers of the Kanpur Mazdur Sabha engaged in sacred oaths invoking the Ganga (Joshi 2003:243); in the Eka movement against oppressive practices of landlords, peasants took oaths on Ganga water and the Quran (Hardiman 2021:88).

71. An elder IFTU leader at the time was rumored to have engaged in taking commissions, causing nervousness and doubts among some workers.

72. One could see a parallel hierarchy in the making, of communist party leaders, union leaders, worker-leaders, and ordinary workers, alongside the company hierarchy of directors, managers, proto-leaders, and ordinary workers.

73. The other resignees were Amar Singh, Raju, and Vijay II.

74. Hanif was the only Muslim at the second ritual. Firoz and Sabbir were in the village. Other Muslim workers (Guddu Khan, Kalim, and Babloo Khan) had left the company.

75. The sacrality of Ganga water, Firoz told me, was akin to that of the holy water of Mecca (*zamzam ka pani*).

76. "*Dekho! Maim Gangajal utha raha hum!*"

77. "*Teri shakl dekhte hi mera mood kharab ho jata hai.*"

78. "*Maim apko bhi nahim dekhna cahta hum.*"

79. "*Ek manager ki haisiyat dekhna cahta hai? Tere ko marumga!*"

80. "*Ap mar sakte haim, maim bhi mar sakta hum.*"

81. "*Tere ko kam nahim karne dumga.*"

82. After his injury, Guptaji did not work on the machine.

83. "*Kam karte nahim ho!*"

84. "*Agar maim kam nahim karta hum to tumhari gand mem dam hai to mera hisab kara do!*"

85. This iteration of restrained working, which was of a more open, defiant, and widespread nature, approached the practice of work-to-rule.

86. "*Maim apko yah ashvasan deta hum ki sansthan ke andar pravesh kar purn utpadan dumga, adhikariyom ke ucit adesh ka palan karumga, aur purn anushasan ke andar rahkar karya karumga.*"

87. Good conduct undertakings have been described as illegal by the government. In the context of agitations at the Maruti Suzuki Manesar auto plant in 2011, in which such undertakings were utilized by the management, the minister of labour and employment stated, "Demanding

of good conduct bonds from workers as per conditions before allowing them to resume work is an arbitrary act and it also amounts to unfair labour practice as given in the Industrial Disputes Act, 1947" (Press Trust of India 2011).

88. "*Jo bhi bat hogi, Okhla mem hogi.*"

89. The list added Amlakant, Balram, Firoz, Mithilesh, Naresh II, Rakesh, Sivam, and Umesh.

90. "It is not religion but revolution which is the opium of the people," writes Weil (Weil 1952a:235). "[A]s a revolt against the essential misery of the working condition it is misleading, for no revolution will get rid of the latter" (Weil 1986c:247).

91. "*Inquilab zindabad! Gair kanuni chantni nahim calegi! Talabandi nahim calegi! Metal Artware ke management hosh mem ao! IFTU zindabad! Mazdur ekta zindabad! Jab lal lal lahrayega, hosh thikane ayega! Jo na mane jhande se, vo manega dande se! Jo na mane batom se, vo manega latom se!*"

92. "*Inquilab zindabad! Tanashahi nahim calegi! Jo hamse takrayega, chur chur ho jayega! Aise management ki kya davai? Juta cappal aur pitai!*"

93. "*Mar gaya sala! Hay hay! Bahut kamina! Le cal Jamuna! Mazdur ekta zindabad!*"

94. Periodic payments to the police were given by the company, according to the manager, to overlook ongoing legal violations.

95. The company might have given the Okhla police a payment to disperse the workers once, not multiple times.

96. "[M]ost interesting was that at each turn he raised his right fist high, shook it in the air above his head, and suddenly brought it down as if crushing some adversary to dust. He repeated this trick every moment. It gave me an eerie feeling," writes Dostoevsky, of a speaker at a fête in *Demons* (Dostoevsky 1994:476).

97. "*Jab admi berozgar ho jata hai, kuch accha nahim lagta hai.*"

98. The company gave settlement amounts of Rs. 17,000–23,000 for its regular workers, which included August wages and two extra months' wages of notice pay, due to the union dispute. By involving the labor officer as a witness, the company was probably protecting itself against future legal claims by the resignees, for example, of coercion or nonreceipt of final dues.

99. "*Malikom ke dalal hosh mem ao! Ghus lena band karo!*"

100. The resignees were Achaibar, Akhilesh, Arun, Avdesh, Balram, Divan, Narayan, Pappu, Prakash, Rakesh II, Ramparvesh, and Shiva. Due to Dr. Das's demonstration that day, the labor officer perhaps thought it wise to witness future settlements outside of the labor office. The DLC might have been playacting, onstage, in posing as an ally to workers and making brusque calls to Khan sahab, while allowing his subordinates to assist the management in its objectives, offstage. According to resignees, the labor officer was handed cash commissions (of Rs. 1,000) for each settlement.

101. Hanif might have refused to lift the Ganga water out of the awareness of his dubious allegiance to the group.

102. Majdoor Samachar-Kamunist Kranti (1996; 1997; 1998).

103. *Faridabad Workers Newspaper* (blog), http://faridabadmajdoorsamachar.blogspot.com/.

104. See Sethi (2012b). In other writings, see Ness (2021:100–101), Ruthven (2021:661–662), and Ullah (2020:385).

105. On the history, content, and activities of *FMS*, see Majdoor Samachar-Kamunist Kranti (2021).

106. "*Khabardar! Gundaraj ke jhuthe sapne; Ham sabhi sthai karmcariyom ko ek mahine se bahar kar diya gaya hai. Ham apni naukri bacane va adharm ke khilaf shram vibhag mem case lar rahe haim. Ham sabhi ko torne ke lie manager kahte haim ki maim Phase II mem dusri nai unit khol raha ham. Agar tum case laroge to maim nahim rakhumga. Agar tum case nahim laroge to maim hisab karva dumga.*" In referencing *adharm*, there were resonances with the mode of

subaltern resistance described by Ranajit Guha as dharmic protest, deriving from "the morality of struggle against adharma" (Guha 1989:268). But the ideal that seemed to motivate the workers' struggles was described less as *dharm* (a word that more commonly meant one's religious community) and more as *haq* (justice).

107. "*Khabardar! Shram adhikari ka notom ke bal par mazdurom ke jivan ke sath khilvar; Ham apni naukri bacane ke lie gair kanuni talabandi ke khilaf lar rahe haim. Har tarikh ke thik ek din pahle management labor officer ko bulakar karmcariyom ko samjhauta patr par sign karakar hisab karvate haim. Phir hamari tarikh par management ata nahim. Hamari tarikh barhti ja rahi hai aur labor officer ki kamai barhti ja rahi hai lekin hamara sangharsh bhi barhta ja raha hai.*"

108. "*Khabardar! Factory ke Kalyugi bhaiyom se satark; Ek bhai ko 3 agast ko bahar kar diya jiska sath dene ke cakkar mem ham sabhi karmcariyom ko dinank 10 agast ko bahar kar diya. Vo bhai pit piche sabse pahle hisab lekar management ka mohra ban gaya. Ajkal 6 baje subah mem soye hue baki mazdur bhaiyom ko jagakar unko torne ke cakkar mem salah deta hai ki jaldi hisab lo, maim abhi manager se bat karvata hum. Hamem kisse zyada khatra hai—management ya kalyugi bhaiyom se?*"

109. While acknowledging that they were doing wage work in factories, workers could avoid calling themselves *mazdurs*, due to identifications as farmers (*kisans*) in the village (who occasionally hired *mazdurs*), and negative associations of *mazdur* with certain forms of difficult, low-paid work (e.g., road work and construction).

110. Bhagvati shared his thoughts on the *Kalyug* in an interview the previous year. "One should try to protect oneself from the *Kalyug*. One should control one's own soul and recognize the good path, good behavior, and a good nature. One shouldn't associate or speak with persons engaged in wrongdoing (*Kalyug se bacne ke lie admi ko koshish karna cahie. Svayam apni atma ko control karna cahie aur acche rasta, acche vyavahar, aur acche nature ko pahcanna. Galat admi ke sath baithna uthna, bol bat karna nahim cahie*)," he said.

111. "*Thoda yah dekh lena ki production thik rahe.*"

112. "*Vishvakarma Bhagvan ki jai!*"

113. "*Calo, machine par baitho! Calu karo!*"

114. Khan sahab made attempts to recruit Naresh and his relatives, with promises of higher earnings, but they were not ready to leave regular jobs at B156.

115. The company, according to legal documents, received complaints about late export shipments during the work stoppage.

116. In a leaflet distributed in Okhla, the union termed the outcome a victory of unity and struggle in adverse, neoliberal conditions. "The victory of the Metal Artware workers shows that struggle alone guarantees the protection of jobs and that to accept or arrange settlements is the work of cowards. Come, let us strengthen the fight for jobs and implementation of labor laws, health insurance, provident fund, bonus, etc. in every factory. If you want to live, learn to die, learn to fight at every step (*Jina hai to marna sikho, kadam-kadam par larna sikho*)," the leaflet concluded.

117. "*Tum aise hamare upar atyacar nahim kar sakte haim. Jab caho to naukri se bahar kar diye. Kabhi koi notice laga diya ki nahim, ispar sign karo to naukri karoge. Kam karo ham samosa nahim demge. Vo atyacar par atyacar kiye jae aur ham cup cap [rahem]. Hamari larai siddhant ke rup mem thi, apne haq ki larai thi, adharm ke khilaf larai thi.*"

118. I am adopting the *FMS* understanding of *talmel* (synchrony) as an alternative method to unity, in characterizing the poster campaign. This usage gradually entered the B156 workers' vocabularies, through exposure to *FMS* (though they could also use *ekta* [unity], in its more horizontal valences, as a synonym for *talmel*). They otherwise utilized the word in its more common usages, as concord, compatibility, and understanding in interpersonal dealings, for example, between machine partners, neighbors, friends, or husbands and wives.

Chapter 4. Struggle Across Borders

1. The company also ceased giving orders to Khan sahab's vendor unit in Ghaziabad. His factory stopped functioning and paying wages. The ex-B156 workers dispersed. Vijay came back to C82.

2. *Pakoras*: vegetable fritters.

3. Their final settlements from Metal Artware Exports and Dhatu Exports, they were told, would be given at the conclusion of the legal dispute.

4. It is unclear why all of the B156 workers were not given such offers (in which case, they might have accepted), but possible reasons include managerial constraints arising from the legal dispute and hesitations due to the lockout contestation.

5. "*Calo, calo, bahar calo!*"

6. "*Kya taklif hai?!*"

7. The sparse case notes by the surgery ward doctors for the following days, indicating a steady decline in the patient's condition, contradicted my direct observations. The case notes might have been written by a doctor after the death, so as to create a plausible story, according to a neurosurgeon from the All India Institute of Medical Sciences.

8. Weil (1986b:163).

9. "*Mazdur admi ka koi thikana nahim hota.*" The saying is invoked to describe workers' changing work situations, residences, and movements (e.g., within the city, to and from the village), and conveys the sense of vulnerability and exposure to hazardous work, illnesses, road accidents, and inadequate medical treatment.

10. "*Ye Ramdev ki lash par union ka jhanda buland karna cahte the.*"

11. "*Pure Okhla mem shor hai! Director I cor hai! Jute maro sale ko! Ramdev sathi amar rahe! Uski maut ka zimmedar kaun hai? Directors I and II javab do! Uski patni ko naukri do!*"

12. "All must pass in this way (*Sabki yahi gatya hai*)," Varmaji added. "All have to become like this, all who are born in this cosmos, in this mortal world. The passing that has occurred, this is truth, it has to happen to all (*Isi sthiti mem sabko ana hai, jitne is Brahmand mem, is mrityulok mem paida hue haim. Jo gati hui hai, yahi satya hai, aisa hona hai*)."

13. "*Calo bhai, bahar calo!*"

14. The B156 workers also gave them Rs. 2,700 of Ramdev's dues from a savings committee in the factory.

15. Ramdev grew up in Madhubani district, Bihar. From an early age, he worked in his family fields and did wage work in others' fields. In his early teens, he went to work in a street-side eatery in Siliguri, West Bengal, before returning and getting married to Shibbo Devi. He traveled to Kurukshetra, Haryana for agricultural work, alongside others from his village, at Rs. 3,000–4,000, for long workdays, for about three years. In 1990, he came to Delhi, began work as a construction helper for Rs. 30–35 a day, then worked at a garment export company for most of the decade. He learned various kinds of work in factories in Govindpuri, Tughlakabad, and Khanpur, including washing, spotting, dry cleaning, cutting, steam pressing, checking, packing, and field purchases, with his monthly earnings rising to Rs. 3,000–3,500. Due to reductions in export orders in 1999, he began learning polishing at a factory in Okhla, on piece rates. A year later, when orders sharply declined, a relative at the head office factory of Metal Artware Exports directed him to B156, where he was hired as a helper in April 2001, at Rs. 1,800 wages. His wages rose to Rs. 2,592, a few months later, when he was regularized.

16. "*Kaun lagaya?! Are sale! Tu janta nahim kitna banta hai?!*"

17. "*Zarurat hai zyada qurbani ki.*"

18. "*Okhla ke andar mahaul ko garam karemge.*"

19. After an agreement mediated by Sonia Gandhi and Left unions, permanent workers were reinstated, while hundreds of contract workers lost jobs. On occurrences of violence in later

years at factories in the Delhi region, see Ness (2016:92–105), Shyam Sundar (2012), and Yadav (2015).

20. *"Metal polish udyog mem ESI-PF lagu karo," "Metal polish kamgarom ki svasthya suraksha ki guarantee karo," "Mask-dastane-gur-pine ka pani sabko do," "Thekedari kilo ke bhav nahim calega," "Sangathit ho. Sangharsh karo."*

21. *"B156 ma saman hai. Yaham jhanda danda lagana mujhse dekha nahim jata."*

22. *"Bahncod side hoke nara laga!"*

23. *"Metal Artware ka cor malik hosh mem ao! C109 ka malik cor hai! Vetan dena parega!"*

24. Govind, the supervisor, who had taken part in the procession, reflected on the activities of the management, which were inviting *karmic* punishments. "This is the blatant exercise of muscle force. It is injustice. We've been always asking them only for work. Now they're doing wrong to us. When will they be punished—will they be, when—no one knows (*Yah khule am dadagiri hai. Anyay hai. Unse ham hamesha kam hi mang rahe haim. Ab vo hamare sath galat kar rahe haim, to uska dand unhem kab milega—milega, kab milega—koi nahim janta*)."

25. *"Ghut ghut ke marne se barhiya hai larai larke maro. Do car din, pamc din ki larai mem hamem ar-par hona cahie."*

26. *"Ham apne hisab se laremge, jaise hamem larna cahie."* Just as workers practiced *apne hisab se kam karna* (auto-regulated working) at the machines, they seemed to advocate *apne hisab se larna* (autonomous struggle guided by their own discussions and deliberations). They seemed to seek strong leaders, to give knowledge and direction, make decisions, handle dealings in the labor office, and protect them from the management and the police. But they also wanted to think for themselves and decide their own activities. They seemed to desire, at once, authority and autonomy.

27. On the Jhalani Tools struggle, see Majdoor Samachar-Kamunist Kranti (1998).

28. *"Do malikom ke bic pis gaya mazdur," "Tankhvah band, malik farar," "Dashahra phika, Dipavali andhkar."*

29. *"Naukri sarkar ki, seva punjipatiyom ki."*

30. *"Metal Artware Exports ke mazdur."*

31. These legal settlements were in the range of Rs. 21,000–35,000.

32. *"Vacancy nahim hai yah. Yah hamara pura Okhla ki vacancy hai!"*

33. *"Kya hai bhaiyya?"*

34. *"Are bhai, tankvah band, malik farar!"*

35. Lallan's words suggest an implicit connection between the military martyrs of the India Gate monument, with its (erstwhile) burning flame, and the B156 workers, who were also martyrs of sorts, bearing witness to the development process and its correlates, struggling against oppression and injustice, with placards as nonviolent weapons.

36. *"VIP ilaka hai. Kabhi bhi action utha sakta hai, ki yaham kya kar raha hai?"*

37. *"Court se bara koi nahim hota."*

38. *"Ham apne haq ke lie lar rahe haim."*

39. *"Apni larai to ham lar rahe haim. Lekin thekedari ke ham khilaf larai lar rahe haim, anya companiyom mem bhi ESI-PF lagu hona cahie. Yah sari batem, to keval mere sath hi nahim haim, anya mazdurom ke bhi sath haim."*

40. *"Jab admi kahim bhi rahta hai, agar jhompri bhi banata hai . . . Maim janta hum svarg nahim. Baki pyar factory se nahim, pyar samaj se hai. Samaj bikhar jaega hamara. Naukri to hamem bahut mil jaegi, factory isse acchi mil jaegi, isse accha kuradan mil jaega. Lekin aisa hamara samaj nahim milega."*

41. In contrast to Rajender's letter of demands, which included excess desiderata, to be conceded during negotiations, the Justice for Workers petition contained only three demands.

42. *"Payment ki bat mat karo! Yaham dikhna nahim cahie! Lath se khopda phar dumga!"*

43. *"Bhai hat jao, phir a jao."*

44. "*Haram zyade kutte! Tum log yaham kyom khare ho?!*"

45. "*Tum khud apne haq ke lie bolo!*"

46. Sher Singh and I also gave written statements.

47. "*Maro pito aur bhagao.*"

48. On the history of nonviolent protests in India, including by those who viewed nonviolence as a provisional, strategic method, see Hardiman (2013:45–47; 2018; 2021).

49. One might see in the placards struggle, and in its implicit nonviolence, an image of what Ashis Nandy describes as a mythic Gandhi, who lives among those who might know little of Gandhi, "a symbol of those struggling against injustice, while trying to retain their humanity even when faced with unqualified inhumanity" (Nandy 2021:267).

50. "*Are tum log samay batao aur date do! Calte haim! Sale sari compani ko ag laga dete haim, phumk dalte haim!*"

51. "*Bahncod ane to do, un salom ko mar karke yahim bicha demge.*"

52. "*Mazdurom ka koi bharosa nahim.*"

53. "*Yah tariqa galat hai! Aise ilake mem thik nahim lagta hai.*"

54. The C109 managers had given her a collection from the management and workers of Rs. 32,000.

55. "*Thik kar rahe ho tum log.*"

56. "There was also feeling there (*Dil mem bhi bat thi*)," said Ramkumar.

57. "*Acchi bat hai, khare raho!*"

58. Weil (1952a:200).

59. "*Hamse hoga sale gatte to phar karke do car sale to maim akele nipat lumga.*"

60. "*Rs. 3,000, 3,500, je mil raha hai, vahi mang rahe haim. Utna utna paise ham log kya karemge? Vo to khatm ho jaega, pata bhi nahim calega.*"

61. "*Sirf 'don't' kat do, tumhare gatte ke sath photo le leta hum.*"

62. "*Isse kuch hone vala nahim!*"

63. "*Dusra admin, bas apna bhar dekh rahe haim, aur kya, sath kya demge. Bas vo sath mem haim, bas yah sun rahe haim. Sath kaham dene vala haim.*"

64. An early story on the struggle appeared in the newspaper *Prabhat Khabar*, which circulated in Jharkhand.

65. "*Sara problem ko solve vo kar leti thi. Mujhe kuch karna nahim tha. Mujhe sirf cycle uthao, pahumco, phalane phalane jagah pe, sangharsh ke lie.*"

66. "*Lekin chorna mat.*"

67. "*Babu, kabhi aisi bat mat karna taki log bag ap pe arop lagaem.*"

68. "*Us time to kuch samajh mem nahim ata tha, itni pareshani. Ghar mem na koi ciz, na paise. Tension to bahut thi ki kya hoga, kaise bacce ko jilaya jae, dudh kaham se laya jae, kaise kharc calae jae. Rona ata tha, bas.*"

69. "*Calo, koi bat nahim, dekha jaega jo hoga.*"

70. "*Itne paise se kam nahim calega.*"

71. "*Kya karte haim sara din? Kuch ho nahim raha hai!*"

72. "*Papa, cup raho. Jao, cale jao.*"

73. "*Kab tak aise karte rahoge?! Kuch nahim hoga! Hisab le lo! Jo de raha hai to le lo!*"

74. "*Do lakh dega tab lumga.*"

75. "*Do lakh de dega?!*"

76. "*Pata nahim dega ki nahim dega! Kuch ho nahim raha hai!*"

77. "*Dekhie, thoda bahut kuch ho hi raha hai, pata nahim lag raha hai, lekin andar andar kuch to ho raha hai. Ab dekho, Tehkhand Mor tak gari leke a ja rahe haim.*"

78. "*Calo, Naresh, calo.*"

79. "*Ham isko map nahim sakte haim.*"

80. This might be read as an instance of what Arjun Appadurai calls the "paradox of patience in the face of emergency" (Appadurai 2013:192).

81. While certain workers were more audible in meetings (e.g., Amlakant, Varmaji, and others), many contributed in distinctive ways to the discussions and the struggle. The Jharkhandis, who were relatively quiet in meetings, were critically active in organizing protests and other activities.

82. "No one was able to realize the importance of these meetings (*Isi meeting ka mahatva koi nahim samajh pae*)," Firoz recounted.

83. This discussion of nonviolent methods reminds one of Weil, who writes:

> We must strive to substitute more and more in this world *effective* non-violence for violence.
>
> Non-violence is no good unless it is effective. Hence the young man's question to Gandhi about his sister. The answer should have been: Use force unless you are such that you can defend her with as much chance of success without violence. Unless you possess a radiance of which the energy (that is to say, the possible effectiveness in the most material sense of the word) is equal to that contained in your muscles.
>
> We should strive to become such that we are able to be non-violent.
>
> This depends also on the adversary. (Weil 1952a:137)

On the effectiveness of nonviolent movements in the twentieth century, see Chenoweth and Stephan (2011).

84. "*Aise faisla nahim hone vala hai. Ap log bahut din gatte dikhaye. Ap log Gandhivadi ban gae haim, lekin tumhem azadi nahim milne vali hai. Ab batao, kab ikkatha hona hai.*" On the importance of causes other than nonviolent resistance in bringing about Independence, see Hardiman (2021:313–314).

85. "*Are raho! Aj nahim to kal dega!*"

86. "To stand with placards is a struggle of weak persons. We don't fight like this. We don't bow down and fight. This is not called a real struggle (*Gatte leke khare hona, yah kamzor logom ki larai hai. Ham aise nahim larte haim. Ham jhuk ke nahim larte haim. Is larai ko larai nahim kahte haim*)," Dr. Das said to Naresh, at a visit to a placard protest in December.

87. "*Chorna mat.*"

88. "*Bhai sahab, are raho!*"

89. Weil (1986b:173).

90. In *Hind Swaraj*, Gandhi writes of the existence of forces opposed to brute force, of soul-force (*atmabal*) and truth-force (*satyagraha*), exhibited in nonviolent activities that noncooperate with perceived injustice (M. Gandhi 2010:72–81).

91. In this commingling of the categories of force, *metaxu*, *ahimsa*, truth force, *haq*, and justice, in the unfolding of the struggle, one could see bridges (*metaxu*) in thought and politics between Weil, Gandhi, and working people.

Chapter 5. Warp and Weft

1. See Virottam (1972:23–24, 63) and Mohan (1973:9, 27).

2. "Distant drums sound appealing (*Dur ke dhol suhavne lagte haim*)" is an oft-heard saying among migrants, in describing images of the city in the village.

3. Interview with Sunil Bidhuri, municipal councillor, November 2005. Other residents gave estimates of 30,000–100,000 migrants. In the late nineties and early 2000s, about 100 units, mostly in dyeing, zinc plating, and lathe work, closed down in Tehkhand due to government sealing drives, displacing 500–1,000 workers. About one quarter of the B156 workers lived in Tehkhand village.

4. To cover these costs and be able to send money home, Naresh felt he needed a basic wage, before overtime, of at least Rs. 5,000.

5. "*Kalyug sayana ho gaya.*"

6. In discussing the effects of tension, Mithilesh invoked a couplet of Kabir: "*Cinta se ghate caturai, dukh se ghate sharir / Lobh se ghate Lakshmi, kah gaye das Kabir* (From worries, you lose your senses, from sorrow, the body diminishes / From greed, wealth flees, so says Kabirdas)."

7. These vendors were mostly Kumhars (Backward Class) from Chando, Anita Devi's village, who were his brothers-in-law (*sale*) in village kin terms.

8. *Gutkha*: a mixture of tobacco, betel nut, and other ingredients. *Ganja*: cannabis.

9. "*Apne admi sab jalte rahte haim. Kaise bahar mem rah rahe haim, do paisa kama rahe haim, kaise accha se kha rahe haim, kapda sahi se pahn rahe haim, kaise age barh rahe haim. Yah sab zyada admin haim. To usko kuch athi karemge to barhiya se roti nahim kha payega, pareshan bhi rahega.*"

10. On spirit possession, shamanic healing, and witchcraft among *adivasis*, see Hardiman and Raje (2008), Kakar (1982), Shekhar (2014), Singh (1993), Sinha (2015), and Sundar (2001).

11. Several of the B156 workers, including Amlakant, Firoz, Naresh II, Rambachan II, Sivam, and Varmaji, articulated beliefs in spirit affliction and shamanic healing. On one occasion, Naresh II and Rambachan II assisted in bringing Anita Devi to a healer in Rambachan II's neighborhood in Faridabad.

12. Souls in the *Kalyug*, it seems from these beliefs, had to struggle with the invasions of unwelcome, disembodied, malicious souls, directed into them by the egoism, envy, and hostility of other, *Kalyug*-distorted souls.

13. "*Usko thode hi pata hai kya karte haim vaham. Dimag kharab hai vaham.*"

14. "*Pahle se adho sharir nahim hai.*"

15. "*Sab ke pet vaham cal rahe haim sab apne bivi bacce pal rahe haim to ham log nahim pal paemge?*"

16. Such trips could cost Rs. 5,000–13,000 each time.

17. In 2005, this paper route became advantageous as Naresh could access press reports on the struggle in the early mornings, share them with the B156 workers, and distribute them at the C109 gate.

18. I am drawing the term *unvanquished* from *Aparajito* (The Unvanquished) (1956) and the work of Ashis Nandy (e.g., Nandy 1983), which seem to gesture to a condition of ongoing struggle against formidable forces, which rises neither to heroic victory nor descends into ignominious defeat, but survives between these poles.

19. On viewing cancer as potentially caused by sorcery, among lower caste women in Tamilnadu, see Van Hollen (2022:197–213).

20. An ESI doctor who was not involved in Madodari Devi's treatment looked at her case papers the following year and observed, "This clearly shows the apathy shown by all these doctors, for the poorest of the people, who come with a lot of faith to them." The doctors had been neglectful and cruel, he felt, due to an absence of empathy and compassion for the patients. "Most of the doctors, when they see a patient, they do not identify the patient with a human being like them. With a misery like them. They think they are just like nothing. Why should they see them properly?" he said.

21. "*Ekdam pura chachan rahi thi yah. Aur vo log khali yaham vaham daura raha tha, yah karo to vo karo. Aur isko dard zyada ho raha tha. Koi doctor dekh bhi nahim raha tha hali. Koi sun nahim rahe the.*" "*Vahan hamari sunvai nahim hai* (We are not heard there) is the dominant expression used to refer to one's encounters with government hospitals and dispensaries," writes Veena Das, in describing the experiences of the urban poor in Delhi (Das 2003:98). Tapesvar's phrase, "*Koi sun nahim rahe the,*" conveys the sense that no one was listening to them, but also, to draw on Weil, no one was attending to her suffering (Weil 1951).

22. *"Ab bekar hai, ab kuch nahim hoga."*

23. *"Pura ghar barbad karke rakh diya, do tin sal se, dava dava dava! Kamre mem pareshan karke rakhi hai! Mariyo nahim rahi hai jaldi!"*

24. For an example of the reverse process, of poor mothers who triage their offspring, see Scheper-Hughes (1992).

25. *"Baithiye na."*

26. As in the struggle across borders, one could see degrees of empathy and solidarity among the Jharkhandis, in times of crisis, but also, tendencies toward insularity, withdrawal, and spectatorship.

27. *"Calio gailak. Miliyo ke na gail."*

28. *"Langra bhi nahim rahne diya bahn. Puri zindagi le liya hai."*

29. *"Barhiya se rahiha, mil julke rahiha, larai jhagra mat kariha."*

30. That morning in Tehkhand, Tapesvar expressed reluctance to buy a new *sari* for the cremation, which cost Rs. 100, or about a day's wages, saying, "What's the point of getting a *sari* (*Ka hoga sari*)?" One was reminded of Premchand's story "The Shroud (*Kafan*)," in which Ghisu says, after the death of his daughter-in-law, Budhiya, "What's the point of throwing a shroud over her? In the end it just burns up. She can't take anything with her" (Premchand 1969b:191). Varmaji angrily said to him, "I don't know whether you ever got her a *sari* before or not, but today, at her last rites, the least you can do is to cover her body. She'll never ask you again (*Pahle pata nahim pahnaya tha ki nahim pahnaya tha baki aj last mem marte dam kam se kam uske tan ko dhak de. Ab dubara tere se kabhi mangne nahim aegi*)." Tapesvar bought the *sari*.

31. On the politics of Rajbhars, including the communal dimensions of narratives of Suheldev, see Amin (2015), Chandra (2017), and Narayan (2009:80–100).

32. *Kabaddi*: a contact sport.

33. "One didn't know when it was day or night, there was that much freedom. There was no kind of tension. Time passed so easily, it felt like we were roaming in heaven (*Din rat kuch malum nahim parta tha, itni azadi rahti thi. Koi kisi prakar ki tension nahim rahti thi. Samay aisa kat jata hai jaise malum parta hai ki svarg mem ghum rahe haim*)," Varmaji says.

34. *"Paise nahim haim."*

35. *"Daru pine ke lie paise rahte haim, aur hamare lie paise nahim haim."*

36. *"Tum kisi kam layak nahim ho! Tum to dhang se baccom ka parvarish nahim kar sakte ho! Tum ek bhikhari se bhi gaye guzre ho!"*

37. *"Cup kar, bahn ki lauri, bhosrivali, dimag kharab kar deti hai!"*

38. *"Hata! Durga Vurga koi nahim hai! Ya sab dhakosla hai!"*

39. In Old Delhi, non-Muslims go to Sufi shrines and mosques for assistance with ailments and afflictions, where they are given amulets (A. Gandhi 2013:200–201).

40. "It's good that he got injured, at least he mended his ways (*Chot lag gaya accha hua, kam se kam sudhar to gae*)," Durgawati said.

41. *"Khatre mem bhi kuch anand hota hai, aur admi us thoda sa anand ke cakkar mem bilkul daldal mem phamsta cala jata hai aur apne bhavishya ko khud andhkar mem dalta hai, aur adharm ko nimantran deta hai ki ao, hamare upar havi ho. To aise maim phamsa."*

42. *"Agar mere ko pata hota itne darubaz haim, maim shadi karti nahim. Maimne apne bhavishya mem kabhi soca hi nahim tha mujhe aise admi milem."*

43. *"Sab nasib ka hi khel hota hai."*

44. *"Kuch karo lagan se! Kuch karke dikhana hai!"* Ironically, the B156 management could use similar words when seeking to motivate polishers to work hard, raise production, and show their capabilities, if they wanted to get ahead in the company.

45. In *Roti Kapada Aur Makaan* (1974), Zeenat Aman's character tells her unemployed, brooding boyfriend, as they sit together in a park in Delhi, that she sometimes wishes that he were her dashing, wealthy, industrialist boss. "Then all my dreams would be fulfilled. Life would

not lag behind, standing in line for buses. . . . [L]ife in big cars would go faster than time (*To mere sare sapne pure ho jate. Zindagi busom ki line mem lagkar piche nahim rah jati. . . . [Z]indagi bari bari carom mem vaqt se tez bhagti*)." She plans to go with her boss on a trip to America, and says, glancing up at the sky, "As soon as I get a passport, my flight takes off! (*Idhar passport bana, udhar havai jahaz ura!*)"

46. Durgawati would wash Varmaji's blackened work clothes at the hand pump in Hari Nagar, seemingly without the embarrassment or shame that was sometimes felt by polishers in their homes. As she scrubbed with detergent, and black grime oozed out, women neighbors would ask her why she was washing such filthy, foul-smelling clothes. "The blackness that is seeping out is the earnings that I live on (*Yahi to sab paise haim, kale kale jitne gir rahe haim, isse kamai khati hum*)," she would respond.

47. Only a few of the B156 workers' wives (e.g., of Prakash, Divan [Prakash's brother-in-law], Ramakant, and Vijay II) worked in Okhla factories. Neelam, Divan's wife, worked for a few months as a B156 helper, doing packing in the upstairs office, but was terminated by the manager. On the ideal of the male provider in working-class families in Delhi, in contexts of precarious work, compulsion, and women's wage work practices, see Grover (2017:36–46) and *The City Beautiful* (2003).

48. Though Varmaji was against allowing his wife to work, in 2005, he passionately urged Ramdev's widow, Shibbo Devi, to fight alongside the B156 workers for a job in the new factory in Okhla, against the wishes of the managers and her relatives (who did not wish to lose *izzat* by permitting her to work), as a way to provide for her children and avoid oppressive dependence on her in-laws.

49. "*Maim kama rahi hum! Tum mere bal-bute par ho!*"

50. In cinema, see *Chakravyuha* (1978), *Ardh Satya* (1983), *Vaastav* (1999), and *Chakravyuh* (2012). On poetry and plays on the Abhimanyu theme, see Lothspeich (2009:106–162). Ratan Thiyam's *Chakravyuha* (Thiyam 1998) is a recasting of the episode in Manipuri theater. Ranjan Palit's documentary, *Abhimanyu's Face* (2001), explores Chhau performance traditions of the Abhimanyu story in West Bengal.

51. The womb story does not appear in the critical edition (Smith 2009:420).

52. In a cognate image, Naresh spoke of feeling entangled in a mesh of affective attachments (*mayajal*), with attendant tensions and responsibilities, with regard to Anita Devi, Guddu, and other family members, from which exit was not easily possible.

53. "*Maim cakravyuh mem par gai. Shadi ho gai. Ab chor to sakti nahim.*"

54. For explorations of love, alongside conflict, in working-class families in Delhi, see Grover (2017), Kakar (1989:65–84), and *The City Beautiful* (2003).

55. "*Tumhare bas ki bat nahim!*"

56. "*Jab admi akela rahta hai, to bahut ajib sa lagta hai. Vivahit jivan aisa hota hai ki sat ath sal agar sath guzar lo, aur phin bikhrav uske andar hota to zindagi bahut bhari nazar ati.*"

57. "*Thand lag rahi hai. Kaun si duty karne jate ho? Kitne kamake lae bahut subere khana mangte ho?*"

58. "*Sangharsh ke dauran yah kahumga ki help bahut ki.*"

59. In 2013, in a loosening of patriarchical *izzat* norms, Varmaji allowed Durgawati to work and stay with Radha, their Nepali landlord, doing cooking, dusting, and other chores in the large house of a fashion designer in Sainik Farms. The job involved more continuous, extended hard work (*mehnat*), she felt, than working in the village home. She earned Rs. 4,000 a month, which rose to Rs. 9,500 by 2019, when she was let go.

60. There were other instances of mixed caste rooming. A few years later, Surinder brought two Scheduled Caste migrants and lived with them in one room. Naresh helped in getting them trained in metal polishing. Two Cheros in Naresh's boundary lived with a Muslim from the village for several months. At times, Naresh ate in these rooms. Chero women, Naresh felt, were

more rigid in observing village norms. When he was living with non-Chero migrants, he would bring his aunt, who lived in the same building, tasty dishes like *sag* (green, leafy vegetable curry), cooked in his room. She would look at the dishes with desire but refused to try them. Anita Devi had cordial dealings with her immediate neighbors in the boundary, who were thought to be Scheduled Caste, but she avoided exchanging food with them.

61. In traveling to the village, the Cheros often relied on the assistance of a young Muslim migrant from Chando, Raizul, whom Naresh called son (*beta*), in village kin terms, who stayed near the Old Delhi railway station, purchased tickets in advance, and when the train arrived, pushed his short, wiry body through the crowds to claim spaces for them on the berths of a general compartment.

62. The non-Chero migrant roomates were from Chando and addressed Naresh in village kin terms, as brother-in-law (*jija*) and aunt's husband (*phupha*).

63. "*Bhai ke tarah rahte haim pardes mem. Ek dusre ka sahara ho jata hai. Milkar khao, kamao. Pardes mem zyada chuachut samjhemge to admi cal nahim payega.*"

64. When he visited the home of a Scheduled Caste (Chamar) migrant in Chando, in whose room he had eaten food in Delhi, he ate snacks and sweets and drank water in the fields (not inside the home), but did not publicize it to other Cheros, to avoid possible disapproval.

65. An exception was Guptaji, whose surname and self-reporting suggested a forward caste (Bania) background.

66. Workers seemed to treat Muslims as a caste, and were less interested in their internal castes.

67. In a study of a hydroelectric project in Orissa, caste ambiguities were present in the workplace and neighborhood, along with a loosening of commensal restrictions, while caste rules were more rigidly observed in home villages (Strumpell 2008).

68. At bathing time, the Jharkhandis also seemed more willing to share soap fragments among themselves, rather than with others.

69. Alongside such discourse, Rajender was flexible in his own eating practices and associative circles. He shared food, with saliva transfers, with Bhagvati, who was his neighbor in the Tata Steel shanty cluster, and sang Bhojpuri songs (*birha*) with a music group that included Bhagvati and other Scheduled Caste workers. Rajender went to Prakash's party.

70. "*Calo, koi bat nahim, pardes hai, calega.*"

71. Uday did not know Prakash's caste, and did not wish to find out, he said, as such knowledge could create undesirable obstacles, in matters such as commensality. B. K. Singh, Naresh's relative and neighbor, advised Naresh to go, as Prakash was a friend and a good person, and because they were distant from the village, so did not have to fear caste expulsion.

72. *Puris*: deep-fried, puffy bread.

73. Varmaji, who lived close by in Hari Nagar, believed Prakash was from a Backward Class (Verma), which is also what Prakash self-reported in interviews.

74. "*Chamar siyar bade hoshiyar / Jaham lut pare, vaham tut pare / Jaham mar pare vaham bhag pare.*" While seemingly believing such generalizations, it is also true that every morning, before coming to B156, Amlakant would stop to sit, chat, and read the paper at the Okhla shop of his closest friend in Delhi, who was from his village and of Scheduled Caste origin.

75. "*Chorie, jat pat se kya hota hai? Ravidasji jat ke Chamar the, jute silte the. Baki dekhie kitne buddhijivi the.*"

76. Arun, Amlakant, and Ramakant identified as Kurmi, Yadav, and Maurya respectively (Backward Classes). Naresh II's caste was ambiguous to the Jharkhandis (he self-reported as Thakur [upper caste]).

77. After a late-night call from Surinder, describing Varmaji's symptoms, I got more closely involved in the diagnosis.

78. The leaders were Lal Mani Prasad, Bahujan Samaj Party (1993 Assembly elections), Surendra Yadav, Janata Dal (1996 Parliament elections), and Indrajeet Mishra, Bharatiya Janata Party (1998 Parliament elections). They won their seats.

79. In the 2000s, Varmaji's brother became a member of the Hindu Yuva Vahini, a Hindu nationalist organization founded by Yogi Adityanath.

80. "*Garv se kaho, ham Hindu haim, Hindustan hamara hai!*"

81. "*Ram Lalla ham ayemge, vahim mandir banayemge! Katue kate jaemge, Ram nam cillaemge!*"

82. "*Tretayug mem Bhagvan paida hue the, jhagra aj kar rahe ho Kalyug mem uske lie.*"

83. "*Jis parmatma ko maim manta hum usi parmatma ko vo bhi mante haim. Aur kya, unke lie special Bhagvan banke ae haim, kya? Ya hamare lie special banke ae haim? Nahim. Hai eka hi vo, baki ham kisi aur dhang se unko dekhte haim aur vo kisi aur dhang se dekhte haim.*"

84. To Varmaji, the Metal Artware Exports managers were contractors of ethical wrong (*adharm ke thekedar*).

85. Among Muslims in Zakir Nagar, the machinations of political and religious leaders were also seen to be a cause of communal violence (Kirmani 2013:129–130).

86. "*Ra se rakshas ki tarah, ja se janta ko, na se nuksan pahumcane vala, aur ta se tikrambazi karne vala.*"

87. "*Us sammelan mem meri koi dilcaspi nahim. Maim Hindu hum. Baki maim nahim manta hum, sab Hinduom ko ikattha karke Mussalmanom ko mar dalna. Nahim.*"

88. Since his early days in Delhi, Varmaji had lived, eaten, and drunk liquor in rooms with Scheduled Caste workers (e.g., Ramjit, Rambhooan, Mahesh). At the factory, Varmaji was one of the few (along with Govind and Rajender) to greet and shake hands with Rajpal, an elder, casually employed, Scheduled Caste worker from Firozabad, Uttar Pradesh, who swept, removed garbage, and occasionally descended into the sewer, in only an undershirt and shorts, with no mask or boots, to manually clear blockages.

89. *Halva*: sweets.

90. "What guarantee is there [that you don't eat beef]? (*Tumhara kya bharosa hai?*)" Durgawati would sometimes say, with a smile, when asking Firoz to bring his own glass or bowl from his room. When Khan sahab visited, he too was served in her separate vessels. Firoz was of the Dhunia caste, a Backward Class in Uttar Pradesh.

91. For example, in 2003, when Priti fell ill, and Varmaji was on night duty, Firoz brought Durgawati and her daughter to a hospital in Badarpur for treatment.

92. This was in stark contrast to the difficulties in arranging blood among the Jharkhandis during Madodari Devi's treatment in 2006.

93. *Papad*: thin, crisp flatbread.

94. "*Utna dur mat jao. Hamem bahut dikkat hoti hai.*"

95. "*Uparvala eka hi hai. Manne ka admi ke har har tariqa alag alag hai, sab alag alag nam se lete haim. Ham Allah karke bulate haim, vo Ram karke bulate haim, vo Isu karke bulate haim. Hamara Bhagvan sahi hai, aur unke Bhagvan bekar hai, yah to galat bat hai. Apni jagah pe sab mazhab sahi haim.*"

96. "*Bismillah Allahu Akbar.*"

97. "*Accha jao, namaz parkar ao.*"

98. "*[K]isi ki dharmik bhavnaom par thes nahim pahumcana cahie. Hamara dharm yah allow nahim karta hai, is ciz ko kabhi anumati nahim deta hai*" (Patwardhan 1992). The political and religious leaders of the Ram temple movement, Lal Das felt, were motivated not by devotion, but by desires for power (*kursi*) and wealth (*paisa*). On Lal Das, see Nandy et al. (1995:47–50).

99. "*Bas, bas!*"

100. On the inversion of social roles during Holi, see Marriott (1966).

101. *Gujiyas*: fried, sweet dumplings.

102. In Tehkhand, this touching could sometimes provoke sudden eruptions of verbal abuses and scuffles among men, with apologies, reconciliations, and a resumption of the festive atmosphere. To Varmaji, such touching was often driven by opportunistic, lustful, *Kalyug*-like feelings (*Kalyugi bhavna*).

103. On a previous Holi, Ramakant ran into Kalim in the lane outside his building in Tehkhand. Though Ramakant ordinarily had only harsh things to say about Kalim's informing and shirking activities, combined with negative generalizations about Muslims, Ramakant smiled, embraced him, and brought him to his room for food and drinks.

104. In the nineties, Naresh would hear of incidents of communal tensions in Palamu, during the festival of Muharram, when Muslims would gather in large numbers, take out processions, and sometimes block roads, which could induce quarrels and altercations with Hindus. These tensions could heighten when Muharram occurred close to the festivals of Ramnavami and Durga Puja. Hindus might block the *taziyas*, and Muslims might not permit Hindus to pass with their deities. On the participation of non-Muslims in Muharram, see Chandavarkar (1994:235), Hyder (2006:54–55, 172), Kumar (1988:215–216), Mohapatra (2007), and Naqvi (2012:60–66).

105. *Chole bhature*: deep-fried, puffy bread with chickpeas.

106. Varmaji took keen interest in a scene in *Khuddar* (1994), in which a police inspector beats a corrupt politican onstage with the latter's shoe, at a political rally.

107. Durgawati served Firoz and the other Muslims in separate vessels and glass bowls, brought by Firoz.

108. Weil (1977:54).

109. The term *tana bana* (warp and weft) arises in multiple sources, including poetry, novels, ethnography, and films. A song ("Jhini Chadariya") of the weaver-poet Kabir invokes the image in describing the body as a complex, intricate, divinely woven garment (Hess 2015:167–168). It is a deep, complex image in Reza's description of the evolving relations among rival families, diverse castes, men and women, Hindus and Muslims, and other persons and phenomena in a village in Ghazipur district, Uttar Pradesh (Reza 2008). It also appears in depictions of weavers in Benaras, to describe social and economic relations between and among Muslims and Hindus (Bismillah 1996; Raman 2010). The image is subtly evoked in the activity of women's quilting in the village, as an implicit metaphor for the difficult work of sustaining families, and the vital interweaving of Hindu and Muslim persons, communities, and inheritances within a precarious and violent social fabric, in *Gaman* (1978).

110. I draw instruction here from Thomas Carlyle's image of organic filaments, "mysteriously spinning themselves," interconnecting elements of society, and giving rise to a new society (Carlyle 1918:183–191; the image is also invoked by Ambedkar [Ambedkar 2014:280, 282]). In migrant worlds, the weaving of integrative filaments is an active, agentive, difficult, though not always self-conscious process. For theological explorations, taking guidance from Walt Whitman's image of a lone spider spinning filaments, akin to one's soul seeking connections in the cosmos, see Tracy (2020b). A Hindi equivalent, which was not audible among the workers, is *tantu* (strings, threads, filaments). For a resonant, ethnographic image of the workings of centrifugal forces (to do with the agricultural development process) and centripetal social connections in a village in Maharashtra, see Appadurai (1990:212).

Chapter 6. Churning

1. "Fate is forged according to one's actions (*Karm ke hisab se qismat banti hai*)," says Sabbir.

2. For resonances of such views in village studies, see Fuller (1992:246–248), Sharma (1973:353, 356, 363), and Wadley and Derr (1989).

3. Migrants come to Delhi and work in factories, says Rajender, to change one's unfavorable fate.

4. On the multiplicity of possible causes and explanations for actions and events, see Babb (1983:173) and Daniel (1983:40–41, 45).

5. "*Ek ghatna mem kai cizem juri hoti haim.*"

6. "*Bhagvan dete haim chappar pharke aur lete haim to gand pharke.*"

7. "*Jitna atyacar hamari company mem ho raha hai, uparvala sab jan raha hai, maim iska badla zarur lumga.*"

8. "*Kya pata ki vo ham logom ke sath jo atyacar kar rahe haim, vo hamare purv janam ki kahani cal rahi ho, aur uske dand ham log bhog rahe hom. Ham purv janam mem unko sataye, vo aj hamem sata rahe haim.*"

9. "Tell me, if everyone were to become [as wealthy as] Director I, then who will rub steel today in this factory? One needs workers. Who will those workers be? Poor folk (*Bataie, agar har admi Director I hi ho jae, to aj Director I ki factory mem steel ko kaun ghisega? Worker to cahie. To worker kaun hoga? Garib log*)," says Rajender.

10. "*Jo amir admi rahemge vo to paise kauri hi mem apna busy rahemge to hamara nam kab lemge. Jo garib admi rahemge, hamara nam lemge.*"

11. The image of marionettes in a divine play also appears in Daniel (1983:40) and Fuller (1992:251–252).

12. "*Ek natak likh rahe haim vo, aur usi ke ham patr ban karke kam kar rahe haim. Jaise filmom mem hota hai, writer kahani likhta hai, uspar adharit vo film banate haim, aur usi director us kahani ke mutabik un sabko nacata hai. Vo katputli haim ham log. Jaise hamem nacaya jata hai vaise ham nacte haim.*"

13. "*Vo apni lila natak khel raha hai. Kisi se galti karvata hai, kisi se dand dilvata hai, kisi ko marvata hai, kisi ko paida karta hai. Ham logom ko aise carha karke ghuma karke apna manoranjan kar raha hai.*"

14. "*Pura agar lila dekhemge to ekdam bilkul niras lagta hai. Kahim kuch anand layak hai hi nahim. Aur Ram Rajya ane vala nahim hai.*" On diverse interpretations of Ram's rule, see Ambedkar (2014:269), Hardiman (2021:47, 280, 283), and Lutgendorf (1991:371–392).

15. "*Nac bhi kai prakar ke haim. Ek bhakti ka nac nacie, ek adharm ka nac nacie.*" In acting ethically and devotedly, one might suggest, one acts nonegoistically, from the true soul-valence, the site of the indwelling divine, and in so doing, attempts to become (agentive) marionettes of God's will.

16. "*Mele mem sab kuch milta hai.*"

17. "*Jaise ma-bap bhejte haim, jao mela ghumne, vahi jaise Bhagvan haim. Vo ek mela mem bheje haim, jao mela mem, aish mauj karo, kasht pareshani karke ao. Khelne ke lie kasht karne sab kuch ke lie jao, ghumo. Phir vapas ham le lemge.*" An image of the world as *mela*, as discernible to the soul upon death, appears in a verse of Kabir, "The swan will fly away, alone / beholding the world as festive gathering (*Ur jayega hams akela / jag darshan ka mela*)."

18. "Wrong actions make it possible to recognize the good (*Bura karm hota hai tabhi acchai ki pahcan hoti hai*)," says Amlakant. In cinema, villains are vitally necessary to make heroes look good, he says. Though audiences may dislike them, and even the actors who depict them (Amlakant's wife, Dulari, was glad when Amrish Puri, who played memorable villains, passed away), they are integral to the workings of films. Sorrow and suffering, arising from the complex gathering of causes, are inescapable in the *mela*. "Everyone gets some jolt, whether one is culpable or innocent (*Thoda bahut jhatka lag hi jata hai sabhi ko, cahe doshi cahe nirdosh*)," says Naresh. But these experiences are to be affirmed within the wholeness of life. "A human being should know both happiness and sorrow (*Sukh aur dukh donom manushya ko janna cahie*)," he says.

19. "Happiness and sorrow are brothers. If bad times come, good times will eventually come; if good times come, bad times will eventually come (*Sukh aur dukh donom bhai haim.*

Aise vaqt bure ate haim, to acche bhi ayemge, acche ayemge to bure bhi ayemge)," says Varmaji.

20. "*Mela mem kaise karna hai kya ciz khana hai kya kam karemge, vo to hamare hath mem hai idhar. Kaise calemge to roti milega, kaise calemge to bhukha rahna hai, kya ciz sikhem, zyada kamaemge. Galat karemge to galat ke phal milega, sahi karemge to sahi ke phal milega. [Bhagvan] dekh rahe haim kaun kaise kar rahe haim, kaise cal rahe haim.*"

21. "*Kalyug hamko nacata hai.*"

22. Migrants seemed to attribute responsibility and blame for distorted activities not on the *Kalyug*, but on the interplay of agentive human beings with the *Kalyug*, thereby keeping alive possibilities for noncooperation.

23. In this distorted field of causes, the innocent can suffer, says Amlakant, invoking the saying, "When grain is ground, insects perish (*Gehum ke sath ghun bhi pis jata hai*)."

24. "*Mela yug ke hisab se cal raha hai.*"

25. For ethnographic studies of discourses in north India on society and ecology in the *Kalyug*, that resonate with these perspectives, see Gold (1998), Halperin (2020), and Pinney (1999).

26. Naresh says, "I am seeing that the person who is doing ethical wrong—making illegitimate earnings, thievery, dacoity, womanizing—he is doing fine. He is living in luxury. He doesn't die that quickly either. The guy who is doing good—who is honorable and acting with humanity—he is the one who is getting a lot of hardships as fruits. He gets hit somewhere by a vehicle and dies. I am slowly coming to think that no, there is no God. It's just a saying that 'you reap as you sow.' (*Dekh rahe haim jaun galat kar raha hai—haramkhori, cori, dakaiti, laundiyabazi—vo sahi se hai. Vo ekdam aish mauj se cal raha hai. Usko mrityu bhi nahim hota hai, jaldi. Aur jaun accha kar raha hai—izzatdar hai, insaniyat mem cal raha hai—usi ko zyada kasht phal mil raha hai. Vo gari se kahum dakka lagke mar gaya. Ab to dhire dhire lag raha hai ki nahim, ab koi hai hi nahim hai. Khali kahavat jaisa hai ke kartavya ke phal [milta] hai*)."

27. "*Unko bhi apne is nirman par dukh hota hoga, ki maimne jo yah banaya hai, yah kya kar raha hai. Bananevala ne sirf insan banaya hai. Lekin banate samay vo yah nahim soca hoga ki maim is khilaune ko jo bana raha hum, yah visphotak bhi hoga.*" God's marionettes, on this reading of the *lila*, are evidently endowed with agency.

28. "*Har admi ko izzat cahie, admi ho cahe janvar ho. Sab ciz izzat khojta hai.*"

29. Large, heavy, black stones believed to be the immanent Shiva are brought and kept near village homes in Palamu. In an ethnography in rural Rajasthan, God is seen to have "turned away from people" due to a decline in ritual and worship (Gold 1998:178).

30. "*Bhagvan bhi sahi nahim rahe. Bhagvan Kalyug ke mutabiq cal rahe haim.*"

31. In a village ethnography in Tamilnadu, Daniel also observes a "Kali Yuga perspective" in which "neither man nor god is capable of exercising much restraint" (Daniel 1983:56).

32. "Ethical wrongs will accumulate to the breaking point (*Pap ka ghara bhar jaega*)," migrants say.

33. The oppression of human beings and the destruction of nature, for example, through the cutting of trees by avaricious contractors and villagers in Jharkhand, says Naresh, create growing, downward pressure on the earth, which at times, the earth can no longer bear. By splitting open, as in the 2001 Gujarat earthquake and the 2004 Indian Ocean tsunami, the earth partly relieves this burden. In so doing, the earth mother goddess (*Prithvi Ma*) destroys some human beings, of the species responsible for the excess weight, but also endures damage and loss to herself, in the destruction of animals, trees, arable lands, and other myriad forms of nonhuman life. The earth mother commits self-amputating sacrifice (*ang sati*), a martyrdom of the divine, not out of anger, but in compelling difficulty. These disasters anticipate the splitting and leveling of the earth at the end of the *Kalyug*. "Until the earth splits and everything goes into it, the *Satyug* (age of truth) will not come (*Jab tak yah phat phat ke andar jayemge nahim, tab tak Satyug ane ka bat nahim hai*)," he says.

34. "Hindus call it dissolution, Muslims call it doomsday (*Hindu dharm usko pralay bolte haim, hamare dharm mem usko Qayamat bolte haim*)," says Firoz.

35. Interweaving is also visible in the narrative of Mathew, a Pentecostal welder from Pathanamthitta, Kerala. Following his schooling in the village, he worked as a metal polisher in Mumbai, then learned welding at an Industrial Training Institute in Kerala. He worked for several companies based in Mumbai and Delhi, which sent him for welding work in north India, West Bengal, Assam, and Kerala, including one stint in Vietnam, before he came to B156. After the coming of Jesus, Mathew says, we are living in the *Kripayug* (age of mercy), when we may still ask God for forgiveness for our sins, borne of the distortive influence of Satan (*Shaitan*) on the soul and our own frailty (*durbalta*). If these prayers are sincere, and accompanied by ethical alterations, deviations might be forgiven by God. As distortions, sins, and oppression intensify, provoking tempests, earthquakes, diseases, and wars, the world will progress into the violent, apocalyptic *Kalyug* (*Kalikalam* in Malayalam), culminating in the emergence of the Antichrist and the Messiah.

36. For resonances of this bifocal vision with Yudhisthira's perspective on *dharma* in the *Mahabharata*, see Malinar (2007:89).

37. "*Admi ko koshish to karte rahna cahie. Yah nahim socna cahie ki jaise cal raha hai vaise calne do. Samaj ko badalne ke lie, sahi samaj lane ke lie, galat admi ko sahi raste par lane ke lie usko koshish karna cahie. Ab vo usmem kaham tak safal ho sakta hai yah to nishcit nahim hai, lekin koshish karna cahie, har admi ko karna cahie—hamem bhi, apko bhi, ya kisi ko bhi—badlav lane ke lie. Kyomki jo speed kam hai, dhire dhire nuksan ho raha hai, admi ka naitik patan dhire dhire gir raha hai, iski vajah yah hai ki ham abhi koshish kar rahe haim is samaj ko badalne ke lie. Dhire dhire barh rahi hai speed. Lekin agar vo koshish rok di jae, to speed ekaek kai guna barh jaegi.*"

38. "*Yah to hamem pata hai ki yah nahim badalna hai, aur age kisi din pura ka pura hi yahi ho jana hai, aur tab vahi Bhatyug vali bat ani hai.*"

39. "*Ham to jani rahe haim ki [Kalyug] rukhega nahim, to age jana hi hai.*"

40. Such efforts, says Uday, are akin to attempts in the village to keep an old, dying man alive. "Like someone knows, this old man is going to die. But still he makes a lot of efforts to keep him alive. No, he thinks, I'm not going to let him die right now (*Jaise admi janta hai, yah burha marne vala hai. Lekin phir bhi usko jilane ke lie bahut koshish karta hai. Nahim isko abhi marne nahim demge*)," he says.

41. Though workers seemed unwilling to embrace the ideology and practice of the communist union and Party, they were not averse to the idea of a revolution that would deliver ameliorations in deprivation and exploitation, even within a decivilizing temporal context. In Dr. Das's reworking of the epochal imaginary, he once said to Varmaji, who was critically referencing the *Kalyug* in the union office, "No, the previous epoch [the *Dvapar*] was not good. There was a lot of oppression in that. The *Kalyug* is going to be good for the working class (*Nahim, pichla yug accha nahim tha. Usmem bahut atyacar tha. Kalyug mazdur varg ke lie accha hoga*)." For Dr. Das, the *Kalyug* would be the age of revolution, not decivilization.

42. Noncooperation, integrative filaments, and devotion are understood here as commingling activities.

43. "*Kalyug ka pura muqabla maim datke kar raha hum jaham tak hamse ho sakta hai.*" In contrast to Michael Taussig's descriptions of workers' contracts with and worship of the devil in Latin America (Taussig 1980), in this discourse, there is a felt duty to resist the workings of the *Kalyug* as devil.

44. "*Qayamat aur dur bhagegi.*"

45. "*Har ek manushya ka kartavya yah cahie ki jiske andar atma hai, usse lagav rakhna, kyomki usmem parmatma ka vas hai.*"

46. "[L]ife is a battlefield, just as it's a festival," says Cornel West. "So you know that you are ready for combat, that you're ever-ready for engagement on the one hand, and yet you try to remain open enough, or even humble enough, to surrender to the fun, or surrender to the love, or surrender to the joy, that you get on the festival side" (Prepidemic Magazine, interview, 2010, http://www.youtube.com/watch?v=oPOIVmLz88I).

47. Pyarelal (1958:65).

48. The modified talisman would also imply attending to the concerns of Gandhi's talisman, including material deprivation, spiritual nourishment, and the deeper autonomy of the demos.

49. As migrants recognize, the *Kalyug* is not all distorted. They draw upon categories, ideals, and resources within the *Kalyug* to take on the *Kalyug*, including concepts of work, respect, justice, nonviolence, duty, fellowship, action, God, and time; the messages of religious traditions, poet-saints, cinema, the union, and the *Faridabad Workers Newspaper*; and their own evolving experiences, reflections, and auto-critiques.

50. The category of *manthan* (churning) appears in multiple sources, including the *Mahabharata* (van Buitenen 1973:73–76), the *Puranas* (Dimmitt and van Buitenen 1978:74–75, 94–98), cinema (*Manthan* [1976]), political writings (Majdoor Samachar-Kamunist Kranti 2020), and the news media. For an invocation of this image to understand economic and ecological processes, see Shrivastava and Kothari (2012:xv–xvi).

51. In certain valences of noncooperation, such as restrained working, migrant workers also enlist the assistance of the demonic soul-valence.

52. For a visual depiction of these gyrations and countergyrations, see the Appendix of Diagrams.

Postscript

1. The B156 workers' connections to the union weakened after the placards struggle and the transfer to Noida. Naresh and other Jharkhandis, when called by the IFTU leaders, continued to go for demonstrations in Delhi. The workers also continued to meet and discuss with Sher Singh, who died in 2025.

2. See Rahman (2020).

BIBLIOGRAPHY

Agrawal, Purushottam. 1994. "'Kan Kan Mein Vyape Hein Ram': The Slogan as a Metaphor of Cultural Interrogation." *Oxford Literary Review* 16, no. 1-2 (July):245–264.

———. 2019. "Vernacular Modernity and the Public Sphere of Bhakti." In *China, India and Alternative Asian Modernities*, ed. Sanjay Kumar, Satya P. Mohanty, Archana Kumar, and Raj Kumar, 168–184. London: Routledge.

Alter, Joseph S. 1992. *The Wrestler's Body: Identity and Ideology in North India*. Chicago: University of Chicago Press.

Ambedkar, B. R. 2014. *Annihilation of Caste: The Annotated Critical Edition*, ed. S. Anand. New Delhi: Navayana.

Amin, Shahid. 2015. *Conquest and Community: The Afterlife of Warrior Saint Ghazi Miyan*. Chicago: University of Chicago Press.

Ananthamurthy, U. R. 2012. *Samskara: A Rite for a Dead Man*, trans. A. K. Ramanujan. New Delhi: Oxford University Press.

Anderson, Kevin B. 2010. *Marx at the Margins: On Nationalism, Ethnicity, and Non-Western Societies*. Chicago: University of Chicago Press.

Appadurai, Arjun. 1990. "Technology and the Reproduction of Values in Rural Western India." In *Dominating Knowledge: Development, Culture, and Resistance*, ed. Frédérique Appfel Marglin and Stephen A. Marglin, 185–216. Oxford: Clarendon Press.

———. 2013. *The Future as Cultural Fact: Essays on the Global Condition*. London: Verso.

Apte, Mahadev L. 1985. *Humor and Laughter: An Anthropological Approach*. Ithaca: Cornell University Press.

Arumugam, Indira. 2015. "'The Old Gods Are Losing Power!': Theologies of Power and Rituals of Productivity in a Tamil Nadu Village." *Modern Asian Studies* 49, no. 3 (May):753–786.

Babb, Lawrence A. 1983. "Destiny and Responsibility: Karma in Popular Hinduism." In *Karma: An Anthropological Inquiry*, ed. Charles F. Keyes and E. Valentine Daniel, 163–181. Berkeley: University of California Press.

Banerjee, Prathama. 2006. *Politics of Time: 'Primitives' and History-Writing in a Colonial Society*. New Delhi: Oxford University Press.

Bate, Bernard. 2009. *Tamil Oratory and the Dravidian Aesthetic: Democratic Practice in South India*. New York: Columbia University Press.

Bear, Laura. 2015. *Navigating Austerity: Currents of Debt Along a South Asian River*. Stanford: Stanford University Press.

Bergson, Henri. 1999. *Laughter: An Essay on the Meaning of the Comic*, trans. Cloudesley Brereton and Fred Rothwell. Copenhagen: Green Integer.

Bhan, Gautam, and Swathi Shivanand. 2013. "(Un)Settling the City: Analysing Displacement in Delhi from 1990 to 2007." *Economic and Political Weekly* 48, no. 13 (March 30):54–61.

Birtchnell, Thomas. 2011. "*Jugaad* as Systemic Risk and Disruptive Innovation in India." *Contemporary South Asia* 19, no. 4 (December):357–372.

Bismillah, Abdul. 1996. *The Song of the Loom (Jhini Jhini Bini Chadariya)*, trans. Rashmi Govind. Madras: Macmillan India.

Bowles, Adam. 2007. *Dharma, Disorder and the Political in Ancient India: The Apaddharmaparvan of the Mahabharata*. Leiden: Brill.

Breman, Jan. 1996. *Footloose Labour: Working in India's Informal Economy*. Cambridge: Cambridge University Press.

———. 2009. "The Great Transformation in the Setting of Asia." Address delivered at the International Institute of Social Studies, The Hague, October 29.

———. 2013. *At Work in the Informal Economy of India: A Perspective from the Bottom Up*. New Delhi: Oxford University Press.

Burawoy, Michael. 1979. *Manufacturing Consent: Changes in the Labor Process Under Monopoly Capitalism*. Chicago: University of Chicago Press.

Carlyle, Thomas. 1918. *Sartor Resartus: On Heroes, Hero-Worship and the Heroic in History*. London: J. M. Dent.

Chakrabarty, Dipesh. 1989. *Rethinking Working-Class History, Bengal 1890–1940*. Princeton: Princeton University Press.

———. 2008. *Provincializing Europe: Postcolonial Thought and Historical Difference*. Princeton: Princeton University Press.

Chakravarti, Uma. 2005. "From Fathers to Husbands: Of Love, Death and Marriage in North India." In *"Honour": Crimes, Paradigms and Violence Against Women*, ed. Lynn Welchman and Sara Hossain, 308–331. London: Zed.

Chandavarkar, Rajnarayan. 1991. "Workers' Resistance and the Rationalization of Work in Bombay Between the Wars." In *Contesting Power: Resistance and Everyday Social Relations in South Asia*, ed. Douglas Haynes and Gyan Prakash, 109–144. Berkeley: University of California Press.

———. 1994. *The Origins of Industrial Capitalism in India: Business Strategies and the Working Classes in Bombay, 1900–1940*. Cambridge: Cambridge University Press.

Chandra, Abhimanyu. 2017. "How Adityanath's Hindu Yuva Vahini Backed the BJP's Attempts to Woo the Rajbhar OBCs Through the Legacy of King Suheldev." *Caravan*, March 10. https://caravanmagazine.in/vantage/adityanaths-hindu-yuva-vahini-backed-bjps-attempts-woo-rajbhar-obcs-legacy-king-suheldev.

Chatterjee, Roma, and Deepak Mehta. 2007. *Living with Violence: An Anthropology of Events and Everyday Life*. New Delhi: Routledge.

Chenoweth, Erica, and Maria J. Stephan. 2011. *Why Civil Resistance Works: The Strategic Logic of Nonviolent Conflict*. New York: Columbia University Press.

Chowdhry, Prem. 2007. *Contentious Marriages, Eloping Couples: Gender, Caste, and Patriarchy in Northern India*. New Delhi: Oxford University Press.

———. 2015. "Popular Perceptions of Masculinity in Rural North Indian Oral Traditions." *Asian Ethnology* 74, no. 1:5–36.

Cleaver, Harry. 1979. *Reading Capital Politically*. Austin: University of Texas Press.

Cohen, Lawrence. 1995. "Holi in Banaras and the Mahaland of Modernity." *GLQ: A Journal of Lesbian and Gay Studies* 2, no. 4 (October):399–424.

———. 1998. *No Aging in India: Alzheimer's, the Bad Family, and Other Modern Things*. Berkeley: University of California Press.

Daniel, Sheryl B. 1983. "The Tool Box Approach of the Tamil to the Issues of Moral Responsibility and Human Destiny." In *Karma: An Anthropological Inquiry*, ed. Charles F. Keyes and E. Valentine Daniel, 27–62. Berkeley: University of California Press.

Das, Veena. 2003. "Technologies of Self: Poverty and Health in an Urban Setting." In *Sarai Reader 03: Shaping Technologies*, 95–102. New Delhi: Sarai.

Deshingkar, Priya, and Shaheen Akter. 2009. *Migration and Human Development in India*. Human Development Research Paper 2009/13. New York: United Nations Development Programme.

Desmond, Matthew. 2016. *Evicted: Poverty and Profit in the American City*. New York: Crown.

Dhand, Arti. 2008. *Woman as Fire, Woman as Sage: Sexual Ideology in the* Mahabharata. Albany: State University of New York Press.

Dimmitt, Cornelia, and J. A. B. van Buitenen, eds. and trans. 1978. *Classical Hindu Mythology: A Reader in the Sanskrit Puranas*. Philadelphia: Temple University Press.

Dostoevsky, Fyodor. 1956. *The Idiot*, trans. David Magarshack. New York: Penguin.

———. 1983. *Memoirs from the House of the Dead*, ed. Ronald Hingley, trans. Jessie Coulson. New York: Oxford University Press.

———. 1992. *The Brothers Karamazov*, trans. Richard Pevear and Larissa Volokhonsky. New York: Alfred A. Knopf.

———. 1994. *Demons*, trans. Richard Pevear and Larissa Volokhonsky. New York: Alfred A. Knopf.

Drèze, Jean, and Amartya Sen. 2013. *An Uncertain Glory: India and Its Contradictions*. Princeton: Princeton University Press.

Duneier, Mitchell. 1992. *Slim's Table: Race, Respectability, and Masculinity*. Chicago: University of Chicago Press.

———. 1999. *Sidewalk*. New York: Farrar, Straus and Giroux.

Edwards, Richard. 1979. *Contested Terrain: The Transformation of the Workplace in the Twentieth Century*. New York: Basic.

Fernandes, Leela. 1997. *Producing Workers: The Politics of Gender, Class, and Culture in the Calcutta Jute Mills*. Philadelphia: University of Pennsylvania Press.

Freud, Sigmund. 1960. *Jokes and Their Relation to the Unconscious*, ed. and trans. James Strachey. New York: W. W. Norton.

Fuller, C. J. 1992. *The Camphor Flame: Popular Hinduism and Society in India*. Princeton: Princeton University Press.

Gandhi, Ajay. 2013. "Porous Boundaries: Hindu-Muslim Demarcations and Crossings in Delhi." In *Topographies of Faith*, ed. Irene Becci, Marian Burchardt, and José Casanova, 189–205. Leiden: Brill.

Gandhi, M. K. 1999. "Discourses on the Gita." In *The Collected Works of Mahatma Gandhi* (Electronic Book), vol. 37 (November 11, 1926–January 1, 1927), 75–354. New Delhi: Publications Division, Government of India. https://www.gandhiashramsevagram.org/gandhi-literature/mahatma-gandhi-collected-works-volume-37.pdf.

———. 2010. *M. K. Gandhi's Hind Swaraj: A Critical Edition*, ed. Suresh Sharma and Tridip Suhrud. New Delhi: Orient BlackSwan.

Gandhi, Ramchandra. 1984. *I Am Thou: Meditations on the Truth of India*. Poona: Indian Philosophical Quarterly Publications.

———. 1992. *Sita's Kitchen: A Testimony of Faith and Inquiry*. Albany: State University of New York Press.

———. 2007. "Two Cheers for Tolerance." *India International Centre Quarterly* 34, no. 1 (Summer):146–151.

———. 2015. *The Seven Sages: Selected Essays by Ramchandra Gandhi*, ed. A. Raghuramaraju. New Delhi: Penguin.

George, Kenneth M., and Kirin Narayan. 2022. "Technophany and Its Publics: Artisans, Technicians, and the Rise of Vishwakarma Worship in India." *Journal of Asian Studies* 81, no. 1 (February):3–21.

Ghassem-Fachandi, Parvis. 2012. *Pogrom in Gujarat: Hindu Nationalism and Anti-Muslim Violence in India.* Princeton: Princeton University Press.

Gidwani, Vinay, and K. Sivaramakrishnan. 2003. "Circular Migration and the Spaces of Cultural Assertion." *Annals of the Association of American Geographers* 93, no. 1 (March):186–213.

Gold, Ann Grodzins. 1998. "Sin and Rain: Moral Ecology in Rural North India." In *Purifying the Earthly Body of God: Religion and Ecology in Hindu India*, ed. Lance E. Nelson, 165–195. Albany: State University of New York Press.

Gooptu, Nandini. 2001. *The Politics of the Urban Poor in Early Twentieth-Century India.* Cambridge: Cambridge University Press.

Government of NCT of Delhi. 2006. *Delhi Human Development Report 2006: Partnerships for Progress.* New Delhi: Oxford University Press.

Graeber, David. 2013. *The Democracy Project: A History, a Crisis, a Movement.* New York: Spiegel and Grau.

Grover, Shalini. 2017. *Marriage, Love, Caste and Kinship Support: Lived Experiences of the Urban Poor in Delhi.* New Delhi: Social Science Press.

Guha, Ranajit. 1983. *Elementary Aspects of Peasant Insurgency in Colonial India.* Delhi: Oxford University Press.

———. 1989. "Dominance Without Hegemony and Its Historiography." In *Subaltern Studies VI: Writings on South Asian History and Society*, ed. Ranajit Guha, 210–309. Delhi: Oxford University Press.

Gupta, Akhil. 2012. *Red Tape: Bureaucracy, Structural Violence, and Poverty in India.* Durham, NC: Duke University Press.

Gupta, Dipankar. 2005. "Whither the Indian Village: Culture and Agriculture in 'Rural' India." *Economic and Political Weekly* 40, no. 8 (February 19):751–758.

Gupta, Monobina. 2016. "Return of the Chamcha Age." *Wire*, June 19. https://thewire.in/culture/return-of-the-chamcha-age.

Halle, David. 1984. *America's Working Man: Work, Home, and Politics Among Blue-Collar Property Owners.* Chicago: University of Chicago Press.

Halperin, Ehud. 2014. "The Age of Kali: Contemporary Iterations of the Kaliyug in the Kullu Valley of the Western Himalayas." *Nidan: International Journal for the Study of Hinduism* 26, no. 1 (July):42–64.

———. 2020. *The Many Faces of a Himalayan Goddess: Hadimba, Her Devotees, and Religion in Rapid Change.* New York: Oxford University Press.

Hamper, Ben. 1992. *Rivethead: Tales from the Assembly Line.* New York: Warner.

Hardiman, David. 1987. *The Coming of the Devi: Adivasi Assertion in Western India.* Delhi: Oxford University Press.

———. 2013. "Towards a History of Non-violent Resistance." *Economic and Political Weekly* 48, no. 23 (June 8):41–48.

———. 2018. *The Nonviolent Struggle for Indian Freedom, 1905–19.* Gurgaon: Penguin Random House.

———. 2021. *Noncooperation in India: Nonviolent Strategy and Protest, 1920–22.* New York: Oxford University Press.

Hardiman, David, and Gauri Raje. 2008. "Practices of Healing in Tribal Gujarat." *Economic and Political Weekly* 43, no. 9 (March 1):43–50.

Hess, Linda. 2015. *Bodies of Song: Kabir Oral Traditions and Performative Worlds in North India.* New York: Oxford University Press.

Hyder, Syed Akbar. 2006. *Reliving Karbala: Martyrdom in South Asian Memory.* New York: Oxford University Press.

Jha, Hetukar. 2001. "A Peasant's View of Peasant Life and Its Categories: A Study of the Proverbs of North India." *Indian Social Science Review* 3, no. 1:101–114.

Joshi, Chitra. 2003. *Lost Worlds: Indian Labour and Its Forgotten Histories.* Delhi: Permanent Black.

Kakar, Sudhir. 1982. *Shamans, Mystics and Doctors: A Psychological Inquiry into India and Its Healing Traditions.* Chicago: University of Chicago Press.

———. 1989. *Intimate Relations: Exploring Indian Sexuality.* Chicago: University of Chicago Press.

Karki, Mohan Singh. 2001. *Kabir: Selected Couplets from the Sakhi in Transversion.* Delhi: Motilal Banarsidass.

Kelley, Robin D. G. 1996. *Race Rebels: Culture, Politics, and the Black Working Class.* New York: Free Press.

Khan, Yasmin. 2016. "Izzat." In *Key Concepts in Modern Indian Studies*, ed. Rachel Dwyer, Gita Dharampal-Frick, Monika Kirloskar-Steinbach, and Jahnavi Phalkey, 128–129. New York: New York University Press.

Kirmani, Nida. 2013. *Questioning the Muslim Woman: Identity and Insecurity in an Urban Indian Locality.* New Delhi: Routledge.

Kishwar, Madhu. 2000. "Yes to Sita, No to Ram: The Continuing Hold of Sita on Popular Imagination in India." In *Questioning Ramayanas: A South Asian Tradition*, ed. Paula Richman, 285–308. New Delhi: Oxford University Press.

Kumar, Nita. 1988. *The Artisans of Banaras: Popular Culture and Identity, 1880–1986.* Princeton: Princeton University Press.

Lal Das, Krishna Shekhar. 1997. "Trade Unions and the New Economic Policy in India: Perceptions and Responses Under Neo-Liberal Reform 1980–1995." Research paper. The Hague: Institute of Social Studies.

Lamb, Sarah. 2000. *White Saris and Sweet Mangoes: Aging, Gender, and Body in North India.* Berkeley: University of California Press.

Lothspeich, Pamela. 2009. *Epic Nation: Reimagining the Mahabharata in the Age of the Empire.* New Delhi: Oxford University Press.

Luedtke, Alf. 1986. "Cash, Coffee Breaks, Horseplay: *Eigensinn* and Politics Among Factory Workers in Germany Circa 1900." In *Confrontation, Class Consciousness, and the Labor Process: Studies in Proletarian Class Formation*, ed. Michael Hanagan and Charles Stephenson, 65–95. Westport, CT: Greenwood.

Lutgendorf, Philip. 1991. *The Life of a Text: Performing the* Ramcaritmanas *of Tulsidas.* Berkeley: University of California Press.

Madhok, Sumi. 2021. *Vernacular Rights Cultures: The Politics of Origins, Human Rights and Gendered Struggles for Justice.* Cambridge: Cambridge University Press.

Majdoor Samachar-Kamunist Kranti. 1996. *A Ballad Against Work.* Faridabad: Majdoor Library. https://libcom.org/article/ballad-against-work-kamunist-kranti.

———. 1997. *Reflections on Marx's Critique of Political Economy.* Faridabad: Majdoor Library. https://libcom.org/article/reflections-marxs-critique-political-economy-kamunist-kranti.

———. 1998. *Self-Activity of Wage Workers: Towards a Critique of Representation and Delegation.* Faridabad: Majdoor Library. https://libcom.org/library/self-activity-wage-workers-kamunist-kranti.

———. 2020. *A Glimpse of Social Churnings: Attempts at Conversational Interactions During Global Covid Lockdowns.* Faridabad: Majdoor Library. https://faridabadmajdoorsamachar.noblogs.org/post/2020/10/18/a-glimpse-of-social-churnings/.

———. 2021. *Fragments and Pathways for Imagining a Near Future.* Faridabad: Majdoor Library. https://drive.google.com/file/d/1CuDUgZ8OWvDtvug8eA-AXUmXTDByE986/view.

Malinar, Angelika. 2007. "Arguments of a Queen: Draupadi's Views on Kingship." In *Gender and Narrative in the* Mahabharata, ed. Simon Brodbeck and Brian Black, 79–96. London: Routledge.

Marglin, Stephen A. 1990. "Losing Touch: The Cultural Conditions of Worker Accommodation and Resistance." In *Dominating Knowledge: Development, Culture, and Resistance*, ed. Frédérique Appfel Marglin and Stephen A. Marglin, 217–282. Oxford: Clarendon Press.

Marriott, McKim. 1966. "The Feast of Love." In *Krishna: Myth, Rites, and Attitudes*, ed. Milton B. Singer, 200–231. Honolulu: East-West Center Press.

Marx, Karl. 1963. "Economic and Philosophical Manuscripts." In *Karl Marx: Early Writings*, trans. and ed. T. B. Bottomore, 61–219. New York: McGraw-Hill.

———. 1977. *Capital: A Critique of Political Economy*, vol. 1, trans. Ben Fowkes. New York: Vintage.

———. 1978. "Contribution to the Critique of Hegel's *Philosophy of Right*: Introduction." In *The Marx-Engels Reader*, 2nd ed., ed. Robert C. Tucker, 53–65. New York: W. W. Norton.

Mazumdar, Indrani. 2001. *Unorganised Workers of Delhi and the Seven Day Strike of 1988*. NLI Research Studies Series No. 026/2001. Noida: V. V. Giri National Labour Institute.

Mazumdar, Indrani, N. Neetha, and Indu Agnihotri. 2013. "Migration and Gender in India." *Economic and Political Weekly* 48, no. 10 (March 9):54–64.

McGregor, R. S., ed. 1997. *The Oxford Hindi-English Dictionary*. Delhi: Oxford University Press.

Mehrotra, Santosh, Jajati Parida, Sharmistha Sinha, and Ankita Gandhi. 2014. "Explaining Employment Trends in the Indian Economy: 1993–94 to 2011–12." *Economic and Political Weekly* 49, no. 32 (August 9):49–57.

Mehta, Deepak. 2000. "Circumcision, Body, Masculinity: The Ritual Wound and Collective Violence." In *Violence and Subjectivity*, ed. Veena Das, Arthur Kleinman, Mamphela Ramphele, and Pamela Reynolds, 79–101. Berkeley: University of California Press.

Misra, Pooja, and Jaya Gupta. 2021. "Impact of COVID 19 on Indian Migrant Workers: Decoding Twitter Data by Text Mining." *Indian Journal of Labour Economics* 64:731–747.

Mohan, Hari. 1973. *The Chero: A Study in Acculturation*. Ranchi: Bihar Tribal Welfare Research Institute for the Government of Bihar, Welfare and Forest Department.

Mohapatra, Prabhu P. 2007. ""Following Custom"? Representations of Community Among Indian Immigrant Labour in the West Indies, 1880–1920." In *Coolies, Capital and Colonialism: Studies in Indian Labour History*, ed. Rana P. Behal and Marcel van der Linden, 173–202. Cambridge: Cambridge University Press.

Montgomery, David. 1979. *Workers' Control in America: Studies in the History of Work, Technology, and Labor Struggles*. Cambridge: Cambridge University Press.

Nandy, Ashis. 1983. *The Intimate Enemy: Loss and Recovery of Self Under Colonialism*. New Delhi: Oxford University Press.

———. 1995. "Sati in *Kali Yuga*: The Public Debate on Roop Kanwar's Death." In *The Savage Freud and Other Essays on Possible and Retrievable Selves*, 32–52. New Delhi: Oxford University Press.

———. 2001. "The Politics of Secularism and the Recovery of Religious Tolerance." In *Time Warps: The Insistent Politics of Silent and Evasive Pasts*, 61–88. Delhi: Permanent Black.

———. 2002. "Telling the Story of Communal Conflicts in South Asia: Interim Report on a Personal Search for Defining Myths." *Ethnic and Racial Studies* 25, no. 1 (January):1–19.

———. 2007. "The Fantastic India-Pakistan Battle: Or, the Future of the Past in South Asia." In *Time Treks: The Uncertain Future of Old and New Despotisms*, 23–39. Calcutta: Seagull.

———. 2013. "Return of the Sacred: Politics of Religion in a Post-Secular Age." In *Regimes of Narcissism, Regimes of Despair*, 95–112. New Delhi: Oxford University Press.

———. 2021. "Gandhi After Gandhi: The Fate of Dissent in Our Times." In *Breakfast with Evil and Other Risky Ventures: The Non-Essential Ashis Nandy*, 260–268. New Delhi: Oxford University Press.

Nandy, Ashis, Shikha Trivedy, Shail Mayaram, and Achyut Yagnik. 1995. *Creating a Nationality: The Ramjanmabhumi Movement and the Fear of the Self*. New Delhi: Oxford University Press.

Naqvi, Saba. 2012. *In Good Faith: A Journey in Search of an Unknown India*. New Delhi: Rupa.

Narayan, Badri. 2009. *Fascinating Hindutva: Saffron Politics and Dalit Mobilisation*. New Delhi: Sage.

———. 2011. *The Making of the Dalit Public in North India: Uttar Pradesh, 1950–Present*. New Delhi: Oxford University Press.

NCEUS (National Commission for Enterprises in the Unorganised Sector). 2007. *Report on Conditions of Work and Promotion of Livelihoods in the Unorganised Sector*. New Delhi: Government of India.

Ness, Immanuel. 2016. *Southern Insurgency: The Coming of the Global Working Class*. London: Pluto.

———. 2021. *Organizing Insurgency: Workers' Movements in the Global South*. London: Pluto.

Ngai, Pun. 2005. *Made in China: Women Factory Workers in a Global Workplace*. Durham, NC: Duke University Press.

———. 2016. *Migrant Labor in China: Post-Socialist Transformations*. Cambridge: Polity.

O'Flaherty, Wendy Doniger. 1976. *The Origins of Evil in Hindu Mythology*. Berkeley: University of California Press.

Omvedt, Gail. 2008. *Seeking Begumpura: The Social Vision of Anticaste Intellectuals*. New Delhi: Navayana.

Parry, Jonathan (in collaboration with Ajay T.G.). 2020. *Classes of Labour: Work and Life in a Central Indian Steel Town*. London: Routledge.

Parry, Jonathan P., Jan Breman, and Karin Kapadia, eds. 1999. *The Worlds of Indian Industrial Labour*, special issue of *Contributions to Indian Sociology* 33, no. 1–2 (February).

Patwardhan, Anand. 1992. *Ram ke Naam (In the Name of God)*. Documentary.

Peña, Devon G. 1997. *The Terror of the Machine: Technology, Work, Gender, and Ecology on the U.S.-Mexico Border*. Austin: Center for Mexican American Studies, University of Texas at Austin.

Pinney, Christopher. 1999. "On Living in the *Kal(i)yug*: Notes from Nagda, Madhya Pradesh." *Contributions to Indian Sociology* 33, no. 1–2 (February): 77–106.

Ponniah, James. 2014. "Alternative Discourses of Kali Yuga in Ayya Vali." *Nidan: International Journal for the Study of Hinduism* 26, no. 1 (July):65–87.

Premchand. 1969a. "The Power of a Curse." In *The World of Premchand: Selected Stories of Premchand*, trans. David Rubin, 36–47. Bloomington: Indiana University Press.

———. 1969b. "The Shroud." In *The World of Premchand: Selected Stories of Premchand*, trans. David Rubin, 186–194. Bloomington: Indiana University Press.

———. 2002. *The Gift of a Cow: A Translation of the Classic Hindi Novel* Godaan, trans. Gordon C. Roadarmel. Bloomington: Indiana University Press.

———. 2017. "Violence Is the Supreme Religion," trans. Alpana Neogy. In *The Complete Short Stories*, vol. 3, ed. M. Asaduddin, trans. M. Asaduddin and others, 86–94. Gurgaon: Penguin Random House.

Press Trust of India. 2011. "Maruti Good Conduct Bond Unfair: Govt." *Indian Express*, November 29. https://indianexpress.com/article/news-archive/web/maruti-good-conduct-bond-unfair-govt/.

Pyarelal. 1958. *Mahatma Gandhi: The Last Phase*, vol. 2. Ahmedabad: Navajivan.

Radcliffe-Brown, A. R. 1952. "On Joking Relationships." In *Structure and Function in Primitive Society: Essays and Addresses*, 90–104. Glencoe, IL: Free Press.

Rahman, Saba. 2020. "Protest Enters 32nd Day: At Shaheen Bagh Protest, Roza, with Gandhi." *Indian Express*, January 22. https://indianexpress.com/article/cities/delhi/protest-enters-32nd-day-at-shaheen-bagh-protest-roza-with-gandhi/.

Raman, Vasanthi. 2010. *The Warp and the Weft: Community and Gender Identity Among Benaras Weavers*. New Delhi: Routledge.

Ramanujan, A. K. 1990. "Is There an Indian Way of Thinking? An Informal Essay." In *India Through Hindu Categories*, ed. McKim Marriott, 41–58. New Delhi: Sage.

Reddy, Gayatri. 2005. *With Respect to Sex: Negotiating Hijra Identity in South India.* Chicago: University of Chicago Press.

Reza, Rahi Masoom. 2008. *A Village Divided*, trans. Gillian Wright. New Delhi: Penguin.

Roy, Arundhati. 2014. "The Doctor and the Saint." In *Annihilation of Caste: The Annotated Critical Edition*, ed. S. Anand, 15–179. New Delhi: Navayana.

Ruthven, Orlanda. 2021. "'Blind Laws' and the Bureaucracy of Rights: Migrant Industrial Workers in Post-Lockdown India." *Journal of Agrarian Change* 21, no. 3 (July):651–667.

Sanchez, Andrew. 2012. "Deadwood and Paternalism: Rationalizing Casual Labour in an Indian Company Town." *Journal of the Royal Anthropological Institute* 18, no. 4 (December): 808–827.

———. 2016. "Profane Relations: The Irony of Offensive Jokes in India." *History and Anthropology* 27, no. 3:296–312.

Sarkar, Sumit. 1989. "The Kalki-Avatar of Bikrampur: A Village Scandal in Early Twentieth Century Bengal." In *Subaltern Studies VI: Writings on South Asian History and Society*, ed. Ranajit Guha, 1–53. Delhi: Oxford University Press.

———. 1997a. "Renaissance and Kaliyuga: Time, Myth and History in Colonial Bengal." In *Writing Social History*, 186–215. New Delhi: Oxford University Press.

———. 1997b. "Kaliyuga, Chakri and Bhakti: Ramakrishna and His Times." In *Writing Social History*, 282–357. New Delhi: Oxford University Press.

———. 2002. "Colonial Times: Clocks and Kali-yuga." In *Beyond Nationalist Frames: Relocating Postmodernism, Hindutva, History*, 10–37. Delhi: Permanent Black.

Scheper-Hughes, Nancy. 1992. *Death Without Weeping: The Violence of Everyday Life in Brazil.* Berkeley: University of California Press.

Scott, James C. 1990. *Domination and the Arts of Resistance: Hidden Transcripts.* New Haven: Yale University Press.

———. 2012. *Two Cheers for Anarchism: Six Easy Pieces on Autonomy, Dignity, and Meaningful Work and Play.* Princeton: Princeton University Press.

Sethi, Aman. 2012a. *A Free Man: A True Story of Life and Death in Delhi.* New York: W. W. Norton.

———. 2012b. "Down and Out on India's Shop Floor." *Hindu*, July 29. https://www.thehindu.com/business/Industry/down-and-out-on-indias-shop-floor/article3697113.ece.

Shah, Svati P. 2014. *Street Corner Secrets: Sex, Work, and Migration in the City of Mumbai.* Durham, NC: Duke University Press.

Sharma, Ursula. 1973. "Theodicy and the Doctrine of Karma." *Man* 8, no. 3 (September):347–364.

Shekhar, Hansda Sowvendra. 2014. *The Mysterious Ailment of Rupi Baskey: A Novel.* New Delhi: Aleph.

Shrivastava, Aseem, and Ashish Kothari. 2012. *Churning the Earth: The Making of Global India.* New Delhi: Penguin.

Shyam Sundar, K. R. 2012. "Industrial Violence and Labour Reforms." *Economic and Political Weekly* 47, no. 41 (October 13):35–40.

Simeon, Dilip. 1997. "O.K. TATA: Mobiloil Change and World Revolution." In *Civil Lines 3: New Writing from India*, ed. Rukun Advani, Ivan Hutnik, Mukul Kesavan, and Dharma Kumar, 4–30. Delhi: Ravi Dayal.

Singh, Sehjo. 1993. *The Women Betrayed.* Documentary.

Sinha, Shashank S. 2015. "Culture of Violence or Violence of Cultures? Adivasis and Witch-hunting in Chotanagpur." *Anglistica AION* 19, no. 1:105–120.

Sitrin, Marina A. 2012. *Everyday Revolutions: Horizontalism and Autonomy in Argentina.* London: Zed.

Sitrin, Marina A., and Dario Azzellini. 2014. *They Can't Represent Us! Reinventing Democracy from Greece to Occupy.* London: Verso.

Smith, John D. 2009. *The Mahabharata: An Abridged Translation*. New York: Penguin.

Strumpell, Christian. 2008. "'We Work Together, We Eat Together': Conviviality and Modernity in a Company Settlement in South Orissa." *Contributions to Indian Sociology* 42, no. 3 (October):351–381.

Sundar, Nandini. 2001. "Divining Evil: The State and Witchcraft in Bastar." *Gender, Technology and Development* 5, no. 3 (November):425–448.

Taussig, Michael. 1980. *The Devil and Commodity Fetishism in South America*. Chapel Hill: University of North Carolina Press.

Taylor, Frederick Winslow. 1998. *The Principles of Scientific Management*. Mineola, NY: Dover.

Thiyam, Ratan. 1998. *Chakravyuha*, Pre-text and reconstructed performance text by Kavita Nagpal. Calcutta: Seagull.

Thompson, E. P. 1966. *The Making of the English Working Class*. New York: Vintage.

———. 1993. *Customs in Common*. New York: New Press.

Tracy, David. 2020a. *Fragments: The Existential Situation of Our Time—Selected Essays*, vol. 1. Chicago: University of Chicago Press.

———. 2020b. *Filaments: Theological Profiles—Selected Essays*, vol. 2. Chicago: University of Chicago Press.

Tulasidasa. 1999. *Tulasidasa's Shriramacharitamanasa (The Holy Lake of the Acts of Rama)*, ed. and trans. R. C. Prasad. Delhi: Motilal Banarsidass.

Ullah, Faiz. 2020. "Digital Media and the Changing Nature of Labor Action." *Television & New Media* 21, no. 4 (May):376–391.

Unger, Roberto Mangabeira. 1984. *Passion: An Essay on Personality*. New York: Free Press.

———. 2001. "Appendix to the New Edition: Five Theses on the Relation of Religion to Politics, Illustrated by Allusions to Brazilian Experience." In *False Necessity: Anti-Necessitarian Social Theory in the Service of Radical Democracy, from Politics, A Work in Constructive Social Theory*, 597–603. London: Verso.

———. 2014. *The Religion of the Future*. Cambridge, MA: Harvard University Press.

van Buitenen, J. A. B., ed. and trans. 1973. *The Mahabharata, 1: The Book of the Beginning*. Chicago: University of Chicago Press.

Van Hollen, Cecilia Coale. 2022. *Cancer and the Kali Yuga: Gender, Inequality, and Health in South India*. Oakland: University of California Press.

Virottam, Balmukand. 1972. *The Nagbanshis and the Cheros*. New Delhi: Munshiram Manoharlal.

Wadley, Susan S., and Bruce W. Derr. 1989. "Eating Sins in Karimpur." *Contributions to Indian Sociology* 23, no. 1 (January):131–148.

Weil, Simone. 1951. *Waiting for God*, trans. Emma Craufurd. New York: Harper and Row.

———. 1952a. *Gravity and Grace*, trans. Arthur Wills. Lincoln: University of Nebraska Press.

———. 1952b. *The Need for Roots: Prelude to a Declaration of Duties Towards Mankind*, trans. Arthur Wills. London: Routledge.

———. 1977. "Factory Work." In *The Simone Weil Reader*, ed. George A. Panichas, 53–72. New York: David McKay.

———. 1986a. "Human Personality," trans. Richard Rees. In *Simone Weil: An Anthology*, ed. Siân Miles, 49–78. New York: Weidenfeld and Nicolson.

———. 1986b. "The *Iliad* or the Poem of Force," trans. Mary McCarthy. In *Simone Weil: An Anthology*, ed. Siân Miles, 162–195. New York: Weidenfeld and Nicolson.

———. 1986c. "Prerequisite to Dignity of Labour," trans. Siân Miles. In *Simone Weil: An Anthology*, ed. Siân Miles, 244–256. New York: Weidenfeld and Nicolson.

West, Cornel. 1999a. "Religion and the Left." In *The Cornel West Reader*, 372–379. New York: Basic Civitas.

———. 1999b. "Prophetic Christian as Organic Intellectual: Martin Luther King, Jr." In *The Cornel West Reader*, 425–434. New York: Basic Civitas.

———. 1999c. "Subversive Joy and Revolutionary Patience in Black Christianity." In *The Cornel West Reader*, 435–439. New York: Basic Civitas.

Willis, Paul. 1977. *Learning to Labor: How Working-Class Kids Get Working-Class Jobs*. New York: Columbia University Press.

Yadav, Anumeha. 2015. "Workers Get More Militant as Space for Unionisation Shrinks." *Scroll.in*, June 24. https://scroll.in/article/736208/workers-get-more-militant-as-space-for-unionisation-shrinks.

———. 2016. "Millions Go on Day-Long Strike Across India to Protest Dilution of Workers' Rights." *Scroll.in*, September 2. https://scroll.in/article/815560/millions-go-on-day-long-strike-across-india-to-protest-dilution-of-workers-rights.

———. 2019. "Neither Reservations nor Agitation Dispel Gloom Among Workers in Delhi's Industrial Areas." *Scroll.in*, January 11. https://scroll.in/article/908830/neither-reservations-nor-agitation-dispel-gloom-among-workers-in-delhis-industrial-areas.

INDEX

ACKNOWLEDGMENTS

Many persons have contributed, directly or otherwise, to this project. I am grateful to my professors and friends at Harvard University for instruction and guidance, from college days and beyond, including Stephen Marglin, Juliet Schor, Prasannan Parthasarathi, David Washbrook, Sanjay Reddy, Thomas Burke, and Roberto Unger. At the University of Chicago, I benefited greatly from the teachings and insights of my advisors Arjun Appadurai, Dipesh Chakrabarty, Bernard Cohn, and John Comaroff. I am indebted to courses and discussions with other professors and friends in and beyond Chicago, including Ralph Austen, Lloyd Rudolph, Susanne Rudolph, Gary Herrigel, Uday Mehta, Faisal Devji, Carol Breckenridge, McKim Marriott, Ronald Inden, John Kelly, David Scott, D. R. Nagraj, U. R. Ananthamurthy, Christopher Pinney, Ravi Vasudevan, Robert Pippin, David Tracy, Paul Friedrich, Peter Hudis, Anil Lal, Vinay Lal, Roby Rajan, Jonathan Magidoff, Madhuri Deshmukh, Tanya Kenkre, and Prithvi Sobhi. At Harvard, more recently, I was fortunate to have close interactions with Parimal Patil, Rahul Mehrotra, Alex Watson, Lee Ling Ting, Amit Basole, Umang Kumar, and Beena Sarwar, and to study with Cornel West. At presentations, workshops, and conferences, I have benefited from the questions and responses of many scholars, including Prabhu Mohapatra, Rana Behal, Chitra Joshi, Dilip Simeon, Jairus Banaji, Mukul Mangalik, Marcel van der Linden, Cláudio Costa Pinheiro, Jan Breman, Jonathan Parry, Jan Lucassen, Aditya Sarkar, James Andrews, Ronald Kassimir, Ajay Gandhi, Lotte Hoek, Thomas Blom Hansen, Hylton White, Anand Yang, K. Sivaramakrishnan, Nandini Sundar, Deepak Mehta, Udaya Kumar, Pradeep Jeganathan, Ann Gold, Frédérique Apffel-Marglin, Leela Gandhi, Peter deSouza, Rudolf Heredia, Shail Mayaram, Rajeev Bhargava, Shahid Amin, David Hardiman, Gyanendra Pandey, Sudipta Kaviraj, Ananya Vajpeyi, Kushanava Choudhury, Durba Chattaraj, Prasanta Chakravarty, Brinda Bose, Immanuel Ness, Milind Wakankar, Farhana Ibrahim, Amita Baviskar, Neeladri Bhattacharya,

Prathama Banerjee, Martin Fuchs, Antje Linkenbach, Chandan Gowda, and Bishnu Mohapatra.

In Delhi, I am grateful for the advice, insights, and close readings of Ashis Nandy, Ramchandra Gandhi, Ajay Mehta, and Sher Singh. The artistry and guidance of Sudharak Olwe, along with Ravi Agarwal and Siddharth Photographix, made the photography possible. I owe great thanks to Geeta Rai for Hindi instruction and Amit Mahajan for research assistance. I have benefited from exchanges and conversations with Purushottam Agrawal, J. N. Mohanty, Indrani Mazumdar, Indu Agnihotri, Jeebesh Bagchi, Aditya Nigam, Dunu Roy, Lalit Batra, Avinash Kumar, Vinay Ranjan, Mohinder Singh, Gananath Obeyesekere, James Scott, Arpana Caur, Vidya Rao, Punam Zutshi, Devasia Antony, Anuradha Veeravalli, Prabodh Parikh, Rahul Roy, Saba Dewan, Sanjay Kak, Arundhati Roy, Basharat Peer, Shalini Grover, Anisa Rahim, Orlanda Ruthven, Vikram Akula, Neelima Khetan, Priyanka Singh, Anish Damodaran, Dinakaran Meenamkunnu, Venkat Rao, Manu Chakravarthy, Uma Nandy, Namita Unnikrishnan, Syed Mohammed Faisal, Maryam Sikander, Shachi Seth, and Aseem Shrivastava. Ramachandra Guha generously gave comments on the manuscript in the final stages. I feel deep gratitude to the B156 workers and their families for allowing me to witness their lives and speak and discuss with them at length. The Murtis, the Rajus, the Sharmas, the Charleses, the Mehtas, the Nandys, the Lals, and the Nehrus gave me a great deal of warmth and hospitality in Delhi. In NJ, my father, mother, brother, Drs. Mani and Jaya, the Thompsons, and close friends Fred, Jandee, Matt, Shannon, Frank, Joann, Charlie, Patti, Christina, Tom, Marty, and Viji have given me love, assistance, and encouragement over many years.

Funding for this project was provided by the Social Science Research Council, the Fulbright-Hays Doctoral Dissertation Research Abroad Program, the National Science Foundation, the American Institute of Indian Studies, the Committee on Southern Asian Studies and the Department of Anthropology at the University of Chicago, and the Lakshmi Mittal and Family South Asia Institute, Harvard University. Materials in the book, in earlier versions, were published in the following articles and books, and are drawn upon here with permission: "Masculinity, Respect, and the Tragic: Themes of Proletarian Humor in Contemporary Industrial Delhi," *International Review of Social History* 51 (Supplement, 2006):203–227 (reprinted in *Coolies, Capital and Colonialism: Studies in Indian Labour History*, ed. Rana P.

Behal and Marcel van der Linden, 203–227 [Cambridge: Cambridge University Press, 2007]); "Togethering Contra Othering: Male Hindu-Muslim Inter-Relations in Proletarian Delhi," *South Asian Popular Culture* 5, no. 2 (October 2007):117–128; "Forces of Truth: A Struggle of Migrant Workers in Delhi," *Ethnography* 13, no. 1 (March 2012):57–70; "A Death in Delhi," in *The Oxford Anthology of the Modern Indian City, Volume II: Making and Unmaking the City—Politics, Culture, and Life Forms*, ed. Vinay Lal, 237–242 (New Delhi: Oxford University Press, 2013); "Matricide and Martyrdom: Cancer and *Karm* in the *Kalyug*," in *Philosophy as Samvada and Swaraj: Dialogical Meditations on Daya Krishna and Ramchandra Gandhi*, ed. Shail Mayaram, 257–271 (New Delhi: IIAS/Sage, 2014); "Abhimanyus in Exile: Entanglements and Bonds Among Migrant Workers in Delhi," in *Studies in Religion and the Everyday: Belief, Practice, Contestations*, ed. Farhana Ibrahim, 63–81 (Oxford: Oxford University Press, 2024); "Interpreting Catastrophes: God, Karma and Martyrdom," in *India and Its Intellectual Traditions: Of Love, Caste, Advaita, the Quest for Power and Other Things—Backwaters Collective on Metaphysics and Politics III*, ed. Vinay Lal, 249–265 (Oxford: Oxford University Press, 2024). The maps and diagrams were prepared by Erin Greb Cartography, Himanshu Baranwal, Punjab Stores, Sahil Chaudhary, and Girish Sharma. I am grateful to Elisabeth Maselli, senior editor, and the University of Pennsylvania Press for bringing out this book.